Dangerous Games

Dangerous Games

What the Moral Panic over Role-Playing Games Says about Play, Religion, and Imagined Worlds

Joseph P. Laycock

UNIVERSITY OF CALIFORNIA PRESS

University of California Press, one of the most distinguished university presses in the United States, enriches lives around the world by advancing scholarship in the humanities, social sciences, and natural sciences. Its activities are supported by the UC Press Foundation and by philanthropic contributions from individuals and institutions. For more information, visit www.ucpress.edu.

University of California Press
Oakland, California

Library of Congress Cataloging-in-Publication Data

Laycock, Joseph.
Dangerous games : what the moral panic over role-playing games says about play, religion, and imagined worlds / Joseph P. Laycock.
p. cm.
Includes bibliographical references and index.
ISBN 978-0-520-28491-3 (cloth, alk. paper)
ISBN 978-0-520-28492-0 (pbk., alk. paper)
ISBN 978-0-520-96056-5 (electronic)
1. Fantasy games—Moral and ethical aspects. 2. Role playing—Moral and ethical aspects. 3. Dungeons and Dragons (Game—Moral and ethical aspects. I. Title.
GV1469.6.L395 2015
793.93—dc23 2014030653

Manufactured in the United States of America

24 23 22 21 20 19 18 17 16 15
10 9 8 7 6 5 4 3 2 1

In keeping with a commitment to support environmentally responsible and sustainable printing practices, UC Press has printed this book on Natures Natural, a fiber that contains 30% post-consumer waste and meets the minimum requirements of ANSI/NISO Z39.48-1992 (R 1997) (*Permanence of Paper*).

For the bard who found me in the tavern and joined my party.

Contents

Preface

"You Worship Gods from Books!"

> My tolerance of this event is not advocacy for all of its content, and those who wish to interpret my remarks in this way do so uncharitably. And if pushed on this, I swear, I will blame the whole thing on Dungeons & Dragons anyway. The 80s tried to beat into my head that my beloved hobby was a gateway to darkness, and lo and behold, here I am. I must have failed a saving throw somewhere along the way.
>
> —Harvard lecturer in ethics and public policy Christopher Robichaud, "Remarks on the Occasion of Harvard's Reenactment of the Black Mass"

When Gary Gygax and Dave Arneson published *Dungeons & Dragons* (*D&D*) in 1974, they created the first commercially successful fantasy role-playing game. In these games, players imagine heroic characters for themselves and produce narratives of their adventures. The point is not only to produce a good story but to allow the players to *experience* an imagined world together. As an art form, the fantasy role-playing game is directed inward. The players do not perform their roles for an audience but for each other. Because of this introspective quality fantasy role-playing games are almost impossible to appreciate or critique without participant observation. This is no doubt why, within the small body of scholarly research on these games, I am unaware of any example in which the scholar has not spent hours playing these games him- or herself. The present study is no exception.

I grew up in Austin, Texas. I was introduced to *D&D* at the age of six at (where else?) a summer camp for gifted children. In those days, children were allowed to spend the afternoon wandering through the woods unsupervised. We were expected to entertain ourselves. We were, after all, "gifted." What we called "Dungeons and Dragons" had almost nothing to do with the game created by Gygax and Arneson. Most of us had never seen multisided dice, and only a few boys with older brothers had seen a gaming book. By middle school I had acquired these mysterious objects and learned to play *D&D* "for real." I was a regular player throughout high school and college and even played the occasional game in graduate school.

In middle school I became involved in live-action role-playing, or LARPing. I joined the Austin chapter of Amtgard, a group that enacted fantasy battles in public parks using padded weapons. In the ninth grade I had "a runner's build" and was not considered athletic. My Amtgard character was an assassin. My college-age teammates would send me on missions to slink behind the opposing team and stab their leaders in the back. If I succeeded at these decapitation strikes, I received praise from adults that I looked up to. If I failed—that is, if I was detected and beaten with foam swords—I was told that I had not died in vain, because I had caused the enemy to divert resources from the front lines. Amtgard felt like a cross between being a normal high-school athlete and a child soldier.

By my senior year I had graduated to another LARP called *Vampire: The Masquerade*. In this game, players pretended to be vampires who were pretending to be human. The game met at the University of Texas at Austin, and most of the players were college students. Players had to be eighteen, so I lied about my age in order to participate. Whereas Amtgard had been loud, violent, and sweaty, *Vampire* consisted primarily of elaborate Machiavellian plots, and most characters wore suits instead of chain mail. LARPing was an alternative world in which my normal adolescent life was reversed: In high school I generally avoided the gym. In Amtgard I dealt death from the shadows. In high school I did not talk to many girls. In *Vampire* I discussed philosophy and politics with female college students in leather corsets.

Experiencing this alternative world caused me to think about the ordinary world in new ways. The pummeling I received in Amtgard taught me that I could be tough. In college I began studying martial arts and eventually took up boxing and weight training. These skills gave me the confidence to work with at-risk youth as a high-school teacher, and I briefly coached boxing. *Vampire* taught me about networking, resourcefulness, and cunning. Every graduate student would be well served by playing *Vampire* before attending his or her first academic conference. I was able to discover these things through LARPing precisely because these games seemed more "real" than playing *D&D* with friends. The high level of organization and the number of people involved meant that my actions had consequences within the alternate reality of the game that forced me to think carefully about what I was doing. The freedom to take risks without suffering permanent consequences when I made mistakes taught me confidence and helped me to grow up.

However, living in Texas, I was also aware that my hobbies marked me as deviant. In middle school, I was occasionally bullied for playing *D&D,* and a neighbor's father was convinced that Amtgard was a Satanic cult. In fact, bullies and evangelical Christians seemed to be in lockstep regarding *D&D*. In the 1980s there was a full-blown moral panic over role-playing games in which such figures as Geraldo Rivera and Tipper Gore warned that games like *D&D* cause young people to lose their minds, commit suicide, and worship the devil. Gamers (those who play fantasy role-playing games) were simultaneously the object of ridicule and fear. Somehow we were perceived as hapless losers who were also dangerous Satanists. As a child, listening to sensational claims about my favorite hobby led me to my first suspicion that grown-ups are fallible. Adults claimed that their authority came from their experience and wisdom, and yet a simple game made them frightened and hysterical.

One experience of antigaming hostility had a particularly lasting impression on me. In the sixth grade, I was discussing the game with a friend when an older student overheard our conversation and began berating us. "You worship gods from books!," he cried with disgust. "That's just sad!" A hostile debate ensued in which he repeated several times that we "worshipped gods from *D&D* books." Although I was not able to properly articulate it as a sixth grader—especially to a larger and more aggressive student—I understood that there were several layers of irony in the accusation that *D&D* players "worship gods from books." First, *D&D* was a game, not a religion. It had nothing to do with worshipping anything. Second, the pantheon of gods in our *D&D* games was imaginary, not real. We knew the gods were imaginary because we had made them up. Third, and most importantly, there was nothing unusual about worshipping "gods from books." Jews, Christians, and Muslims all worship a God that they have come to know primarily through a sacred text. The bully, who made it clear that he had the full support of his church in condemning our hobby, most certainly worshipped a God from a book. This encounter caused me to suspect that the attack on fantasy role-playing games was fueled by deep-seated fears and desires that the attackers themselves were only dimly aware of.

This book began as an attempt to understand these hidden fears and desires behind the moral panic over role-playing games. Why did a fantasy game fill Christian critics with such fascination and horror? Why did stories about a a game of imagination that drove people insane receive so much attention from talk shows, psychiatrists, and law enforcement? These questions led to an exploration of how we define such concepts as "reality," "fantasy," and "religion." I found that fantasy games like *D&D* often can resemble religions. But religious worldviews can also resemble a shared fantasy. This second insight likely motivated much of the religious antagonism toward fantasy role-playing games. By accusing gamers of delusion and heresy, religious claims makers policed the boundaries between religion and fantasy, assuaging their own doubts about the status of their worldview.

Researching this book was often a frustrating and depressing undertaking. I read every available book, tract, and article on the supposed dangers of fantasy role-playing games. In doing so, I was constantly confronted by passages such as these:

> Players of the game designate a "Dungeon Master" who has god-like control over the fantasy world. The Dungeon Master puts players in situations. For example, the Dungeon Master may decide that a "Fighter" player will fight a "Magic-user" player in a castle full of trap doors and serpents.[1]

> Even a manticore takes a back seat to a dragon, of which there are four different species: white, black, red, and brass. Brass is the worst. All dragons breathe fire and spew sleep, magic, and fear all over the place.[2]

The authors of these passages claimed that playing *D&D* leads to suicide. But to anyone who has ever played a fantasy role-playing game it is obvious that these two authors are claiming authority about something they know nothing about. *D&D* is a form of storytelling not a series of gladiatorial spectacles in which a dungeon master pits players against one another. And as any *D&D* player knows, there are more than four varieties of dragons, and brass dragons are peaceful and benevolent. The claims maker was simply too lazy to find a suitably nightmarish *D&D* monster to frighten her audience.

To examine claims that these games cause violent crimes it was also necessary to sift through the details of numerous suicides, murders, and other tragedies that were blamed on fantasy role-playing games. While role-playing games were always tangential to these cases, I could see how it would be comforting to believe a game was solely to blame for these events. The true causes of these deaths were almost always more complicated and more tragic. The most disturbing cases of all were events such as the massacre at Columbine High School in which there was no obvious motivating factor. In this sense, the panic over role-playing games was also linked to problems of theodicy and the need to live in a world that appears sensible and sane.

As human beings, we all desire to inhabit a world that is ordered and meaningful in which our lives have purpose. To create these worlds we take the chaotic elements around us, and together we imagine a new order in which they are given meaning. In this sense, fantasy role-players and their religious critics are engaged in similar projects. They are both constructing new worlds in which tragedy is rendered sensible, and if the forces of chaos cannot be annihilated, we can at least fight them as heroes.

It is important to note that while my analysis focuses on Christian criticism of fantasy role-playing games, I do not take these critiques as representative of Christian views in general. The creators of *D&D* were themselves Christian, and groups such as the Christian Gamers' Guild contain pastors among their ranks. The attack on fantasy role-playing games was led by a coalition that included both secular and religious voices. However, while law enforcement and mental health professionals lent authority to the attacks on games, the claims themselves originated in the New Christian Right, a cluster of conservative evangelical movements that emerged in the 1970s. While the New Christian Right has drawn support from conservative Catholics, Jews, Mormons, and secularists, it is at its core Protestant, and its political interests lie primarily in maintaining the cultural hegemony of American Protestantism.

Similarly, in drawing a connection between religion and fantasy, I do not mean to deride religious worldviews as irrational or to dismiss religious truth claims as "mere fantasy." As a sociologist in the tradition of Émile Durkheim, I assume that we require a socially constructed framework in order to interpret the world. All such frameworks are in a sense "fantasies," and there is no Archimedean point from which we may perceive the world without recourse to our culturally inherited biases. Furthermore, religious ideas have consequences for individuals that can be studied psychologically and consequences for society that can be measured empirically. Religion matters, whether or not it is the product of human imagination. What the panic over fantasy role-playing games suggests is that nominally imaginary worlds also have an effect on how we make sense of the world and ourselves. This interpretive function is similar to that of a religious worldview in nature if not degree. Thus, rather than dismissing religion as mere fantasy, I am proposing that fantasy is likewise a very serious thing. Finally, it should be noted that just because religion is a social reality that can be studied sociologically, this does not preclude the possibility of a metaphysical reality beyond the data available to sociologists.

Many people supported and encouraged me in writing *Dangerous Games*. Daryl Bridges, an avid gamer and Unitarian Universalist minister, read the earliest drafts of the manuscript and provided his insight. Paul Cardwell—a game designer, chair of the Committee for the Advancement of Role-Playing Games (CAR-PGa), and an ordained Methodist minister—also read through drafts and and lent his expertise. David Frankel, an artist who moved in gamer circles with me at Hampshire College, designed the cover. Douglas Cowan and David Bromley, two sociologists of religion whom I respect very much, offered encouragement and suggestions. Finally, my editor, Eric Schmidt, was willing to take a chance on an unusual project and provided excellent support.

INTRODUCTION

Fantasy and Reality

Our relationship with the world which we entered so unwillingly seems to be endurable only with intermission.
—Sigmund Freud, *A General Introduction to Psychoanalysis*

The vistas [religion] opens and the mysteries it propounds are another world to live in; and another world to live in—whether we expect ever to pass wholly over into it or no—is what we mean by having a religion.
—George Santayana, *The Life of Reason*

Role-playing games are games in which players pretend to be someone else, typically a fictional character.[1] Imaginative play is an intuitive activity for human beings. For children, especially, imaginative play is a means of formulating models of how the world works, acquiring new skills, and becoming socialized.[2] In games such as "house" children pretend to be adults performing the domestic duties of their parents. Other simple role-playing games involve imaginary conflicts such as "cops and robbers" or "cowboys and Indians." These games also lead to the cultivation of new skills. Developmental psychologists have identified a form of play dubbed "mastery play" in which children engage in behaviors that require new levels of courage or physical coordination. On a playground, mastery play might include such activities as going down a slide or traversing monkey bars. Children often engage in mastery play and role-playing simultaneously. While pretending to be superheroes or other idealized figures, children sometimes find they have courage and abilities they did not know they had.[3] Adults also use role-playing games to develop new competencies. The US military has used simulations to develop strategy since the nineteenth century. Today the military utilizes role-playing games not only to improve decision making during combat, but also to train peacekeeping forces to interact with other cultures. Governments use role-playing games to develop contingency plans for new safety threats. Corporations have increasingly used role-playing games in lieu of training videos to teach employees new skills. Surgeons use a variety of simulations to hone their skills, and other health-care professionals use role-playing to rehearse interacting with patients.[4] Of course, when adults use their imaginations in this way, their activities are usually referred to as "exercises" rather than "games."

WHAT IS A FANTASY ROLE-PLAYING GAME?

The term "fantasy role-playing game" refers to a much more specific genre of games. In these games, players generally assume the roles of heroes in a fantastic setting. Fantasy role-playing games may either be played while seated at a table (tabletop role-playing) or the players may move around a designated space to simulate the actions of their characters (live-action role-playing). In some ways fantasy role-playing games resemble such childhood pastimes as cops and robbers. However, they usually entail complicated systems of rules to determine the outcome of a character's actions. On the playground, a child might simply point his index finger and declare, "Bang! I got you!" The child's playmate might lie down and play dead or (more likely) respond that the imaginary bullet missed, that he has survived because he is wearing a bulletproof vest, that he caught the bullet in his teeth, and so on. In a fantasy role-playing game the outcome of a gunshot might be determined by a variety of mechanisms, such as rolling dice or a match of rock-scissors-paper between the players. Many games feature rules to represent a dizzying range of factors. To determine whether a bullet hit its mark, a game might weigh such factors as the model of the gun, the distance of the shot, the agility and preparedness of the target, mitigating circumstances such as mist or the glare of the sun, and so on. While not all fantasy role-playing games have cumbersome rules, most cannot be played without an impartial referee who adjudicates the outcomes of the characters' interactions within the imaginary world.

Despite the often daunting rules of fantasy role-playing games, they remain popular even in an era when computer games make such complicated game mechanics unnecessary. Wizards of the Coast is one of the largest publishers of fantasy role-playing games in the world. They are also the current copyright owner of *Dungeons & Dragons* (*D&D*), the game that defined the genre when it appeared in 1974. In 2000, Wizards of the Coast sent a postcard survey to more than 65,000 respondents, age twelve to thirty-five, in more than 20,000 American households. The poll concluded that about 6 percent of the population or about 5.5 million people play tabletop role-playing games. Of these, half are habitual players or "gamers" who play at least once a month.[5] In 2012, 41,000 people attended Gen Con, the gaming convention originally created by Gary Gygax.[6] In addition, various celebrities, including action star Vin Diesel, comedians Robin Williams, Mike Myers, and Stephen Colbert, and science-fiction writer Robert Heinlein, have admitted to playing *D&D*.[7] Director Steven Spielberg also appreciated *D&D* and used it to assess the acting ability of children while casting *E.T.*[8]

Game designer and novelist Greg Stafford has argued that role-playing games actually constitute a new art form "as legitimate as sculpture, drama, or prose fiction."[9] (Significantly, Stafford is also a practicing shaman and sits on the board of directors of the magazine *Shaman's Drum*. The artist, the shaman, and the gamer are all in the business of traveling between worlds. As we will see, these journeys may involve similar mental faculties.) Lawrence Schick, who designed several products for *D&D*, adds that fantasy role-playing is an improvisatory art akin to jazz. It is also a performance art like dance. The performance is ephemeral and can be appreciated only while it is occurring. However, unlike dance, role-playing games direct the performance inward, toward the players, rather than outward toward an audience. Daniel Mackay argues that there is also an enduring aesthetic object produced by role-playing games in that the players create a shared set of stories. These stories are occasionally shared with others through blogs, magazines, and other outlets.[10] Schick addresses arguments that role-playing cannot be art because it is often violent and juvenile, noting: "It is true that most role-playing is oriented toward acting out adolescent power fantasies—but what of it? The same can be said of fiction and film. Real artistry is rare in every art form."[11]

John Eric Holmes, a professor of neurology as well as a science-fiction writer and game designer, wrote an article for *Psychology Today* entitled "Confessions of a Dungeon Master," in which he speaks candidly about some of the darker aspects of his favorite hobby. Holmes's players were not adolescent boys but medical students, doctors, and nurses. And yet, he notes:

> Almost always, the personalities of the characters turn out to be combinations of people's idealized alter egos and their less-than-ideal impulses. . . . There is hardly a game in which the players do not indulge in murder, arson, torture, rape, or highway robbery. I have even had players tell me that their characters had stopped on the way to underground dungeons to spray-paint graffiti on the walls![12]

Role-playing games often function as a journey into the player's mind, uncovering both exalted ideals and repressed impulses. However, this is not a private journey but a shared one. Holmes notes that playing *Dungeons & Dragons* resembles a sort of collective madness:

> This "alternate universe" feel to the world of Dungeons and Dragons is produced by its *social* reality. It is a shared fantasy, not a solitary one, and the group spirit contributes to the tremendous appeal of the game. You always wanted a world of magic and mystery to explore, and now a group of your friends gathers every two or three weeks to explore it with you. For a few hours, everyone agrees to accept that world, to accept your pretense that you are a magician who can throw exploding balls of fire from one hand. The fantasy has become a reality, a sort of *folie à deux,* or shared insanity.[13]

In sum, fantasy role-playing is a unique cultural form that taps into some of the most fundamental aspects of human experience. It combines imaginative play, which comes naturally to children, with complex rules and mathematical models. It is described as a "game," but often resembles art, psychotherapy, or madness more than traditional games. The worlds created within the game are reflections of the individual personalities of the players, but the process through which they come to seem "real" is a collective one.

Sociologists know that categories such as "insanity" and "reality" are themselves largely social constructions. Peter Berger famously observes that humans, alone among the animals, are not slaves to their instinctive modes of behavior. Instead, humans are able to imagine the world and their lives in an infinite number of ways. The price of this freedom is the threat of chaos—that infinite possibilities present us with a world that is infinitely meaningless. And so humans must engage in "world-building," a collective process through which a society comes to understand the world in a particular way.[14] Science, religion, and other models of reality that help us to interpret our world can be understood as both the tools for and the products of world-building. From this perspective, the manner in which imaginary worlds are collectively constructed in the context of fantasy role-playing games is similar to the process through which all human meaning is created.

THE MORAL PANIC OVER FANTASY ROLE-PLAYING GAMES

Anyone who was aware of fantasy role-playing games in the 1980s and 1990s was equally aware of claims that these games were socially, medically, and spiritually dangerous. A coalition of moral entrepreneurs that included evangelical ministers, psychologists, and law enforcement agents claimed that players ran a serious risk of mental illness as they gradually lost their ability to discern fantasy from reality. It was also claimed that role-playing games led players to commit violent crimes, including suicide and homicide, and to the practice of witchcraft and Satanism. In North America, the United Kingdom, and Australia, activists mobilized against these games. Several school districts and colleges banned gaming clubs and removed gaming books from their libraries. In the United States, activists petitioned federal agencies to require caution labels on gaming materials, warning that playing them could lead to insanity and death. Police held seminars on "occult crime" in which self-appointed experts discussed the connection between role-playing games and an alleged network of criminal Satanists. Dozens of accused criminals attempted the "*D&D* defense," claiming that they were not responsible for their actions but were actually the victims of a mind-warping game.

The anxiety over fantasy role-playing games conformed to a well-known social model of a moral panic. Sociologist Stanley Cohen famously gives the following definition of a moral panic:

> A condition, episode, person or group of persons emerges to become defined as a threat to societal values and interests; its nature is presented in a stylized and stereotypical fashion by the mass media; the moral barricades are manned by editors, bishops, politicians and other right-thinking people; socially accredited experts pronounce their diagnoses and solutions; ways of coping are evolved or (more often) resorted to, the condition then disappears, submerges or deteriorates and becomes more visible.[15]

Like all moral panics, the fear of fantasy role-playing games eventually declined. This was partly because mainstream society became used to the idea of games like *D&D*. Fantasy role-playing was no longer a new form of media and thus no longer threatening. At the same time, the rise of computer games featuring increasingly realistic violence offered new fodder to draw the attention of moral entrepreneurs.[16]

The moral panic over fantasy role-playing games was a revealing period in the history of the New Christian Right. Claims about the dangers of these games were always embedded within a larger "subversion narrative" in which society was threatened by insidious forces that sought to seduce and corrupt young people. Historian of religion David Frankfurter notes that the monstrous conspiracies featured in subversion narratives are "intrinsically parasitical" in that the conspiracy requires our children to perpetuate itself.[17] Fantasy role-playing games were amenable to these sorts of conspiracy theories precisely because the games occurred in the minds of children and adolescents. While the elements of this subversion narrative remained the same, the exact nature of the conspiracy evolved throughout the decades. The fear of new religious movements formed the context through which critics first interpreted role-playing games. In the 1970s, the college campuses where fantasy role-playing games were designed and played were perceived by some as locations where dangerous "cults" recruited impressionable young people. In the 1980s, the subversion narrative shifted focus from marginalized religious movements to an imagined network of criminal Satanists. Fantasy role-playing games were portrayed as a powerful recruitment tool for the Satanists. Moral entrepreneurs warned parents that Satanic rituals were being conducted by their own children in the guise of a game. Fears about role-playing games resurfaced throughout the 1990s, particularly in the wake of the massacre at Columbine High School in 1999. Here the subversion narrative shifted again, and the fear of Satanists was replaced by a more abstract fear of "goths," "super predators," or youth who were otherwise defective and lacking a conscience. Fantasy role-playing games were presented as a component of a morally bankrupt culture that was producing a generation of remorseless killers. In each case, fantasy role-playing games were linked to fears of a generation that would rise up and kill its parents. While the imagined forces corrupting young people changed from decade to decade, the subversion narratives were always closely tied to fears of the religious and moral other. In this sense, the history of the panic over fantasy role-playing games is really a history of far darker fantasies that haunted the American psyche.

While the panic receded, a generation that came of age in conservative churches in the 1980s can recall being warned about the spiritual and psychological dangers of *D&D*. Some churches offered special youth programs on the topic that included videos and displays of gaming materials. The panic also shaped a generation of gamers. Groups like CAR-PGa (the Committee for the Advancement of Role-Playing Games) were created to monitor and counter claims that fantasy role-playing games lead to madness, crime, and occultism. Today, there is a growing genre of "gamer autobiographies" written by former players who have become writers and journalists. These are self-deprecating accounts of being social misfits who enjoyed a highly stigmatized hobby. These authors often express puzzlement that gaming is no longer considered deviant. Ethan Gilsdorf comments: "When I left this pop-cultural world, it was disdained by the mainstream. When I returned, D&D *was* the mainstream."[18]

Claims about the dangers of role-playing games still survive in enclaves of conservative evangelical culture such as the *700 Club*. An article entitled "Dungeons and Dragons: Adventure or Abomination," originally published by the Christian Broadcasting Network in 1986, has been reprinted in Christian publications as recently as 2011.[19] In April 2013, Pat Robertson appeared on the *700 Club* where he answered an e-mail asking, "Is it safe for a Christian to enjoy video games that have magic in them, if the person playing the games is not practicing the magic?" Robertson responded that Christians should not play such games adding that *Dungeons & Dragons* had "literally destroyed people's lives."

In 2011, Don Rimer, a retired police officer from Virginia Beach, Virginia, utilized the popularity of vampire media such as *Twilight* and *True Blood* to revive fears of teenagers driven to violence by fantasy role-playing games. In a newspaper article about the growing threat of "occult crime," Rimer warned: "Fantasy role-playing like Dungeons and Dragons . . . and vampire gaming are alive and well. There are people who take gaming to another level, one that results in deaths and suicides. In the world of gaming, there is evil."[20]

Politically, opposition to fantasy role-playing games was a conservative issue, and conservative politics provides another index of lingering fears over fantasy role-playing games. In 2008, official McCain campaign blogger Michael Goldfarb equated *New York Times* writers with adults living in their parents' basement, "ranting into the ether between games of dungeons and dragons." After receiving an irate response from the gaming community, he issued an apology: "If my comments caused any harm or hurt to the hardworking Americans who play Dungeons & Dragons, I apologize. This campaign is committed to increasing the strength, constitution, dexterity, intelligence, wisdom, and charisma scores of every American."[21] Goldfarb used *D&D* as metonymy for immaturity but also revealed that he was familiar with the game and did not regard it as dangerous or objectionable.

Another index of current attitudes toward fantasy games developed during the 2012 election cycle when Colleen Lachowicz, a social worker from Maine, ran for the state senate as a Democrat. Her Republican opponents discovered that she regularly played the online fantasy game *World of Warcraft,* and gained access to comments she had made during the game. Republican strategists sent out mailers alerting voters to Lachowicz's interest in the game and even created the website colleensworld.com, which featured comments she had typed while playing the game, and pictures of her character, an orc assassin named Santiaga. The site declared, "Maine needs a state senator that lives in the real world, not in Colleen's fantasy world."[22] Some of the comments featured on the site were simply Lachowicz's political views, which were often expressed bluntly as a result of the (seemingly) private setting of the game. Other comments, however, were clearly meant as the words of Lachowicz's character, Santiaga. When CNN covered the story, Lachowicz gave an interview by phone during which a news anchor demanded an explanation for the comment, "I love poisoning and stabbing! It is fun." The rhetoric that Lachowicz "lives in a fantasy world" was calculated to build on thirty years of claims that fantasy role-playing games contribute to violent behavior and an inability to discern fantasy from reality. In the end, however, the strategy backfired. Not only did Lachowicz win the election, but outraged gamers around the country donated $6,300 to political action committees that supported her campaign.[23]

This incident repeated itself in 2014 when Jake Rush, a Republican congressional candidate from Florida, was outed by supporters of the Republican incumbent for his involvement in a live-action *Vampire* game. Once again, there were allusions that Rush suffered from multiple personalities, and disturbing statements made by Rush during the game were presented out of context. Rush doubled down, releasing a statement outlining his experience in gaming and theater and accusing his opponents of playing "a game" by diverting attention from actual political issues.[24]

While claims about the dangers of fantasy role-playing games linger on, this book regards the moral panic over these games as a historical event that began in 1979, peaked in the mid-1980s, and then slowly declined throughout the 1990s. Aside from its historical significance, the panic is an important case study for the sociology of knowledge. At stake in the claims made about fantasy role-playing games is the problem of how such categories as "fantasy" and "reality," "madness" and "sanity," are defined. The ability to define these categories is the single most powerful form of control over the social order.

THE STUDY OF FANTASY ROLE-PLAYING GAMES

"Ludology," or the study of games, began in the early twentieth century with the work of Dutch medievalist Johan Huizinga and French intellectual Roger Caillois. Huizinga and Caillois argue that "play" is a distinct mode of human behavior and that much of culture has developed from play. In his opus *Homo Ludens,* Huizinga argues that the rules of games, which are arbitrary, context specific, and disinterested from the logic of means and ends, formed the basis of myth and ritual, which in turn led to the development of law, commerce, craft, art, and science. Each of these institutions, Huizinga maintains, has a unique set of conventions and "rules," and is rooted in the "primeval soil of play."[25] In contemporary scholarship, the advent of role-playing games and the immersive virtual realities of computer games and other "new media" have led to a revival of ludology.

While there is currently a burgeoning field of scholarship on the nature and significance of fantasy role-playing games, the most important scholarly study of these games is also one of the earliest. In 1983 Gary Alan Fine published *Shared Fantasies: Role-Playing Games as Social Worlds.* To produce this book, Fine became not only a theorist of fantasy role-playing games but an anthropologist. In the early 1980s, he spent months playing with a group that ran games in a public community room at a police station in Minneapolis, Minnesota. (The first edition of his book begins with an apology to his wife, who tolerated the fact that his research frequently required him to stay out until four in the morning.) Fine's labors yielded two important insights about fantasy role-playing games. First, Fine addresses a critique frequently raised by outsiders that these games are "pointless," lacking a clear objective, winner, or even a definitive conclusion. Fine counters that playing these games is "autotelic"—that is, an end unto itself. The fun of the game does not arise from winning, but rather from "engrossment." Players participate in fantasy role-playing games for the experience of playing the game and mentally inhabiting another world.[26]

Second, Fine employs a sociological theory known as "frame analysis." Outsiders are sometimes disturbed that gamers become absorbed in a world that is not real. The human ability to experience alternate "worlds" and alternate definitions of reality was first studied by William

James and then by Alfred Schutz. These thinkers describe how human beings can direct their attention toward different worlds of meaning and that these worlds are "real" so long as we attend to them. Madness, of course, is a classic example of a private subjective world. But art, science, and religion also present distinct worlds to experience. All of these discrete worlds exist alongside the world of practical realities or what Schutz calls "the world of daily life." Gregory Bateson further develops this theory in an essay entitled "A Theory of Play and Fantasy" that analyzes such activities as play and ritual. Bateson notes that play and ritual are unique contexts of communication wherein the ordinary meaning of signs is changed. For instance, a clenched fist is a sign of aggression. However, if the clenched fist is "only play" it can mean something else entirely. Bateson coins the term "frame" to describe these contexts of metacommunication in which signs do not carry their ordinary meanings. Erving Goffman develops Bateson's model into an entire theory of social organization called "frame analysis."[27]

Fine draws on this body of theory to explain that fantasy role-playing games operate by using three frames or "interrelated systems of meaning."[28] The first frame is commonsense reality or the world of daily life. The second frame is that of the rules of the game. These are models of how the fantasy world works and the mechanisms through which players direct the course of the fantasy. The third frame is the content of the fantasy itself. This world is not inhabited by the players but rather the characters whose roles players assume. Most of the time players are able to move fluidly back and forth between the three frames. For instance, a player might make the following statement: "Are you friend or foe? I'm rolling for charisma. Pass the chips." Here the player moves from frame three to frame two to frame one. The question, "Are you friend or foe?," is understood to be spoken by the character—perhaps in response to meeting a stranger in the wilderness. The statement, "I'm rolling for charisma," is understood to be the action of the player. Many games assign characters with an attribute such as charisma that determines their effectiveness in social interactions. This is often a numerical value that is combined with a die roll to determine what happens in the fantasy world. It is assumed that the character, who exists within the context of the fantasy world, does not think of herself as having a set of numerical attributes. Finally, the imperative, "Pass the chips," can be understood through the frame of commonsense reality: the player would like another player to hand her some chips. Most of the time, a group of players knows instantly which frame everyone is referring to at any given moment.[29]

Occasionally, problems do arise from the relationship between the three frames. Players may attempt to act on information that they know but that their character does not. For instance, when her character approaches a door, a player may notice the dungeon master—the title of the referee and storyteller in *D&D*—staring intently at her notes and suspect that opening the door will trigger some sort of trap. The player may then insist that her character will not open the door before meticulously checking and rechecking for signs of a trap. Because this action is based on the observations of the player rather than her character, it is considered a form of cheating. The term "metagame thinking" is sometimes used to describe acting on such knowledge.[30]

More rarely, problems can arise when characters possess information that players do not. An example of this is an urban legend told in some gaming circles about a gazebo. In this story, a player announced that his character was venturing into a field and asked the dungeon master what he saw. The dungeon master responded, "You see a gazebo." The player, presumably a young teenager, did not know what the word "gazebo" meant, and so did not know what his character was seeing. Rather than admit his ignorance, the player assumed that a "gazebo" was a fantastic and potentially dangerous creature. The player responded, "What is the gazebo doing?" The dungeon master, not understanding the question, replied, "Nothing. It's a gazebo." The player responded, "I call out to it." The dungeon master answered, "OK. Nothing happens." The player, still cautious that the gazebo might present a threat, announced, "I fire an arrow at it." The dungeon master responded, "You hit. Now it's a gazebo with an arrow sticking out of it." The player anxiously asked, "Did I hurt it? Did my arrow have any effect?" The gazebo story demonstrates an instance where frame two has broken down. The character, who exists in frame three, does not need to know the term "gazebo." In the context of the fantasy, the character could presumably see that in the field there is a small, open-air structure. In fact, the character would have seen the exact shape, dimensions, and color of the gazebo. But because of the player's lack of vocabulary, the dungeon master was unable to convey what the character in the fantasy saw. In some versions of this story, the dungeon master became frustrated and announced, "The gazebo eats you! You're dead!" Here, the third frame has broken down. It is no longer clear to anyone what is happening within the fantasy.

A recurring concern about entertainment that employs alternate frames of meaning is that such pastimes can create a situation in which players become "lost in fantasy" and lose their ability to discern fact from fiction. The gazebo anecdote is significant because it reveals what actually happens in fantasy role-playing games when the three frames of reality become confused: it is simply a miscommunication dismissed as either irritating or humorous. This is because, while confusion can arise in the second and third frames, the first frame of reality—that of commonsense reality—is not impaired through normal fantasy role-playing.

In justifying his research on fantasy role-playing games, Fine explains:

> Fantasy gaming is, to be sure, a unique social world, treasured for its uniqueness, but like any social world it is organized in ways that extend beyond its boundaries. Just as the mechanics of the wheel can explain tractors and dune buggies, lazy susans and escalators, so does the understanding of one social world provide sociologists with the tools necessary to understand others, which may have no more than a tangential similarity. Fantasy gaming, then, has the potential to open the door to a universe of meanings, if only we would enter.[31]

Much of the emerging literature on fantasy role-playing games has not been as innovative or as theoretically rigorous as Fine's. Instead of applying the insights learned from fantasy role-playing games to other cultural phenomena, current studies of fantasy role-playing games have focused heavily on the nature of the games themselves. Much ink has been spilled over such problems as whether fantasy role-playing games are more like a game, a narrative, or a performance. To remain relevant, the study of fantasy role-playing games must expand its horizons and seek new directions of analysis.

One of the best books in the field since Fine is Mackay's *The Fantasy Role-Playing Game: A New Performing Art.* Mackay outlines four structures at work in fantasy role-playing games, which he calls the cultural, formal, social, and aesthetic. However, he hints at a fifth structure that he calls "the spiritual." Mackay presents fantasy role-playing games as part of a search for meaning in the face of modernity, and a response to the experience of disenchantment. He writes:

> The role-playing game is a natural response to the frosting of the windows of otherworldliness that has occurred in much of contemporary art, thought, and culture. It is a worldly entertainment that manufactures, through a shared social experience, otherworldly playgrounds from the images of American culture.[32]

Mackay's insight that fantasy role-playing games fulfill a need for contact with the otherwordly suggests that claims makers were not entirely wrong in asserting that fantasy role-playing games function as a pseudo-religion. The present study examines the moral panic over fantasy role-playing games in order to explore how fantasy games function as a religion, and, conversely, how religion functions like a shared fantasy.

FANTASY ROLE-PLAYING GAMES, RELIGION, AND THE SOCIAL CONSTRUCTION OF REALITY

The controversy over fantasy role-playing games is an important study in the contested nature of imagined worlds. Moral entrepreneurs claimed that games like *D&D* were occult religions that masqueraded as games in order to indoctrinate young people. Gamer apologists responded that it was the claims makers themselves and not the gamers who struggled to distinguish fantasy from reality. The polemics of this debate have served as a distraction from the complex relationship between fantasy role-playing games and religious worldviews. Many gamers responded to charges that their pastimes promoted madness and heresy by framing fantasy role-playing games as "harmless escapism." But this emphasis on "mere escapism" ignored the fact that experiences within the frame of a fantasy world *do* shape the way players think about and experience the world of daily life. Like the children who engage in mastery play while pretending to be superheroes, gamers often report gaining new competencies through role-playing. An example of this can be found in the following letter, which was written by a soldier serving in Saudi Arabia as part of Operation Desert Shield in 1990 and published in *Dragon*, a magazine for fantasy role-playing games:

> I am the only person in my six-member family (including both parents) to graduate from school, and the only person in my family to graduate from college. I have AD&D [*Advanced Dungeons & Dragons*] games to thank for much of that. I was introduced to gaming when I was 16, when my friends and I discovered the AD&D game. At the time, I was a fairly withdrawn underachiever. Through gaming, I learned that any obstacle can be overcome through some very simple principles: teamwork, faith in friends, faith in your own abilities, perseverance, and dedication. These principles were buried behind piles of discarded soda cans and empty potato chip bags, and I learned them while surrounded by loyal friends who faced creatures that would make Arnold Schwarzenegger run in fear. In the meantime, my "normal" peers spent their weekends getting drunk, getting high, and taking part in other "normal" activities. By playing this "dangerous" game, my friends and I became adults.[33]

This author responds to claims that *D&D* is an unwholesome game that corrupts its players, by demonstrating that the game has changed him for the better. This account demonstrates that the experiences of frame three—his heroic adventures with his friends—resulted in a tangible effect in frame one. Rather than escapism, this reveals a reciprocal relationship between the fantasy world and the world of daily life. This relationship between two worlds not only makes the games fun to play but is often a source of great meaning for players.

The rhetoric of the panic also required gamer apologists to dismiss and ignore the relationship between fantasy role-playing games and religious innovation. One of the most persistent claims made by critics of fantasy role-playing games was that these games are a "catechism of the occult" and that players inevitably graduate from imagining magic to the actual practice of witchcraft and Satanism. There is almost no statistical evidence to refute or deny this claim. One poorly worded survey found no link between fantasy role-playing games and such activities as "casting spells" or "demon-summoning."[34] However, it is easy to find anecdotal evidence of individuals who practice religious traditions such as paganism that include a magical worldview, and who have also previously enjoyed fantasy role-playing games.[35] So while most people who role-play wizards will not become practicing magicians, a few will. Correlation does not prove causation, and these individuals likely had an interest in magic that preceded their interest in either role-playing or magical religious traditions. Moral entrepreneurs were also incorrect in claiming that players assume that because their characters have magical abilities, they do as well. Instead, the connection between fantasy role-playing games and magical religious practices appears to lie in the reciprocal relationship between fantasy and reality. The experience of an imaginary world allows us to think about our own world differently. Berger argues that in order for the social realities that people create to remain meaningful and to seem real and legitimate they require a social "base" that he dubs "plausibility structures."[36] Sociologists who study the milieu of contemporary magical belief have suggested that popular culture, especially the science-fiction and fantasy genres, may indirectly support these belief systems by shaping plausibility structures.[37] So while players never mistake the fantasy world of frame three for the everyday world of frame one, thinking about plausible models of magic and the supernatural for purposes of organizing a fantasy world may contribute to thinking about plausible models of magic in the real world. In fact, playing fantasy role-playing games can cause players to reassess any number of paradigms and assumptions, including religious and scientific ones.

Frames, Play, and Paracosms

Bateson describes frames as metacommunicative contexts in which the ordinary meaning of language and signs is changed. He notes that animals also utilize frames, especially play. Watching monkeys at the zoo, Bateson noticed that signs that would normally indicate aggression were interpreted differently while the monkeys were "at play." He also realized that the ability to discuss the context in which gestures are given and statements are made indicates an awareness that signs are signs and distinct from the objects they signify. To be aware of frames is to be aware of the symbolic order. For Bateson, play is a critical form of metacommunication because it facilitates a more sophisticated understanding of signs. He writes:

> It appears . . . that play is a phenomenon in which the actions of "play" are related to, or denote, other actions of "not play." We therefore meet in play with an instance of signals standing for other events, and it appears, therefore, that the evolution of play may have been an important step of human communication.[38]

In play we can step outside the ordinary system of signs and their meanings so that signs can be repurposed and put to new uses. This means that play entails a form of agency in which the symbolic order can be reflected on and reassessed.

In fact, a key element of play—particularly imaginative play—is *bricolage* or the creative rearrangement of symbolic elements. The psychologist Lev Vygotsky argues that by imposing the imaginary order of play onto reality—for instance, imagining that a banana is a phone—children acquire the ability to distinguish referent from object. He concludes that the ability to repurpose signs through imaginary play is necessary for developing abstract thought.[39] Developmental psychologist Alison Gopnik argues that children spend so much time engaged in play and imagination because these are the means through which they formulate causal theories of the world.[40]

Imaginative play, then, is a special frame through which new meaning and new frames can be produced. It is an engine for what Peter Berger calls "world-building." Fantasy role-playing games especially are about creating alternative worlds that seem uniquely real. In psychological literature, the term "paracosm" is sometimes used to describe the sort of detailed and engrossing imaginary worlds found in fantasy novels and role-playing games. Paracosms are a special frame created through imaginative play in which signs do not have their ordinary meaning. They are also a product of *bricolage* in which elements from the real world as well as historical and fictional narratives are reassembled into a pleasing new world. Most paracosms are created by children. However, paracosms created and maintained by adults are especially consistent and detailed. J.R.R. Tolkien's "Middle Earth" is a classic example of a paracosm having its own history and even invented languages. The four Bronte siblings created a paracosm called "Gondal." Before creating Narnia, C.S. Lewis created a childhood paracosm called "Boxen" with his brother Warren.[41] Paracosms are different from the delusions of the mentally ill, which tend to be both simplistic and immediate rather than complex and fantastic. Most importantly, paracosms provide a sense of joy and control while delusions inspire the opposite of these feelings.[42] However, while even children can distinguish their paracosms from reality, human beings do sometimes lose track of the frames they create and become "lost in play."

Play and the Sacred

Religion is also concerned with the experience of alternative worlds. Huizinga sees clear connections between play and religious ritual, both of which he describes as occurring within a "magic circle" separated from ordinary life. In fact, Huizinga's definition of play appears to anticipate frame analysis:

> Summing up the formal characteristics of play, we might call it a free activity standing quite consciously outside "ordinary" life as being "not serious" but at the same time intensely and utterly absorbing the player. It is an activity connected with no material interest, and no profit can be gained by it. It proceeds within its own proper boundaries of time and space according to fixed rules and in an orderly manner. It promotes the formation of social groupings that tend to surround themselves with secrecy and to stress their difference from the common world by disguise or other means.[43]

It is apparent in this definition that play shares similarities with what religion scholars call "the sacred." For Émile Durkheim, the chief criterion of the sacred is that it is "set apart and forbidden." Like play, the sacred can exist only so long as it is kept separate from the profane realm of ordinary space and time.

Caillois addresses this connection between Durkheim and Huizinga explicitly in an appendix to *Man and the Sacred.* He concludes that while both play and the sacred exist in opposition to the world of the profane, they are not equivalent to each other. For Caillois, play is distinct from both the profane and the sacred.[44] It is a third realm from which we can both reflect on ordinary reality and imagine the possibilities of the sacred.

In *Religion in Human Evolution* Robert Bellah builds on the work of Huizinga to argue that play is a feature of human biology that naturally led to ritual and then to the emergence of religion. Bellah describes play as "a new kind of capacity with a very large potentiality of developing more capacities." It is "the first alternative reality" from which the frames of science, philosophy, and religion are ultimately derived.[45] These connections between play and the sacred have a direct bearing on the controversy over fantasy role-playing games. Despite being "just games," activities like playing *D&D* may inform the way players think about religious values and truth claims. Conversely, some of the religious claims made by moral entrepreneurs resemble a form of play.

The Corruption of Play and the Construction of Reality

Bateson notes that while we are capable of employing frames deliberately, we are often unconscious of frames. We can fail to notice how a particular context is changing the meaning of signs. We may even transition between frames without realizing it. Bateson regards the delusions of schizophrenics as a failure to navigate these frames of metacommunication, such that thoughts and metaphors are misinterpreted as ordinary reality. However, mental illness is not required for a frame to break down. Alfred Radcliffe-Brown's ethnography of the Andaman Islands describes a peacemaking ritual wherein the two participants strike each other. Sometimes this ritual collapses into actual violence. The meaning of the blows is no longer interpreted through the metacommunicative frame of the ritual but as a simple assault. Play can also break down and become reality. Bateson notes that there are even forms of play that revolve around the question of whether or not signs are actually meant as play. Hazing initiations, for instance, are meant to induce anxiety in the initiate as to whether the initiators are "serious."[46]

Huizinga, Caillois, and Bellah argue that ritual, religion, and other cultural institutions are all products of play. Like paracosms these are new frames that have emerged from the frame of play. Unlike paracosms, culture is not regarded as imaginary or invented. On the contrary, most cultural institutions are taken for granted as part of "the real world." Thus the creative process that occurs in play can yield worlds of fantasy as well as socially constructed worlds that are—for all intents and purposes—real. Play can also produce interstitial worlds that are more than imaginary but are not yet accepted as reality.

Caillois speaks of "the corruption of play." Play becomes corrupt when it ceases to be separate from the profane world. Instead of playing for "the sake of play," corrupted play becomes entangled in the logic of means and ends. This is not the same as a game becoming "serious." Huizinga and Caillois never claim that play cannot be serious. Corrupted play is not about intensity so much as duration. The frame of the game is lost, and what was once voluntary becomes compulsory. Huizinga addresses this problem in *In The Shadow of Tomorrow.* Writing in 1936, Huizinga had seen the horrors of World War I and the rise of Fascist movements in Europe. He concludes that the Enlightenment has failed and that Western civilization is on the verge of collapse. Modern people, he warns, exhibit a form of dangerous "puerilism" that manifests in the decline of critical thinking, superstition, and totalitarianism. He regards the corruption of play as a fundamental part of the problem, writing:

> A far-reaching contamination of play and serious activity has taken place. The two spheres are getting mixed. In the activities of an outwardly serious nature hides an element of play. Recognized play, on the other hand, is no longer able to maintain its true play-character as a result of being taken too seriously and being technically over-organized.[47]

Huizinga acknowledges that this "contamination" has always existed in all cultures, but (like all doomsayers) claims that this was the worst it had ever been.

It is possible for the frame of play to shift without the players realizing it, and for play to "become real." During the decades of the moral panic over role-playing games, there were several highly publicized cases in which adolescent males who played role-playing games committed murders. In 1986, sixteen-year-old Sean Sellers murdered a convenience store clerk and later his mother and stepfather. Sellers had played *D&D* and was a self-styled Satanist. He had a coterie of like-minded teens with whom he associated, one of whom assisted him in his first murder. Ten years later, Rod Ferrell, also sixteen, murdered the parents of his friend Heather Wendorf. Ferrell had a passing interest in *D&D* and the game *Vampire: The Masquerade.* Like Sellers, he was the leader of a small group of teens who identified as vampires. One of these friends was present during the murders. Both cases received tremendous media attention because they played into a deeply embedded fear of a fallen generation that would murder its parents. Moral entrepreneurs interpreted these crimes either religiously as a manifestation of demonic forces or medically as a sort of pathology induced by dangerous games. However, a more cogent explanation of these crimes can be found in ludology.

In his work *Kamikaze Biker,* Ikuya Sato presents an ethnography of Japanese motorcycle gangs known as *bosozoku.* Typical *bosozoku* members were adolescents from affluent families. The Japanese media regarded the gangs as a serious social problem, and several social theorists explained the impulse to join a biker gang in pathological terms. Sato argues that for Japanese adolescents becoming a biker is a form of imaginative play in which they perform a romanticized and heroic role. Playing this role is pleasurable because it provides a sense of meaning, agency, and identity. The danger is that the play-world of the *bosozoku* becomes "real" when activities made in the context of play result in irrevocable consequences. If a *bosozoku* commits an assault or a rape while performing a role, he can no longer cast off the role and return to his life as an ordinary middle-class adolescent. Sato explains how the frame of the play-world can collapse into the frame of practical realities:

> When action becomes serious rather than playlike, one is at the mercy of an alternative definition of reality. Detached or liberated from traditional institutions and sacred symbolism, he may have originally engaged in action-seeking as a way of escaping from boredom. But he may, at the end of his search for new freedom, find himself entrapped in the web of a quasi-sacred and quasi-mystical symbolism of a cult, fanatic-ideology, or criminal underworld.[48]

Sato's model is a better explanation of the crimes committed by Sellers and Ferrell. Sellers and Ferrell each led a group of like-minded adolescents who performed the roles of Satanists and vampires. Moral entrepreneurs and the media labeled these groups "cults," with all of the pathological and heresiological claims that the term implies. However, these groups are more accurately understood as play-groups engaged in a dangerous form of imaginative play. By committing murder, Sellers and Ferrell collapsed the play-world in which they merely pretended to be dangerous criminals. Fantasy and reality became synonymous.

MORAL PANIC AS CORRUPTED PLAY

The moral panic over role-playing games can also be interpreted as a form of corrupted play. The claims makers used their imaginations to produce horrifying and vivid descriptions of what supposedly happens during fantasy role-playing games. Many of these claims makers constructed elaborate conspiracy theories involving Satanists and, in some cases, Jews, Freemasons, the Catholic Church, and other popular scapegoats. Most importantly, they invariably presented themselves as heroes—part detective and part exorcist—who alone were able to identify and uproot the demonic forces threatening America.

In his book *Religion of Fear,* Jason Bivins analyzes such expressions of conservative evangelical culture as the tracts of Jack Chick, claims about heavy metal music, and "judgment houses," in which churches compete with traditional Halloween haunted houses by showing visitors scenes of hell. Bivins identifies what he calls "the erotics of fear," in which moral entrepreneurs appear to be fascinated with, and even to take vicarious pleasure in, the very ideas and activities they condemn. In line with Bivins's analysis, the manner in which claims makers constructed heroic worlds for themselves strangely mirrored that of the gamers they condemned. They engaged in a similar process of *bricolage,* borrowing tropes from popular culture to construct a fantasy world. (In many cases, the same horror films and television shows that shaped Satanic conspiracy theories during the 1970s were also incorporated into the creation of *D&D.*) Through the erotics of fear, fantasy role-playing games provided pleasure to the claims makers as well as to the gamers. Games like *D&D* offered a particularly rich source of symbols and tropes from which new conspiracy theories and subversion narratives could be constructed. Moral entrepreneurs delighted in plumbing these games for new evidence of occultism and other objectionable practices. By claiming that *D&D* was not a game but "real" occultism these moral entrepreneurs effectively cannibalized the fantasies of others: the contents of paracosms were ripped from the frame of imaginative play and dragged into the frame of conspiracy theory.

In an essay cowritten with Daniel Martin, Gary Alan Fine notes that both gamers and their critics were engaged in a project of reenchantment. Martin and Fine explain:

> To engage actively in fantasy role-playing and creative imagination *is* to enchant. In framing fantasy role-playing games as occultist activities, crusading groups share with Dungeons and Dragons players a sense of "the world reenchanted." What is different is that fantasy role-players, in contrast to members of the crusading groups, define these activities as inherently social, imaginative, and limited rather than cosmological and self-defining.[49]

The key difference is that while gamers confine their heroic fantasies to the frame of play, the claims makers do not. Several observers have claimed that moral entrepreneurs are delusional and engage in a form of projection when they accuse gamers of becoming lost in their own fantasy.[50] More precisely, the claims makers refuse to draw sharp boundaries between the frames of reality, imagination, and wishful thinking. Tellingly, Huizinga claims that one of the many symptoms of the puerilism that plagues modern society is a tendency to blame problems on conspiracies perpetuated by Jesuits, Freemasons, and other "phantasms of organized satanic forces."[51] Conspiracy theories represent a creative rearrangement of familiar elements, not unlike the new forms created in play. In fact, moral entrepreneurs sometimes seemed surprised when their claims were subjected to rational criticism, as if they were meant within a liminal frame between literal truth and fiction. In this sense, their activities resemble the corrupted play of Sean Sellers and Rod Ferrell. As with these teenage murderers, this corrupted play resulted in real human suffering. During the 1980s, the heroic fantasies of these claims makers contributed to Satanic panic in which innocent people were accused and imprisoned.[52]

This inability to negotiate discrete frames of meaning that fueled moral panic in the 1980s can be linked to the rise of the New Christian Right. The conservative evangelical movement that formed in the 1970s emphasized biblical literalism and promoted leaders who derived their charisma from their personas as postbiblical characters. Biblical literalism adopted the modernist assumption that stories have value only if they are true in a historic and scientific sense. The project of biblical interpretation is paradoxically a "generative" one, as literalists are constantly required to "discover" new truths in a text that is allegedly simple and unchanging. Similarly, New Christian Right leaders such as Jerry Falwell sometimes invented details about themselves in order to present their personal narratives as an extension of biblical narratives. These distortions were not regarded as dishonesty; instead they were a sort of creative confusion between literal and creative frames of communication.[53] In other words, conservative evangelical culture during the decades of the panic was attempting to be creative and literal simultaneously. The frames of literal truth, allegory, and imagination were mingled so that all claims could be presented as authoritative in a way that appealed to modernist notions of truth. This situation entails a sort of "epistemological messiness" that fosters corrupted play. Satanic conspiracy theories can be read as an extreme example of this tendency to creatively confuse frames and to treat metaphorical claims as literal truths.

RELIGION AS FANTASY: THE TERROR BEHIND THE PANIC

In some ways, the reaction of moral entrepreneurs to fantasy role-playing games was entirely predictable. New forms of media are frequently regarded with suspicion. Before the arrival of *D&D*, television, radio, and novels were each branded as immoral influences.[54] These games were particularly amenable to subversion narratives because they were marketed to children and adolescents. One of the elements Stanley Cohen assigns to a moral panic is a suitable victim, one that the public can identify with. In the 1980s, moral entrepreneurs presented gamers as victims—adolescent boys of above-average intelligence and sensitivity, but naive and vulnerable to corruption. Fantasy role-playing games also fit into a narrative of infiltration and seduction because they were simultaneously domestic and otherworldly. *D&D* books were a familiar sight in a teenager's bedroom, but their pages were filled with pictures of demons and weapons. Youngsters might appear to be safely sitting in the living room, but their minds could be in realms of unspeakable evil. Finally, Cohen notes that moral panics require a suitable enemy, one with few resources to fight back.[55] Few people were going to defend an obscure hobby, and even the most successful gaming companies had very narrow profit margins and could allocate very few resources to resisting claims that their games were part of a Satanic conspiracy. All of these factors made fantasy role-playing games an ideal target for moral entrepreneurs.

But while the panic over role-playing games was similar to other concerns about the unwholesome influence of media, there were several peculiar features to the claims made about these games. Christian critics in particular suggested that fantasy role-playing games were threatening in a way that other objectionable media such as violent movies and heavy metal music were not. Christian critics claimed that fantasy role-playing games were not simply an unwholesome form of media but a deviant religion. Playing these games, they claimed, was not really leisure but a religious practice in which players knowingly or unknowingly conducted rituals in the service of "occult" deities. Joan Robie, author of *The Truth about Dungeons and Dragons,* explains: "People everywhere (young and old) are searching for truth. Some are looking to New Age philosophies, others are turning to what they call the 'old religion'—paganism, which is in reality witchcraft and Satanism. Some turn to role-playing games like *Dungeons and Dragons.*"[56] Robie, a conservative evangelical, assumes that players do not indulge in these games for pleasure, but rather out of a search for truth necessitated by the spiritual vacuum of modern society.

Also curious was the fact that Christian critics of fantasy role-playing games appeared alienated from the games' obvious provenance in Christian cosmology. The creators of *D&D* were themselves Christian, and many of the supernatural elements of the game are inspired by the Bible and Christian tradition. More than other fantasy role-playing games, *D&D* frames the world in stark terms of good and evil. Many of the monsters that the heroes must dispatch, such as witches, demons, and vampires, are derived from Christian folklore and demonology. However, critics saw these elements not as evidence of the game's provenance in Christianity but rather of its link to Satanism. Robie goes on: "Despite Gygax's denial that the game is occult, there are many references to traditional Christian terms, such as atonement, deity, faith, fasting, resurrection, God, prayer and Divine Ascension, that are treated in a blasphemous manner in the players' handbook and various other D&D guide books."[57] Similarly Rus Walton warns: "The 'games' purposefully and constantly use Biblical terms and phrases blasphemously."[58] There is nothing objectively blasphemous about how biblical and Christian terms are used in *D&D*. Robie and Walton assume a priori that if Christian terms appear in fantasy role-playing games then their use must be blasphemous. The essence of their claim is a paradox: the admittedly Christian elements of *D&D* prove that it is an anti-Christian, "occult" game. For some reason, elements of Christian cosmology that should have been familiar were identified as strange and demonic. These Christian critics of *D&D* became alienated from their own cultural tradition.

Finally, in explaining why a game of fantasy is spiritually dangerous, several Christian critics of fantasy role-playing games concluded that the imagination itself is heretical because imagining another world amounts to a rejection of God's creation. In an essay entitled "Escaping Reality: The Dangers of Role-Playing Games," Baptist pastor and former gamer Vince Londini explains:

> Most born-again souls that get caught up in role-playing games probably have never thought this point through. But, what you're really telling God when you play any game that glorifies what God opposes or ignores His existence is, "Thanks for creating the World, dying for my Sins, saving my soul, sealing me with your Spirit, and preserving your Word for my instruction; but, I'd rather spend my time pretending to explore an imaginary world

> whose authors rebel against Your existence by not including You. I know you understand that I need to have my fun."[59]

Not only is God not central to most fantasy role-playing games, he argues, but fantasy worlds are by definition not the worlds given to us by God. Accordingly, Londini contends that science-fiction-themed role-playing games are just as bad as those involving spells and magic because both magic and futuristic technology are not real, and therefore thinking about such topics is a form of "ignoring" God and his creation.

Evangelical theologians Peter Leithart and George Grant make a similar argument in their book *A Christian Response to Dungeons and Dragons: The Catechism of the New Age.* For them, the problem is not only that fantasy role-playing games ignore God (some fantasy role-playing games do include an omnipotent, monotheistic deity). Instead, they suggest that reality is an extension of God's will, and therefore imagining an alternative reality is a form of rebellion against God. They explain:

> Ultimately, all extreme identification with a role is a sin, because it involves a rebellious rejection of the role to which God has assigned us. This motive is apparent in many of the D&D enthusiasts. . . . They hate their God-given role in the God-directed drama of history, and they play D&D in order to create their own identity and their own history.[60]

Londini, Leithart, and Grant also assert that games like *D&D* lead to violence and the practice of witchcraft. But they regard the ability to imagine and mentally inhabit other worlds as a much more serious threat.

These peculiarities—the persistent claim that a form of leisure is secretly a religion, the interpretation of Christian game elements as "occultism," and the suspicion of the imagination itself—suggest that there were deeper, more existential fears at stake in Christian critiques of fantasy role-playing games besides those explicitly stated by the claims makers. Bivins suggests that the condemnations of conservative evangelicals point toward inner doubts, writing: "At bottom, the religion of fear's most pressing concern is that the monster may lurk within as well as without."[61] I suggest that much of the energy that evangelicals put into framing fantasy role-playing games as either madness or a heretical religion was actually a defense mechanism to assuage their own doubts. The realization that a game of imagination can resemble a religion naturally leads to the suspicion that one's religion could likewise be a game of imagination. One way to suppress this suspicion was to cast fantasy role-players as delusional and evil and to pave over the connections between *D&D* and Christianity by insisting that *D&D* is an "anti-Christian" game. In this sense, the moral panic over role-playing games provides an insight into the strategies through which religious worlds are maintained in the face of contradictory evidence.

This book proceeds in two parts. Part 1 provides a historical account of the panic regarding the creation of fantasy role-playing games in the 1960s and 1970s through the decline of the panic at the end of the twentieth century. The panic is located within the larger cultural and religious developments of the era in order to show how claims about fantasy role-playing games reflected a larger set of anxieties. Part 2 analyzes the relationship between play, imagination, and the sacred. As a case study, the panic demonstrates how religious claims resemble play, and how play can share functions with religion.

Chapter 1 describes the origin of fantasy role-playing games. *D&D* evolved from "wargaming," a hobby based on military strategy, but also drew from cultural developments of the 1960s such as nostalgia for a mythic past and a new ethos that emphasized cooperation over competition. Chapter 2 suggests that *D&D* has always been a "religious" game, both in the substantive sense of dealing with metaphysics and morality and in the functional sense of utilizing narrative and ritual to create a sense of connection to another world.

Chapter 3 discusses the beginning of the moral panic in the 1970s. In 1979 James "Dallas" Egbert disappeared from Michigan State University. His family hired a private investigator, William Dear, who claimed that Egbert had become mentally trapped in a fantasy world as a result of playing *D&D*. Dear's hypothesis proved to be entirely wrong. However, his account of searching for Egbert became the first narrative of the delusional gamer. This narrative repeated itself throughout the 1980s and eventually formed the basis of an insanity defense that was attempted unsuccessfully in dozens of criminal cases. The public found Dear's story of a gifted college student who became a victim of his own fantasy compelling because it drew from a number of cultural currents of the 1970s. In addition to popular discourse by authors such as Alice Miller on the plight of "gifted children," the story built on the cult controversy of the 1970s and associated fears of brainwashing and cult leaders.

Chapter 4 discusses the height of the panic in the 1980s. In that decade, Satanic panic fused the anxiety over fantasy role-playing games to a much larger set of social anxieties. It was now claimed that these games were not only hazardous to one's mental state, but part of a Satanic conspiracy and a millennialist end-times scenario. In this era of the panic, Patricia Pulling emerged as the most influential opponent of fantasy role-playing games. Her career as a moral entrepreneur began after her son, Irving "Bink" Pulling, committed suicide in 1982. Like the disappearance of Egbert, Bink's death provided a sort of narrative anchor that energized a movement and made the crusade against games meaningful. Pulling went on to found BADD (Bothered About Dungeons and Dragons) and to reinvent herself as an occult crime investigator. Pulling worked closely with law enforcement, medical professionals, and the media to convince the public that fantasy role-playing games were a serious social problem.

Chapter 5 discusses a new round of controversy that occurred in the 1990s. Although the panic over Satanism was in decline, fears of fantasy role-playing games were folded into a more general fear of "super predators" and murderous youth. In the aftermath of the massacre at Columbine High School in 1999, Pat Robertson and others cited *D&D* among the causes of the shootings. The 1990s also saw the rise of the White Wolf game company, which specialized in dark games about supernatural creatures living in the modern world. White Wolf produced games such as *Vampire: The Masquerade,* which influenced several alternative religious groups emerging in the 1990s, including a community of self-identified vampires. This connection demonstrates the ability of role-playing games to shape plausibility structures. These games also became a source of renewed controversy for moral entrepreneurs and self-styled occult crime experts, demonstrating the resiliency of claims about fantasy role-playing games. Although the claims made during the panic never completely died, the historical overview concludes with the beginning of the war on terror in 2001. The threat of terrorism provided a new national fear that left little energy for concerns about deviant youth or fantasy role-playing games.

Chapter 6 explores how fantasy role-playing games serve a religious function by allowing players to experience an alternative world. The paracosms created for fantasy role-playing games are a reflection *of* the real world in that they are pastiches of familiar elements such as films, novels, historical settings, and other symbols. This *bricolage* gives artistic expression to the experience of the players. However, fantasy role-playing games are also a reflection *on* the real world. Paracosms create a mental space from which the real world can be reflected on and analyzed. In constructing a plausible fantasy world, players have the opportunity to reassess their models of reality. In this way, fantasy role-playing games provide a form of radical agency. While fantasy is often dismissed as "escapism," the door between fantasy and reality opens both ways. The fantasy world is not an "escape" but an annex that allows players a mental space from which to reassess their worlds. Historically, the ability to step outside of the known world and look back on it from an alternative and more idealized reality has come from religion.[62]

Chapter 7 explores the anxiety that paracosms and fantasy incite in moral entrepreneurs and attempts to locate these fears within the history of Western thought. Claims makers regarded imaginary realities as unproductive, spiritually dangerous, and a form of delusion. They also consistently argued that fantasy role-playing games are not, in fact, imaginary and that players are engaging in spiritual and religious realities when they play. There are a number of historic sources for this suspicion of the imagination, including condescending attitudes toward myth and fictional narratives that arose during the Enlightenment, capitalist notions that the imagination is unproductive, and biblical inerrancy that often refuses to distinguish between the frames of myth, science, and historical truth. One reason the suspicion of the imagination is so enduring is that all hegemonic movements are threatened by play and the imagination. The ability to step outside of the symbolic order empowers individuals to question ideology and formulate new ideas about the social order. This makes imagination especially threatening in the hands of those whom hegemonies most seek to control, such as adolescents.

Chapter 8 explores claims that moral entrepreneurs are themselves lost in fantasy and projecting their own confusion onto gamers. It is true that many of the most prominent opponents of fantasy role-playing games held fantastic worldviews in which they battled literal demons as well as global conspiracies. Evangelical publisher Jack Chick promoted the work of several individuals who were diagnosed by medical experts as suffering from paranoid delusions and mental disturbance. I argue that fantastic claims and conspiracy theories were not a medical pathology but a form of corrupted play in which the frames of fantasy and reality collapsed. The construction of conspiracy theories and subversion narratives is a creative process and a form of meaning production that frequently parallels that of fantasy role-playing games.

The conclusion considers the implications of this study for future controversies over how such concepts as play, madness, and religion are defined. I argue that "the sacred canopy" provided by a religious worldview can be regarded as a kind of fantasy role-playing game. It provides us with a meaningful world to inhabit and roles to fulfill. It is the product of play, and it is maintained by the continued effort and participation of the players. This does not mean that the sacred canopy is a "delusion" or that we can fully step out from under it. However, a better understanding of the processes through which human beings create and maintain meaningful worlds allows us to be more deliberate in how we use our frames of meaning. By being attentive to the frames of metacommunication we can avoid corrupted play and truly learn to walk between worlds, experiencing enchantment without delusion.

PART I

The History of the Panic

CHAPTER 1

The Birth of Fantasy Role-Playing Games

Imagination is but another name for super intelligence.

—Edgar Rice Burroughs, *Jungle Tales of Tarzan*

All men dream: but not equally. Those who dream by night in the dusty recesses of their minds wake in the day to find that it was vanity: but the dreamers of the day are dangerous men, for they may act their dream with open eyes, to make it possible.

—T. E. Lawrence, *Seven Pillars of Wisdom*

Dungeons & Dragons inspired countless other fantasy role-playing games, defining the genre.[1] The origins of Gary Gygax and Dave Arneson's extremely successful game did not lie in theater or storytelling but in wargaming—a hobby in which players simulate historical battles using miniature soldiers. Wargaming developed in the nineteenth century, primarily as a training exercise for Prussian military officers. It was eventually adapted for civilian leisure, but it has remained an obscure hobby. Not only does wargaming demand a serious interest in military history, but the rules frequently require complex mathematical calculations and charts that most people would regard as a tedious exercise rather than entertainment. Thus wargaming was an unlikely midwife for the genre of fantasy role-playing.

D&D combined two very different ways of thinking about the world. On the one hand, it entailed a preoccupation with mathematical models and rules, the roots of which can be traced back to Prussian officers perfecting "the science of war." On the other hand, it reflected the cultural trends of the 1960s, including a fascination with history, myth, and fantasy as well as a renewed appreciation for values such as cooperation and imagination. This combination of mechanistic and romantic thinking was developed by a group of wargamers at the University of Minnesota and in Lake Geneva, Wisconsin. In traditional war games two players control armies, with each acting as a sort of abstract commander. As in an actual battle, each game ends with a winner and a loser. However, some wargamers began to experiment with scenarios that involved numerous factions, which might or might not be adversarial toward each other. These experiments in wargaming required an impartial referee to mediate between players. Others were changing the genre of wargaming by including elements of the fantastic. Where traditional war games reenacted famous historical battles, by the 1960s some players were designing rules for battles that involved dragons and wizards. Finally, the scale of the conflict shifted from entire armies to individual heroes. Together, these changes resulted in a new game that had much broader appeal than war games ever had. It was a game that resembled both science and art, combining the analytical and the creative functions of the brain. But something else happened: the new genre of game somehow smacked of religion in a way that wargaming had not.

THE EVOLUTION OF *DUNGEONS & DRAGONS*

While Gary Gygax did eventually write a number of fantasy novels, the creators of *D&D* were not artistically inclined in the ordinary sense. C.S. Lewis and J.R.R. Tolkien, both members of Oxford's literary circle "the Inklings," shared interests in mythology, theology, and writing. By contrast, Gygax and Arneson were wargamers who would have been more at home discussing the comparative merits of crossbows and longbows than Anglo-Saxon poetry. However, the most important development of the fantasy role-playing game was not the content of the fantasy but the ability to create plausible simulations of an alternate reality. This was something that Gygax and Arneson learned from war games.

War games are almost as old as warfare itself. Simple games designed to represent battle existed in Egypt and Mesopotamia as early as the third millennium. Go was created between 206 BCE and 8 CE and was a favorite game of Chinese generals and statesmen. Chess, the classic war game, is believed to have originated in the Gupta empire of northwest India in the sixth century CE. While chess entails strategy and employs the symbols of feudal warfare (knights, castles, etc.), it is a symbolization of war rather than a simulation. In Europe, war games changed following the Enlightenment. Enlightenment thinkers believed that war, like anything else, could be understood scientifically and simulated using mathematical models. In Prussia, military officers attempted to make an increasingly accurate simulation of warfare using models to represent all of the factors that determine the outcome of a battle. This process began with Christopher Weikhmann, who created an expanded version of chess called *Koenigspiel* (The King's Game) in 1664. Weikhmann claimed his game "would furnish anyone who studied it properly a compendium of the most useful military and political principles."[2] In 1780, Johann Christian Ludwig Hellwig, master of pages to the German Duke of Brunswick, developed a game called *Kriegspiel* (War Game). The game was played on a board with 1,666 squares. Squares were painted different colors to represent different types of terrain. Pieces could move a different number of squares depending on what type of terrain they were crossing.[3] The pieces represented units rather than individual soldiers and were designated as infantry, cavalry, and artillery. Hellwig even created rules to represent entrenchment and the use of pontoons. In 1798, George Vinturinus of Schleswig expanded on Hellwig's game to create "New Kriegspiel." This game expanded the board to 3,600 squares and featured a sixty-page rule book.[4]

War games were revised again following the Napoleonic Wars. In 1811 Baron George Leopold van Reiswitz and his son developed a new game that they called *Instructions for the Representation of Tactical Maneuvers under the Guise of a Wargame*. This game introduced many of the elements that came to define modern wargaming as a genre. It did away with a board entirely and was instead played on a "map" consisting of a special table covered in sand. Ceramic models could be placed on the table to represent terrain. Units were represented by miniature soldiers, colored red and blue respectively. Each unit had a different "speed" and could move a different distance across the map each turn. The game also featured dice to determine the success of actions, and an umpire to adjudicate the outcome. The game was prescribed for Prussian officers, but the rules were so complex and tedious that some officers were reluctant to play it. In 1876, Colonel von Verdy du Vernois produced a simplified version of the game that removed the dice and delivered more authority to the umpire, who was expected to be a veteran officer who could draw on his own combat experience to determine what the results of each player's action would be.[5] This role was an early forebear of the dungeon master.

For the Prussian military, war games were not understood to be an "escape" from reality. On the contrary, the experience that officers gained while playing these games was expected to have immediate application in the real world. Game designers also understood that the more realistic and detailed their models of warfare were, the more the simulation would prepare officers for actual combat. In 1870, the militia army of Prussia defeated the professional army of France. The Prussian success was attributed to war games, and other Western militaries began to develop similar training exercises. In 1880, Charles Totten, a lieutenant in the United States Army, developed a game called *Strategos.*[6] Within a decade, German-inspired war games were introduced to the US Army and incorporated into the curriculum of the Naval War College.

War games were not easy to learn, and it was some time before anyone attempted to create a war game for civilians. The science-fiction writer H.G. Wells was among the first to create an "amateur" war game. In 1913, he created a game entitled *Little Wars: A Game for Boys of Twelve Years of Age to One Hundred and Fifty and for That More Intelligent Sort of Girl Who Likes Boys' Games and Books.*[7] A pacifist, Wells was not interested in creating a game that would train better officers. *Little Wars* was meant to be fun and possibly even to satisfy impulses that might lead to actual wars. This book also contained over a hundred photographs depicting battlefields that featured miniature soldiers and scenery. These photographs added nothing to the strategy of the simulation but were a source of pleasure for the players. In this sense, *Little Wars* marked a transition in wargaming from science into art.

Evidence of what may be the earliest transition from wargaming to role-playing appeared in the pages of *Life* magazine in 1941. An article entitled "*Life* Visits the Planet Atzor" described nineteen-year-old Frederick Pelton of Lincoln, Nebraska, who had organized a club around a fantasy world called Atzor. Each member of the club created a persona who ruled a nation of Atzor. The group held parties in which attendees would hold court in their personas. Aztor parties were attended in costume, which generally resembled the dress of European royalty. The club eventually expanded to 400 young Nebraskans, many of whom were women and played queens and empresses. Court gatherings usually resulted in declarations of war, and battles were resolved using miniatures. But Atzor involved much more than simulated battles. Club members produced Atzorian currency, a passport and postal system, and even a dictionary of the planet's language, Samarkandian.[8] Atzor became a paracosm, and the war game became a sort of performance art. Daniel Mackay suggests that the increasing emphasis on aesthetics in war games was a backlash against the cult of reason and efficiency that had, paradoxically, inspired military simulations in the first place.[9]

The first commercially successful war game was *Tactics* designed by Charles Roberts in 1953. He later formed the company Avalon Hill and published *Gettysburg,* a game in which players could simulate one of the most storied battles of the Civil War. *Gettysburg* was a huge success, and by 1962 Avalon Hill was the fourth largest producer of adult board games.[10] It is significant that the first truly successful war game in America was about Gettysburg. This battle was not only the turning point of the American Civil War; it was a sacred event, vital to the story that Americans tell themselves about their nation. In the Gettysburg Address, Lincoln spoke in explicitly religious language about consecrating and hallowing the battlefield as a sacred space. The carnage of the battle, according to Lincoln, had also been "the birth of a new freedom." The popular appeal of war games, then, did not lie simply in models and calculations but in revisiting and reenacting moments of historical and cultural significance. *Gettysburg* was commercially viable because it allowed Americans to experience and participate in a moment of sacred history while sitting at their kitchen tables.

Dave Wesley and Braunstein

By the 1960s, a subculture had formed around wargaming. There were several magazines for wargamers, and wargaming clubs had begun to appear on college campuses. As with *Gettysburg,* wargamers turned to military history for new conflicts to simulate. Where the military games of the nineteenth century had been attempts to simulate current technology, wargamers created simulations for World War II, the Crusades, and the campaigns of Roman generals. Dedicated groups would arrange series of games known as "campaigns" in which each battle determined the starting conditions of the next. Campaigns added a further sense of realism and immersion into another time and place.

The first step in the transition from war games to fantasy role-playing games occurred with an experimental game called "Braunstein" hosted by Dave Wesley at the University of Minnesota in 1968.[11] Wesley enjoyed war games but disliked their competitive nature. Too often games degenerated into bickering. Another problem was that games lasted for hours and allowed for only two players. In college wargaming clubs, it was not uncommon to see bored wargamers sitting idly, waiting for their chance to play. Wesley discovered a copy of Totten's

Strategos in the university's library. Like the Prussian war games, *Strategos* called for a disinterested referee to supervise the game. This was an element that had been dropped from war games like *Tactics* that were intended for a popular audience. Reintroducing a referee offered one way of resolving the arguments that marred the games.

But Wesley also wanted to create a non-zero-sum game that was not inherently competitive.[12] In the 1960s, opposition to the Vietnam War and militarism had inspired interest in noncompetitive games. The so-called New Games movement began with Stewart Brand, the editor of *The Whole Earth Catalog* and a member of Ken Kesey's "Merry Pranksters." In 1966, an antiwar group asked Brand to create a public activity to oppose the war in Vietnam. Brand responded with a game called *Slaughter*. As the name implied, *Slaughter* was a full-contact game. It featured a six-foot ball painted to look like Earth. There were virtually no rules other than to push the ball to the other side of the field. Teams were not declared but rather formed spontaneously. Curiously, whenever the ball neared one end of the field, some players would spontaneously decide to change objectives and begin pushing the ball in another direction. Much like fantasy role-playing games, *Slaughter* was "pointless," as there was no way of ending the game or determining a winner. However, its proponents defended it as art. If nothing else, *Slaughter* seemed to be an interesting critique of the Cold War as an equally pointless struggle by the two superpowers to "steer the planet." Brand went on to found the New Games movement, which emphasized play for the sake of play over competition.[13] Whether or not Wesley was aware of the New Games movement, his experiment at the University of Minnesota bore a family resemblance to *Slaughter*.

In *Strategos*, Totten emphasizes that the referee "must remember that anything which is physically possible may be attempted—not always successfully." Wesley expanded on this idea to create an entirely new kind of war game. He took a game published in *Strategy and Tactics* magazine called *The Siege of Bodenburg* to use as a springboard for his experiment. *The Siege of Bodenburg* was designed by Henry Bodenstedt, the proprietor of a hobby shop in New Jersey. It is a relatively simple war game in which an army of knights defends a medieval town against an invading force of Huns. The game called for miniature knights and Huns that could be purchased at Bodenstedt's shop. Wesley renamed the town "Braunstein" and set the siege during the time of Napoleon. More importantly, he modified the game to include multiple players as well as a referee. As with a traditional war game, two of the players assumed the role of the French and Prussian commanders. Wesley included more players by allowing them to assume the roles of various parties in Braunstein: the mayor, the banker, the university chancellor, and others. When interest in Wesley's experiment attracted twenty people, he found roles for all of them. Each role had its own objectives and goals. With autonomy came chaos. The game did not develop the way Wesley had imagined it and resembled an undisciplined brawl. The Prussian and French commanders announced that they had agreed to fight a duel, and Wesley was forced to improvise rules for this contingency. Wesley felt his game was a failure, that the players had taken over the game, and that the rules he had lovingly created no longer applied.[14] The players felt differently about Braunstein. They had enjoyed their chaotic struggle over the town. One particularly enthusiastic player was Dave Arneson, a student at the University of Minnesota. He recalled his experience of the game: "As a local student leader, I tried to rally resistance to thwart a French attack. (I ended up arrested by the Prussian General because I was 'too fanatical.')"[15] Wesley's experiment had failed as a strategy game, but it had triumphed as a role-playing game. He created more scenarios including a game set during the Russian Civil War and another set during a Latin American coup. Local gamers came to use the term "Braunstein" (or "Brownstine") generically to describe this new genre of open-ended war games.

The cooperative spirit of *Braunstein,* which was reflected by the New Games movement, also marked a "ritual turn" in war games. Claude Levi-Strauss argues that while games and rituals often resemble each other, games are *disjunctive* while ritual is *conjunctive.* In games with winners and losers, players or teams begin the game as equals, and differences are established between them. By contrast, ritual creates a union between groups that are initially distinct, such as congregation and priest. Levi-Strauss cites the Gahuku-Gama people of New Guinea, who play football continually until both teams have won an equal number of matches—a process that often takes days. For the Gahuku-Gama, Levi-Strauss argues, football is not a game but a ritual.[16] The Gahuku-Gama learned football from the British but "ritualized" the game, giving it a conjunctive function. Wesley made a similar move with *Braunstein.* As wargaming developed into an autotelic pastime, it increasingly came to resemble ritual.

Gary Gygax and Chainmail

The same year that Wesley organized *Braunstein* at the University of Minnesota, Gary Gygax organized the first annual "Gen Con," a convention for wargamers. It was held in the Horticultural Hall in Lake Geneva, Wisconsin, which Gygax rented for fifty dollars. There were ninety-six attendees, which was just enough to cover the costs. Gygax was not a university student. In 1958 he married Mary Jo Powell, with whom he had four children. He worked odd jobs and took night classes at a junior college where he made the dean's list. He was admitted to the University of Chicago, but decided instead to take a job as an insurance underwriter for the Fireman's Fund in Lake Geneva to support his family. Later, he ran a small shoe-repair business out of his basement.

Gygax was a leader of a wargaming group called United States Continental Army Command. As the group's interests and membership expanded, it was renamed the International Federation of Wargaming.[17] A subgroup of Gygax's International Federation of Wargaming was called the Castle and Crusade Society. The society was dedicated to simulating medieval battles and appealed to a rising interest in fantasy and medievalism under way in the 1960s. Wargaming was not the only outlet through which Americans were attempting to recreate the medieval past. In 1966, Diana Paxson of Berkeley, California, founded the Society for Creative Anachronism (SCA). This was an organization dedicated to "living history." Members dressed in costume, assumed personas as feudal lords and ladies, and gathered for feasts and others events. They revived medieval arts such as weaving, cooking, dance, calligraphy, archery, horsemanship, and fencing. The SCA, now larger than ever, also organizes battles in which combatants don metal armor and battle with weapons made from rattan. Significantly, the group describes its goal as recreating the Middle Ages "as they ought to have been."[18] That is, group members are not interested in strictly recreating history but rather in celebrating aspects of medieval culture that are interesting and appealing to them. The SCA is more an art form than a rigorous historical endeavor. For the counterculture of the 1960s, the Middle Ages were not merely the past, but an alternative world that seemed more personally satisfying. Gygax made a similar move toward reenacting history "as it ought to have been" through wargaming.

Gygax was introduced to *The Siege of Bodenburg* by Jeff Perren, the owner of a hobby shop in Lake Geneva. Like Wesley, Gygax loved the game and immediately set about modifying it. He expanded the rules from four pages to sixteen. In 1969, Gygax and Perren debuted their new medieval war game in the magazine of the Castle and Crusade Society, calling it *Chainmail*. In 1971, *Chainmail* was published by Guidon Games and retailed for three dollars. It was a relatively popular product, selling a hundred copies a month. A second edition, featuring a "fantasy supplement," was published the following year. Gygax drew the fantasy elements from pulp science fiction and fantasy novels of the 1950s and 1960s, particularly Tolkien, whose Lord of the Rings trilogy had gone through twenty-five successive printings between 1965 and 1969. Now in addition to medieval units such as cavalry, footmen, and archers, players could also include units of hobbits, dwarves, elves, goblins, orcs, trolls, several varieties of dragons, elementals, balrogs, and ents.[19]

Chainmail also featured rules for battle between individual soldiers rather than units. Gygax devised rules for "heroes," individuals who could single-handedly change the outcome of a battle. The idea of the hero was also inspired by fantasy novels, notably Robert E. Howard's character Conan the Barbarian. In addition to powerful warriors, there were rules for wizards or "magic users," who could summon forth fireballs and lightning bolts to devastate enemy units. The *Chainmail* fantasy supplement demonstrated that the models of simulation on which war games were based could be applied to anything that the human mind could conceive. As Ethan Gilsdorf explained, "The trolls and fireballs may be fanciful, but they have to behave according to a logical system."[20]

Dave Arneson and Blackmoor

While Gygax and Perren were the first to successfully publish a war game with elements of fantasy, similar changes were under way in wargaming groups throughout North America and the United Kingdom. "Ancient" wargaming referred to games that simulated battles fought by the Romans or earlier cultures. As early as 1957, Tony Bath of England created *The Hyboria Campaign,* a war game using "ancient" rules but based on Howard's Conan stories. Bath also experimented with a war game called *Tolkia* based on Tolkien's writings. Although Bath sometimes designed fantastic elements for war games, his British peers generally discouraged these endeavors.[21] More often, fantastic elements were introduced to war games spontaneously out of whim or boredom. Mark Barrowcliffe describes playing war games in the early 1970s before discovering *D&D*. He recalls a game in which the players were simulating the Siege of Leningrad. In addition to Soviet and Nazi forces, his gaming group added a number of dragons, wizards, and a giant slug.[22]

A similar moment of whim occurred in 1969 during a game hosted by Dave Arneson. Ever since participating in Wesley's *Braunstein* games, Arneson had continued to experiment with new forms of wargaming.

Arneson recalled refereeing an ancient war game involving a battle between Britons and Romans:

> As far as the fantasy part, I was the first one to come up with a violation of the basic concept of warfare of the period. We were fighting an ancient game. Very dull again. And I'd given the defending brigands a Druid high priest, and in the middle of the battle, the *dull* battle, the Roman war elephant charged the Britons and looked like he was going to trample half their army flat, the Druidic high priest waved his hands and pointed this funny little box out of one hand and turned the elephant into so much barbeque meat. This upset all of the participants in the game a great deal and the fellow playing the Druidic high priest was, well, he was laughing his head off in a corner. That was absolutely the only thing in the game that was out of the ordinary, but they weren't expecting it and it was of course, Star Trek was then playing, firing a phaser was adding science fiction to an Ancient game.[23]

Although the Druid wielded a phaser rather than magic, many historians of role-playing games regard this moment as the birth of the fantasy role-playing genre. It is also significant that Arneson's decision was inspired by *Star Trek*. The popular culture of the 1960s provided a rich milieu of fantastic elements from which wargamers regularly borrowed.

Arneson continued to design games that combined the format of *Braunstein* with elements of fantasy. His early projects drew from the Lord of the Rings trilogy as well as *Dark Shadows*, a popular soap opera of the 1960s that featured a vampire, a witch, and other supernatural characters. His greatest success was a game called *Blackmoor*, which he created in 1971. Arneson recalled that he created *Blackmoor* as a result of "watching five monster movies on *Creature Feature*, reading a Conan book and stuffing myself with popcorn, doodling on a piece of graph paper."[24] Initially, the premise of the game was that the players themselves had been hurled through a time warp into a medieval world full of monsters and magic, not unlike *A Connecticut Yankee in King Arthur's Court*. They did not play the role of a historical persona as in *Braunstein*, but rather played as university students in a fantastic setting. Arneson recalled:

> In the first campaign, all of the PCs [player characters] were assumed to have come through a time/space warp into the strange new world of Blackmoor. Thus, the players *could not expect* to know everything and all information from the locals would be related by the referee. So here were these 20th-century types; naturally the first thing they wanted to do was arm themselves to the teeth with firearms. I determined that they could arm themselves on the condition that they tell me how they made the weapons. Building weapons actually turned out to be quite interesting. The bottom line was that

firearms gave the players a fighting chance to survive and learn about the world before they ran out of bullets. Some of the lads had fun with hot air balloons and steam engines, but no one knew enough metallurgy to overcome some very basic problems.[25]

While *Blackmoor* employed a pseudo-historical setting in a manner similar to wargaming or the SCA, its strange premise was unprecedented. *Blackmoor* functioned like the "campaign" war games in that each session of play changed the imaginary world, creating a sense of continuity and realism. Each gaming session felt like a return to an alternative world. As Arneson continued to run games of *Blackmoor,* the players eventually assumed the roles of characters native to the fantasy world. Their adventures now almost always focused on individual interactions rather than battles, and so Arneson had to devise new rules. He met Gygax at the first Gen Con in 1968 and employed some of the *Chainmail* rules for *Blackmoor*. He also introduced a number of new concepts. Notably, he allowed players to improve their characters after each game, making them stronger. This became the basis of a "level system," now featured in many fantasy role-playing games, in which characters become more powerful as they gain experience.[26]

Arneson also shifted the game from the battlefield of traditional war games into large indoor settings such as castles, caverns, and mines. In one of Arneson's most successful games, the characters were sent to infiltrate Blackmoor Castle through its sewer to open the gates. The game was essentially a medieval commando raid. To reach the gate, the characters had to traverse the castle's dungeons, which were full of various guards and monsters. This premise helped to direct the flow of the game because the indoor environment presented players with a finite number of options. Similar scenarios became standard for fantasy role-playing games. The indoor environments of the games were known as "dungeons" regardless of the actual nature or purpose of the space. Arneson explained: "A dungeon is nice and self-contained. Players can't go romping over the countryside, and you can control the situation."[27]

Dungeons & Dragons

In 1972, Arneson attended Gen Con in Lake Geneva and ran his Castle Blackmoor scenario for convention goers. Gygax was impressed, and the two began collaborating via phone and mail. Their first collaboration was a game about naval combat called *Don't Give Up the Ship!,* published that year by Guidon Games. The game featured mechanics gleaned from both *Blackmoor* and *Chainmail* including armor class (a number indicating how difficult an object is to damage), hit points (a number indicating how much damage a target can withstand), and morale (a number representing fighting spirit).[28] In August 1973, Gygax formed a company called Tactical Studies Rules (TSR) with his childhood friend Don Kaye and Brian Blume, a wargamer he had met through Gen Con. Kaye kickstarted the company with $1,000 in start-up funds that he borrowed against his life insurance policy. The company's first product was a war game called *Cavaliers and Roundheads,* set during the English Civil War.[29] Gygax did not invite Arneson to join his company. He later explained: "Dave was never considered as a partner. We didn't figure he was the kind of the guy who would be too good at running a business."[30]

Gygax and Arneson continued to collaborate on what they called "The Fantasy Game." Initially there were only three types of characters that players could role-play: heroes, wizards, and a religious class called "clerics."[31] The game also included an experience system from Arneson's *Blackmoor* campaign in which characters could "level up" after successful adventures. There was no way to "win" the game, and the continual development of characters became the closest thing the game had to an objective.

It was Gygax who decided on a name. He wanted to continue a pattern of paired nouns already used in the Castle and Crusade Society and *Cavaliers and Roundheads.* He drew up two columns of words that included men, magic, monsters, treasure, underworld, wilderness, castles, dragons, dungeons, giants, labyrinths, mazes, sorcery, spells, swords, trolls, and so on. Then he ran various combinations of words by his play testers, who included Don Kaye and his children Ernie and Elise. He ended up deciding on "Dungeons & Dragons" because the alliteration pleased his youngest daughter, Cindy.[32] These sorts of names, often alliterative, became standard for fantasy role-playing games. Tony Bath created an ancient war game called *Pelfast and Pila* that depicted Roman armies. The first games to imitate *D&D* had names like *Tunnels and Trolls, Chivalry and Sorcery,* and *Heroes and Horrors.* There was a superhero game called *Villains and Vigilantes,* a fan magazine called *Alarums and Excursions,* and even a role-playing game based on the novel *Watership Down* called *Bunnies and Burrows,* in which players assume the roles of sentient rabbits. (In BADD literature that was distributed to law enforcement, Patricia Pulling warned of *Bunnies and Burrows,* "These rabbits are not like 'Peter Cottontail' they have human attributes, engage in violent/aggressive confrontations.")[33] Later, evangelical critics of fantasy role-playing games demonstrated that they could create alliterative titles too. One anti-*D&D* tract began: "Adventure or abomination? Creativity or cruelty? Diversion or demonology?"[34]

In December 1973 the first 150-page manuscript was sent off to Graphic Printing in Lake Geneva. Gygax felt the new game needed a bigger publisher than Tactical Studies Rules, so he went to Avalon Hill, the largest war game publisher in the business. He promised that *D&D* would sell 50,000 copies, but Avalon Hill declined. Arneson later stated of their decision, "They couldn't understand a game with no winners and losers that just went on and on."[35] And so Tactical Studies Rules scraped together $2,000 in start-up costs, much of which was contributed by Brian Blume.[36] In January 1974, the tiny company published 1,000 copies of a booklet titled *Dungeons & Dragons: Rules for Fantastic Medieval Wargame Campaigns Playable with Paper and Pencil and Miniature Figures*. The booklet was soon developed into a boxed set. The game came in a brown cardboard box with hand-applied labels on the front and sides. Inside were three half-sized booklets labeled "Men & Magic," "Monsters & Treasures," and "Underworld & Wilderness Adventures." But owning these three booklets was not enough to play *D&D*. The box also contained a list of equipment that was not included but necessary to play the game:

> *Dungeons and Dragons* (you have it)
>
> *Outdoor Survival* (a game available from the Avalon Hill Company used to play travel across the wilderness)
>
> Dice—the following different kinds of dice are available from TSR
>
> 1 pair 4-sided dice
>
> 1 pair 20-sided dice
>
> 1 pair 8-sided dice
>
> 1 pair 12-sided dice
>
> 4 to 20 pairs 6-sided dice
>
> Chainmail miniature rules (available from TSR Hobbies)
>
> Other Supplies:
>
> 1 3-Ring Notebook (for the referee and each player)
>
> Graph paper (6 lines per inch is best)
>
> Sheet Protectors (the heaviest possible)

3-Ring Lined Paper
Drafting Equipment and Colored Pencils
Scratch Paper and Pencils
Imagination
1 Patient Referee[37]

By all accounts the game was hopelessly confusing for anyone who did not already have a detailed knowledge of wargaming. In 1978, a journalist perused one of the forty-six-page rule booklets and remarked that it, "at least on first reading, is only marginally less complicated than a Ptolemaic analysis of planetary motion."[38] It is hardly surprising that Avalon Hill was unwilling to take a chance on this game. Gygax's basement, which was still filled with shoe-repair equipment, was converted into an assembly plant. Gygax, Kaye, and Blume all worked to assemble boxes, as did Gygax's wife and children. There was no money for marketing, and so it was necessary to advertise the game by word of mouth. It took eleven months to sell the first 1,000 copies, but the game was becoming popular. Mimeographed copies of *D&D* began circulating around college campuses. Gygax began to receive letters and phone calls, sometimes late at night, asking for clarifications about the rules. The game became popular in the military (the cultural birthplace of wargaming) and American servicemen spread *D&D* to Europe.[39] Soon the British company Games Workshop became *D&D*'s first European importer.

After an initial slow start, business picked up rapidly. In 1975, Avalon Hill decided they would like to purchase *D&D* after all. They made Gygax an offer, which was soundly rejected. In January that same year Don Kaye, who had borrowed the initial start-up funds to create TSR, died of a heart attack. He was eventually replaced by Brian Blume's brother, Kevin. Kaye's stake in the company was taken over by his wife, Donna, whom Gygax and the Blume brothers found "impossible to work with." So they simply dissolved Tactical Studies Rules and reincorporated as TSR Hobbies.[40]

Gygax and Brian Blume produced a second role-playing game, *Boot Hill,* set in the Old West. However, the company's main source of revenue was *D&D,* and TSR began to produce supplemental products at a feverish rate. An article in the *New York Times* entitled "Dungeons and Dollars" compared TSR's products to Gillette's business model of selling a cheap razor that would keep customers returning for blades.[41] In

1976, TSR began publishing *Dragon,* a magazine dedicated to *Dungeons & Dragons* and other fantasy role-playing games. In 1977, J. Eric Holmes offered to rewrite the game to make an introductory version for younger players. By March 1979, the company was selling 7,000 copies of the *D&D* basic set each month to an estimated 300,000 players.[42] In 1980, its gross income was $4.2 million.[43]

D&D rapidly became a subculture unto itself. Although fantasy role-players and wargamers still saw each other at conventions and hobby shops, role-players had become a distinct group. More traditional wargamers came to be referred to as "grognards," a Napoleonic term meaning "grumblers" and referring to the conservative Old Guard.[44] Players immediately began creating new rules, monsters, and character classes, some of which TSR published in subsequent books. As the game developed, TSR began thinking about the distinction between the mechanics for playing the game (frame two) and the imaginary worlds in which games occurred (frame three). Arneson had continued to host adventures in his land of Blackmoor, while Gygax ran a game in his own fantasy world that he dubbed *Greyhawk*. Both games represented ongoing stories and used similar rules, but featured different characters and imaginary lands. In 1975, TSR published *Greyhawk* as a supplement based on Gygax's world. TSR also hired Arneson, who produced a supplement called *Blackmoor* later that year. These became *D&D*'s first "campaign worlds," ready-made worlds of fantasy that could be used in the game. The worlds of *Blackmoor* and *Greyhawk* reflected the personalities of their creators and gradually yielded new elements that were added to the game. For *Blackmoor,* Arneson invented a new character class called the assassin, an expert in poison and murder, and the monk, a martial artist inspired by kung fu movies of the 1970s.[45] Gygax also created new character classes, notably the thief and the paladin, a holy warrior.[46]

Most players were as inventive as Arneson and Gygax (if not more so) and set about creating their own fantasy worlds. Many also began tinkering with the rules or creating entirely new games. In the late 1970s, an employee at a food co-op in San Francisco's Bay Area named Deanna Sue White became a minor celebrity as a result of her campaign world "Mistigar." About thirty people played characters that inhabited Mistigar and directed the course of its wars and politics. Those who could not attend games in person did so by correspondence, writing or calling White to explain what their characters were doing. Mistigar became so famous that a nearby group of *D&D* players calling themselves "the

Black Lotus Society" hatched a plot to "invade" Mistigar by joining the game as evil characters who would conquer and pillage White's paracosm rather than protect it. But Mistigar was so beloved that when other players caught wind of this plot, they had their characters slay the characters of the Black Lotus Society.[47] The battles for Mistigar demonstrate how quickly these shared fantasy worlds inspired an emotional investment on the part of players.

THE RISE AND FALL OF TSR

Almost as soon as *Dungeons & Dragons* was created, competitors began to produce similar games. One of the first of these was *Tunnels and Trolls,* published by Ken St. Andre of Phoenix, Arizona, in June 1975. St. Andre's game was originally marketed as "like D&D," which resulted in a cease-and-desist letter from TSR's lawyers. In 1984, Avalon Hill decided a fantasy role-playing game might be marketable after all and produced *Powers and Perils.* By 1989 there were over 300 such games on the market.[48] In general the creators of these games did not see themselves as imitating the ideas of Gygax and Arneson. Tinkering with and improving on existing games had always been part of the culture of wargaming. Many of the new games were presented as smoother or improved versions of *D&D.*

Gygax believed that gaming was good preparation for business and often ran his company like a war game. He saw other fantasy role-playing games not as a sincere form of flattery but as opponents to be defeated. Lawrence Schick, who worked for TSR, explains:

> As publisher of Dungeons and Dragons, TSR felt that role-playing was their special territory. As far as they were able, they tried to call the shots in the industry. They engaged in petty "turf" wars with other publishers and convention organizers, threatened legal action on the slightest provocation, and generally acted like the bully of the block.[49]

Some gamers began to feel that TSR were not artists producing a new art form but greedy capitalists who exploited other people's love of their game. The slogan "D&D is too important to leave to Gary Gygax" began to appear in independent magazines for fantasy gaming. One issue of *Alarums and Excursions* featured a description of a new *D&D* monster called a "Gygacks," which began: "These bull-headed men exactly resemble Minotaurs, but are extremely and annoyingly Lawful in nature. When encountered, they will insist upon everything being done their way, although they will insist that they favor individuality and diversity."[50]

TSR's lawyers sent out a number of cease-and-desist letters to gamers who sought to publish their own additions to *D&D*. Ironically, TSR was being sued by the estates of various fantasy authors whose work it adapted into games without permission. An early game called *Warriors of Mars,* based on the novels of Edgar Rice Burroughs, earned a legal action from Burroughs's estate. In 1977, TSR was sued by Hollywood mogul Saul Zaentz, who had acquired certain rights to Tolkien's works the year before. Zaentz claimed that terms such as "dragon," "orc," and "elf" were all protected, and demanded a million dollars in damages. TSR settled out of court, and *D&D* creatures that were clearly derivative of Tolkien, such as hobbits, ents, and balrogs were renamed halflings, treants, and balor demons.[51]

In November 1976, Arneson ceased to be an employee of TSR, leading to another series of lawsuits. As the cocreator of *D&D,* Arneson was entitled to lucrative royalties. So Gygax made some minor changes and began calling the product *Advanced Dungeons & Dragons* (*AD&D*). TSR continued to describe all of its new products as "Advanced" in order to avoid paying royalties to Arneson. Arneson sued TSR on five separate occasions.[52] These lawsuits were sometimes mentioned by the media and moral entrepreneurs to demonstrate that *D&D* was entangled in "controversy."

Undaunted, Gygax's next project was to create an "entertainment" division for TSR. The CBS network created a *Dungeons & Dragons* cartoon show that aired on Saturday mornings from 1983 to 1986. The premise of the cartoon was the same as Arneson's original *Blackmoor* campaign. It featured a group of teenagers who board a "*Dungeons & Dragons* ride" at a carnival and are magically transported to a world of magic and monsters. Each episode portrayed the teens' continued efforts to return home. Gygax went to Los Angeles to work on the show and had plans for other projects, including a *Dungeons & Dragons* movie. He rented a mansion on Summitridge Drive in Beverly Hills where he enjoyed a hot tub, chauffeured Cadillac rides, and a barn set up with a sand table so that he and his writers could play *Chainmail.* This lifestyle caused his expenses to approach $10,000 a month.[53]

Back in Wisconsin, TSR had begun to unravel. Gygax and his partners had assumed that the explosive growth of the last decade would continue unabated. At 600 employees, they had overstaffed the company. The Blumes had also invested in expensive computer equipment, office furniture, and a fleet of company cars. They invested in a salvage dive to recover the wreck of the steamship that had sunk in Lake Geneva in 1891. There were rumors that the company owned a mansion on the Isle of Man and had discussed purchasing a railroad company in order to vertically integrate shipping.[54] By 1984, TSR was $1.5 million in debt, and it was rumored that the Blumes were seeking to sell the company. Gygax returned to Lake Geneva, where he persuaded the board of directors to fire Kevin Blume. He published a new *D&D* rule book to raise money, but to pay off TSR's debts he needed new investors. In Los Angeles, he had met Lorraine Dille Williams, who had experience as an administrator for hospitals and nonprofits. She was also the granddaughter of John F. Dille, a newspaper magnate who had turned the science-fiction character Buck Rogers into a syndicated comic strip. Williams inherited the rights of the Buck Rogers character as well as a valuable collection of Buck Rogers memorabilia. She initially turned down Gygax's offer to invest in TSR but agreed to advise him on managing the company.[55]

In May 1985, Gygax exercised a stock option that gave him a controlling interest in TSR. He named himself CEO and hired Williams as a general manager. Williams was impressed by the value of TSR's intellectual property and used her business acumen to take over the company. She bought out the Blume brothers, who were already planning to leave TSR, giving her a majority share. Gygax responded by taking Williams to court, claiming that the Blume brothers had not given adequate notice of sale. The trial lasted five days, but in the end a judge awarded ownership of TSR to Williams.[56] Now both Gygax and Arneson were legally barred from the game they had created. In 1992, Gygax designed a new fantasy role-playing game called *Dangerous Dimensions* for a rival game publisher, Game Designers' Workshop. Williams sued on behalf of TSR, claiming that the game's alliteration (two "D" words) was too much like *Dungeons & Dragons*. Gygax changed the name of his game to *Dangerous Journeys*.

Williams proved to be a far more capable leader than either Gygax or the Blume brothers. However, she approached the company from a purely business perspective and had no interest in war games or role-playing. It was rumored among TSR employees that she boasted of having never once played a role-playing game.[57] When she took control of TSR, she initially declared that she would change the focus of the company to making board games about TV soap operas.[58] Fortunately for fans of *D&D*, this did not come to pass. Williams's tenure as head of TSR saw the creation of several new campaign worlds. These worlds, with names like Faerun, Krynn, and Ravenloft, provided a background for further storytelling. In edition to publishing game supplements, TSR published 242 novels set in these worlds as well as several computer games.[59]

The company experienced another crisis in the mid-1990s. *D&D* was more popular than ever, but the company had published more supplemental products than a saturated market was willing to consume. Meanwhile, new games were eating away at TSR's market. The biggest of these was a card game called *Magic: The Gathering* published by Wizards of the Coast. Although *Magic* was not a role-playing game, it contained elements of fantasy and attracted the same market. More importantly, *Magic* was sold in the form of inexpensive "packs" that contained a random assortment of cards. Some players were willing to spend exorbitant amounts of money in search of rare cards.

Despite these obstacles, 1996 was the best sales year in the history of the company with $40 million in sales. However, a clause in TSR's distribution contract turned this triumph into a disaster. In 1981, TSR entered a distribution agreement with Random House, which shipped TSR products to small bookstores, such as B. Dalton and Waldenbooks. At the end of the year, the contract allowed Random House to return any unsold products to TSR, at which time TSR would have to pay for the products as well as a handling fee. That year, TSR had invested heavily in hardcover fantasy novels as well as a new game called *Dragon Dice*. *Dragon Dice* was TSR's answer to *Magic: The Gathering*. Instead of packs containing random cards, players were encouraged to purchase boxes containing randomly patterned dice. Both of these products flopped, and at the end of the year nearly a third of TSR's products were returned. After paying Random House, the company did not have the capital for printing, and finished products sat unprinted. TSR had also fallen behind on payments to a logistics company that handled printing, warehousing, and shipping. The logistics company stopped working with TSR and refused to ship existing products out. Furthermore, they had all of the production plates for TSR's best-selling products, meaning the company could not do business with someone else. Williams immediately began searching for someone to purchase TSR and assume its debts.

TSR was initially purchased by a collectible card game company called Five Rings Publishing. Soon after, in June 1997, Wizards of the Coast bought out both companies. The wild success of *Magic: The Gathering* combined with the economic conditions of the Internet bubble had left Wizards of the Coast with several million dollars of capital waiting to be invested. Because of the crisis at TSR, it was widely assumed that Gen Con would not be held, for the first time since 1968. The convention had grown into a massive affair that drew in players from around the world. Wizards of the Coast decided that Gen Con must happen and made hosting the conference a priority. Next, Wizards of the Coast sought out the creators of TSR's greatest product. Arneson received a settlement, and Wizards of the Coast was finally able to drop the word *Advanced* from *D&D*. Wizards of the Coast also paid a settlement to Gary Gygax and gave him their blessing to develop any new games he wished. Gygax went on to produce a game called *Lejendary Adventure* in 1999 and collaborated on a game called *Castles and Crusades* in 2005.[60]

Gygax died in March 2008. At Gen Con, the din of the exhibit hall was halted in order to hold a moment of silence for the man who had founded the conference. The Gen Con staff also had a special plaque dedicated to Gygax, which read:

> The first DM,
> He taught us to roll the dice.
> He opened the door to new worlds.
> His work shaped our industry.
> He brought us Gen Con,
> For this we thank him.[61]

In Lake Geneva, Gygax's funeral was followed by an impromptu session of gaming that quickly developed into an annual event called "Gary Con." Journalist David Ewalt compared his experience attending Gary Con to a Muslim undertaking the hajj.[62] At the time of this writing, Wizards of the Coast is working to erect a memorial to Gary Gygax in Lake Geneva.[63] Dave Arneson died one year after his former partner. Although his death did not receive the same media attention as Gygax's, a mourner posted on Arneson's online obituary:

> My brother loved your games Dave. . . . He was taken too early as you were too. Please say hello to him in Heaven from me and sit down and play a few rounds of Dungeons and Dragons with him. He was very good and will give you a run for your money, or whatever you play for in Heaven. See you when I get there.[64]

CHAPTER 2

Dungeons & Dragons as Religious Phenomenon

I don't think it's an exaggeration to say that, at this time, my devotion to the game became almost religious.

—Mark Barrowcliffe, *The Elfish Gene*

No living, normal man can be reduced to his conscious, rational activity, for modern man still dreams, falls in love, listens to music, goes to the theater, views films, reads books—in short, lives not only in a historical and natural world but also in an existential, private world in an imaginary Universe. It is primarily the historian and phenomenologist of religions who is capable of recognizing and deciphering the "religious" structures and meanings of these private worlds or imaginary Universes.

—Mircea Eliade, *The Quest*

In his autobiography, *The Elfish Gene,* Mark Barrowcliffe describes his attitude toward the *Dungeons & Dragons* as "almost religious." *D&D* first appeared in the 1970s in the midst of a moral panic over cults. In 1978, one reporter opined, "The game inspires the sort of fanatic devotion usually associated with mind-bending religious cults."[1] This vague sense that there was something "religious" about this new game continued into the 1980s. BADD and similar groups eventually claimed that fantasy role-playing games were not only *similar* to a religion but actually *were* a dangerous religious movement masquerading as entertainment. As one concerned citizen warned in a letter to the editor, "I believe Dungeons and Dragons is a cult and more than 'just a game.'"[2]

Neither players, journalists, nor moral entrepreneurs were ever very good at explaining *why* fantasy role-playing games seemed religious. BADD's approach was to simply ignore the imaginary frame of the game. BADD claimed that if players assume the existence of deities, religious traditions, and rituals within the context of the game, then they must also believe in these religious elements outside of the game. This claim is, of course, absurd. Players do not share the religious worldviews of their characters any more than an actor playing Shylock is necessarily Jewish. Fantasy role-playing games cannot be said to be a "religion" in the same way that Christianity, Judaism, or Buddhism is a religion. However, BADD's claims were successful in part because they appealed to a much broader sense that *D&D* was not an ordinary game and that there was something very serious at stake for those who played it.

Those who study religion know that the label "religion" is notoriously vague and can be used to signify a variety of meanings. While *D&D* is not a religion according to most definitions, there are aspects of the game that could be thought of as *religious*. Furthermore, I suspect that outside observers sensed a religious function at play in *D&D* but lacked the background in religious studies to articulate how exactly the game related to their understanding of religion as a category. Claims that fantasy role-playing games are "a cult" were, in part, attempts to express this idea.

There are three ways in which fantasy role-playing games may be usefully compared to religion. First, there are many elements of *D&D* that are substantively religious—that is, they concern morality, gods, rituals, and the supernatural. In many cases, these elements reflect the religious worldviews of the game's creators. When moral entrepreneurs claim that *D&D* is a religion, they focus exclusively on these substantive elements. However, the important religious functions of the game lie elsewhere. Chess has "bishops," but no one would claim that this qualifies it as a religion.

Second, the most significant function that *D&D* shares with religion is the possibility of experiencing a more idealized time and place. As Gary Alan Fine notes, the pleasure of becoming engrossed in an alternate reality is the raison d'être of the game. When players and journalists speak of a "religious devotion" to fantasy role-playing games, they refer to the intensity with which players pursue this experience of engrossment. The worlds of fantasy role-playing games are radically different from our own, and they are often worlds in which moral forces such as good and evil are more vivid and more intensely experienced.

This nostalgia for a world of heightened meaning has a long history in the West going back at least to the romantics of the eighteenth century. In the 1960s many tried to make sense of a century characterized by mechanized warfare and existential doubts by looking to other times and places—first to history, then to mythology and worlds of fantasy. Fantasy role-playing developed alongside fiction, historical reenactment, and wargaming as the most intense and direct method of experiencing another world. In providing this connection to a realm of heightened meaning, fantasy role-playing has a function in common with myth and religious ritual.

Finally, by inhabiting another world we are able to look back at our own from a new perspective. This too is a function that fantasy role-playing games share with religion. While the truth claims of religious worldviews generally cannot be proven empirically, they exert an observable influence on the way that people order their world. Religion provides models of humanity's place in the cosmos and enables us to think in ways that were previously impossible. The imaginary worlds of fantasy role-playing games provide similar models and can, in some cases, provide a similar form of agency. This agency is largely what is at stake when religious critics of fantasy role-playing games describe these games in heresiological terms as "occultism." The word "heresy" is derived from the Greek *hairesis,* meaning "choice." Because fantasy worlds allow gamers to imagine things that were once unimaginable, they also present choices that were once inconceivable.

SUBSTANTIVE ELEMENTS OF RELIGION IN *DUNGEONS & DRAGONS*

Both creators of *Dungeons & Dragons* were devout Christians. Dave Arneson was affiliated with the Way International and performed missionary work during the 1980s. Gary Gygax became a Jehovah's Witness when he married his first wife. In his history of *D&D,* Jon Peterson discovered several articles by Gygax in gaming magazines and newsletters that reveal his faith. On several occasions he announced that he was retiring from wargaming in order to dedicate more time to his faith. In February 1969, Gygax published a short article in the newsletter for the International Federation of Wargaming explaining that while he was grateful for the Christmas cards he received, as a Christian he did not celebrate Christmas. The article goes on to claim that Christmas was a pagan invention, and cites numerous passages from the New Testament supporting the thesis that Christians ought not to celebrate Christmas. In another article, in the wargaming magazine *Graustark,* Gygax explains his objection to the Vietnam War in millennialist terms:

> You know, the Bible Book of Revelation describes the dual Anglo-American world power as an animal that resembles a two-horned lamb with a mouth of a dragon and calls it a false prophet. . . . The US cloaks its actions in lamb-like motives (that is what are declared to be altruistic reasons for aggressive wars) but you'd better believe that it speaks like a dragon! . . . Now it's the "False Prophet" because it is misleading the nations (like backing the U.N., the "Image of the Wild Beast" and they all derive their power from Satan).[3]

In an interview given at Gen Con in 2007, Gygax explained that he had been reluctant to talk about his identity as a Christian during the era of the panic: "I was afraid it would give Christianity a bad name because I did D&D."[4]

Christianity left an indelible mark on Gygax and Arneson's game. There was no need to include religion, in the substantive sense, in a game set in a medieval fantasy world. But religion and morality are certainly part of *D&D.* Even before the creation of *D&D,* Gygax's *Chainmail* featured a rule called "alignment" in which every creature has a moral essence, defining it as an entity of either law or chaos. Some of the first character classes Gygax created for the game were explicitly religious ones: the cleric and the paladin. Finally in 1976, TSR published *Gods, Demi-Gods, and Heroes.* This was essentially a crash course in comparative mythology and presented rules for including gods and religions in fantasy worlds. This was only the fourth supplement ever produced for the game.

A number of early game designers found these elements off-putting. Ken St. Andre explains that themes of religion and morality in *D&D* were among the key reasons he created his own game, *Tunnels and Trolls:*

> [*Tunnels and Trolls*] was written largely as a revolt against Gygax's game. First to go were funny sided dice—my game would use all six-sided, which can be obtained from any old Monopoly or Yahtzee game. Next, let's get rid of clerics. Religion was not very important in my life, so why should it clutter up my game? . . . Next to go was alignment. Why should characters be Good, Evil, Lawful, Chaotic, or Neutral? In the real world people made their own choices and characters.[5]

St. Andre is certainly correct that there seems to be an unusual amount of religion in *D&D,* and that great emphasis is placed on a system of morality that is narrowly defined. Ironically, it was precisely these elements of religion and morality that were cited by moral entrepreneurs as evidence that *D&D* is anti-Christian.

Alignment

Alignment is a feature of game mechanics that frames the morality of all intelligent beings in the game. Alignment is often less the sum total of a character's moral choices than an aspect of the character's essential nature. Of the hundreds of fantasy role-playing games that have emerged since *D&D,* virtually none have framed morality in such stark and absolute terms. In 1979, TSR published a pamphlet entitled *What Is Dungeons and Dragons?* It explained, "D&D . . . furnishes a world in which everything is categorized and labeled; there is no mistaking good and evil."[6] In edition 3.5 of *D&D,* published in 2004, the idea of alignment is explained through the following story:

> In the temple of Pelor is an ancient tome. When the temple recruits adventurers for its most sensitive and important quests, each one who wants to participate must kiss the book. Those who are evil in their hearts are blasted by holy power, and even those who are neither good nor evil are stunned. Only those who are good can kiss the tome without harm and are trusted with the temple's most important work. Good and evil are not philosophical concepts in the D&D game. They are the forces that define the cosmos.[7]

The idea of a Manichaean universe divided between good and evil is especially prominent in the writings of Tolkien and C. S. Lewis. In Tolkien's *Two Towers,* Frodo attempts to bind Gollum with an elvish rope, but the rope burns Gollum's flesh.[8] Gollum is a creature of evil while the elves (and their creations) are good. Thus the rope burns Gollum simply because of his moral essence. Here, morality is so absolute that it resembles chemistry, and certain combinations of essence lead to predictable results.[9]

One year before the Lord of the Rings trilogy was published, Poul Anderson's novel, *Three Hearts and Three Lions,* appeared in the *Magazine of Fantasy and Science Fiction.* Although the novel was a relatively obscure work it introduced an important feature to the dualism of the fantasy genre, reframing it in a quasi-scientific register as a battle between the forces of law and chaos. The novel begins during World War II, and the protagonist, Holger Carlsen, is a Danish engineer fighting in the resistance movement against the Nazis. An explosion sends him to a parallel world resembling the Middle Ages. This world is also defined by a great war, a war between the forces of Law and Chaos. Holger joins the side of Law, associated with humanity and the Roman Catholic Church. The forces of Chaos include witches and pagans as well as creatures of "the Middle World," such as elves, trolls, and faeries.

Three Hearts and Three Lions was a major influence on *D&D*. Several monsters in the game appear to be inspired by Anderson's story, and Holger's persona as a champion of Law influenced Gygax to create the paladin class.[10] The novel may even be the inspiration for the original premise of the *Blackmoor* campaign. In fact, had Anderson been born two decades later, he would likely have played in this campaign. Anderson graduated from the University of Minnesota in 1948, and in the 1960s he became a founding member of the Society for Creative Anachronism.

Although *Three Hearts and Three Lions* is not an especially well-written novel, it contains much for a game designer or a scholar of religion to ponder. Several passages in the novel are dedicated to Holger's scientific musings on Law and Chaos, which he eventually decides resemble "modes of existence" more than forces. Chaos draws strength from war, while peace and order are only possible under Law. However, Law and Chaos are not precise equivalents of good and evil. For the faerie creatures Law is as painful and intolerable as Chaos is for humans. Law is stifling, and Chaos creatures seek to "restore some primeval state where anything could happen."[11]

Science is the enemy of Chaos because Chaos uses magic to run roughshod over the laws of the physical universe. The three Abrahamic religions are also allied with Law and condemn witchcraft. Thus rationalism and transcendent religion are allies against a magical worldview associated with archaic religion. Anderson's moral universe was not so different from the ideas of Max Weber, who claimed that transcendent religion had led to an "iron cage" of rationalization and the disenchantment of the world.

Finally, Anderson's model applies to our world as well as to the fantasy world. Holger muses:

> This business of Chaos versus Law, for example, turned out to be more than religious dogma. It was a practical fact of existence, here. He was reminded of the second law of thermodynamics, the tendency of the physical universe towards disorder and level entropy. Perhaps here, that tendency found a more . . . animistic . . . expression. Or, wait a minute, didn't it in his own world too? What had he been fighting when he fought the Nazis but a resurgence of archaic horrors that civilized men had once believed were safely

> dead? . . . The same fight was being waged, here the Nazis and there the Middle World but in both places, Chaos against Law, something old and wild and blind at war with man and the works of man.[12]

Here Law and Chaos are not only the premise of a fantasy novel but a model of the great conflicts of the twentieth century. They are a theoretical framework through which Anderson interprets the carnage that defined the era in which he came of age. Holger's adventure in a fantasy realm serves to better articulate Anderson's model of the underpinnings of World War II by using the fictional narrative to cast idealized moral forces into relief.

A decade after *Three Hearts and Three Lions,* Michael Moorcock used Anderson's cosmic battle between Law and Chaos as the basis for many of his novels. However, while Anderson used Law and Chaos as a pseudo-scientific version of Christian morality, Moorcock created a universe where Law and Chaos appear to supersede notions of good and evil, rendering them obsolete. His most famous character was Elric of Melniboné. Moorcock created Elric after an editor for the pulp magazine *Science Fantasy* said he would like to publish something similar to Robert E. Howard's stories about Conan the Barbarian. At the time, Moorcock was in a dark period of his life, resulting from a combination of poverty, heavy drinking, and unrequited love. He writes: "I do recall with great pride, my main achievement of the winter of 1960 or 1961, which was to smash entirely an unbreakable plate-glass door in a well-known restaurant near Piccadilly. . . . I mention this, to give a picture of my mood at the time of Elric's creation."[13]

Whereas Anderson used his fantasy to construct a moral universe that could account for the apparent evil of World War II, Moorcock created a fantasy that articulated his moral uncertainty and doubts about humanity. The Elric stories depict a nihilistic universe in which humanity is caught in the middle of a meaningless battle between forces beyond its comprehension. Elric is an antihero who reflects Moorcock's own sense of alienation. He is an emperor by birth and the last heir to the decadent and wicked empire of Melniboné, which worships the forces of Chaos. Whereas Conan is a physical paragon, Elric is an albino and requires drugs to maintain his strength. In a war with his cousin, Elric destroys the last great city of Melniboné and chooses a life of exile and adventure. To gain the power to defeat his rivals, Elric makes a Faustian bargain with the demon Arioch, one of the Lords of Chaos. He also wields "Stormbringer," a sentient and evil sword that drinks the souls of its victims and transfers their life force to Elric. Elric despises Stormbringer but is addicted to its power and lacks the strength of will to relinquish it. Moorcock explains: "Elric, for me, symbolized the ambivalence of mankind in general, with its love-hates, its mean-generosity, its confident-bewilderment act. Elric is a thief who believes *himself* robbed, a lover who hates love. In short, he cannot be sure of the truth of anything, not even his own emotions or ambitions."[14] At the end of the series, Stormbringer kills those closest to Elric before finally slaying its wielder.

The creators of *D&D* were so inspired by the Elric stories that *Gods, Demi-Gods, and Heroes* contained rules for Elric and the various demons and supernatural beings described in his world. In 1979, TSR published an adventure called *White Plume Mountain* in which the heroes can recover a sinister sword named "Blackrazor," an obvious derivative of Stormbringer. In 1981, Ken St. Andre produced a fantasy role-playing game called *Stormbringer* based directly on the Elric stories. Meanwhile, evangelical crusader Bob Larson was so horrified and fascinated by the Elric stories that he devoted an entire page to the character's idolatrous exploits in his book *Satanism: The Seduction of America's Youth*.[15]

Chainmail, which first introduced the concept of alignment, mentions both Anderson and Moorcock explicitly. *D&D* attempted to simultaneously include both the dualism of Tolkien and Anderson, with its moral and religious certainty, and the dualism of Moorcock, with its existential malaise. Each creature's moral essence is defined using both a law-chaos axis and a good-evil axis. A "chaotic good" character shirks rules and authority but respects human life and dignity. A "lawful evil" character seeks personal gain at the expense of others but does so within the confines of the law. Both axes also offer the possibility of neutrality for a total of nine alignments. "True neutral" refers to characters that are neutral on both axes.

It was quickly discovered that the concept of alignment has applications outside of the context of the game. The website for Wizards of the Coast features a quiz to determine what your alignment is. (According to the quiz, I am "neutral good." While I am generally law-abiding, the life of an untenured professor entails frequent moving, the inability to make long-term plans, having fewer ties to a community—in sum, chaos.) However, many gamers rejected the idea that individuals have a moral essence. Many game systems developed after *D&D* included an element similar to alignment that defined the character's nature, but none were ever as morally absolute as the *D&D* alignment system. Indeed, alignment in *D&D* is not realistic or based on empirical observation. Alignment is a theoretical model that helps to order the world. Its usefulness is not that it is realistic but that it is consistent and can be applied to anything capable of moral behavior.

Perhaps because alignment serves a religious function in offering a model of morality, it has drawn the attention of religious critics of *D&D*. One might think that conservative Christians would approve of a game that frames good and evil in such stark and immutable terms. After all, this is a moral universe that is heavily influenced by Christianity. Instead, critics of *D&D* claimed, paradoxically, that alignment was designed to blur the lines between good and evil, rendering these concepts meaningless.

Larson boasts of an encounter on his radio show *Talk Back* in which he rhetorically defeated a gamer who called the show. Larson explains: "One caller, Charles, explained that the roll of the dice gave him a character who was 'neutral-good' with 'chaotic-lawful' attributes. 'That's contradictory,' I challenged Charles. 'In reality, good is not neutral. The very idea of ethical neutrality supposes that our world exists in a moral vacuum."[16] Of course, anyone who has played *D&D* knows that players choose the alignment of their characters instead of rolling dice. Similarly, Larson does not understand the two axes. Law and chaos are at opposite ends of the same axis, and therefore "chaotic-lawful" is not one of the nine alignments, law and chaos being on the same axis. Misunderstandings aside, Larson's comment demonstrates a view that was widely held by religious critics of *D&D* that alignment promotes moral relativism rather than moral certainty.

A variation of this critique is that while *D&D* does present valid concepts of good and evil, it does not presume that good will ultimately triumph, and gives players no incentive to choose good over evil. Peter Leithart and George Grant argue: "Most FRPs take place in a thoroughly Manichaean universe where law and chaos are equally powerful and, in a strange sense, equally 'good.' . . . In such a universe, magic can be either white or black, good or evil. And it doesn't matter which."[17] Carl Raschke, a religion professor, is one of the few academics who embraced the moral panic over Satanism and fantasy role-playing games in the 1980s. He takes this argument even further in his book *Painted Black,* where he suggests that *D&D* is actually a "pedagogy" intended to teach children that evil and occultism are more effective than good. In fact, Raschke claims that the word "alignment" was chosen because it sounds like "astrology." His implication is that the very term "alignment" is an attempt to steer players toward yet another occult science.[18]

It is true that the game mechanics give no specific advantage to good characters. However, as in the real world, characters that are cooperative and trustworthy often succeed where selfish characters do not. Perhaps for this reason, Fine found that 80 percent of all players he studied chose to play "good" or "lawful" characters.[19] On the other hand, Barrowcliffe recalls that in his clique of troubled teenagers evil characters were preferred because no one wanted to be seen as "a goodie-goodie."[20]

More importantly, one could make the opposite argument to Leithart and Grant—that if good is guaranteed to win, then goodness becomes merely a means to an end rather than an end unto itself. In 1984, the *Dragonraid Adventure Learning System* was published as the first Christian fantasy role-playing game. Unlike *D&D, Dragonraid* really was a pedagogical tool for religious training. Heavily influenced by the allegorical Christian fantasy of C.S. Lewis, the game takes place in the fantasy world of "EdenAgain." The characters are called "the TwiceBorn" and serve "the Overlord of Many Names." The adventures require players to demonstrate evangelical values through their characters, and if they fail to do so, they lose the game. The mechanics of the game also allow the TwiceBorn to roll different dice from the villains, giving good a statistical advantage over evil. While this system is designed to promote Christian values, the absence of free will casts doubt on whether the players have any interest in these values or are merely seeking to win.

Dragonraid is a window into Christian fears about fantasy role-playing games. This is a role-playing game that really was created to modify the beliefs and values of the players. *Dragonraid* requires the players, rather than their characters, to participate in religious rituals. Players must memorize "Wordrunes," which are actually Bible verses. Certain events in the game require players to recite a Wordrune successfully to determine what happens. The religious opponents of fantasy role-playing games often claimed that players were required to memorize and chant "occult" phrases in order to cast spells in the game. Ironically, *Dragonraid* is the only known role-playing game that requires players to perform any sort of formal recitation as part of the mechanics of the game.

Ironically, BADD and similar groups attacked *Dragonraid* as an even more subtle attempt to lure Christians down the path to occultism. These attacks essentially destroyed the intended market for *Dragonraid* and seriously damaged sales during the 1980s.[21] The attack on *Dragonraid* suggests that religious critics of fantasy role-playing games were sensitive to the religious elements of role-playing games but were also profoundly alienated by any appearance of Christian cosmology in these games.

Fantasy Religions

Not only is *D&D* set in a moral universe, but imaginary religions play an important role in the game. One of the basic character classes introduced in 1974 was the cleric, a hero whose powers come from her religious devotion to one or more deities.[22] With the possible exceptions of Robin Hood's Friar Tuck and Edith Pargeter's brother Cadfael, clerics are not stock characters in medieval legend and fiction. Few of the fantasy writers who influenced *D&D* featured overtly religious heroes. Gygax and Arneson appear to have conceived of the cleric through a combination of three influences: (1) the prevalence of the Catholic Church in medieval European society, (2) their own background in biblical literature, and (3) the depiction of Christianity in horror films of the 1960s. As in *Three Hearts and Three Lions, D&D* assumes that religion and magic are completely different forces. While the powers of both clerics and wizards are described as "spells," they do very different things. Many of the original cleric spells have obvious provenance in the Bible. Like Moses, clerics can temporarily part bodies of water or turn a wooden staff into a serpent. Like the prophet Elijah, they can purify tainted food and water, raise the dead, or call down fire on their enemies. Like the apostles, they can cure various wounds and illnesses and speak in tongues. Even a cleric spell called "conjure animals" appears to reference a story in 2 Kings in which a gang of boys mocks the prophet Elisha for his bald head. In retaliation, Elisha curses them in the name of the Lord, causing two she-bears to emerge from the woods and kill forty-two of the children. In the first edition of the game, "conjure animals" specifically summons two large bears. Clerics also have the power to repel undead creatures by holding up their holy symbol. Gygax listed Bram Stoker as one of his influences, and this ability appears to reflect numerous Dracula films in which a vampire hunter repels the undead using a crucifix.[23] According to David Ewalt, Arneson had a player who wanted to play a vampire and another who wanted to play a vampire hunter. The ability to repel the undead was created as a special ability for the vampire hunter. Both players wanted to create these characters after watching the soap opera *Dark Shadows*.[24]

As with alignment, religious critics of *D&D* interpreted the cleric not as evidence of the game's provenance in Christianity but rather of occultism and heresy. Leithart and Grant cite the "sticks to snakes" spell as evidence that *D&D* contains "genuine occultic techniques."[25] In a stark example of the "erotics of fear," Raschke perused the *D&D* "red box" starter set intended for children as young as twelve and concluded that the cleric "uses sexual magic to get her way." Nothing in the rules or the narrative would suggest this. Apparently, Raschke simply found a drawing of a female cleric alluring.[26] Albert Dager, in one of the earliest religious critiques of *D&D,* objected that characters can purchase supplies such as wolvesbane, holy water, and garlic to ward off evil creatures. He writes: "It is not without knowledge that *Dungeons and Dragons* was devised. But it is the knowledge of an evil that mingled the Babylonian mystery religions with a luke-warm 'Christianity.'"[27] Dager's odd reference to Babylonian mystery religions is a code word for Catholicism. Here he builds on a claim made by some evangelical Protestants that Catholicism is not "really" Christianity, but a form of Babylonian paganism disguised with Christian trappings. Dager is the only religious critic to acknowledge Christian influences of the game, but he does so by framing these influences as heretical. In fact, the "Catholic" elements of the game cited by Dager are derived from horror films, notably those produced by Hammer Studios during the 1960s, in which Catholic objects such as crucifixes and holy water are portrayed as tools against monsters.

While *D&D* features religious characters, the original rules did not describe fantasy religions. When Gygax's circle of players wanted to know what their clerics prayed to, he created a being called "Saint Cuthbert." Gygax's saint was directly based on Saint Cuthbert of Lindisfarne, a seventh-century monk and bishop. Alfred the Great claimed to have a vision of Saint Cuthbert while repelling an invasion of Danes, and Cuthbert remains an important saint in northern England. In an adventure published in *Dragon* in 1985, the characters must magically travel to twentieth-century Earth and retrieve the mace of Saint Cuthbert from the London Museum. The adventure implies that *D&D*'s Saint Cuthbert and Saint Cuthbert of Lindisfarne are one and the same.[28] Gygax likely opted for a medieval saint because he wanted to present a religion that resembled medieval Christianity without bringing the Judaeo-Christian deity into his fantasy game.

The 1977 supplement *Eldritch Wizardry* introduced further religious elements to the game. In addition to a new "druid" character class, this supplement introduced demons for the first time. Many of the monsters in this supplement, such as the succubus, were drawn from Christian demonology. Rules were provided for a demon prince named "Orcus," the name of a Roman god of death referenced in Virgil's *Aeneid.* Another demon prince is named "Demogorgon," a name that appears in several early modern and romantic narratives, including Milton's *Paradise Lost,* Edmund Spenser's *The Fairie Queen,* Lodovico Ariosto's *Orlando Furioso,* and Percy Bysshe Shelley's *Prometheus Unbound.* C.S. Lewis concludes that the name "demogorgon" first arose as a corruption of the demiurge mentioned in Plato's *Timaeus,* and then entered Western literature.[29] Critics regarded the use of demonic names in *D&D* as evidence that the game's creators were part of a demonic cult. In reality, these names only evidenced their background in classics and Western literature.

The prominence of original fantasy religions in *D&D,* as opposed to adaptations of Christian saints and demons, can be attributed largely to the influence of a philologist named M.A.R. Barker. Philip Barker was born in 1929 and grew up in rural Idaho. His next-door neighbors were a Basque family, and Barker developed an interest in philology in part because he was jealous that his neighbors could tell secrets in another language.[30] He studied Indian languages in college and in 1951 received a Fulbright scholarship to do further research in southern India.

It was during this trip that he converted to Islam and changed his name to Muhammad Abd-al-Rahman Barker. He explained: "I adopted Islam while I was over there, for purely theological reasons. It seemed like a more logical religion."[31] He received a doctorate from Berkeley, where he wrote his dissertation on Klamath, a vanishing Native American language. In 1972 he took a position at the University of Minnesota—the alma mater of Poul Anderson and the home of the *Braunstein* and *Blackmoor* games. It was here that he became interested in wargaming.

Even before discovering wargaming, Barker had been developing a paracosm for much of his life. His world was called Tékumel, and he had imagined an entire history, nations, and social structure for its inhabitants. Like Tolkien, he had used his expertise in philology to construct new languages for his imaginary world. But where Tolkien shared his fantasy with the world through his novels, Barker did so through a role-playing game.

Barker sent a manuscript to TSR for a new game called *Empire of the Petal Throne* set in the world of Tékumel. Barker's fantasy was infinitely more vivid and rich than the campaign worlds of *Blackmoor* or *Greyhawk.* Arneson declared, "As far as I am concerned, Phil Barker's world of Tékumel is the most original and detailed fantasy world ever published."[32]

In 1975, TSR published Barker's game as a variation on *D&D*. The game came with a preface from Gygax:

> I must ask the reader to view the world of Tékumel in comparison with J. R. R. Tolkien's Middle Earth. A study of the background detail and society of each will force the reader to the conclusion that the former work is, if anything, at least as painstakingly and lovingly detailed as that of the acknowledged master of the fantasy world in toto.[33]

But Barker's world is far darker than Middle Earth. Where Tolkien was inspired by Celtic mythology and Anglo-Saxon literature, Barker drew on his experience in South Asia as well as milieu of dark science-fiction in the vein of Lovecraft. Tékumel is similar to Earth but hotter and wetter, its climate resembling that of India rather than that of Europe. Millennia ago it was terraformed by space-faring humans and their extraterrestrial allies. For a time, Tékumel was home to a utopian civilization in which humans lived side by side with creatures from other worlds. Then the world underwent a cataclysm:

> Upheavals beyond comprehension, a time when the stars went out, and volcanoes, earthquakes, and tidal waves rolled across the land. It is clear now that through some freak of space, some fault in the fabric of Time itself, the solar system of Tékumel was cast into some great other-dimensional "hole in the sky." . . . The stars had gone out forever, and with them went all communication and commerce with the suns of Humanspace. Now the planet, its sun, its moons, and its four uninhabited sister worlds flew on alone into the terrible dark.[34]

Empires of the Petal Throne is set thousands of years after this cataclysm, when the inhabitants of Tékumel have rebuilt their world and adapted to an alternate universe where magic is more powerful than technology. The inhabitants now possess a medieval level of culture, but the fabulous machines of their ancestors are sometimes discovered in remote parts of the world.

Tékumel is also a world in which the worship of rival pantheons is a part of daily life. Barker explains the prevalence of religion in his fantasy:

> Tolkien had this Britisher's sort of attitude that religion is something you do in church, and . . . It doesn't really do that much to your daily life . . . Whereas I'd been living and working in societies where religion is just permeating the atmosphere . . . Even the simple villagers are behaving in ways that they consider related directly to religion, rather than secular politics or something like this.[35]

Barker's religions were the antithesis of his adopted religion of Islam. They featured numerous gods, elaborate rituals, and human sacrifice. He also built on the work of Anderson and Moorcock by featuring both gods of stability (the Tlomitlanyal) and gods of change (the Tlokiriqaluyal). The latter include such entities as the Five-Headed Lord of Worms, Master of the Undead (Sarku), and the Green-Eyed Lady of Sins (Dlamelish). Fine, who spent many hours playing *Empire of the Petal Throne,* quotes one player: "The difference between good and evil is that the evil guys [the worshippers of the evil gods] like to sacrifice humans every day, while the good guys do it only once or twice a week."[36] Barker's fantasy religions were so detailed and convincing that eventually a supplement was produced called *The Book of Ebon Bindings,* which describes the religions and demonology of Tékumel.

D&D was, on the whole, a much brighter game than *Empire of the Petal Throne.* What Barker demonstrated was that the creation of fantasy religions could be a way of creating richer fantasy worlds, as well as a useful plot device for devising interesting adventures. *Gods, Demi-Gods, and Heroes* was the first attempt to provide religions for a fantasy game. The original text featured a mural of Egyptian deities on the cover and outlined the pantheons of the Egyptians, Hindus, Greeks, Celts, Norse, Finnish, Aztecs, Mayans, Chinese, and Japanese. In 1980, a revised version was printed as *Deities and Demigods.* Its cover featured two dueling priests. In the sky behind them was an armored man battling a dragon, a cosmic reflection of the priests' earthly battle. The warrior and the dragon are reminiscent of the *Enuma Elish,* in which the god Marduk slays the dragon Tiamat, the classic Western myth of law and chaos. Although intended as a supplement for the game, these books were a terrific entrée into comparative mythology.[37] Barker had demonstrated that education and research could produce richer fantasy worlds. In fact, it was the educational aspect of *Deities and Demigods* that religious critics found so objectionable. Bob Larson reported with horror that the book contained an appendix listing the traditional holy days of all the gods and goddesses. Conservative evangelical authors John Ankerberg and John Weldon warned that readers were encouraged to do "further research" on mythology. The book recommended such titles as *The Egyptian Book of the Dead* and *The Golden Bough* by James Frazer. Ankerberg and Weldon described Frazer's classic of anthropology as "a compendium on occult practices."[38] For groups like BADD, *Deities and Demigods* was the smoking gun that proved *D&D* was not a game but a doorway into the occult. An article in *Christianity*

Today featured a child peeking over the top of an open copy of *Deities and Demigods.*[39] In 1985, TSR changed the title of the book to *Legends and Lore,* but this did little to dissuade religious critics of the game.

Of course, gamers were not required to incorporate any of the pantheons of *Deities and Demigods* into their games. They could use monotheistic religions, gods and religions from their own imagination, or avoid the issue entirely by simply having good and evil clerics. A Christian gamer wrote *Dragon* to explain that in his campaign world all clerics are "neutral good Jehovians."[40] A representative from the Christian Gamers Guild argued that by using polytheistic pantheons in *Deities and Demigods,* TSR was actually showing respect for monotheistic religions. He explained: "People often complain about the polytheism in the game. But then, what would they prefer? Would they want Game Masters around the world deciding the will of the True and Living God?[41] As with the issue of alignment, there was no way to include religion in the game that could not be interpreted as anti-Christian.

THE RELIGIOUS FUNCTIONS OF *DUNGEONS & DRAGONS*

When journalists and gamers compare *D&D* to a religion, they are not referring to the fact that *D&D* assumes a conflict between good and evil or contains rules for clerics and gods. Instead they mean that there is something about the *experience* of the game that is similar to religious devotion. As Fine points out, the purpose of the game is to produce an experience of engrossment. For this reason, any comparison of *D&D* and religion must begin with phenomenology. Mircea Eliade's theory of "the sacred" is a useful tool for approaching the longing for meaning that attracts people to *D&D* and sometimes inspires fanatical interest in the game.

Before discussing Eliade, it is necessary to his address his critics. A number of religion scholars have mounted attacks on the use of phenomenology as an approach to religious studies. The phenomenology of religion has been accused of having a general lack of conceptual clarity and rigor.[42] Done poorly, it can become a form of "couch-potato scholarship" that leads to theoretically unsophisticated research.[43] It can also become a form of "crypto-theology" that sneaks religious commitments into scholarship.[44] Despite these concerns, I justify the use of Eliade for two reasons.

First, it has to be understood that the phenomenology of religion is properly used as a hermeneutic and a way of interpreting the experience of religious subjects.[45] It provides the religion scholar with a way of thinking about descriptions of religious experience that she is not privy to. This makes it a particularly useful tool for studying a game that is primarily concerned with experience. For example, in an interview for *Wired,* Gygax describes how as a boy he desired to be a hero, explaining: "There's a call to adventure. It's something in the inner psyche of humanity, particularly males."[46] We cannot study Gygax's longing for adventure empirically, but we can attempt to interpret his description of this experience by comparing it with other data.

Second, the creators of *D&D* came of age in the United States during the mid-twentieth century, when thinkers like Eliade held a significant cultural influence. In *The Politics of Myth,* Robert Ellwood outlines how by the 1960s many in the West had become disenchanted with the promise of the Enlightenment. The state of modernity was not defined by knowledge and hope but by alienation and uncertainty. Technology had not produced a utopian society but horrifying weapons. The disenchanted turned to myth, in which they saw "avenues of eternal return to simpler primordial ages when the values that rule the world were forged."[47] A letter printed in *Alarums and Excursions* in 1975 on whether firearms should be allowed in *D&D* made it clear that some players saw *D&D* as an antidote to the reality of the Vietnam War. The author writes: "I'm not a wargarmer except for D&D. I think that if you use those things that make the 6:00 news a horror, you've done serious damage to the unique character of that game."[48]

Leading this return to myth were what Ellwood calls "the midcentury mythic trinity" consisting of Carl Jung, Joseph Campbell, and Mircea Eliade. The return to myth went hand in hand with the surge of fantasy fiction that influenced *D&D*. In some cases, game designers made deliberate attempts to apply the theories of the mythicists. Ed Greenwood created a campaign setting called "Forgotten Realms" that drew heavily on a paracosm he created as a youth during the 1960s. Forgotten Realms became one of *D&D*'s most popular fantasy worlds of all time. Greenwood remarks on his creation:

> The setting wasn't created to fulfill a market niche, but to fulfill a human need for legend, mythology, and discovery. If you place any weight in the writings of Joseph Campbell—and it's hard to imagine a D&D player who wouldn't be affected by *The Power of Myth, The Hero with a Thousand Faces,* or *Myths to Live By*—then it's easy to understand why someone else's sincere attempts to create a personally fulfilling world of powerful myth would resonate with so many people.[49]

The game designers shared the same assumptions as Ellwood's mythicists and may have been engaged in the same sort of "crypto-theology." In fact, the game mechanics featured in *Deities and Demigods* is not unlike the projects of Jung, Campbell, and Eliade. They represent an attempt to take the sacred stories of every culture and break them down into a set of universal factors.

The influence of the mythic trinity did not fade with the baby boomers. When White Wolf published *Vampire: The Masquerade* in 1991, it defined a second generation of role-playing games that placed greater emphasis on narrative and reflected the concerns of Generation X. The end matter of the second edition listed the works of Campbell, Eliade, and Jung as inspirations for the game.[50]

Eliade's theory of religion assumes the existence of a sui generis category of phenomena that exists across cultures, which he calls "the sacred." The chief criterion of the sacred is that it exists in contradistinction to the profane or quotidian reality. The sacred is also a realm of heightened meaning and reality compared to which the profane world is merely a shadow. Human beings cannot live without meaning and so are always attempting to reach out to the sacred. Religion, for Eliade, is humanity's attempt to access, commune with, and participate in the sacred.

The sacred acts not only like a separate place but like a separate time. Myths describe acts of creation that occurred in a primordial sacred time in which the world was formed and/or imbued with meaning. Storytelling and religious rituals recreate these myths. Eliade argues that for archaic man, myths and rituals created an experience of time travel in which humanity returned the world to its state of primal meaning. He describes sacred time as *illud tempus* (that time) because it is not understood to exist in a normal chronological fashion. Sacred stories exist simultaneously in the past and in the present, where they are reenacted through ritual. By accessing sacred time, myths and rituals provide an infusion of meaning that renews the world and even offers the possibility of reordering it.

For Eliade, religion is very much preoccupied with *nostalgia* and a longing to return to a time when things really mattered. Humanity is not only nostalgic for the primordial time of creation but for "the sacred history of the tribe." Modern man still experiences this nostalgia but, because of the ascendancy of scientific rationalism, understands time as irreversible. Modern people are trapped in a world of profane time, what Eliade calls "Dead time, the time that crushes and kills."[51] Without myth and ritual, modern man seeks to access worlds of heightened meaning through literature (an experience of fictional worlds) and history (an experience of the past).

It is debatable whether all cultures throughout human history have understood time and meaning as described in Eliade's theory. However, Eliade himself certainly felt alienated from the modern world and experienced a romantic longing for the past.[52] Gygax also expresses something like living in an age of "dead time." In *What Is Dungeons and Dragons?* he writes:

> Our modern world has few, if any, frontiers. We can no longer escape to the frontier of the West, explore Darkest Africa, sail to the South Seas. Even Alaska and the Amazon Jungles will soon be lost as wild frontier areas. Furthermore, adventures are not generally possible anymore. . . . It is therefore scarcely surprising that a game which directly involves participants in a make-believe world of just such nature should prove popular.[53]

An even starker expression of nostalgia and yearning for transcendence comes from John, a gamer interviewed for an article about *D&D* that appeared in the magazine *New West* in 1980:

> Ever since I was ten, I've wanted to drop out of this world. There are so many flaws. A lot of things are unfair. When I'm in my world, I control my own world order. I can picture it all. The groves and trees. The beauty. I can hear the wind. The world isn't like that. My beliefs, morals, sense of right and wrong are much stronger since playing D&D. . . . It's hazardous. Your vocabulary, your mental quickness increases, but school seems increasingly boring and droll. Your grades drop. The more time you spend in your fantasy world, the more you want to walk away from the burdensome decisions in life. . . . The more I play D&D, the more I want to get away from this world. The whole thing is getting very bad.[54]

BADD and similar groups cited this quote over and over again as evidence that fantasy role-playing games cause players to gradually dissociate from reality. Critics of *D&D* assume that when John says, "The whole thing is getting very bad," he is referring to his addiction to fantasy. However, this is not clear. John could also be expressing that the world he is seeking to get away from is getting very bad. Applying Eliade's hermeneutic to John's quote, there is a clear sense of the sacred and the profane. The fantasy world is not only more bright and vivid, it is the realm of moral meaning. By contrast, the real world is a place of boredom and suffering. John describes it as flawed and unfair. Furthermore, the fantasy world provides a perspective by which the real world is to be measured. The real world is judged as flawed and unfair inasmuch as it fails to meet the ideal standards of the fantasy world. John's description of the dichotomy between "his world" and "this world" is not unlike the traditional Christian understanding of the world as fallen to sin and the hope for the world to come.

Nostalgia and the Search for the Sacred

The first edition *D&D Player's Handbook* contained a cartoon of warriors and wizards playing a fantasy role-playing game called *Papers and Paychecks*. For the heroes in the cartoon, "reality" is adventuring, and their "fantasy" is a banal existence working in an office or writing papers. The cartoon points to an important function of fantasy role-playing games. In theory, one could create a game called *Papers and Paychecks* that simulated living in the twentieth century. When small children play "house," this is essentially what they are doing—role-playing domestic duties. But the unstated purpose of fantasy role-playing games is to experience a reality that is alternative to our own. The quality of being "wholly other" has always been the first criterion of the sacred in the phenomenology of religion, going back to Rudolf Otto. This suggests that fantasy role-playing games are religious in a way that playing house and other games of imagination are not.

Furthermore, the history of fantasy role-playing games points to an ongoing quest for an experience of an alternative reality. The origins of *D&D* lie in fantasy, and the origins of fantasy lie in historiography. Historiography, according to Eliade, is the product of modern man's nostalgia for sacred time. It is an attempt to "discover our solidarity" with vanished peoples.[55] This idea is echoed by sociologist Dean MacCannell, who observes that "for moderns, reality and authenticity are thought to be elsewhere; in other historical periods and other cultures, in purer simpler life-styles."[56] *D&D* evolved from wargaming, which, along with the Society for Creative Anachronism, was an attempt to reenact and participate in an idealized past. The first commercially successful war game was *Gettysburg,* which literally allowed Americans to reenact "the sacred history of the tribe."

The fantasy genre, which began in England in the late nineteenth century and spread to the United States a few decades later, was part of this effort to form a bridge between the modern world and the idealized past. Richard Mathews explains that fantasy fiction is characterized by "a narrative frame that unites timeless mythic patterns with contemporary individual experiences."[57] Many twentieth-century fantasy authors borrowed tropes and symbols that took their significance from historiography, and rearranged them to create paracosms. In essence, an idea of sacred time was repurposed to create an idea of sacred space.

This transition from sacralized history to sheer fantasy is apparent in the way the work of G.K. Chesterton influenced Robert E. Howard as well as C.S. Lewis and Tolkien. Chesterton's *The Everlasting Man* is a work of Christian apologetics that presents a historical argument for the divinity of Jesus and the truth of Christianity. A chapter about the war between Rome and Carthage entitled "War of the Gods and Demons" had a particularly strong influence on Tolkien and Lewis. Chesterton's horrific depiction of Hannibal's Baal-worshipping troops assaulting Rome was a likely inspiration for the forces of Mordor besieging Minas Tirith in *The Lord of the Rings*.[58] Similarly, Chesterton's epic poem *The Ballad of the White Horse* is set in ninth-century Britain and describes a coalition of Celts, Romanized Britons, and Anglo-Saxons under King Alfred in a battle of Christians against heathen Danish and Norse invaders. In the preface to this book, Chesterton notes that his story is not historically accurate and that the fight to defend "Christian civilization from Pagan nihilism" did not occur in a single epic battle but across several generations. Chesterton explains: "It is the chief value of legend to mix up the centuries while preserving the sentiment; to see all ages in a sort of splendid foreshortening. That is the use of tradition: it telescopes history."[59] Like the Society for Creative Anachronism, *The Ballad of the White Horse* depicted "the Middle Ages as they should have been." Chesterton's ballad made a lasting impression on Robert E. Howard, who praised it in letters to his friend Clyde Smith.[60] The fantasy world he created for Conan took the idea of "telescoping history" to an unprecedented degree. In Howard's world of Hyboria, Conan's adventures brought him into contact with cultures and groups reminiscent of medieval Europe, precontact Mesoamerica, Russian Cossacks, and Elizabethan pirates.

The settings of most fantasy role-playing games offer a similar pastiche of historical sentiments. Greenwood's *Forgotten Realms* campaign includes an imitation of nearly every premodern human culture from Vikings to feudal Japanese to Bedouin nomads. Sacred time is repurposed to create sacred space. In his discussion of historiography, Eliade predicts such a transition, writing, "It was to be expected that modern man, fallen under the domination of Time and obsessed by his own historicity, should try to "open himself" to the World by acquiring a new dimension in the vastness of the temporal realm."[61] In fact, Greenwood originally conceived of his world as one that exists parallel to our own. In this idea for the campaign world, "Earth's fantastic legends derive from a fantasy world that we've now lost the way to—hence, the Forgotten Realms." Here the Forgotten Realms are not simply imaginary but a reality from which we are separated by a gulf of time and space. In the end, TSR decided to emphasize that the Forgotten Realms were completely imaginary. Greenwood explains, "Concerns over possible lawsuits (kids getting hurt while trying to 'find a gate') led TSR to deemphasize this meaning."[62]

Fantasy fiction is concerned not only with constructing new worlds from mythic themes but with facilitating an experience of this world for the reader. In his history of the origins of *D&D,* Jon Peterson writes on what he calls "the visitation theme" in fantastic literature, in which protagonists are transported from the ordinary world to a fantastic one. This theme can be found in such early literature as *Alice in Wonderland* (1865) and *The Wonderful Wizard of Oz* (1900). But Edgar Rice Burroughs's stories about John Carter's adventurers on Mars, first published in 1912, had the greatest influence on twentieth-century fantasy literature. Peterson explains, "Fantastic adventure it too exciting, too immersive, to be appreciated only from afar: its fans wanted to get involved with it."[63] The longing to be transported to a world of heightened meaning and adventure appears in *Three Hearts and Three Lions,* the early scenarios of Arneson's *Blackmoor* campaign, and even in the premise of the *Dungeons & Dragons* cartoon show. This impulse to inhabit a sacred narrative led naturally from fantasy fiction to fantasy role-playing. Like religious ritual, role-playing can be understood as a collective act in which an alternative reality is temporarily made present. Barrowcliffe explains:

> D&D is, I believe, something virtually unique and unprecedented in human history. . . . It's more interactive than any other sort of narrative I can think of. . . . This is why D&D is so addictive when it's played right. It's like the best story you've ever heard combined with the charge a good storyteller feels as he plays his audience. I think there's a basic human need to listen to stories but also to tell them. In D&D you get that tingle you imagine when you think of the ancient storytellers, dusk falling, the camp fire burning and the first line being read. It's not like hearing "In a hole in the ground lived a hobbit," it's like saying it *for the first time* and to a rapt audience that is dying for your next sentence.[64]

What Barrowcliffe appears to be describing is how the collective storytelling of fantasy role-playing games creates an experience that seems to transcend time. The story is both unfolding and being retold simultaneously. In the final paragraph of *Myth and Reality,* Eliade writes, "Traces of such a mythological behavior can also be deciphered in the desire to rediscover the intensity with which one experienced or knew something *for the first time.*"[65] One wonders if Barrowcliffe ever read Eliade.

The Transformative Power of Role-Playing Games

Religion scholars debate not only what religion *is* but what religion *does.* So far, I have attempted to show how the fantasy worlds experienced during role-playing games resemble religious models of sacred time and space. Eliade speaks of nostalgia for sacred time, and fantasy role-playing is often framed as "escapism." However, the transcendent realms accessed through myth, ritual, history, and literature offer more than just a respite from the banality of the profane. The sacred is also the means through which order is imposed on the profane world. As such, visions of sacred times and spaces have real and measurable consequences in this world. To explore this aspect of religion and role-playing games it is necessary to move from the phenomenology of religion to the sociology of religion.

Sociologists of religion often speak of the so-called Axial Age characterized by religious innovations that occurred between roughly 800 and 200 BCE in India, China, Israel, and Greece. In each location, religious elites—prophets and philosophers—developed a clear vision of a transcendent reality that is both radically different from our own and a source of ideals by which our world must be ordered and evaluated. The Axial Age is better understood as an ideal type than an actual historical event. Each of the Axial cultures had reached a level of technological sophistication that could support a class of elites who could spend their time thinking exclusively about religious and philosophical ideals. So-called pre-Axial cultures also have traditions of sacred realms, and the difference seems to be one of degree rather than essence.[66] Nevertheless, in the wake of these transcendent visions, each culture experienced a radical change in the social order.

An idea of transcendence created a mental space that facilitated numerous other ideas. Cultures that were able to imagine a completely different reality began to rapidly acquire other changes as well. Benjamin Schwartz writes of the Axial Age:

> If there is nevertheless some common underlying impulse in all these "axial" movements, it might be called the strain towards transcendence. . . . What I

> refer to here is something close to the etymological meaning of the word—a kind of standing back and looking beyond—a kind of critical, reflective questioning of the actual and a new vision of what lies beyond.[67]

The philosopher Kenneth Burke coined the verb "to beyond" in an attempt to describe such a process, wherein achieving a higher perspective causes one to think about and interpret the world differently[68] The sociologist Shmuel Eisenstadt suggests that this Axial vision made the project of world history possible. Like the North Star, the transcendent vision provided a means of measuring the movement of a society, either closer or further from its sacred ideal. History developed as a way of recording the distance between a society and its ideal state. The ability to evaluate the world from the perspective of a transcendent realm also brought with it a new capacity for abstract thought. "Second-order" worlds of knowledge including science and metaphysics are also products of the Axial Age.[69] The roots of *D&D* lie in a romantic nostalgia that led modern seekers first to history and then to fantasy, combined with an ability to create models and simulations that wargaming inherited from the Enlightenment. If we take Eisenstadt seriously, both the romantic attitude toward the past and the ability to recreate it through simulation are ultimately products of the Axial Age.

Unlike the transcendent realities described by Chinese sages, Israelite prophets, Platonic philosophers, and Indian holy men, the worlds of fantasy role-playing games are not assumed to be real. Despite John the gamer's immense dissatisfaction with the real world, he understands that the world of his fantasies is only imaginary. But these imaginary worlds still have the same ability to change how we perceive our own world. There is the same effect of "drawing back" whether one thinks about the world from the perspective of Platonic forms or the Forgotten Realms. In sum, role-playing games have some of the same transformative power as religious worldviews not because they make truth claims, but because they provide an ability to construct models of reality.

Ian Barbour, a philosopher of religion and science, notes that models occur in both religion and science. In both cases, models are not a description of the world but an "imaginative tool" used for ordering experience. Unlike myths or paradigms, models are taken "seriously, but not literally." They are "symbolic representations of aspects of the world which are not directly accessible to us."[70] *D&D* is essentially a game of models. All of the rules are negotiable so long as they adequately order experience. As one edition of the *Dungeon Master's Guide* explains to aspiring dungeon masters, "Consistency is the key to a believable fictional world."[71] *D&D* evolved from war games that attempted to simulate war using a scientific model. But as the war games became more open-ended and acquired elements of fantasy and metaphysics, they developed religious models as well. Barbour argues that while scientific models order the natural world, religious models order history and human experience. They concern "the object of man's trust and loyalty, the character of his ultimate concern, the final justification for his values."[72] By this definition, alignment, which has its roots in Poul Anderson's attempts to impose moral order onto the conflicts of the twentieth century, is a religious model.

In both science and religion, models lead to the development of new ideas. In ordering one particular problem, models produce "surplus meaning," which can be applied toward the interpretation of other phenomena. A model is "a continuing source of plausible hypotheses."[73] By creating a model of a transcendent world, the Axial Age radically accelerated social change. In the same way, fantasy role-playing games produce a surplus of meaning that, at least for some gamers, serves to order the way they think about questions of meaning, morality, and even the supernatural. Fantasy worlds create an additional mental space from which gamers can step back and reflect on what reality is. In this sense, fantasy role-playing games have some of the same transformative power as religions. Like religions, the imaginary worlds of role-playing games have an ability to influence how gamers order their world, sometimes in small ways, sometimes in radical ones. Far from "brainwashing" players, these games entail a form of radical agency. The "beyonding" achieved by constructing imaginary worlds empowers players to reorder the world in ways that were previously unimaginable and unthinkable.

CHAPTER 3

Pathways into Madness: 1979–1982

The more I research, the more I learn about the long-term effects of fantasy role-playing games. They are, unquestionably, oppressive mind robbers. Rather than free the imagination, they imprison it. But, above all, I detest them because they ultimately rob some young persons of life itself.

—Jerry Johnston, *Why Suicide?*

Remember, it's not your children's fault that they're being drawn into a Satanic world of nightmare. It's their gym teacher's fault for making them feel outcast when they couldn't do one single pull up.

—The Dead Alewives, *"Dungeons and Dragons"*

The public response to *D&D* was shaped by growing fears about cults and the vulnerability of young minds. By the mid-1970s, *D&D* was a common pastime across college campuses. However, this was also a decade rife with collective paranoia. Journalist Francis Wheen described the flavor of the 1970s as "a pungent *mélange* of apocalyptic dread and conspiratorial fever."[1] Political institutions, cultural trends, and even our own sense of self were the objects of new-found suspicion. The Cold War had given rise to the concept of "brainwashing," the idea that it was possible to forcibly reprogram someone's personality. The term was first coined in 1950 by CIA operative Edward Hunter. Hunter noted that a few American POWs returning from the Korean War appeared to have genuinely become advocates of Communism. He attributed this shift in attitude to the use of mysterious and sinister techniques that the Chinese had cultivated over thousands of years.[2] The 1962 film *The Manchurian*

Candidate introduced the idea of brainwashing to the American public. By the following decade, a number of highly publicized psychological studies were raising similar fears that identities and personalities were neither static nor secure. In 1971, Robert Jay Lifton, a psychiatrist who had had worked with veterans who had allegedly been subjected to brainwashing, published an article in *Archives of General Psychiatry* entitled "Protean Man." Lifton characterized the twentieth century as an age of mass carnage in which the pace of history had accelerated and mass media had come to dominate culture. He argued that as a result of these changes, human beings no longer had a stable sense of self. Their beliefs, values, and their very identity had become unhinged and could now shift at a moment's notice.[3] With "Protean Man," Lifton ushered in suspicions that our autonomy as individuals was fragile and subject to invasion, manipulation, and poisoning from any number of sources.

Heightened concern about the mind and its frailties developed alongside fears about the spread of cults. America's Protestant establishment watched with horror as young people began to participate in previously unknown religions, many of which originated in Asia. The concept of "brainwashing" made it possible to interpret interest in new religious movements in medical terms as a kind of disease. In 1977, Dr. Eli Shapiro declared that "destructive cultism is a sociopathic illness, which is rapidly spreading throughout the U.S. and the rest of the world in the form of a pandemic."[4] The panic over cults in the 1970s combined religious fears of the heretical other with medicalized notions of brainwashing and mental illness. This constellation of anxieties formed the context through which critics understood *D&D*. Like young people who joined new religious movements, *D&D* players were not regarded as immoral but rather as innocent victims whose minds were being manipulated by powerful psychological forces that science was only beginning to understand.

In 1979 sixteen-year-old James "Dallas" Egbert disappeared from Michigan State University. His family hired private detective William Dear to locate the missing student. Dear homed in on Dallas's interest in *D&D* and constructed a highly imaginative scenario in which Dallas had become the victim of his own fantasy world. At one point, he even suggested that a mysterious "dungeon master" might have warped Dallas's mind and was now using him as bait to lure investigators into his mad game. Dear's theory was sheer fantasy, but it resonated with the public because it built on a foundation of popular psychology and anxieties about young people in a changing culture. The claims made by

Dear during his investigation became the genesis of a narrative about the mental dangers of fantasy role-playing games. His claims also established a paradoxical understanding of players as simultaneously mentally gifted and lacking in mental autonomy.

RUMORS OF MIND CONTROL

Several highly publicized events shaped the way that critics interpreted *D&D* in the 1970s. In the so-called Stanford Prison Experiment conducted in 1971, Philip Zimbardo created a mock prison in the basement of the Stanford psychology building and recruited students to play the roles of guards and prisoners. Guards were given batons and mirrored sunglasses as symbols of their authority, while prisoners were made to wear smocks and had chains attached to their ankles. The results were disturbing: several of the "guards" exhibited sadistic behavior and abused prisoners. For reasons of safety and moral concerns, the experiment was shut down after only six days. Zimbardo concluded that the abusive behavior came about primarily because of the roles assumed by the students rather than because of inherent personality traits. One newspaper ran the headline "Pseudo Prison Turns into Brutal Reality."[5] The experiment appeared to have dark implications for role-playing and cast doubts on whether ordinary people were capable of safely maintaining multiple frames of meaning.

In 1973, Flora Rheta Schreiber published her novel, *Sybil.* The story was based on the life of Shirley Ardell Mason, a psychiatric patient diagnosed with multiple personality disorder (now called dissociative identity disorder). Mason allegedly had multiple personalties that did not share the same set of memories. She would find herself in strange places, unable to remember which personality had brought her there or why. Schreiber's book suggested that Sybil/Mason had created these personalities as a coping mechanism to deal with the stress of childhood sexual abuse at the hands of her mother. In 1976, *Sybil* was adapted into a made-for-TV movie. Several psychologists have since cast doubt on the Mason case, suggesting that Mason was highly suggestible and was being coaxed by her psychiatrist to produce multiple personalities.[6] Regardless, *Sybil* engendered renewed interest in multiple personality disorder.[7] Our personalities, it seemed, were not solid and stable but could be sundered. The right negative influence, such as an abusive parent, could be enough to create an entirely new personality. *Sybil* prepared the American public to interpret fantasy role-playing as a kind of mental illness in which another personality, the character, takes up residence in the mind of the player.

In 1974, the same year that *D&D* was published, nineteen-year-old Patricia "Patty" Hearst, granddaughter of newspaper magnate William Randolph Hearst, was kidnapped from her Berkeley apartment. Her abductors were part of a militant leftist movement calling itself the Symbionese Liberation Army (SLA). Two months after her abduction, the SLA released a tape to the local radio station in which Hearst claimed allegiance to the SLA and said that she was assuming the name "Tania." Days later, Hearst was videotaped during a bank robbery wielding an M1 Carbine, apparently aiding her captors. In 1975, the FBI located Hearst and arrested her for armed robbery. At her trial, Robert Jay Lifton and clinical psychologist Margaret Singer appeared as expert witnesses. They claimed that Hearst had been brainwashed by her captors and was not responsible for her actions. Both Lifton and Singer had studied cases of alleged brainwashing during the Korean War and claimed that religious cults were currently engaged in brainwashing young Americans. The prosecution countered that Hearst had, in fact, exercised agency in choosing to join the SLA. Hearst was convicted and initially sentenced to thirty-five years in prison. However, President Jimmy Carter commuted her sentence after only twenty-two months. In the court of public opinion, many felt that she had been brainwashed and that deviant groups like the SLA did have the power to control the way people think. Teenagers like Hearst were believed to be especially vulnerable to brainwashing.

Fears of brainwashing ultimately gave rise to "cult deprogramming" in which self-described deprogrammers offered to locate young people who had joined new religious movements, abduct them (often using violence), and impose their own regimen of abusive behavior on them to "deprogram" the effects of mind control. The father of deprogramming was a high-school dropout named Ted Patrick. In 1971, Patrick was sought out by a woman in San Diego who wanted help convincing her son to leave a group called the Children of God. Patrick feigned interest in joining the group in order to observe their recruitment techniques. After reading Lifton's work on mind control, Patrick concluded that the Children of God were engaged in brainwashing. He remarked, "If toughened US soldiers couldn't fight it in the 1950s, what chance did fresh-faced teenagers have in the 1970s?"[8] Patrick had no professional training before embarking on this unusual career. His views demonstrate how saturated mainstream American culture had become with the idea of brainwashing. Cult deprogramming soon became a cottage industry. Deprogrammers were generally hired by parents who objected to their son or daughter's new interest in a religious or political group. Several deprogrammers were convicted of kidnapping and false imprisonment, including Patrick. Dear claimed to have worked as a cult deprogrammer before being hired to search for Dallas. Whether or not this is true, cult deprogramming formed the cultural context through which Dallas's disappearance was interpreted.

As a new cultural form, fantasy role-playing was regarded by many outsiders as one more fad in a vast milieu of new and ephemeral ideas that included new religious movements. Moira Johnston describes *D&D* as "a coming together of two forces of the seventies—fantasy books and encounter groups."[9] Anticult organizations generally interpreted *D&D* as a more subtle manifestation of the cult phenomenon. A tract by the Daughters of St. Paul, a conservative Catholic organization, lamented that the medical establishment had not attempted to frame *D&D* as a mental illness, as it had with new religious movements:

> To date no de-programmers have surfaced to aid worried parents whose children have become D&D cultists. While *Dungeons and Dragons* has been compared to the organized cults, there is no professional group in Canada or the United States which has acknowledged the game as an addiction. Mental health clinics generally are not concerned with it. Thus more families must become informed of the hazards of *Dungeons and Dragons* in order to prevent its introduction into the home, neighborhood and school. As absolute prohibition of the game must be maintained.[10]

This passage also demonstrates the alignment of established religions with the medicalization of new religious movements. For the Daughters of St. Paul *D&D* was regarded as both a medical problem and a heretical cult.

Another cultural precedent for the public response to Dallas's disappearance was the book *Jay's Journal* by Beatrice Sparks, published in 1978. This book was presented as the "edited" diary of a Mormon teenager with genius-level IQ who had taken his own life. "Jay" was based on sixteen-year-old Alden Barrett of Pleasant Grove, Utah, who committed suicide in 1971. Barrett had kept a diary, which his family turned over to Sparks, a Mormon youth counselor whose previous work *Go Ask Alice* was a best seller. Sparks adapted this material into what she deemed an appropriate cautionary tale for teenagers by presenting Jay as a heavy drug-user and a Satanist. Only a small fraction of the content of *Jay's Journal* has any basis in Barrett's diary. The material that Sparks introduced is so fantastic that it hard to imagine how readers could have taken it seriously: Jay learns witchcraft from an old hag, is able to levitate and perform other supernatural feats, ritually murders a kitten, performs a cattle mutilation with his Satanic peers using an electrified bow and arrow, and is finally possessed by a demon with the unlikely name of Raul.[11] *Jay's Journal* sold over 100,000 copies and helped to spark the Satanic panic of the 1980s. It also worked to establish the narrative of teenagers as "brilliant victims" who are, paradoxically, vulnerable because they are geniuses. Much of the diary describes how Jay is fascinated with the occult because he wants to study it scientifically. Sparks presents Jay as a Faustian character whose curiosity leads him to damnation. This was the same narrative through which Dear interpreted Dallas's disappearance and eventual suicide.

THE DUNGEON MASTER

Collective anxiety about the fragility of minds and personalities made the 1970s an inauspicious time to introduce a game that centered around mental engrossment in a fantasy. It was perhaps inevitable that the media would link *D&D* to popular fears about brainwashing and cults. On July 11, 1979, the *Los Angeles Times* published an article called simply "Dungeons and Dragons." While the article was not intended as an attack on *D&D*, it described children losing interest in ordinary activities, suffering from depression after their characters die, and hoping for spells that would bring back the dead. It also had unusual sexual references, noting that monsters may spare characters with high charisma so that they can impose their romantic or sexual wills on them, and that one player's character is a "slightly gay" cleric. Significantly, the article explains that "the player who is the dungeon master . . . functions as a cross between God and a psychologist, analyzing players' characters' abilities and giving each as much challenge as tolerable. . . . At his whim, the dungeon master can easily have players killed off or just as easily allow them to advance with little difficulty."[12]

One month later, on August 15, 1979, Dallas Egbert disappeared from Michigan State University. Dallas was only sixteen and had allegedly been a child prodigy. He had a high IQ and was said to have been repairing computers for the Air Force at the age of twelve. Following his disappearance, a note was found in his dorm room that read simply, "To whom it may concern: Should my body be found, I wish it to be cremated."[13] His parents, James and Anna Egbert, offered a $5,000 reward for any information leading to his recovery.[14] On August 22, Dallas's uncle hired private investigator William Dear. A former Florida highway patrolman, Dear presented himself as a larger-than-life figure and sometimes demonstrated narcissistic characteristics. One of his goals in taking the case may have been to establish himself as a famous detective.[15] The disappearance of a child prodigy from a wealthy family had all the makings of a major news story. Dear made the story even more sensational by linking Dallas's disappearance to his interest in an odd and controversial new pastime. In his memoir, Dear cast himself as a compassionate hero on a quest to save a vulnerable child genius from a web of destructive fantasy. In telling this story, Dear built on a decade's worth of anxieties about young people being preyed on and brainwashed by cults and other subversive forces. This story became the master narrative about the dangers of fantasy role-playing games.

While Dallas did have an interest in *D&D*, he had never participated in any games at Michigan State University. He did, however, have a number of social, mental, and emotional problems before his disappearance. Dallas felt immense pressure from his parents to perform academically. He was also a member of MSU's gay council and was apparently coming to terms with his own sexual identity. He suffered from epilepsy and would occasionally have seizures. Finally, he used recreational drugs and would allegedly manufacture PCP and other dangerous substances.[16] On the night of his disappearance, Dallas entered a network of steam tunnels underneath the university. He brought a bottle of Quaaludes with him, intending to end his own life. He survived the suicide attempt and went into hiding at a friend's house. Dallas continued to travel for several weeks, staying with acquaintances, many of whom he had met through the gay community. His hosts were aware that people were looking for him and were generally reluctant to shelter him for long. He eventually ended up in New Orleans, where he again attempted to poison himself. After this second suicide attempt, he contacted his family. Dear was sent to collect him in Morgan City, Louisiana, on September 13. Dallas's month-long disappearance was more than enough time for the media to create a story about the dangers of *D&D*. Dear did make a statement to the press that Dallas's disappearance had not been related to *D&D*, but this retraction received nowhere near the attention that the original headlines had. Furthermore, Dear continued to capitalize on fears of *D&D* in his memoir, *The Dungeon Master*. Dallas enrolled in a new college after returning home, but in August 1980 he committed suicide using a handgun.

After agreeing to help locate Dallas, Dear arrived at the MSU campus with a five-man team of investigators. Dear quickly learned about an elaborate network of steam tunnels beneath the campus. Students would explore the tunnels or even use them to move between buildings on cold days. Sometimes groups of students would organize live-action fantasy role-playing games inside the tunnels. While conducting its own exploration of the steam tunnels, Dear's team found graffiti that read, "This Way to Middle Earth," and even a sort of tableau of a mannequin seated at a table that had been built in an empty chamber. Dear learned of Dallas's interest in *D&D* and hypothesized that he had disappeared into the steam tunnels to play a new and more immersive form of *D&D* and never returned. Dallas, he suggests, was undergoing some kind of psychotic break in which he had become so engrossed in his role that his identity as a college student had been completely forgotten. Dear explains:

> Dallas might actually have begun to live this game, not just to play it. Dungeons and Dragons could have absorbed him so much that his mind had slipped through the fragile barrier between reality and fantasy, and he no longer existed in the world we inhabit.[17]

After concluding that Dallas's disappearance was somehow related to *D&D,* the question became whether Dallas was a mad genius luring others into his game of fantasy or actually the victim of a cult-like group that had induced his break with reality. In *The Dungeon Master,* Dear vacillates between presenting himself as Dallas's rescuer or his victim. He ponders: "We've sat here many an hour, all of us wondering—is Dallas the dungeon master? Or if he isn't the dungeon master, is there some other dungeon master who has pulled all of us into this game by using him as some sort of pawn?"[18]

There were a number of problems with Dear's theory even before Dallas was discovered. First, while Dallas had participated in role-playing games in the steam tunnels, the students who organized these games had asked him not to come back because they suspected that he was on drugs.[19] Second, Dear understood that *D&D* is normally played sitting around a table and not acted out in steam tunnels and other settings. Because of this, he assumed that the games in the steam tunnels represented an unhealthy or obsessive form of *D&D* in which players were making increasingly elaborate efforts in the game to escape reality. In fact, live-action role-playing, or LARPing, is simply another genre of role-playing games and not a more intensive form of so-called tabletop games. Live-action role-playing groups such as the Society for Creative Anachronism (SCA) actually preceded tabletop fantasy role-playing games like *D&D*. By 1979 the SCA and similar groups had also formed chapters at numerous colleges.

These flaws made Dear's hypothesis no less appealing to the press. Dear talked about *D&D* at a press conference, creating an immediate sensation. Newspapers across the country ran headlines such as "Game Cultist Still Missing," "Dungeons and Dragons' Cult May Lead to Missing Boy," and "Fantasy Turned Real Life May Have Killed Student."[20] These articles also announced to the nation that Dallas was gay—a lapse of journalistic ethics that may have contributed to his eventual suicide. Law enforcement found Dear's theory plausible. A police captain commented: "I personally think if he's alive, he's playing. . . . We're pawns in this game and we're being utilized to satisfy his own needs."[21]

In 1980, Dear told reporters he would "never reveal" what had transpired during Dallas's month-long absence, and that he had found him "locked in a dingy room with two single beds in an undisclosed location."[22] We now know that this is not how Dear found Dallas at all. Nor did Dear keep silent about Dallas's absence. When Dear published *The Dungeon Master* in 1984, Dallas's family expressed outrage and saw the book as a form of exploiting their son's death. Dallas's aunt said of *The Dungeon Master:* "I think it's a big bluff to make [Dear] look good. It's all a publicity stunt to make him a star and get him public attention. . . . Really, nothing he did brought the boy back." Carla Hall interviewed Dear about his book for the *Washington Post.* She found Dear's appearance pretentious, remarking: "There are the rings on his fingers: Great, globby hunks of gold, one of which—the one resembling a small meteorite—he takes off and lets clunk on the table to show you how heavy it is. Inside his tooled, black cowboy boots is a strap constructed to secure a knife." Dear told Hall that he was worth $3 million and that people in England called him "the real James Bond." Hall was suspicious of these claims and concluded that Dear "has his fantasies too."[23]

Dallas's mother claimed that much of *The Dungeon Master* is not accurate.[24] In fact, there are details of Dear's book that are almost certainly invented in order to present Dear as the heroic figure he purported to be. For instance, he begins the book by describing a previous adventure in which he and his team rescued a child from a cult:

> Once Dick and I recovered a child from a religious cult that had kidnapped her in Erie, Pennsylvania. We put our helicopter down in an empty schoolyard and got the girl, but then we had to deal with armed cult members. I

> handed the child to Dick and told him to run for the copter, and I saw the struggle of loyalties in his face.[25]

Exactly what "cult" did Dear heroically fight off single handedly? How was this story kept out of the papers? And why did Dear write a memoir about crawling through steam tunnels in an unsuccessful search for a missing college student instead of this death-defying helicopter raid?

This story demonstrates how the panic over fantasy role-playing games evolved from the panic over cults. Dear appears to regard cult deprogrammers as heroes and even seems envious of their exploits. Several passages of *The Dungeon Master* express both horror at and fascination with cults. Dear describes hiding in a tree near the campus during his search for Dallas. After lurking in the tree for hours, he spied a small group of students conducting a fireside ceremony. They reportedly cried, "Great Gurdjieff, guide us to the goodness of God's goals!"[26] Dear reflects on this scene: "I was interested in how many such cults, and of what variety, existed on this and other campuses. There were probably many, and one we didn't even know about might have counted Dallas as a member."[27]

Although Dear takes a secular approach to the dangers of *D&D*, *The Dungeon Master* is a classic text in the erotics of fear. Dear regards *D&D* as dangerous, alien, and completely alluring. He describes employing numerous investigative techniques in order to better understand it. However, all of these efforts amount to what the anthropologist E. E. Evans-Pritchard describes as the "If I were a horse" way of thinking. By engaging in these activities, Dear did not gain new insight into the case. Instead, he simply performed his own hypothesis about a delusional gamer.

One of the first "clues" discovered by Dear was a corkboard in Dallas's room. Nothing was affixed to the board except for thirty-eight white and blue pushpins and thumbtacks. Most of the pins were in an apparently random pattern, but some had been arranged into a rectangular shape that vaguely resembled a handgun. Dear became obsessed with the significance of this corkboard and was certain it was some sort of code that could lead to Dallas's whereabouts. He had members of his team fly over MSU in a plane to see if any of the buildings resembled the shape formed by the pushpins. Photos of the corkboard were sent to TSR for analysis.[28] As Dear tells it, when Dallas was found, he explained that each pin on the corkboard represented an alcove in the steam tunnels, and that someone intimately familiar with the tunnels could have discerned that one alcove was missing. This was the alcove where

Dallas had initially gone to overdose on Quaaludes.[29] While this story could be true, it seems more likely that Dear obsessed over a mundane and irrelevant detail and then avoided embarrassment by fabricating this confirmation after Dallas's death. Dear's strange analysis of the corkboard, with his obsession with extraneous details, foreshadowed literature produced by BADD and similar groups that also focused on detecting and deciphering "codes" that were supposedly used by young people involved with fantasy role-playing games and cults. Many of these books contain appendixes enumerating the significance of "occult" symbols such as pentagrams and peace signs, which the authors claim indicate involvement with cults.

In addition to exploring the steam tunnels, Dear heard that Dallas had engaged in "trestling," an activity in which one lies in the center of a railroad track and allows the train to pass just overhead. Dear admits that he lay in the center of a train bridge but then thought better of it as the train approached. He felt that this experience gave him a clearer insight into Dallas's fantasy world, remarking, "The train could have been the dragon bearing down upon him."[30]

Dear also played *D&D*. Rather than finding a gaming group to join, he offered a student fifty dollars to visit him at his motel room and run a game. Dear added, "Sixty if the game is a good one." One can only imagine what a college student thought about this proposition from a forty-two-year-old man. However, the student did show up with a friend, and the three of them played a short game with one dungeon master and two players. I suspect that Dear's description of the *D&D* game is accurate. *The Dungeon Master* includes copies of Dear's character sheet as well as that of the other player. More significantly, Dear's description of the game sounds too frustrating and banal not to have really occurred. The adventure contained almost no plot. The characters simply drifted through a meaningless gauntlet of orcs and other monsters until the dungeon master grew bored and ended the scenario. Dear and the college student neither role-played nor cooperated. Instead, they spent the game using their abilities to steal from, extort, or otherwise manipulate each other. Oddly, the character sheets do not list alignments. Both Dear and the college student played their characters as amoral scoundrels. Dear was not concerned with claims that the game promoted violence or immoral behavior, only its ability to absorb people into fantasy.

Despite these limitations, Dear claims he enjoyed this experience and became even further convinced that Dallas was acting out a *D&D* game in the steam tunnels. Later, while describing his exploration of the tunnels, Dear remarks: "Being in the tunnel really was similar to that game of Dungeons and Dragons I had played in my motel room. For me that game had been exciting enough, because my imagination is a good one. But maybe if I had played the game more, I would have wanted more. These tunnels were practically guaranteed to set your imagination racing, but *you didn't need an imagination down here.*"[31]

Dear did have a good imagination. In fact, the narrative he created about a man lost in a fantasy can be regarded as a form of projection. In the conclusion of *The Dungeon Master,* he muses:

> It occurred to me that Dallas *had* been, in a way, a dungeon master. By disappearing, leaving clues, and setting up alternative outcomes for his adventure, he had created a game in which the other adventurers—me and my men, his parents, anyone who was involved—never knew what to expect.[32]

But save for the dubious example of the corkboard, Dallas had not created the adventure Dear describes: it was Dear who had imposed a fantasy scenario onto real events, casting himself as the hero. In doing so, he became the first critic of *D&D* to engage in a form of corrupted play. Dear presents himself at his most heroic when he arrives in Morgan City to "rescue" Dallas. When Dear finally finds Dallas he is surrounded by the Louisianans with whom he had been staying. They want to know who Dear is and why he is taking Dallas. Dear responds by brandishing his gun. As he tells the story, "These unfortunates *liked* to fight. In Texas they're called shit-kickers, and pain doesn't affect them. Not yours. Not theirs."[33] This account strikes me as a deliberate effort by Dear to embellish his story with a violent climax and to present himself as a conquering hero. The Louisianans serve the same narrative function in Dear's story as the orcs in his *D&D* game: a mindless horde that can only be dealt with through violence.

The sensation created by Dear and his book had a number of lasting consequences. The story had inadvertently served as a massive marketing campaign for *D&D*. Gary Gygax remarked, "Ultimately, it was immeasurably helpful to us in name recognition. We ran out of stock!"[34] By some accounts, TSR's sales quadrupled.[35] However, critics of *D&D* took Dear's story quite seriously. *The Dungeon Master* produced a vivid depiction of what a delusional gamer would look like, if Dallas had, in fact, been one. In this sense, Dear allowed the media and his readers to "know of" the psychological dangers of *D&D*. They could vividly imagine the stages that led from enjoying a game of *D&D* to a complete break with reality. In 1981, two novels were published about gamers suffering psychotic breaks induced by their hobby: *Hobgoblin* by John Coyne and *Mazes and Monsters* by Rona Jaffe. Jaffe's novel was a fictionalized account of Egbert's disappearance and went on to become a best seller. The trope of the delusional *D&D* player was now firmly established in the American consciousness.

Dear's speculations and musings also helped to establish the two key players in this tableau: the gamer as a gifted but vulnerable youth, and the dungeon master as a sinister cult leader. In *The Dungeon Master*, Dallas paradoxically appears as both of these players because Dear's theory shifts from moment to moment. Together, these two figures of player and dungeon master, convert and cult leader, provide the crucial ingredients cited by Stanley Cohen for creating a moral panic: a suitable victim and a suitable scapegoat.

The very title of Dear's book serves to frame "the dungeon master" as something far more significant than a role in a game. For instance, Dear claims he met a gamer who told him:

> You must remember that the dungeon master, although supposedly an impartial arbiter, can abuse his position and take on the status of God. He can do whatever he wants. If the dungeon master believes that a particular character is weak, he can send that character off on his own. Not just in the game, not just in his head. He can send him on a *real* mission. "You have to prove you're worthy to play with us," the DM might say. "You have to show your mettle. I have a mission that you must complete."[36]

There is no evidence of dungeon masters ever giving their players quests to perform outside the context of the game. Regardless, subsequent attacks on *D&D* continued to frame the dungeon master as a figure who poses as a god, wields the power of mind control, and dominates the players both in and out of the game. A psychiatrist with ties to BADD warned: "The most powerful role in the game is that of Dungeon Master, the player/god who runs and controls the game. He can't control the characters completely but he can restrict a character's actions—and he can destroy (kill) him."[37] A school-board member called for *D&D* to be banned, claiming: "The game is run by a 'Dragonmaster' and this smacks of mind control. I don't see how the players can think for themselves."[38] BADD founder Patricia Pulling makes a more direct connection between dungeon master and cult leader, explaining:

> One does not have to live in a commune under the control of an individual or group to be alienated. . . . The Dungeon Master (DM) exerts enormous control over the players in a game of "Dungeons and Dragons." He has the

> final say in the game, and he creates the world in which the adventure takes place. He has total authority in the world he creates.

Finally, Carl Raschke's description of the dungeon master is both overtly religious and completely the product of his own imagination. He writes:

> Half-demon, half-Mephistopheles, he is the one who already "knows" the tenor of life's darkest secrets, which the rest of us pursue like blindfolded, and often errant, idiots. The dungeon master can be "sadistic." Rarely is he benign, and the young players quickly internalize this "religious" view of affairs.[39]

Other rumors developed about the control dungeon masters held over their players. BADD claimed a woman left her career in order to be a full-time dungeon master, and that her players paid for her house, groceries, and expenses.[40] A pastor claimed that players could save the lives of their characters by paying the dungeon master.[41] In some cases, Gygax was framed as a sort of grand cult leader or mastermind behind the cult of *D&D*. A tract by the Daughters of St. Paul warned parents, "You may have just discovered that your son has joined the legion of unsuspecting students who have become victimized by a master con-artist: Gary Gygax."[42]

As Gary Alan Fine points out, none of these claims had any basis in reality. Fine's observations of how dungeon masters interact with their players led him to conclude: "As I have noted, players jokingly refer to the referee as God, but, like any god, if his demands get too imperious, he may find himself without believers. Players have the ultimate control—by leaving the game."[43] However, it was not necessary for the claims makers to witness a game in order to form their opinions about dungeon masters. The press that followed Dallas's disappearance was more than enough to present *D&D* as a plausible threat, particularly when it came on the heels of a decade-long moral panic over cults.

MAZES AND MONSTERS

Rona Jaffe's novel *Mazes and Monsters* appeared after the media frenzy created by Dear's investigation and three years before the publication of *The Dungeon Master.* Unlike Dear, Jaffe did not present her narrative as fact. It was set at the fictional Grant College in Pennsylvania, where students played a fictional fantasy role-playing game called *Mazes and Monsters*. Jaffe was inspired by newspaper stories about Dallas's disappearance and played several games of *D&D* as research for her novel. In many ways, her fictional portrayal of fantasy role-playing games was closer to reality than Dear's. Dear approached *D&D* from the perspective of a cult deprogrammer—as an outside force that is seductive and dangerous. Jaffe regarded the retreat into fantasy as a symptom rather than a disease. Her book suggested that if youth were losing their grip on reality, it was the fault of a neglectful society rather than some subversive force. In an interview about her book, she explains:

> This is the first generation where people will not be able to live as well as their parents. They grow up in a house with two cars and lots of room and they get married and they don't know if they'll ever have a house. They don't even know if they'll ever be able to afford a kid. . . . The '60s were a time when the kids all got up—there were more of them because of the babyboom— and decided they wanted to change things. In the '70s, when people got disillusioned and realized they couldn't change things, they started to investigate their own heads. That was what we called the "me" generation.[44]

This was a thesis that had already been proposed in 1979 by Christopher Lasch in his book *The Culture of Narcissism*. Lasch had suggested that after the political turmoil of the sixties, Americans had lost hope of improving their lives and were now retreating inward, convincing themselves that exploring and improving the self is what really matters.[45]

Mazes and Monsters reached a much wider audience than *The Dungeon Master*. The book was a best seller, and in the fall of 1982 CBS adapted it into a made-for-TV movie. Dallas's role as a young man lost in a world of fantasy was played by Tom Hanks. While Jaffe did not frame *D&D* as a religious cult, her narrative was equally useful to critics of fantasy role-playing games. If Dear provided a suitable scapegoat in the form of the dungeon master, Jaffe perfected the suitable victim by portraying the plight of brilliant but sensitive youth, whose destructive retreat into fantasy was an indictment of a failed society.

Jaffe's novel revolves around a game of *Mazes and Monsters* played by four college students, two of whom appear to be inspired by Dallas. Each of the characters suffers from an emotional problem as a result of a broken home, parental pressure, or a corrupt society. Their game serves as a psychodrama through which they embrace aspects of themselves that society has denied them.

Jay Jay Brockway shares several characteristics with Dallas: he is sixteen, comes from a wealthy family, and has an IQ of 190. His mother is a bohemian divorcee, too self-absorbed to understand her son. Whenever Jay Jay returns from college, he finds that his mother has redecorated his room in line with the latest styles. She is consistently surprised that her son has his own style and tastes and is unappreciative of her efforts. Jay Jay's character is a sprite named "Freelic the Frenetic of Glossamir." Like Jay Jay, Freelic is an outsider, being a different species than his friends. But Freelic is under no compunction to conform. As a sprite, he is free to "be himself" and revel in his fey nature.

Daniel Goldsmith comes from a well-to-do Jewish family in Brookline, Massachusetts. He secretly wants to pursue a career as a game designer but does not know how to tell his parents, who expect him to pursue a traditional path to success. His character is a "charlatan" (Jaffe's take on the thief character class) named Nimble. Goldsmith's choice to play a charlatan reflects his inner conflict over his career aspirations.

Kate Finch was nearly raped at knifepoint one night while doing laundry in her dormitory. Her character is Glacia, the Fighter. While Kate is vulnerable, Glacia is armored and powerful. By playing Glacia, Kate is continuing to heal and deal with feelings resulting from her attack. Jaffe draws several connections between the dungeons explored in the game and the dark and solitary laundry room. *Mazes and Monsters* provides an alternate reality, "where she would take revenge on creeping, soft-breathing things, where she would flash her sword and kill, and conquer."[46] Kate/Glacia also appears to be a stand-in character for the author. Jaffe remarks on her experience playing *D&D* as research for the book: "I wanted to be a fighter. I'm an elf in real life—who wants to be an elf in a game?"[47]

Robbie Wheeling is the newest member of the gaming group. He is drawn to fantasy to escape a broken home life. His older brother became a drug addict and began fighting with his parents. He eventually disappeared during his sixteenth birthday party and never returned. The loss of the firstborn child has destroyed his parents' marriage and caused his mother to become an alcoholic. Wheeling's character is a "holy man" (Jaffe's version of the cleric) named Pardieu (French for "by God"). Pardieu is a pacifist and has taken vows of poverty and chastity. Robbie enjoys playing this character because it "gives him peace."[48]

Jaffe's story unfolds along the lines of the scenario presented through Dear's press conferences. Many elements of the investigation are included, and creative license is taken to fill in gaps in the story. Dallas is split between the characters of Jay Jay and Robbie. Jay Jay is a young, physically slight, and occasionally suicidal genius. It is Jay Jay who persuades his group to engage in a live-action version of *Mazes and*

Monsters in some caverns near the college (Jaffe's version of MSU's steam tunnels). However, it is Robbie who suffers a psychotic break and wanders away from campus, unable to remember the reality beyond the game. As Pardieu, he embarks on a quest to New York City to find "the Great Hall." "Hall" was the name of Robbie's brother. Pardieu's quest is a projection of Robbie's desire to find his brother, who ran away to New York, as well as his irrational belief that if he can find his brother, his family will somehow be whole again.

Jaffe's description of the media frenzy following Robbie's disappearance borrows several elements from the Dallas case. Psychics arrive to help in the investigation, a detail that is also mentioned by Dear. Sales of *Mazes and Monsters* also spike following the media coverage of Robbie's disappearance. The other characters discover Robbie's whereabouts after finding a mysterious note in his room that features a maze with a heart in the center. The note is Jaffe's version of the corkboard that Dear obsessed over. However, unlike Dear's investigation, in Jaffe's story it is possible to find the missing person by following clues. Robbie's friends deduce that a reference to "the Two Towers" actually refers to the World Trade Center and go to find Robbie in New York.

Much like Dear's account of playing *D&D* and climbing through steam tunnels, *Mazes and Monsters* invites the reader to imagine what the world would look like to a confused and frightened gamer suffering a psychotic break. Several passages of the story describe Robbie wandering around New York City as Pardieu and interpreting everything he sees as part of a medieval fantasy. He believes the subway train is a dragon—a theory that Dear proposed after hearing that Dallas had engaged in trestling. One of the most striking of Robbie's misinterpretations results from his conversation with a prostitute. Robbie is living on the street where he befriends a young prostitute, whom he misidentifies as a princess of the sprites. The prostitute, in turn, misidentifies Robbie as a drug addict who has resorted to prostitution. She says that Robbie reminds of her Holden Caulfield and gives him the following advice:

> You're never going to get a john when you're stoned like that. . . . You're kind of old for these chicken hawks, but you *are* cute. . . . There are leather queens and piss freaks and S and M's, but unless you get a real masochist weirdo nobody's going to want you like this. They'll think you've been smoking angel dust.[49]

In his persona as a fantasy holy man, Robbie assumes that "angel dust" is a magical item. He also misinterprets the prostitute's advice as instructions for locating a messenger who can help him in his quest. This causes him to enter a hotel room with a john. A farce ensues as the two men misunderstand each other's actions. The john finally grows impatient and grabs Robbie's penis. Robbie interprets the sexual aggression as a demonic assault:

> He had been tricked! This was no man, but a succubus, intent on rape. Pardieu knew of such things, and once a succubus entered your body you were in its power. He flung the spell of paralyzation, heart beating wildly now with fear. *The spell did not work!* How could this be possible? This was a most powerful demon indeed, but Pardieu had other charms, other spells. He gulped down the remainder of his potion of invisibility. The dragon had not seen him—nor would this succubus now. The succubus was holding him tightly, trying to place its mouth on him, determined to rape what it could feel but could not see. Pardieu was terrified. He twisted to get away from the demon's grasp, but the strength of his adversary was greater than his own. Fasting and privation had made him weak, and a succubus was a hundred times stronger than even a healthy mortal. Pardieu unsheathed his sword, and with a last mighty rush of strength he pushed the sword into the monster's chest.[50]

In reality, Robbie has not stabbed a succubus with a sword, but stabbed a very confused john with a pocketknife. After this encounter, he briefly becomes Robbie again. Much as in the scenes of dissociative amnesia depicted in *Sybil,* he is frightened and unable to remember why he is folding a bloody pocketknife.

While the encounter with the john may strike modern readers as funny, in 1981 readers likely regarded this scene as horrific. Jaffe's story linked *D&D* to other concerns about the perils faced by American youth—namely, drugs and sexual predators. Robbie is all the more helpless in the face of these dangers because he is absorbed in a fantasy. In fact, one of the theories discussed by Dear is that Dallas had been abducted by a "chicken hawk"—a slang term for a homosexual man who preys on young runaways.

In the end, Robbie's friends find him and are able to break him out of his persona as Pardieu. Jay Jay, Daniel, and Kate return Robbie to his parents and quit playing *Mazes and Monsters.* Jaffe writes: "The odyssey they had just been through had been their transition to real life. They didn't need the game to be friends, or for anything else. Maybe they had once, but they didn't need it now."[51] At the end of the story, the three friends visit Robbie at his parents' house only to find that he has lost his mind and become Pardieu permanently. He believes the house is a medieval inn where he is staying between adventures. His parents indulge this fantasy and place a coin under his pillow every night. Robbie/Pardieu believes this is a magical coin and returns it to his parents every morning as payment to the "innkeepers." Robbie's friends also enable his delusion, and the story ends with them embarking on one last adventure together. Jaffe concludes her story, "They saw nothing but the death of a hope and the loss of their friend."[52]

Jaffe did more research on *D&D* than Dear, and her narrative discusses positive aspects of fantasy role-playing that critics of these games generally ignore. For instance, Jaffe appreciates that running games is an art form and that creating imaginary worlds is not a delusion but a creative act. She describes Daniel preparing his game:

> The world he had created, here in his room, with his close friends participating so eagerly, was the best of all possible worlds. It was worth all the trouble he had gone to this summer to create a new adventure. Michelangelo couldn't have felt any better when he finished painting the Sistine Chapel. A work of art was a work of art, no matter on what level.[53]

Jaffe is also the only critic of *D&D* who takes seriously the moral and religious elements built into the game. Much of the novel focuses on Robbie's persona as a "holy man," and the moral ideals that come with playing this role. Jaffe describes Robbie/Pardieu's reflection on the use of violence:

> He thought that a Holy Man had more responsibilities than anyone else. He had to make more complicated choices, and he could heal as well as hurt. That was good, for Pardieu did not like to cause destruction, even of evil beings. He could slash with his sword as well as any but Glacia, but it made him feel guilty to kill, even though he did it only in self-defense. If he could use his magic spells to charm wicked spirits into being good, it was better.[54]

Jaffe's emphasis on pacifism and compassion is quite different from most critics of fantasy role-playing games, who claim these games promote sadism and desensitize players to violence.

But despite these concessions, *Mazes and Monsters* ultimately pathologizes role-playing as a psychologically dangerous pastime. It also shows the influence of the anticult movement. As a holy man, Robbie/Pardieu appears to brainwash himself. He has a dream in which "the Great Hall" appears to him and announces: "The qualities of a Holy Man are these: piety, humility, and chastity. Celibacy, my dear Pardieu. A Holy Man must walk alone."[55] Following this dream, Robbie takes on greater and greater austerities, blurring the line between himself and his character, and ultimately leading to his psychotic break. Jaffe writes:

"His new monastic regime of giving up meat, alcohol, and sex made him feel cleansed. He had also given up all sweet and artificial deserts, eating only an occasional piece of fruit. He had lost weight, but that was natural. He felt closer to the purity of his spirit."[56] The signs that Robbie is no longer a healthy college student and succumbing to the dangers of fantasy role-playing are that he *stops* underage drinking and ends his sexual relationship with Kate. (By contrast, his psychologically "healthy" friends drink constantly throughout the entire book, even stopping their search in New York so that Jay Jay can prepare a pitcher of Bellinis.)

As Robbie continues to cultivate the virtues of chastity and sobriety, his friends interpret this behavior as cult activity. Kate worries, "Oh God, maybe he's going to become a Hare Krishna or something!"[57] After his disappearance, Jay Jay suggests he may have joined "one of those cult groups."[58] In fact, this narrative of religious austerities leading to mental illness and the loss of autonomy had been introduced to the American public by Lifton. Lifton introduced the term "milieu control" to describe the intense religious regimens associated with "cults." "Milieu control," he claimed, was used in brainwashing, and one of the best ways of maintaining milieu control was to establish a "demand for purity," in which mind control is achieved from framing all things as pure or impure.[59] In essence, Jaffe casts Robbie as his own cult leader, mentally dominating himself. Tellingly, one critic of fantasy role-playing games later referred to *D&D* as "Do-It-Yourself-Brainwashing."[60]

Jaffe also hints that fantasy role-playing games lead to an interest in mysticism and the occult, a claim that is not found in *The Dungeon Master.* As Robbie continues to descend into madness he rereads "Tolkien and Castaneda."[61] While both of these writers would have been widely read on a college campus in 1980, they are not in the same genre at all. J.R.R. Tolkien wrote fiction while Carlos Castaneda wrote on metaphysics, allegedly from the perspective of a Yaqui shaman. After the publication of *Mazes and Monsters,* religious critics repeatedly claimed that fantasy role-playing games are a bridge to the study of magic and ultimately, organized Satanism.

Finally, Jaffe's greatest contribution to the emerging narrative about fantasy role-playing games was that they were a form of dangerous psychodrama through which young people were attempting to repair the damage caused by an uncaring society. In her novel, she ponders, "Was it their parents' fault, or life's fault that they had to escape into a fantasy world of invented terrors?"[62] Not only does Jaffe present the game as an idealized reality, but the party is a substitute for what the players actually need—a traditional family. In an interview, Jaffe explains:

> The games . . . present a stalwart band of friends. It's a fellowship of people who have a good mission. They're going to conquer evil and they're also going to make good. They're going to get fortune. They're going to protect the weak ones. That's what the family used to represent. You stuck together in adversity. You protected the weak ones. You had a common goal which was to achieve material things.

In the novel, Daniel reflects: "If anything, the game is an outlet for our fantasies. We work out all our problems in the caverns and then we leave them there."[63] The message of *Mazes and Monsters* is that while fantasy role-playing games may have some value as a coping mechanism, the form of escapism they provide is ultimately destructive.

There is, in fact, a body of literature discussing the value of fantasy role-playing as a form of psychotherapy.[64] But while fantasy role-playing games can serve as one outlet through which people confront emotional issues, Jaffe's story implies that *all* gamers suffer emotional problems. It presents role-playing at best as a crutch and at worst as a dangerous pathology. By allowing readers to "know of" the emotional pain experienced by gamers, *Mazes and Monsters* contributed to an understanding of gamers as victims whose creativity and intelligence made them even more vulnerable to the dangers of a morally decadent world.

GAMERS AS BRILLIANT VICTIMS

The media sensation over Dallas's disappearance, as reflected through Dear and Jaffe, provided the public with a profile of the sort of person likely to become trapped in a fantasy world. At the same time, psychologists were working to develop a profile of the sort of person likely to join a cult.[65] The profiles presented by moral entrepreneurs of who was likely to become a delusional gamer, join a cult, or become involved with Satanism were essentially the same. In 1988 the magazine *Woman's Day* published an article entitled "A Parent's Primer on Satanism." It claimed that "bright, bored, underachieving, talented, and even gifted teens are susceptible to cults."[66] Patricia Pulling was somewhat more specific. She explained, "A white male who is intelligent, creative and curious is the most likely to be seduced by the occult."[67]

There is a long history of identifying certain classes of people as having an inferior grasp of reality. In the nineteenth century, there were concerns that women should not read novels because they had trouble distinguishing fiction from reality.[68] In 1981, the year that *Mazes and Monsters* was published, a pair of psychologists proposed that roughly 4 percent of the population have "fantasy prone personalities." These "fantasizers" were said be frequent daydreamers, susceptible to hypnosis, and to sometimes have trouble distinguishing fantasy from reality.[69] What was unusual about the profile of the delusional gamer was that it was a stereotype wracked with paradox. Like Dallas, the delusional gamers were believed to be young and of above-average intelligence; however, their superior intellects somehow made them less able to discern fantasy from reality. According to the moral entrepreneurs, fantasy role-playing games did not simply seduce youth, they seduced the best and the brightest youth.

Occasionally, critics would attempt to account for this paradox. Carl Raschke explains, "Bright children may fall for *D&D* because the ordinary world is too drab and boring for the ambitions of genius."[70] Boredom might account for interest in the game (or any hobby, for that matter), but not why intelligent children are more susceptible to delusion. One of the most fanciful explanations came from Rebecca Brown, an evangelical writer who interprets fantasy role-playing as part of an apocalyptic end-times scenario. Brown claims that fantasy role-playing games are specifically designed to target and corrupt gifted children. She writes:

> One of Satan's biggest tools in our country today is the occult role-playing fantasy games which have become so popular. Satan is using these games to produce a vast army of the most intelligent young people of this country; an army that the Anti-Christ will be able to tap into and control in an instant.[71]

More often, moral entrepreneurs either do not realize or do not address the paradox of gamers as brilliant victims. Stanley Cohen notes that claims made about "folk devils" are often contradictory.[72] Such claims are not conclusions based on empirical observation but attempts to support specific social agendas.

The idea of gamers as brilliant victims built on discourse about child abuse and the neglected emotional needs of children that flourished in the early 1980s. In 1979, the year of Dallas's disappearance, psychologist Alice Miller published her influential book *Prisoners of Childhood: The Drama of the Gifted Child*. Psychiatrist Joel Paris notes that psychoanalysis generally assumes that minor troubles in childhood can result in larger problems in adulthood, but that Miller turned this assumption into "a religion." He also quotes a *New York Times* article that proclaimed Miller "the missing link between Oprah and Freud."[73]

Dear built on the momentum created by Miller in his presentation of Dallas as an abused genius. He claimed not only that Dallas was gifted but that his intelligence was "one in a million." In one passage he emphasizes that society had failed in its moral duty to care for and nurture its young genius:

> One in a million. I couldn't stop thinking about that. Was this country so rich in talent that it could afford to treat its geniuses cavalierly, like so many pieces of meat on an assembly line? No, worse than that. A hunk of meat would get more attention; Dallas had been ignored, provided with no direction, permitted to transmogrify haphazardly into God only knew what.[74]

While both gamers and moral entrepreneurs have claimed that people who play fantasy role-playing games are more intelligent than the rest of the population, there is little evidence to support this conclusion. Gary Alan Fine observes that while gamers have a great deal of specialized knowledge, there is no evidence that their global knowledge is any higher than that of nongamers.[75] How then, did gamers come to be seen as brilliant victims? The answer seems to lie in the experience of families like the Egberts attempting to make sense of their son's suicide. In the years following Dallas's suicide, several other young men from affluent white families took their own lives, including the son of Patricia Pulling. The families were left with a paradox: they believed their sons to be gifted and bound for success, and yet their sons had taken their own lives. Furthermore, according to the theories of Miller and others, if a gifted child did commit suicide it was the parents who were most likely to blame. The narrative of a deviant game that specifically targeted gifted young men and drove them mad helped to render this paradox sensible. It some cases, it may also have shielded parents from feelings of guilt. Finally, because families like the Egberts and the Pullings were white and privileged, far more media attention was directed toward these suicides, causing a handful of cases to appear as an epidemic.

PSYCHOLOGICAL CLAIMS

As the fear of fantasy role-playing games became medicalized, claims makers presented their ideas as scientific, often alluding to psychological research that did not actually exist. One evangelical critic of role-playing games cautioned, "Psychologists have claimed, time and again, that when someone lives in the realm of fantasy for an extended length of time, the lines dividing fantasy and reality become distorted, fuzzy."[76] There are no studies to support such a claim. Instead, some studies have suggested that games of make-believe actually help children to differentiate between fantasy and reality.[77] However, the idea of gradually being engulfed in a fantasy sounded plausible, particularly to journalists.

As the media reported claims about the psychological dangers of *D&D*, TSR launched a campaign to show that *D&D* was beneficial for young minds. In 1983, the following text was added to the *Player's Handbook:* "Players are not characters; it is important to remember that the player and the character are two different persons. The more the two are kept apart, the better your games can be." TSR also hired famous psychologist Joyce Brothers as a consultant. Brothers promoted the game as a useful exercise that contributed to the creativity, intellectual development, and emotional development of young players. Brothers also emphasized that *D&D* kept young people out of trouble and was an alternative to drugs and alcohol. She recommended that *D&D* be offered in schools as an extracurricular activity because of its educational benefits.[78] Despite the negative press surrounding fantasy role-playing games, this campaign did gain some traction. Even at the height of the panic, several public libraries still encouraged clubs for role-playing games. The Association for Gifted-Creative Children endorsed *D&D*, claiming that it encouraged children to read more challenging works, such as Shakespeare, Tolkien, and Isaac Asimov.[79] Henrietta Wilson, a reading teacher, also praised *D&D*, commenting: "My students know how to read. But they don't know how to synthesize information, how to take what they have and reconstitute it. If *D&D* can help them get analysis and synthesis down pat when they're adolescents, what can they do when they're in their twenties or thirties?"[80] Gygax was even invited to speak at teachers' conventions.[81] However, some in the gaming industry found these claims disingenuous and felt that role-playing games were simply fun and did not need to be educational. Game designer Steve Jackson cynically remarked: "Games are very educational. Scrabble teaches spelling, Monopoly teaches cash-flow management, and *D&D* teaches us to loot the bodies."[82]

So did fantasy role-playing games promote madness and suicide, or were they actually a wonder of education? Between 1987 and 1998 a number of psychological studies were done to assess the various claims about role-playing games.[83] Most of these relied on survey data and attempted to quantify supposed links between gaming and feelings of alienation and depression or criminal behavior. The studies generally did not assess claims that role-playing games are actually beneficial. Occasionally, the psychologists appeared to have as poor an understanding of the games as the moral entrepreneurs. One study on whether *D&D* could be linked to feelings of "alienation" explained that *D&D* has "26 levels," and that upon attaining the 26th level, a player can become a dungeon master. This is not accurate, and it is not clear how the researchers came by this information. The study concluded that "the negative effects of playing the game are still unknown and perhaps nonexistent."[84] In fact, none of the studies found a significant correlation between playing role-playing games and feelings of alienation, depression, suicide, criminal behavior, or involvement in Satanism. As far as psychological studies could prove, *D&D* was neither a pathway into madness nor an opiate through which an emotionally battered generation sought to escape its pain. However, by the 1980s the panic over fantasy role-playing games was beginning to shift from a medical register to a supernatural one. New and fantastic claims were emerging about these games that psychologists were not equipped to measure or assess.

CHAPTER 4

Satanic Panic: 1982–1991

Some may think the games and books harmless, that they are strictly for fun, fantasy, and entertainment. Beware! They are not! Parents who buy or allow such games and books and tapes are playing with dynamite—and their children's souls. They open their homes, and their children, to the subtle introduction of the occult, to Satanism and the malignant world of psychotherapy (mind alteration, values modification). There is nothing benign about these games; they are part of the increasing spread of Satanism and various forms of the occult, a push that will increase in tempo and fervor as Satan's time grows shorter.

—Rus Walton, *Biblical Solutions to Contemporary Problems*

Didn't the grown-ups understand what losers we were? That all we did was roll dice and shout and stuff our faces with snacks?

—Paul La Farge, "Destroy All Monsters"

In his book *Schemes of Satan,* evangelist Mike Warnke claimed that before committing suicide in 1980, Dallas Egbert had written a suicide note that stated in part, "I'll give Satan my mind and power." This quotation was followed by a footnote citing Egbert's obituary, which appeared in the *New York Times* on August 18, 1980. However, the obituary mentions only the original note left in Egbert's dorm room before his disappearance in 1979. It says nothing about a second note and certainly nothing about Egbert pledging his allegiance to Satan.[1] This is probably not a case of shoddy research, but deliberate dishonesty. In 1972 Warnke published his religious best seller *The Satan Seller* in which he claimed that before becoming an evangelical Christian he had been a Satanic high priest. *The Satan Seller* describes how Warnke controlled a secret empire of 1,500 Satanists throughout California who dealt drugs, abducted people, and engaged in human sacrifice. In 1992 an article in the Christian magazine *Cornerstone* utterly debunked the claims made in *The Satan Seller,* drawing on testimony from people who knew Warnke in college.[2] In *The Truth about Dungeons and Dragons* Joan Robie also claims that Egbert left a suicide note containing the line "I'll give Satan my mind and power." Robie offers a different but equally inaccurate citation—an article from *School Library Journal* that describes Egbert's disappearance but says nothing about a suicide note. In fact the article Robie cites defends *D&D* and portrays the game's critics as hysterical.[3]

Conservative evangelical critics like Warnke and Robie effectively rewrote Egbert's suicide, adding a connection to Satanism where none existed. These bibliographic deceptions are significant because they demonstrate how a second layer of claims was made about fantasy role-playing games in the 1980s. The anticult movement of the 1970s provided the context through which critics interpreted *D&D*. In the 1980s, moral entrepreneurs continued to frame their attack on role-playing games in both religious terms as a "cult" and in medicalized terms as a form of brainwashing. But a new claim came to dominate discourse about fantasy role-playing games: that these games were actually designed to promote criminal behavior and suicide because they had been created by an invisible network of criminal Satanists.

Sociologist David Bromley identifies Satanic panic as the second wave of the cult scare of the 1970s.[4] While the anticult movement focused on actual religious groups, Satanic panic revolved around an entirely fictitious conspiracy. It was alleged that a vast criminal network of Satanists lived among the populace. The Satanists operated at all levels of society, from powerful politicians to teenage vandals. They allegedly performed bizarre rituals, conducted human sacrifices, and worked to undermine traditional morality. Like cult leaders, Satanists were believed to use a variety of techniques to corrupt young people and convert them to their cause. Critics of fantasy role-playing games claimed these games were one of the most effective and ingenious tools for the spread of Satanism.

Stories of Satanic cults began in conservative evangelical circles but were increasingly adopted by secular authorities such as counselors, social workers, and law enforcement. Claims about the connection between fantasy role-playing games and Satanism gained a secular spokesperson in 1982 when Patricia Pulling's son, Irving "Bink" Pulling, committed suicide. Pulling created BADD (Bothered About Dungeons and Dragons) and began a campaign in which she claimed that fantasy role-playing games were a direct path toward involvement in Satanism. Although Pulling endorsed many of the claims raised by evangelicals about Satanists, as a secular Jew she was able to present Satanism as a nonsectarian issue that threatened all members of society. For a decade, BADD rode the wave of Satanic panic. Pulling appeared at law enforcement seminars on "cult crime," on talk shows, and in courtrooms where she offered her services as an expert witness. BADD also motivated gamers to respond with their own campaign to counter such claims. Eventually, the panic over role-playing games lost its momentum as a result of a variety of factors: claims of Satanic cults were largely debunked, violent video games offered a new and more vivid target for moral outrage, and BADD became moribund with Pulling's death in 1997.

However, the belief in Satanic conspiracies has died an extremely slow death.[5] Many Americans still believe in criminal Satanic cults, and fantasy role-playing games are still part of a tableau of "occult crime." At the time of this writing, the police department of Natchez, Mississippi, features a website outlining the "warning signs of occult involvement." One of the first items on the list reads: "Heavy into fantasy games. Note: Fantasy games have no rules or guidelines. They encourage creativity without boundaries. The player loses the boundary between reality and fantasy."[6] This warning demonstrates how the concerns first brought forth by William Dear and Rona Jaffe about delusional gamers merged into an even darker fantasy involving human sacrifice and "occult crime."

RUMORS OF SATANISM

It is not entirely clear how rumors of Satanism came to seem plausible to Americans living in the late twentieth century. Philip Jenkins argues that the origins of Satanic panic lie in the pulp fiction of the 1930s, notably Dennis Wheatley's 1934 novel *The Devil Rides Out,* which concerns a modern-day Satanic cult.[7] Rumors of Satanic cults turned into a national preoccupation in the 1960s alongside the anticult movement. While nothing resembling the cult described in Wheatley's novel ever existed, Anton LaVey did found the Church of Satan in 1966. LaVey spouted antinomian polemics and openly challenged Christian values, but he never practiced any sort of blood sacrifice and required his followers to obey secular laws. Nevertheless, his group appeared to confirm claims that Satanic cults really existed. In 1969, the murders carried out by Charles Manson and his "family" convinced many that the teenage counterculture was engaged in criminal Satanism on a large scale. After Manson's arrest, the *Los Angeles Herald Examiner* ran a front-page article titled "Hippie Commune Witchcraft Blood Rites Told."[8] All of this coincided with a popular fascination with the demonic demonstrated in such films as *Rosemary's Baby* (1968), *The Exorcist* (1973), and *The Omen* (1976). Like *The Devil Rides Out,* these films invited audiences to imagine a Satanic threat lurking beneath the surface of modern society. *Jay's Journal* (1978) exploited these fears and connected them to larger concerns about adolescents.

Panic over Satanism intensified in the following decade. In 1980 the book *Michelle Remembers* became a best seller. Michelle Smith suffered from depression and had been seeing a psychiatrist named Lawrence Pazder for several years. In 1976, after having a miscarriage, Michelle commented that she needed to tell him something, but did not know what it was. Over the next fourteen months, Padzer led Smith through hundreds of hours of hypnosis. During this time, Smith repeatedly regressed to the age of five and relived experiences that supposedly took place in 1954. Smith alleged that her mother had been part of a Satanic cult that had tortured her extensively: she had been forced to assist in murders and infanticide; she had been confined within an enormous effigy of Satan; her teeth had been removed, and horns and a tail had been surgically grafted onto her body. She had also witnessed the assemblage and animation of a Frankenstein-like monster and met Satan himself—whose return to Earth was prevented when Smith resisted her family's Satanic conjuring ritual. *Michelle Remembers* presented all of these stories as not only true, but as "too horrible to have been invented." Smith and Pazder formed a romance after "recovering" these memories and eventually married.

Michelle Remembers inspired other people to experience similar "recovered memories," leading to widespread belief in "Satanic Ritual Abuse" or SRA. Autobiographies of SRA became a kind of genre, with titles such as *Satan's Underground* (1988) and *Suffer the Children* (1989). The most famous legal case of the SRA panic was the McMartin Preschool trial, which lasted from 1984 to 1990. In 1983, Judy Johnson accused an employee, Raymond Buckey, of sodomizing her child. In response, the police sent a form letter to approximately 200 parents, asking them to question their children about such topics as sodomy, pornography, and bondage. The letter resulted in hundreds of children—both current and former visitors to McMartin—being interviewed by an abuse therapy clinic. During these sessions, children reported seeing day-care providers fly, being taken in hot-air balloons, and being led to tunnels under the school. Eventually, eight employees of the McMartin Preschool were charged with 321 counts of child abuse involving forty-eight children. Despite the total absence of material evidence, the prosecution persisted for seven years, even after Johnson, the original accuser, was hospitalized with acute schizophrenia. Prosecuting the case cost the public over $15 million.[9] The scandal of the McMartin Preschool trial did little to debunk the myth of Satanic cults. In fact, the case demonstrated that the public was prepared to believe almost anything relating to Satanic conspiracy.

In 1988, Geraldo Rivera hosted a special entitled "Exposing Satan's Underground." The special became a high-water mark for Satanic panic. The program featured cult experts, who explained that teenagers were the most likely to be seduced by Satanism, and that heavy metal music indoctrinated young people through "back masking" or subliminal messages that can be discerned only when a song is played backward. In 1992, an FBI report concluded that there was not an organized network of Satanists covertly abusing thousands of children or conducting human sacrifices, but this hardly mattered to the general public.[10] In 1994, 70 percent of people surveyed for the women's magazine *Redbook* reported belief in the existence of abusive Satanic cults, and 32 percent agreed that "the FBI and the police ignore evidence because they don't want to admit the cults exist." Finally, 22 percent reported their belief that cult leaders use brainwashing to ensure that the victims do not tell.[11] Throughout the 1990s, numerous people, many of them teachers and day-care providers, were accused of SRA. Many were acquitted only after being bankrupted by legal fees. Others were fired, driven out of their communities, or forced to give over their children to child protective services. Some were given lengthy jail sentences for crimes that were almost certainly never committed.[12]

It is difficult to understand how this could have happened in a society that has public education and modern forensics technology, and values individual rights. Bromley attempts to make sense of the panic by suggesting that claims about Satanists abducting and abusing children were an attempt to articulate social concerns and frustrations that could not be expressed otherwise. The real threat, he argues, was that a changing economy in which both parents frequently worked required Americans to rely increasingly on strangers to care for and raise their children. The covenantal sphere of family life was being compromised by the contractual sphere of the market, and parents felt helpless to halt this process. Bromley explains:

> Quite simply, parents have been losing control over the socialization process to various external service providers that operate relatively independently of individual families. Visible evidence of family resistance to this trend is found in the plethora of family-based, grassroots movements seeking to reassert control by nominating as social problems such family-related issues as drug use, missing and abducted children, heavy metal rock music, fantasy games, religious cults, sexuality and violence in the media, pornography, drunk driving, incorrigibility, suicide, and abortion. In most, instances, however, parents cannot reassert familial control by increasing their own involvement in child-rearing; success in the competitive contractual sphere requires a committed pursuit of self-interest.[13]

Bromley's analysis can be interpreted as a confusion over frames. He suggests that claims of Satanic cults may be "metaphorically true even if empirically false."[14] Many Americans truly did feel the presence of an invisible force that seemed to be all around them, corrupting their children and undermining the values of the family. This anxiety was expressed in symbolic terms, and these symbols were then mistaken for reality. Day-care providers were frequently accused of SRA because they were the most readily available manifestation of the contractual sphere on which modern parents depended to raise their children. In persecuting professionals who cared for their children, claims makers were attacking the symbols of their problem rather than problem itself.

Claims that fantasy role-playing games were a form of Satanism or "occultism" seducing America's youth were usually framed as part of a losing battle between traditional family values and a decadent, secular world. Peter Leithart and George Grant begin their book on the spiritual dangers of *D&D* with just such a narrative:

> Parents are concerned. And well we should be. Our children are growing up in a very hazardous world. Not only are they forced to pick their way through a complex maze of conflicting values at school, in the neighborhood, and out in the marketplace, but they are even being assaulted in the "safety" of their own homes. . . . Amazingly, though, the chief weapon used in this spiritual raid on our children is a game—just a simple little game. It is called *Dungeons and Dragons*. Even more than simple cartoons, toys, comics, books, videos, and music, this simple little game has served to make our children a "generation at risk."[15]

The Daughters of St. Paul, a conservative Catholic group, made a similar claim. Their pamphlet states: "The truth is that *Dungeons and Dragons* appeared on the market at exactly the 'right time.' In the recent past, moral decadence and anarchy has seemingly prevailed in the name of 'equal rights.' . . . The legitimate authority of Christian parents has been denigrated and ignored."[16]

Fantasy role-playing games were especially amenable to this narrative of a secret invasion of the domestic sphere, because they were simultaneously familiar and alien, domestic and fantastic. These were games marketed to young people that promised to "transport" players to fantastic worlds full of magic, monsters, and violence. Children could be sitting peacefully in the living room while mentally being in a dark temple or a scene of demonic sorcery. If day-care center providers could be seen as agents of a Satanic conspiracy, then fantasy role-playing games could serve as an even more palpable symbol of the sinister forces that had come to compromise the family.

EARLY SKIRMISHES

One of the first incidents in which Christian parents mobilized against role-playing games occurred in April 1980 in Heber City, Utah, a predominantly Mormon community of about 5,000 people. Significantly, Heber City is about a half hour's drive from Pleasant Grove, Utah, where the events described in *Jay's Journal* allegedly occurred. The local public school in Heber City offered *D&D* as an after-school activity for gifted children. A coalition of concerned parents demanded that the school ban the game, leading to a clash between parents and administrators. Molly Ivins covered the story for the *New York Times* with the headline "Utah Parents Exorcize 'Devilish' Game." Although the conflict in Heber City happened less than a year after the disappearance of Dallas Egbert, the parents had a different set of concerns than those raised by William Dear. Dear had suggested that *D&D* was psychologically dangerous and could potentially lead to delusion. The coalition in Heber City regarded the game as a deliberate attempt by an invading force to corrupt their children. Some opponents of the game were described as "John Birch-types" and claimed it was a form of Communist subversion, but the majority of the coalition claimed that the forces behind *D&D* were supernatural. One parent stated, "I can feel the devil right here in the media center," referring to the space where the game was played. Norman Springer, a nondenominational Christian minister, said of *D&D:*

> Oh it is very definitely antireligous. I have studied witchcraft and demonology for some years and I've taught against witchcraft. The books themselves have been taken from mythology and from witchcraft and they are filled with demonology, filled with pictures and symbols that you could find in any basic witchcraft book and use the same terminology. . . . These books are filled with things that are not fantasy but are actual in the real demon world and can be very dangerous for anyone involved in the game because it leaves them so open to Satanic spirits.[17]

These claims of witchcraft and demonic presence were distinct from earlier psychological claims made about role-playing. Eventually, groups such as BADD would merge these two threats, suggesting that *D&D* was both psychologically dangerous, because it led to delusion, and spiritually dangerous, because it contained elements of "real" witchcraft and demonology.

The PTA at the school in Heber City initially voted to keep the *D&D* program, but the coalition returned with greater numbers. When Cecil Black, a teacher, and Mike Tunnel, a librarian, defended the game, parents accused them of practicing witchcraft themselves. This persistence proved effective. Tunnel remarked: "I am getting bitter. Frankly, I'm not thick-skinned enough. I'm not a crusader." When the PTA voted not to ban *D&D* for a second time, the coalition turned to the state school board, which was more receptive. Board member Irma Christensen remarked: "This kind of game brings out murder, poisons and assassinations, negative kinds of things. It is satanic. You can take my word for it." In the end, the superintendent caved to the pressure and banned the game. As with the Egbert case, controversy only raised interest in the game. Before the program was canceled, it was necessary to turn students away because of overcrowding. Even after the ban, many of these students simply continued to play the game outside of school.[18]

In August, Moira Johnston published an article in the magazine *New West* entitled "It's Only a Game—Or Is It?" She opined, "The games are creating controversies as potentially volatile as the teaching of Darwinian theories in the thirties."[19] Although the article had more good to say about fantasy role-playing than bad, it contained several tantalizing accounts of the demonic. Johnston describes playing a game with her son run by game designer Greg Stafford. Johnston recalls an encounter between their characters and a mysterious woman they meet on the road:

> Greg knows that she is a succubus, that luscious demon of mythology who descends on men when they are asleep in lonely outposts and lures them to

> sexual intercourse. Greg will bring her back on some other run, perhaps in her male form as an incubus who impregnates women as they sleep.

This account of a child being introduced to the concept of a succubus appeared to confirm a narrative that *D&D* was seductive, demonic, and directly aimed at corrupting the innocence of children. Not surprisingly, moral entrepreneurs quoted Johnston's article extensively for the next two decades.

Critics also began to claim that *D&D* was a "catechism of the occult" and a recruiting ground for dangerous occultists. Conservative evangelical writer Gary North pioneered this claim in a passage that was quoted in numerous other anti-*D&D* tracts:

> After years of study of the history of occultism, after having researched a book on the subject, and after having consulted with scholars in the field of historical research, I can say with confidence, these games are the most effective, most magnificently packaged, most profitably marketed, most thoroughly researched introduction to the occult in man's recorded history.[20]

If the media response to the Dallas Egbert case gave rise to the contradictory image of the gamer as a brilliant victim, Satanic panic gave rise to a new contradiction. As Lizzie Stark notes in her ethnography of role-players, "The stereotype about gamers tries to have it both ways. On one hand, there's the powerless buffoon of a man, good at math but a social failure, and on the other hand, there's the satanic priest who is covertly trying to recruit children into his coven."[21]

By 1981, some evangelicals regarded opposition to *D&D* as a powerful symbol of Christian identity. An article appeared in *Christianity Today* entitled "D&D: A Fantasy Fad or Dabbling in the Demonic?" The article ends with rhetorical question:

> Here is something for today: a game that takes lots of time, accumulates status with each $12 addition, mixes demons, demi-gods, dragons, and monsters in violent encounters, makes a fad of fantasy—all in a world created by a "strictly neutral" Dungeon Master. Who could possibly oppose such a game but a bunch of Christians?[22]

The author not only calls on Christians to condemn *D&D*, but presents opposition to *D&D* as evidence of Christian virtue: in an age of denigrated social values, Christians alone possess the wisdom and virtue to see evil where less conscientious people see a harmless children's game.

For some evangelicals, opposition to *D&D* was not only a social responsibility but a form of spiritual warfare. In her book *Prepare for*

War, Rebecca Brown describes doing informal counseling with gamers. She not only believed that the young men she spoke to were demonically possessed and had supernatural powers, but that they *knew* they were possessed and were lying about it. She describes giving the following advice to a gamer named "Bob" whose character was allegedly an "80th degree cleric": "Bob, let's get honest. Your powers come from demon spirits and your deity is actually a demon which affects every aspect of your life, not just the game. It rules you. Did you know that you can be set free from the rule of your deity?"[23]

Not only gamers, but gaming books were interpreted as demonic opponents. In 1981, Tom Webster, a nondenominational minister from Hutchinson, Kansas, announced that he planned to collect $1,000 to purchase *D&D* books so that he could burn them. Such a gesture is senseless as a form of financial pressure: companies make a profit regardless of who buys their books or for what purpose. However, Webster's plan does make sense as an attempt to destroy demons housed within the books. He explained, "When you play with demonic spirits, that's not a game. When you deal in any way with demonic spirits, they're alive and they've got power."[24] Gamers in Oregon and Washington reported similar incidents of pastors burning *D&D* books. There were even rumors in evangelical circles that screams had been heard coming forth from *D&D* books after they were thrown into a fire.[25]

The quintessential cultural artifact of the panic was a comic book entitled *Dark Dungeons,* published in 1984 by Chick Publications.[26] The comic opens with a game of *D&D* with six young players engaged in an adventure run by "Ms. Frost," presumably a teacher. In the second panel a player named Marcie flies into hysterics when her character, a thief named "Black Leaf," is killed. Ms. Frost and the other players are indifferent to her suffering and banish her from the game, while another character, a cleric named "Elfstar," survives the adventure and is promoted to level eight. Ms. Frost informs Elfstar's player, Debbie, that she has now learned enough from *D&D* to be initiated as a Pagan priestess in the Church of Diana. Ms. Frost teaches Debbie actual magic, which she uses to cast a "mind bondage spell" on her father that compels him to spend $200 on *D&D* books. Meanwhile, Marcie hangs herself in her bedroom, leaving a note that reads: "It's my fault Black Leaf died. I can't face life alone!" Shocked by her friend's death, Debbie is brought to an evangelical meeting. A former witch who is now a pastor calls on the congregation to burn *D&D* books. The pastor then performs an exorcism over Debbie, which banishes the demons that entered her through playing *D&D*.

Dark Dungeons is so over the top that it has delighted gamers as much as disturbed them. Gaming conventions have held contests in which copies of *Dark Dungeons* are distributed with all of the text blanked out. Attendees compete to rewrite the comic with the most amusing captions. *Dark Dungeons* is also a stark example of a new set of claims that emerged surrounding fantasy role-playing games during the 1980s. As in the previous wave of panic, *Dark Dungeons* portrays players gradually dissociating from reality, identifying with their characters, and committing suicide. However, it also portrays *D&D* as a crash course in occultism that leads to the cultivation of literal supernatural powers. Debbie does not simply *believe* she can cast a spell on her father, she actually has magical abilities, because playing *D&D* has allowed demons to take up residence within her. Finally, *Dark Dungeons* portrays an invasion of the domestic sphere as teenagers are indoctrinated into witchcraft by their teachers and then turned against their parents. All of these elements comprised a complex web of claims made about fantasy role-playing games during the 1980s.

THE RISE OF BADD

By 1981, *D&D* was firmly established as a demonic threat within the culture of the New Christian Right. However, the general public remained more curious than concerned. This changed after June 9, 1982, when sixteen-year-old Irving "Bink" Pulling of Hanover County, Virginia, committed suicide by shooting himself in the chest. Bink's mother, Patricia Pulling, blamed her son's death entirely on his involvement with *D&D*. Bink had been in his school's gifted and talented program, where several games of *D&D* had been offered as a reward for completing classroom assignments. In the months following her son's death, Pulling constructed a narrative in which Bink had been seduced, driven mad, and ultimately killed by fantasy role-playing games. This narrative resonated with a growing cultural concern about youth suicide.[27] Pulling's persona as a bereaved mother became the foundation of her charisma as a moral entrepreneur. Her book, *The Devil's Web: Who Is Stalking Your Children for Satan?*, begins with her account of her discovery of her son's body. She describes how she and her husband had returned from a shopping trip to purchase Bink a boom box for making good grades. They had also bought train tickets so that the whole family could take a trip to Disney Land once school let out. Their home was on a sizable plot of land and had a long, winding driveway leading up the house. As the car neared the house, Pulling could "sense" something was wrong and demanded that her husband speed up. Rounding a turn, she could see her son's body lying on the front porch. Pulling describes rushing to it, cradling it, and ultimately having to be dragged away. When the police arrived, they allegedly asked, "Are you or your husband devil worshippers?" Pulling and her son were Jewish, and she initially assumed the question was anti-Semitic. The officers then presented *D&D* materials from her son's room and initiated the bereaved mother into the lore of Satanic panic.[28]

Bink had left a suicide note, and police told the *Washington Post* only that it contained "unexplainable-type things."[29] Although Pulling never revealed the exact contents of the note, she stated that in it "he equated himself with Adolph Hitler and the Antichrist, and said that he had been summoned to commit murder, couldn't bring himself to hurt anyone else, and so must end his own life to rid the world of this evil."[30] Searching his room, she also found "violent, sadistic poetry." It seemed that there been a part of Bink's life that Pulling had been unaware of and that he had been suffering in silence for some time.

Stanley Cohen suggests that when a disaster occurs, a natural psychological response is to do an "inventory" of all of the present factors. Because they are in a state of shock when they perform this inventory, communities often err when responding to disasters, mistaking correlation for causation.[31] Instead of focusing on any number of factors that might have contributed to her son's suicide, Pulling focused exclusively on his involvement with *D&D*. As game designer Jeff Freeman explains it, "Instead of becoming a left-wing gun-control nut, Pat Pulling became a right-wing game-control nut."[32]

While researching this book, I sought out a source who had been able to observe Bink closely before his suicide. This source agreed to share information on the condition that his or her name be withheld. According to this source, Bink only played *D&D* at school for a total of nine hours. In this person's opinion, Bink's suicide had been an act of aggression toward his mother. Both of his parents had been having affairs before the suicide. Bink shot himself in the chest with a .38 caliber pistol that belonged to his mother, and his choice to commit suicide on the front porch appeared to be a deliberate attempt to shock and horrify his parents when they returned home. Faced with this possibility, it is little wonder that Pulling chose to believe her son's death was caused entirely by a game he played at school.

Pulling's interpretation of her son's suicide came to revolve around a note found in a folder of gaming materials. It read: "Your soul is mine.

I choose the time. At my command, you will leave the land. A follower of evil. Killer of man." The note was a prop used by a dungeon master during a game. Bink's character had been cursed with lycanthropy, and the heroes had to seek a way to lift the curse before the character became a werewolf. The dungeon master was an English teacher at Bink's school, and the simple poem was a creative and interesting way to introduce the plot of the adventure. But the idea of a curse was also highly amenable to a narrative that *D&D* corrupts children. In an explanation that drew on the cult scare of the 1970s, Pulling writes:

> When my son died and I saw the death curse that had been given to him, I thought that surely no one would take such a curse seriously; surely no one would follow a "command" to commit suicide. Then I began to think about the 900-plus people of Jonestown who committed suicide at the command of a deranged leader named Jim Jones.[33]

She eventually arrived at the following theory of her son's suicide: Bink had been brainwashed from playing *D&D* to the point where he had to literally act out a curse by murdering his own family. The only way that Bink could resist this conditioning and spare his family was by taking his own life.[34] In this scenario, Bink had not really committed suicide at all: he had heroically martyred himself in order to save his family from the deadly effects of fantasy role-playing games.

Not all critics of *D&D* presented Bink's death in quite this way. One BADD pamphlet stated simply, "The Pulling boy had a werewolf spell or curse placed upon him and he shot himself."[35] Like so much of the panic over role-playing games, this narrative operated in a kind of double register. In public discussions about the dangers of role-playing games, Pulling explained that the curse was a form of psychological trauma that caused her son's suicide. But among audiences engaged in spiritual warfare, Bink had been killed by a literal curse brought about by the game through supernatural means.

In reality, Bink's suicide had nothing to do with *D&D*. Pulling claimed that her son had been "perfectly normal" before his involvement in the game. However, his classmates explained that he had been suffering from emotional problems unrelated to the game; some claimed Bink had trouble fitting in and became depressed when he could not find a campaign manager to run for class office. He had written "Life Is a Joke" on the blackboard in one of his classes.[36] Far more serious evidence came from BADD sources. A document produced by Pulling for law enforcement contains a "sample character sheet" outlining a character named "Narthöl." Although the player's name appears to have been removed with correction fluid, it is apparent from the remaining script that Narthöl was one of Bink's characters. Pulling most likely discovered the character sheet in Bink's room.[37] The sheet features a box in the top right that players may use to draw a sketch of their character or a personal insignia that the character uses. In the box, Bink drew a sun containing a bow, a sword, and a quiver of arrows. Above the sun is a swastika. This detail, combined with Pulling's statement that Bink compared himself to Hitler in his suicide note, suggests that Bink was fascinated with Nazism, despite being Jewish.

A more alarming detail comes from Robert Hicks of the Virginia Department of Criminal Justice Services. Pulling regularly gave lectures about her son to law enforcement groups that believed in Satanic conspiracy theories. (Hicks refers to such individuals as "cult cops.") Using his law enforcement credentials, Hicks accessed a transcript of one of these lectures published by Larry Jones, an ex-law enforcement official who went on to found a group called Cult Crime Network, Inc. Hicks explains:

> [Larry] Jones published a transcript of a lecture Pulling gave in 1986 at the North Colorado / South Wyoming Detectives' Association Seminar in Fort Collins, Colorado. Pulling stated then—but not in any of her own publications or subsequent interviews—that several weeks before his death, her son had been displaying "lycanthropic" tendencies such as running around the backyard on all fours and barking. Pulling was also quoted as saying that, within the month before her son's death, nineteen rabbits he had raised were inexplicably torn apart, although no loose dogs were seen, and a cat was found disemboweled with a knife.[38]

If this account is true, then Bink displayed numerous signs of emotional disturbance before his suicide. Pulling apparently revealed these details only to audiences that were predisposed to blame *D&D* for Bink's suicide.

Pulling found support from the New Christian Right almost immediately. Several groups helped to cover legal expenses for a series of lawsuits, including the California-based SALT (Sending America to Light and Truth), which had already been campaigning against *Dungeons & Dragons* for several years. In 1983, Pulling sued Dr. Robert A. Bracey III, the principal of Bink's school, for over $1 million. The lawsuit claimed that the "curse" given to her son in the context of a *D&D* game had been "intended to inflict emotional distress upon [Bink] at a time when he . . . was already under extreme psychological distress and emotional pressure from playing the game." The case was thrown out after a circuit judge ruled that Bracey, in his capacity as an official for the state of Virginia, had legal immunity.[39] Undaunted, Pulling attempted to sue TSR for $10 million. A judge threw his case out, also citing freedom of speech.[40] Although these lawsuits were unsuccessful, they had a chilling effect on school boards across the country. As in Heber City, Utah, several school districts opted to avoid *D&D* rather than invite controversy. In response to Pulling's lawsuit, the local school board in Arlington, Virginia, decided to ban *D&D*.[41]

In 1983, after the courts had refused to support any of Pulling's lawsuits, she founded BADD. The group exerted far more influence than a simple lawsuit. BADD literature was distributed throughout schools, churches, and police stations. By 1985, the organization had earned tax-exempt status, and its newsletter had 500 subscribers.[42] BADD members were not only in the United States, but also in Canada, the United Kingdom, and Australia. Pulling reinvented herself as an occult crime investigator who could discern Satanic plots behind everyday occurrences. She was an unlikely expert. At the time of her son's death, she held a two-year associate of arts degree from J. Sargent Reynolds Community College in Richmond, Virginia. Nevertheless, she became a regular guest on the talk show circuit, appearing on *The Gil Gross Show, Geraldo, Sally Jesse Raphael, Donahue, 60 Minutes,* and other shows. The *700 Club* repeatedly endorsed Pulling as an expert on Satanism.[43] Tipper Gore—then wife of Tennessee senator Al Gore—joined the campaign against *D&D*. Her book *Raising PG Kids in an X-Rated Society* contained a chapter on the rising threat of Satanism. She described the suicide of Bink Pulling and branded *D&D* as an "occult themed game."[44] This celebrity led game designer Michael Stackpole to remark: "As far as games are concerned, Patricia Pulling is the Exxon Valdez of ignorance. She is full of it, she's leaking it all over, and it is left to the rest of us to clean up."[45] Pulling's authority did not come from her mastery of facts or cogent arguments but rather from her persona as a bereaved mother, the strength of the coalition she formed with law enforcement and other moral entrepreneurs, and her ability to articulate general anxieties about changing social mores as evidence of an evil conspiracy.

In *The Devil's Web,* Pulling describes her search for answers following her son's suicide. She claims that, like Dear and Jaffe, she researched *D&D* by playing it. She writes:

> I went to a local college and hung around until I spotted some young men carrying "Dungeons and Dragons" books under their arms. I introduced myself and asked them if they would show me how to play this game. They

> said they would, but openly wondered why a woman in her mid-30s was hanging around a college campus looking for someone to teach her to play "Dungeons and Dragons." . . . We played for several hours a day every day for a month.[46]

Unlike Dear's strange account of playing *D&D* with college students, this story is almost certainly not true. Gaming groups gather in hobby shops or advertise using posters. It is unlikely that anyone would find a gaming group in the manner described by Pulling. Furthermore, not even the most fanatical gamers play every day for hours. But the biggest problem with this claim is that Pulling's writings demonstrate complete ignorance of even the most basic elements of *D&D*, including the difference between characters and players and the role of the dungeon master. This story is only credible to an audience that likewise knows nothing about role-playing games.

Pulling also cultivated her new persona by becoming a licensed private investigator with the Commonwealth of Virginia. This required a forty-two-hour licensing course and a one-hour exam, which she passed on October 6, 1987.[47] Much like Dear, she came to present herself as a larger-than-life figure who faced danger at every turn. Like many Satanic conspiracy theorists, she hinted that Satanists were attempting to silence her for speaking out. She writes: "I often was verbally attacked by avid 'Dungeons and Dragons' players. They spoke with the kind of vigor that many people exhibit when they talk about their religion. I received some obnoxious and nasty letters and phone calls, some of which included death threats."[48]

In 1989, authorities raided the ranch of Adolfo de Jesus Constanzo in Matamoros, Mexico. Constanzo was the leader of a drug cartel and practiced an eclectic mix of magical traditions that he believed would secure his power as a drug lord. Authorities discovered the bodies of several murder victims, which had apparently been killed as sacrifices. Although Constanzo was not a Satanist, claims makers labeled these murders "Satanic," and some attempted to prove a link between Constanzo and figures such as Charles Manson. Although Pulling was never involved in the investigation, she flew down to Matamoros to pose for pictures alongside ritual objects left at the crime scene. A picture in her book *The Devil's Web* shows her pointing to a ritual caldron called an *nganga*. The caption reads, "Investigator Pat Pulling points to the nganga, cross, cigars and body parts found in the sacrificial 'Shed of Death' at Matamoros, Mexico." The caption is meant to imply that Pulling was somehow involved in the investigation or is generally called by law enforcement to deal with dangerous cults. In reality, Pulling was essentially a tourist who sought to exploit Constanzo's crimes to present herself as an expert on "occult crime."

Pulling's aspirations to be taken seriously as an expert on the occult would not have gone far had she not received continual support from law enforcement. It was local police who introduced Pulling to theories about Satanism, and Pulling reciprocated by producing material for cult cops about role-playing games and other "occult" threats. Hicks writes:

> Perhaps the most remarkable phenomenon is Pulling's extraordinary influence on the police, with whom she has an almost symbiotic relationship. Pulling provides the cult cops with misinformation and then makes claims at her seminars based on her access to confidential information provided by cult cops conducting criminal investigations.[49]

Hicks attended seminars on "cult crime" in Arlington and Petersburg, Virginia, where Pulling was introduced as having "innumerable" degrees, honors, and awards. Although law enforcement agents generally attended such seminars only out of personal interest, those who did attend represented a variety of agencies. Thus, Pulling was able to boast in *The Devil's Web,* "Pat instructs the FBI, local police forces, sheriff associations [*sic*] and others, and is recognized by these groups as our nation's leading occult authority."[50]

In addition to working with religious groups and law enforcement, Pulling also reached out to psychiatrists and moral entrepreneurs concerned with violent media. *The Devil's Web* is a veritable who's who of the Satanic cult scare. The foreword is by Maury Terry, an investigative reporter who claimed that David Berkowitz, the "Son of Sam" killer, had been part of a Satanic conspiracy. The back contains endorsements from Tipper Gore and the producers of both *60 Minutes* and *Entertainment Tonight.* The acknowledgments list dozens of cult cops and mental health professionals around the country who were friendly to theories of Satanic abuse.

Several mental health professionals were willing to join Pulling in making claims about *D&D*. Pop psychology books that endorsed BADD appeared with titles like *Suicide: Knowing When Your Teen Is At Risk* and *Why Suicide? What Parents & Teachers Must Know to Save Our Kids.* Charles Ewing, a forensic psychologist with a PhD from Cornell and a JD from Harvard, labeled *D&D* "an occult fantasy game" in his book *Kids Who Kill.*[51] Another forensic psychologist, Stanley Semrau, lectured on the psychological dangers of *D&D* at BADD-sponsored conferences.

One of the most important alliances Pulling formed was with Thomas Radecki, a psychiatrist and founder of the National Coalition on Television Violence (NCTV). While Radecki did not claim that *D&D* was Satanically motivated, he did insist that it was a dire social problem. He told *Christianity Today,* "I don't believe TSR . . . wants to do harm or promote violence, but this game is detrimental to millions of people."[52] Radecki also showed no qualms about presenting fallacious statistics, such as the claim that one in eight Hollywood movies contains a rape scene.[53] BADD and NCTV essentially became one organization, with Pulling and Radecki traveling the country together and organizing concerted campaigns against TSR.

Perhaps the greatest source of Pulling's charisma was simply her ability to present a vision of a monolithic evil. David Frankfurter, in his discussion of evil conspiracy theories, argues that the proponents of these theories derive their authority from their ability to frame misfortune and anxiety in terms of evil. The greater their ability to discern an evil influence behind everyday tragedy and general unease, the more compelling their claims are to their audience.[54] Pulling made sense of her son's death by blaming it on an evil game connected to a Satanic conspiracy theory. As the leader of BADD, she was able to offer others the same tool for constructing meaning out of pain and loss. Not surprisingly, some of her most loyal lieutenants in BADD were also bereaved parents.

Rosemary Loyacano's son, Steve, committed suicide by carbon monoxide poisoning in 1982. She describes searching his room and finding angst-ridden references to Satan along with *D&D* materials. Like Pulling, she assembled a similar narrative of her son's death. As she explains it, "We found out another young boy in the same class had introduced him to satanism. I believe he used Dungeons and Dragons as a tool to interest my son in this." Significantly, she explains how she arrived at this conclusion over a period of months: "Little by little we pieced it together with the aid of friends." These "friends" were likely cult cops and moral entrepreneurs like Pulling. Eventually Loyacano became a moral entrepreneur herself, traveling the country and giving slide shows of BADD claims about *D&D*.

Patrick Dempsey, a retired police officer from Seattle, also became a leader in BADD after his son, Michael, committed suicide in 1981. Dempsey's interpretation of Michael's death was even more overtly supernatural. He describes an argument before his son killed himself and relates how Michael's voice changed as if demonically possessed. That night, Michael shot himself. Dempsey describes smelling "sulphur and garlic" at the scene of the suicide. Although it would be normal to smell sulphur in a room where a gun has just been fired, Dempsey interprets this as a sign of demonic activity. Later, a conservative evangelical tract reported that "witnesses saw him trying to summon up D&D demons just minutes before his death."[55] Whether *D&D* induced mental illness or summoned literal demons, Loyacano and Dempsey found the claims of BADD appealing because they took a senseless and painful loss and rendered it sensible.[56]

BADD'S CAMPAIGN

BADD developed a variety of tactics to demonize fantasy role-playing games. The group's most effective tactic was simply to assert—to anyone who would listen—that fantasy role-playing games contributed to criminality, particularly homicide and suicide. These claims were particularly effective with parent-teacher associations, and games were banned in several school districts. The rhetoric used by BADD was a classic example of a moral panic in that it presented a massive social problem where, empirically and statistically, no problem existed. Pulling's authority as an expert was finally challenged in 1989, when she announced that approximately 8 percent of the population of Richmond was "involved with Satanic worship at some level." A reporter questioned this statistic, pointing out that 8 percent of the population equaled 56,000 people. This meant that Richmond was home to more Satanists than Methodists. Pulling responded that her figure concerned not just Satanists but also "occultists," including New Agers, witches, and others. When asked how she arrived at this figure, she responded that she estimated that 4 percent of Richmond's teens as well as 4 percent of the adults were involved in Satanism and occultism, adding up to 8 percent of the population. When a reporter countered that these figures would not add up to 8 percent of the total population, Pulling simply responded that 8 percent was "a conservative estimate" anyway.[57]

Critics of *D&D* did not think in terms of probability or statistics. They measured reality using narrative rather than numbers: the more stories of teenage suicide, the worse the problem. BADD's chief tactic was to maintain a list of teenage males who played *D&D* and had either committed suicide or a violent crime. This list started with Dallas Egbert and Bink Pulling and continued to grow. Tipper Gore quoted Pulling's claim that *D&D* "has been linked to nearly fifty teenage suicides and homicides."[58] Critics of BADD described this rhetoric as Pulling's "trophy list." Some versions of the list would contain press clippings describing the case. Hicks points out that many of these cases are unreliable or are presented in a dishonest fashion. One item came from the tabloid the *Weekly World News*. In some cases, the edges of the news clippings were cropped so as to edit out any mention of other factors in these suicides, such as a history of mental illness.[59] Other claims makers, such as psychiatrist Charles Ewing and religion scholar Carl Raschke, also employed this tactic, in which the nature and scale of "occult crime" are implied by simply presenting a list of incidents with little or no commentary. The alleged pattern that unites these incidents is implied rather than stated so as to suggest that the pattern is self-evident.

The trophy list was an effective form of propaganda because it appealed to a natural psychological tendency to perceive patterns. Mathematician John Allen Paulos used BADD as an example of the "broad base fallacy," in which an argument is made by citing an absolute number of cases rather than the probability of a given phenomenon. Paulos calculated that if three million people play the game and the average rate of suicide for people age fifteen to twenty-four is approximately 12 in 100,000, then there should naturally be about 360 cases of *D&D* players who commit suicide.[60] Statistically speaking, the trophy list suggested that *D&D* drastically *reduces* the rate of teen suicide. Similarly, psychologists Suzanne Abyeta and James Forest have suggested that role-playing games have became associated with criminal behavior because of a phenomenon called the "availability heuristic." This is a psychological phenomenon in which the supposed probability of an event is calculated on the basis of how many examples come to mind. Thus, if someone can readily think of even a few cases of criminal behavior related to role-playing games, they may simply accept that such games frequently lead to criminality.[61] Finally, sociologists have noted that the logic demonstrated by the trophy list is instrumental in fomenting moral panics. Stuart Hall describes a phenomenon known as "convergence" in which two or more activities are linked in a way that falsely implies a connection between them. Hall explains:

> One kind of threat or challenge to society seems larger, more menacing if it can be mapped together with other apparently similar phenomena—especially if by connecting one fairly harmless activity with a more threatening one, the danger implicitly is made to appear more widespread and diffused.[62]

Thus, serious cases such as the suicides of Dallas Egbert and Bink Pulling are "converged" with a hobby played by millions in order to portray a threat that appears to be both dire and widespread.

By using these tactics, BADD persuaded large segments of the public that fantasy role-playing games were a deviant and dangerous activity. To measure media bias against role-playing games, Paul Cardwell, who has served as chair of the Committee for the Advancement of Role-Playing Games (CAR-PGa) for over two decades, examined 111 news articles about role-playing games printed between 1979 and 1992. Of these, 80 were predominantly negative. At the height of the panic, Gary Gygax began receiving death threats in the mail and even hired a bodyguard. *D&D* was frightening enough that in 1985 Winston Matthews sought to capitalize on this fear in his campaign for the position of Virginia's attorney general. He made banning *D&D* in public schools the core of his platform.[63]

While the media often endorsed BADD's claims, federal agencies were far more skeptical. Knowing that companies such as TSR were protected from lawsuits under the First Amendment, BADD sought the help of federal agencies. In 1985, NCTV and BADD petitioned the FTC to require a warning label on *D&D* products explaining that the game had caused "a number of suicides and murders." They even demanded that a similar warning air before each episode of the *Dungeons & Dragons* cartoon show.[64] The FTC directed BADD to the FCC and the Consumer Product Safety Commission, which refused to docket BADD's petition.[65] A letter from the Consumer Product Safety Commission to Thomas Radecki explained that the supposed risks of injury caused by gradual dissociation from reality and demonic possession were "too indirect" to fall within the commission's jurisdiction.[66]

BADD in the Schools

Jason Bivins notes that for the New Christian Right, schools are a site not only of political struggle, but of cosmic struggle against the forces of evil.[67] In the wake of Pulling's campaign, schools in Connecticut, Vermont, New York, Virginia, Colorado, Wisconsin, California, Ohio, and New Mexico banned *D&D*.[68] As in Heber City, Utah, these decisions often followed long battles between coalitions led by evangelical groups and students and parents who supported the games. Typical of such battles was the conflict that arose in the public school district of Putnam, Connecticut. Panic ensued in 1985 when thirteen-year-old Roland Carter hanged himself. A state trooper who investigated the incident concluded that Carter's suicide was closely connected to his drug use. However, Roland E. Creme, a physician, became convinced that Carter's death was a result of his involvement with *D&D*. Armed with pamphlets from BADD and a group called the Christian Information Council, Creme began a petition to ban *D&D* in Putnam schools and gathered 600 signatures. The Putnam Board of Education initially refused to take this seriously but as pressure grew and the media focused increasing scrutiny on Putnam, the board caved.[69]

The fight over role-playing games in public schools led BADD to devise a new claim: that *D&D* is a religion and that its presence in public schools violates the separation of church and state. One BADD document explains:

> The Supreme Court has ruled that religion is not to be taught in schools (Public). Currently pending the courts are some 2,500 cases filed by the ACLU aimed at getting religion out of public schools. Clearly religion is not to be taught in public schools or in related programs (Extra-curricular activities included) according to the present day thinking of the courts.[70]

In both Putnam, Connecticut, and Sacramento, California, claims makers stated that having a *D&D* club was tantamount to state sponsorship of witchcraft. As Creme explained to the *New York Times,*

> Witchcraft, Satanism and occult practices are incorporated in the game. If a kid can't talk about God, he certainly shouldn't be allowed to talk about Satan. . . . If one were to have a game where one had figures or characters from a Bible and one was required to act out the liturgy of the mass, I'm sure there are a lot of people who would object.[71]

Aside from the patently false claim that *D&D* is a religion for purposes of constitutional law, BADD's characterization of the Supreme Court's position is inaccurate. While the court has ruled that public schools cannot mandate student prayer or devotional study of the Bible, it has never stated that religion cannot be studied in a nonsectarian manner. In *Abington Township School District v. Schempp* (1963) Justice Tom C. Clark opines, "It might well be said that one's education is not complete without a study of comparative religion or the history of religion and its relationship to the advancement of civilization."[72] With this in mind, the game elements that BADD found objectionable, such as learning about world mythology, actually contribute to the goals of public education.

Even after the panic, the New Christian Right has continued to use this tactic in an attempt to banish materials they find objectionable from public schools. In 1991, a group called the American Family Association supported a civil suit seeking $1.16 million in damages from the

Willard, Ohio, school board, claiming that the *Impressions* social studies curriculum violated the establishment clause by forcing children to participate in "occult rituals."[73] In 1999, the same argument was used to claim that J.K. Rowling's Harry Potter series should not be allowed in school libraries.[74] The irony is that the individuals behind these protests frequently objected when the establishment clause prevented government entanglements with Christianity, such as mandating Christian prayers in schools.

BADD and Law Enforcement

Perhaps the most disturbing tactic used by BADD was the creation of secret documents for law enforcement about role-playing games. These were presented as resources created by "experts" that might help police to solve crimes related to role-playing games. However, the information in these documents was not available to the general public. Cardwell describes his difficulty in obtaining these documents:

> The first of B.A.D.D.'s attempts to control the police was *Law Enforcement Primer on Fantasy Role-Playing Games*. This was available free to anyone writing on a police department letterhead, but is terribly secret from the rest of society. I had considerable difficulty getting this document because my local police chief feigned cooperation, then notified B.A.D.D. what I was trying to do. He seemed really proud of that deception. I finally located a copy through CAR-PGa, which has police among its members and shortly thereafter from several gaming sources. It is no longer very secret as most serious game researchers already have a copy. However, it is still a secret from most of the general public, who have no idea their police are involved in organized attacks on innocent citizens.[75]

Through Cardwell, I obtained copies of "A Law Enforcement Primer on Fantasy Role Playing Games" and "Interviewing Techniques for Adolescents" by Patricia Pulling. These were copies of copies that had been produced on a photocopier, and they contained marginalia from previous readers. One page lists all of the fantasy role-playing games of which Pulling was aware when she created the document. Several of these games involve creating characters by rolling three six-sided dice. In the margins next to such games, someone has written "666!" apparently excited to have discovered evidence of a Satanic conspiracy.[76]

A document called "Interviewing Techniques for Adolescents" warns police about the danger of fantasy role-playing games as follows:

> Many of them [players] have described things like when they get into situations in real life they think about a solution as to what their character in the game might do. How he/she, the player/character, would handle a situation. There is another problem in that because this game deals with supernatural things and powers like ESP some youngsters think that they gain these powers and that they can do anything that they are indestructible. Some even think that they are super powerful and some think that they have become deified. . . . Another problem is the amount of authentic occult material included in this "game" which in some creates a "seeding" process or curiosity to delve deeper into the occult.

The document also warns that role-playing games are a tool for behavior modification and that rules like alignment work to undermine societal values and create a distorted notion of right and wrong. The dangers described by Pulling effectively recapitulate all of the anxieties of the previous two decades: sensitive youth unable to distinguish fantasy from reality, brainwashing, Satanism, and a subversion narrative in which society itself is under assault.

"Interviewing Techniques" also provides a suggested list of questions for interrogating adolescent gamers. The list includes such items as "Find out the details of the person's character," "Demand to know who the 'Dungeons Master' is," "Has the individual had any curses placed on his/her character?" and "Has he read the Necronomicon or is he familiar with it?" The document explains, "The purpose of this type of questioning is not to establish cause and effect but rather give the investigator possible reasons for bizarre behavior, possible motive if none is apparent."[77] In other words, law enforcement officers were encouraged to blame role-playing games for crimes involving young men where no motive was evident, particularly suicides, senseless acts of violence, and tragic accidents. In an interview about Satanic crime, Carl Raschke explains: "If you're not looking for it, you don't see the evidence. But if you're looking for it, you see evidence everywhere."[78] Following Pulling's advice, law enforcement officers who were so inclined could now find evidence of mind-warping games behind any number of crimes. For instance, when two adolescent brothers were found under a railroad trestle in Colorado, dead from self-inflicted gunshots, police assumed the deaths had something to do with *D&D*. One officer explained, "My understanding is that once you reach a certain point where you are the master, your only way out is death. That way no one can beat you."[79] The officer's "understanding" of the game was undoubtedly informed by groups like BADD.

Suddenly there seemed to be a grand pattern linking numerous cases of youth violence and suicide. An article that appeared in the *Chicago Tribune* in 1985 demonstrates the "feedback loop" between media and law enforcement that often fuels moral panic:

> Last September, the body of a bright 17-year-old California boy washed up on a San Francisco beach, presumably a suicide victim.
>
> In early November, a 12-year-old Colorado boy fatally shot his 16-year-old brother and then himself. Two days later in a suburb north of Chicago, a boy and a girl, both 17, killed themselves by running the family car in a closed garage.
>
> Two weeks ago in Arlington, Tex., a 17-year-old drama student walked onto a classroom stage, put a sawed-off shotgun to his head and fired.
>
> And last week in Goddard, Kan., James Alan Kearbey, a 14-year-old Eagle Scout candidate, allegedly walked into his junior high school and opened fire with a rifle, killing the principal and wounding three others.
>
> What these seemingly disparate tragedies have in common is a complex fantasy role-playing game called Dungeons & Dragons. In each case, the youths involved had been avid players of a game that requires no boards, no moving pieces—just an active imagination and a sharp mind.[80]

Suicides often function as a sort of Rorschach test onto which many causal explanations can be imposed. Claims about *D&D* became an especially facile way of interpreting the suicides of young men. *D&D* was also blamed in at least five cases in the 1980s involving patricide or matricide. These cases were especially conducive to a subversion narrative in which an invading force turned children against their parents. In 1985, nineteen-year-old Ronald Lampasi of Laguna Hills, California, shot and killed his father and wounded his mother. The Lampasis had adopted Ronald and his two sisters when they were young. Mr. Lampasi had admitted to molesting his adopted daughters, and Ronald claimed to have been molested as well. Despite this obvious motive, the deputy district attorney claimed that Ronald had shot Mr. Lampasi while acting out a game of *D&D*.[81]

The following year, Wyley Gates of Canaan, New York, allegedly shot and killed his father along with his brother, his cousin, and his father's live-in girlfriend. With no apparent motive, the police focused on his interest in *D&D*. Investigators examined 300 of Gates's floppy disks in search of evidence that the murder had been planned as part of a *D&D* game. A front-page article about the murders even quoted rules about assassination from a *D&D* book.[82]

Accidents were also amenable to this narrative. In 1987 a man in Mobile, Alabama, was arrested in the shooting death of his roommate.

The two had been playing "Russian roulette," taking turns pointing a .22 caliber pistol at their heads and pulling the trigger. This should have been an open-and-shut case, except that while searching the apartment police found "parts of a Dungeons and Dragons game." They decided this was somehow relevant to the shooting death, leading the Associated Press to run the headline "Man Charged in Dungeons and Dragons Death."[83]

In a similar case, fifteen-year-old David Ventiquattro of Watertown, New York, shot his eleven-year-old neighbor while playing with a shotgun in his bedroom. Tellingly, a judge called the case one of the "most senseless, motiveless slayings" he had ever seen. Ventiquattro initially explained to police that this had been an accident. However, after an eight-hour interrogation in which Ventiquattro was not allowed to speak with his parents or an attorney, police successfully persuaded the horrified boy to confess that he had shot his playmate as part of a *D&D* game, that he had believed his friend was evil, and that it was his mission to "extinguish evil." An appellate court later ruled that this confession was inadmissible.[84]

The narrative produced from this coerced confession bears a strong resemblance to *Mazes and Monsters,* where Robbie/Pardieu believes he is fighting a succubus while actually stabbing someone with a pocketknife. By applying the sort of logic offered by Pulling, law enforcement effectively brought Jaffe's novel to life. It should also be noted that while Robbie/Pardieu imagined his pocketknife was a sword, it was never explained how exactly a 20 gauge shotgun played into Ventriquattro's medieval fantasy.

In fact, an obvious common factor of all of these cases is children and young teenagers with unsupervised access to firearms. The panic over role-playing games frequently provided a convenient distraction from the more tangible and politically loaded problem of gun control. Months after the massacre at Columbine High School in 1999, moral entrepreneur Bob Larson published *Extreme Evil: Kids Killing Kids,* which blames the massacre on violent video games, gothic music, and fantasy games, including *D&D*. Larson also suggests that killers Eric Harris and Dylan Klebold were bisexual, practiced Wicca and vampirism, and were under the influence of demons. But while citing all of these unlikely factors, Larson repeatedly dismisses any discussion of gun control as a conspiracy by the entertainment industry, writing, "By shifting their focus from human responsibility to an inanimate, cold piece of steel, their conscience is off the hook."[85]

BADD in the Courts

A side effect of blaming senseless crimes and accidents on role-playing games was the rise of the "*D&D* defense," in which individuals accused of violent crimes claimed they were not responsible for their actions because playing *D&D* had left them mentally impaired. This defense was precipitated by the discourse of the 1970s with its fears about the mind and its frailties. In 1978, two years after Robert Jay Lifton and Margaret Singer claimed that Patty Hearst had been the victim of brainwashing, Dan White's attorney attempted the "Twinkie defense," claiming that White's overindulgence in junk food was an index of his mental incompetence before murdering Harvey Milk. In the wake of BADD's campaign, several accused criminals attempted the *D&D* defense and found that the likes of Patricia Pulling and Thomas Radecki were willing to testify on their behalf.

In 1984, Darren Molitor and Ron Adcox of St. Louis, Missouri, tied their friend Mary Towey up in her basement as a prank during a drunken party. Molitor put an ace bandage around her neck "to mess with her mind," and the pair went upstairs to continue drinking. When they returned to release the girl, they found that she had died from asphyxiation. They buried her in the woods and fled to Atlanta, Georgia, where the FBI apprehended them. Molitor was charged with first-degree murder. In court, he claimed that *D&D* was responsible for Towey's death because he had become "desensitized" to violence through hours of play. Radecki and Pulling supported this claim and volunteered to testify as expert witnesses. A judge ruled that testimony about *D&D* was irrelevant, and Molitor was convicted.[86] However, Molitor continued to correspond with BADD from prison and insisted that *D&D* had caused him to kill his friend. Pulling was also consulted in the trial of Sean Sellers, a self-described Satanist who murdered his mother and stepfather in 1986. His attorney claimed that his addiction to *Dungeons & Dragons* caused his criminal behavior. Sellers was convicted and eventually executed in 1999.

In 1988, Daniel Kasten of Long Island was convicted of shooting his adoptive parents after they threatened to stop paying for his college tuition because of his low grades. Although this crime had a clear motive, Kasten's attorney offered an insanity defense. Kasten had allegedly told a psychologist that he was not responsible for his crimes because his mind was under the control of a mind flayer, a tentacled monster from *D&D* that eats human brains. Kasten was also convicted.[87]

The same year Chris Pritchard of Washington, North Carolina, along with two accomplices, was convicted of murdering his stepfather and of the attempted murder of his mother. Pritchard stood to inherit $2 million from his parents' death. However, police chief John Crone theorized that Pritchard and his accomplices had suffered a break with reality brought about by *D&D*. Crone visited the local hobby store and found a published adventure that involved sneaking into a castle, killing an evil overlord, and taking his treasure. He theorized that the teens were acting out this adventure at the time of the murder. (Gamers have been unable to find a published adventure matching Crone's description). Pritchard's attorney, Bill Osteen, was happy to advance this narrative. In court, he read from *Understanding the New Age* by *Los Angeles Times* religion writer Russell Chandler. Chandler cites Christian claims makers who contend that *D&D* leads to the acquisition of "mediumistic and occultic powers." Osteen explained to the jury, "I submit that Chris Pritchard, at the time this dastardly act happened, was changed to such an extent . . . that he had moved himself into a position of imagined power and control over his own destiny, which he now understands is not his to determine." Pritchard was sentenced to life plus twenty years. During sentencing, the judge remarked: "The genesis was Christopher Pritchard. The midwife may have been Dungeons and Dragons and drugs—I would not argue with that—but the genesis was Christopher Pritchard."[88]

As the panic wore itself out, these cases became increasingly farcical. In Ohio, Alabama, and Washington, the *D&D* defense was attempted by offenders who had murdered convenience-store owners and bank tellers while committing armed robbery. All were convicted. One individual brought in a *Newsweek* article in which Pulling was quoted and insisted that the jury read an entire stack of *D&D* manuals. The court ruled that such a request would be "unduly confusing and time consuming." Another individual attempted the *D&D* defense, and then, in 1994, when the panic had subsided, claimed that his trial had been unfair because testimony about his interest in *D&D* had biased the jury against him.[89]

The defense was only marginally successful once. This case involved a fourteen-year-old boy from Orangeville, Ontario, who had strangled two children at his school. Radecki testified that the boy was mentally incompetent because of his involvement with *D&D*, and that no fewer than 131 murders could be linked to the game. An Ontario psychiatrist (who played *D&D* and taught the game to his children) diagnosed the boy with schizophrenia, and he was found not guilty by reason of insanity. At the time, minors could not be sentenced for more than three years under Canadian law, so the charge of insanity amounted to a longer sentence, allowing the state to incarcerate the boy indefinitely.[90] Generally, while cult cops were willing to believe that *D&D* led to criminal behavior, judges and juries were unwilling to excuse criminals because of their hobbies. At one insanity trial at which Radecki testified, it took the jury only fifteen minutes to throw out the *D&D* defense. In another murder trial, in which a woman had persuaded her son to kill her mother-in-law using a crossbow, a potential juror was excused from jury duty simply for acknowledging that the *D&D* defense was plausible.[91]

In 1988 Radecki claimed that more than fifty defendants had been convicted after using the *D&D* defense.[92] But Pulling and Radecki were never discouraged that the *D&D* defense failed, because the defense allowed them to use the courtroom as a public pulpit to advance their agenda. Publishers and television networks scrambled to capitalize on the Christopher Pritchard case, resulting in two books, *Cruel Doubt* by Joe McGinniss and *Blood Games* by Jerry Bledsoe. In 1991 and 1992, both books were adapted into made-for-TV dramas, *Cruel Doubt* and *Honor Thy Mother,* the former of which featured Gwyneth Paltrow. All of this media served to galvanize the association between *D&D* and murder in the public consciousness. Newspaper articles about these trials often described Pulling and Radecki as "national authorities" on role-playing games. Some of the convicted criminals continued to insist that *D&D* had caused them to commit crimes, and became assets for BADD. In this way, BADD continued to gain an influence that was disproportionate to its limited size, resources, and expertise.

RESISTANCE

Gary Gygax dismissed the claims of moral entrepreneurs as "witch-hunting balderdash."[93] Months after Molly Ivins reported on the allegations in Heber City that *D&D* was a Satanic game, an ad appeared in *Dragon* magazine entitled "Real-Life Clerics: TSR Hobbies Needs You," soliciting the help of clergy who were friendly to *D&D* and could speak to the game's positive influence.[94] In 1984 TSR created an in-house document called the "TSR Code of Ethics" that limited the portrayal of evil characters and stressed the teamwork aspects of the game. One clause of the code stated, "Evil shall never be portrayed in an attractive light, and shall be used only as a foe to illustrate a moral issue."[95] In 1989 TSR produced a second edition of *D&D* that removed any mention of demons or devils, assassins, or Asian-inspired monks. Despite such efforts, BADD and its allies were effectively able to steer the public conversation about fantasy role-playing games throughout the 1980s.

In some cases, game companies simply accepted these fears and adapted their business strategies accordingly. Rule books for *Rifts,* a fantasy role-playing game by Palladium featured the following warning:

> Warning! Violence and the Supernatural. This book may be inappropriate for young readers. **The fictional world of Rifts** is violent, deadly, and filled with supernatural monsters. Other-dimensional beings, often referred to as "demons," torment, stalk, and prey on humans. Other alien life forms, monsters, gods, demi-gods, as well as magic, insanity and the supernatural are all elements in this book. Some parents may find the violence and supernatural elements of the game inappropriate for young readers/players. We suggest parental discretion.
>
> **Note that Rifts and the Rifts Conversion Book are works of fiction!** NONE of the monsters, characters, magic, powers or depictions are real. None of us at Palladium Books condone or encourage the occult, the practice of magic, the use of drugs, or violence.[96]

The description of demons, violence, magic, and insanity in this warning appears to be as much an effort to excite adolescent game-players as to demonstrate company responsibility and ward off a lawsuit. Much like the producers of violent movies and heavy metal music, some role-playing game companies simultaneously objected to and profited from the negative media attention generated by moral entrepreneurs.[97] In 1982, the year that Bink Pulling committed suicide, sales of *D&D* products rose to $22 million, up from $14 million the year before.

As a result of this discourse, an entire generation of gamers who came of age during the 1980s recalls being stigmatized for their favorite pastime.[98] Comedian Stephen Colbert recalls:

> We were close to the Bible belt, and ministers were preaching on TV against it, saying that it was a cult, telling stories about kids going too far, playing in the sewers and getting swept away when it rained or getting carried away and believing that the games were real and hurting each other with swords or trying to do incantations, demon worship.

Similarly, author Laurell K. Hamilton describes her experience in college:

> I went to a small Christian college, and the fact that I played *D&D* at all was something some people equated with Satan worship. You had to be careful whom you even told about it. It was hard to find people. Nobody wanted to fess up.[99]

In 1997, the alternative rock group Marcy Playground wrote their song "A Cloak of Elvenkind." In the Lord of the Rings trilogy and *D&D*, elven cloaks are used to hide from enemies. The song describes a teenage boy hiding his gaming books in his closet to shield them from the puritanical gaze of his mother. The lyrics are nostalgic and appeal to a shared memory of hiding from the combined authority of parents and moral entrepreneurs.

As the claims of BADD gained traction, gamers became increasingly more organized. Many responded to claims about role-playing and Satanism with satire. One apologist for role-playing games argued that *Monopoly* is more wicked than *D&D* because "the goal is to take everyone's money and thereby demoralize everyone else and be the richest and only person left owning any property."[100] An article on the Internet entitled "Chess: The Subtle Sin" parodied an essay called "Should a Christian Play Dungeons and Dragons?" Chess, it was argued, is an occult game designed to undermine Christian values. The most powerful piece is the queen, which contradicts biblical commands that women should be submissive.

As school boards continued to ban *D&D*, students began to take more direct action. In a letter to *Dragon* magazine, one gamer wrote, "I think that we'd better get organized somehow or the mainstream may drown us."[101] In 1983, the school district of Alamagordo, New Mexico, removed *D&D* from its after-school program. The superintendent explained that this step had been taken because parents, led by Christian coalitions, had complained that the game involves the occult. A group of twenty-five grade students responded with a petition condemning the ban. The petition laid the charges of deviance on the claims makers, stating, "It is a sick mind that would find the occult in the game."[102] Nicholas Ordnoff, a sophomore, published a similar indictment of the claims makers in a letter to the editor of the *Charleston Gazette:*

> I do not understand why some people think these games are satanic. Is it because the games have illustrations? Has anyone taken a second look at the pictures we hang in art museums, such as George Grosz's "I am Glad to be Back" or David Alfaro's "Echo of a Scream?" Or, do people come to this conclusion from personal experience? Probably not, because most people who have played speak highly of the game. If games really influence behavior, then people who play Risk would try to take over the world, and people who play Monopoly would buy and rent railroads. If they played Twister—I do not want to imagine.[103]

In 1987 *Entertainment Tonight* featured a two-part special entitled "Games That Kill" and hosted by Geraldo Rivera. Rivera announced that over ninety deaths "had been linked" to fantasy role-playing games.[104] The Game Manufacturers Association responded by publishing a pamphlet entitled "Games Don't Kill: A Look at the Claims," written by Greg Stafford. The following year, a group of gamers met at a convention and decided to organize CAR-PGa as a countermovement to BADD. The following ad for CAR-PGa appeared in a gaming magazine:

> As most of you have found, personally or second hand, there is a well-organized and well-funded bunch of people out there trying to ban our games. . . . There is an organization, open for your participation, that is fighting back against these charges, by conducting research into the benefits of RPG, and by fighting the illegal use of tax money for sectarian indoctrination. We seldom get in the mass media, but we do get results.[105]

CAR-PGa was successful at monitoring and investigating the claims makers. Using the Freedom of Information Act, Paul Cardwell obtained copies of correspondence from Patricia Pulling and Thomas Radecki in their attempt to lobby federal agencies to mandate warning labels that role-playing games cause suicide. Cardwell also received support from Senator Lloyd Bentsen (D-TX), who communicated with the Consumer Product Safety Commission on CAR-PGa's behalf.[106] Robert Hicks supplied CAR-PGa with insider information about BADD's connection to police. Pierre Savoie, a PhD student in chemistry at the University of Toronto, began to investigate the background and credentials of the claims makers. His findings were published in an article entitled "The Whole Loon Catalogue" that appeared in the gaming magazine *Shadis*. Savoie found that most of the literature condemning role-playing games quoted religious tracts that were quoting still other religious tracts. In attempting to reach the bottom of this discourse, he uncovered a realm of deviant conspiracy theories. For instance, John Torrell of Christian Life Ministries was quoted in the *Weekly World News* as an expert on the psychological dangers of *D&D*. Savoie found that in his other writings, Torrell had warned that Ronald Reagan had signed a secret surrender treaty with the USSR during a 1986 summit in Reykjavik, Iceland.[107]

Like the grade-school petitioners in Alamagordo, CAR-PGa frequently reversed BADD's claims on the accusers. CAR-PGa manifestos sometimes referred to the claims makers as "cultists." One such document states, "One of the principal things that makes the B.A.D.D.ies bad is their total contempt for law and their campaign to subvert the police into being accomplices in their crimes."[108] This turned the subversion narrative on its head: for CAR-PGa it was actually the moral entrepreneurs who threatened society and sought to undermine traditional values.

CHRISTIAN GAMERS

The escalating conflict between gamers and claims makers was hardest on gamers who were also Christian. Gamers for whom Christianity was an important part of their identity often felt persecuted by both sides: regarded as Satanic by their fellow Christians and mocked as ignorant bigots by their fellow gamers. Christian gamers developed their own discourse to counter the theological rhetoric of antigaming moral entrepreneurs. For instance, Michael J. Young, a game designer and chaplain for the Christian Gamers Guild, responded to concerns about occultism by arguing that Christians have far more to fear from materialism and atheism than "imaginary magic." He also challenged the reading of scripture employed by the claims makers. Christian opponents of *D&D* frequently cited 1 Thessalonians 5:22: "Abstain from all appearance of evil." Their argument, essentially, was that imagining demons and monsters involved the appearance of evil and was thus unbiblical. Young offered a different reading, arguing that this quotation is not a warning to avoid things that literally appear evil but to avoid evil in all its varied appearances.[109]

Paul Cardwell of CAR-PGa is also ordained as a Methodist minister. In his analysis of BADD documents, he suggests that the type of Christianity that supports claims of Satanism is really a form of folk piety that is not rooted in biblical tradition. BADD makes much of the fact that *D&D* characters are created by rolling three six-sided dice. Cardwell counters that the numerals "666" do not appear in the "textus receptus." The King James Bible describes the number of the beast as "six hundred, three-score and six," and in some translations this number is six hundred and sixteen. Cardwell writes, "Obviously, B.A.D.D. is not only appealing to the superstitious, but to those who know nothing about RPG, and/or those who don't read the Bible but merely want to appear religious."[110]

Another case of gamers demonstrating superior religious literacy occurred when Gali Sanchez, a writer who had designed several *D&D* adventures, appeared on the *700 Club*. Sanchez argued that *D&D* was basically a good game, but expressed concern that it contained elements of "actual" occultism. An article produced by the Christian Broadcasting

Network reported, "Sanchez related the history of a god called Moloch."[111] TSR did publish rules for a demon lord named Moloch, a name that is derived from a deity worshipped by the ancient Canaanites. When Sanchez revealed this connection on the *700 Club,* it was presented as a smoking gun proving that *D&D* was actually a form of ancient pagan worship disguised as a game. What is strange is that the *700 Club* had apparently never heard of Moloch. Moloch or Molech is mentioned eight times in the Hebrew Bible and again in the Acts of the Apostles. This figure also makes an appearance in *Paradise Lost.* Moloch appears in *D&D* because the game's creators had a knowledge of biblical tradition that their Christian critics frequently lacked. In fact, the leading news source for the New Christian Right had to learn about this biblical personage from a game designer. This was a stark example of the way Christian critics of fantasy role-playing games were alienated from elements of Christian tradition, and interpreted Christian elements of the game as occultism.

The cleverest demonstration of religious literacy by gamer apologists came from Pierre Savoie, who took aim at a tract entitled "Games Unsuspecting People Play" by Louise Shanahan, writing for the conservative Catholic group the Daughters of St. Paul. The tract came to Savoie's attention after he manned a booth for the games club at a college event for incoming students. One student explained that her Catholicism prohibited her from playing role-playing games. Another Catholic freshman raised his hands in fright when he saw the booth. By tracing the genealogy of anti-*D&D* literature, Savoie found that Shanahan's tract borrowed heavily from other moral entrepreneurs who were virulently anti-Catholic. In particular, Shanahan quoted Albert Dager, who describes Catholicism as a Babylonian mystery religion. Savoie exploited this discovery to the hilt, producing his own tract entitled "Catholics! Have You Been Duped by *Anti-Catholics?*" He also wrote a letter to the editor that was published in the *Catholic Register* in Toronto. Instead of defending *D&D*, he attacked Shanahan on sectarian grounds, asking, "How could a *conservative* Catholic group publish a tract with such blatant *anti-Catholic* references?" (The word "conservative" was presumably emphasized to suggest that anyone who endorsed the tract was not only a bad Catholic, but a bad conservative.) The Daughters of St. Paul responded by placing a disclaimer sticker on the tract, which distanced the organization from its contents and stated that the original article was published in *Our Family* magazine in Battleford, Saskatchewan.[112]

THE FALL OF BADD

BADD's fall was as sudden and rapid as its rise to prominence. A key factor was resistance from gamers that pressured the media into viewing claims about gaming and violent crime more critically. In March 1991, Shawn Novak, sixteen, stabbed a seven- and a nine-year-old to death in Virginia Beach, Virginia. His lawyers attempted the *D&D* defense, claiming that Novak had become confused with his character at the time of the murders. Even though the murders happened in the backyard of BADD and the *700 Club*, the narrative that Novak was motivated by *D&D* received little attention from mainstream media. When an article suggesting this appeared in the *Washington Post*, it was answered with two letters to the editor from gamers that excoriated the media for its lack of insight and ethics.[113] That same month, a librarian from Virginia Beach wrote an article for the *School Library Journal* defending the library's decision to offer *D&D* materials. She writes, "If . . . a parent's concern centers on the rumors that Dungeons and Dragons fosters madness, crime, or cult membership, it is possible to show that this is modern folklore on a par with the tanning machine turned into a microwave."[114]

The year 1991 also saw the publication of *The Psychology of Adolescent Satanism* by clinical psychologist Anthony Moriarty. Although Moriarty took warnings about teenage Satanism quite seriously, he condemned Patricia Pulling and BADD as hysterical and counterproductive.[115] *D&D* was no longer alien and new. Police were less inclined to focus on *D&D* as a factor in violent crimes, and the "*D&D* defense" was a proven failure. At the same time, video and computer games were becoming increasingly realistic, providing a new source of violent media for moral entrepreneurs to focus on.[116]

Soon the leadership of BADD began to collapse. Thomas Radecki was forced to retire from public life amid scandal. He had claimed to be on the faculty of the University of Illinois Champaign-Urbana medical school. Cardwell investigated and found that Radecki had briefly held the "clinical faculty" status given to doctors who are accredited to practice at a teaching hospital. But this title was revoked in 1985, long before Radecki stopped claiming to be a faculty member at the medical school. In March 1992, he quit NCTV and turned it over to his Beverly Hills colleague, Carole Lieberman. Shortly thereafter, his license as a physician was revoked for five years for "immoral conduct of an unprofessional nature with a patient." Radecki's license was eventually restored, but in 2012 he voluntarily surrendered it, amid charges that he was trading prescription drugs for sexual favors.[117]

Patricia Pulling briefly became the head of NCTV before she contracted cancer and died in 1997. A column in *Dragon* announced her death. Michael Stackpole credited Pulling with "forcing the industry to grow up." He was quoted: "She shined one hell of a light on us, so we had to learn how to deal with the outside world. Without that, we might not have had the strong growth of the late '80s and early '90s."[118] Indeed, the gamers who endured BADD's assault came of age and became the producers of popular culture. *D&D* has been depicted as a harmless diversion in such television series as *The X-Files, Freaks and Geeks, Buffy: The Vampire Slayer,* and *The Big Bang Theory.* What was once regarded as deviant and frightening has now been generally accepted into the mainstream. However, claims about fantasy role-playing games and their connection to madness and Satanism continue to smolder in some religious communities. John Walliss, in his article "The Road to Hell Is Paved with D20s," describes an interview with a Christian gamer from the United Kingdom that took place in 2009. She assumed no one from her church would care that she enjoyed *D&D.* Instead she recalls:

> *I had no idea the can of worms I was opening.* I got letters. One lady in our home study group wrote me this letter saying, "*I can't believe that you have gone over to the devil.* You're doing *Satanic* things." . . . There was even someone in the Church Elder's Council who said, "I don't know much about *D&D*. All I know is that it's Satanic."[119]

Beyond the sphere of mainstream discourse, the narrative of a Satanic game that undermines society and drives children mad continues to hold sway. In the wake of tragedy or senseless violence this narrative is quickly revived.

CHAPTER 5

A World of Darkness: 1991–2001

White Wolf calls this approach "Gothic-Punk," an apt a name as any for a game where atmosphere reigns supreme. Cities are dark clusters of decaying buildings and gloomy streets. Political corruption and corporate greed are taken for granted. Outcast youths find solace in street gangs and death-rock music. In this world of hopelessness, "the end" is not coming, it is here.

—Rick Swan, review of *Werewolf: The Apocalypse*

As high as America's body count is today, a rising tide of youth crime and violence is about to lift it even higher. A new generation of street criminals is upon us—the youngest, biggest, and baddest generation any society has ever known.

—William J. Bennett, John J. DiLulio, Jr., and John P. Walters, *Body Count*

Beginning in the late 1980s, a second generation of role-playing games emerged that moved away from the genre's roots in wargaming. Games such as *Amber: Diceless Roleplaying* (1991) featured mechanics that were designed to emphasize storytelling and narrative rather than meticulous simulation or complex combat scenarios. There was also a shift toward "urban fantasy": while the premises of fantasy role-playing games continued to feature magic and supernatural beings, these elements were often moved from a fantastic world like Middle Earth and into an otherwise familiar modern setting. *Shadowrun* (1989) remains an extremely popular example of the new generation of games. The game is set in the mid-twenty-first century and assumes that magic returned to Earth in the year 2011. With the return of magic, dragons and other magical beasts reappeared in modern cities, esoteric rituals once again caused magical effects, and many ordinary humans were mutated into elves, dwarves, orcs, and trolls. Meanwhile, Western civilization has developed into a brutal oligarchy in which corporations wage war against each other. Players assume the roles of mercenaries, cybercriminals, and magicians who either hire themselves out to corporate interests or fight to protect ordinary people. Urban fantasy games were partly a way for new games to compete with *D&D*, which appeared to have cornered the market on medieval fantasy games. But these settings also appealed to players because they made the fantastic seem both more intellectually sophisticated and more plausible. *Shadowrun* invites players to imagine a world where dragons expand their hoards by becoming CEOs, and Texas A&M University is now Texas A&M&M (Agriculture and Military and Magic).

The new generation of fantasy role-playing games also departed from *D&D* in atmosphere and style. *D&D* was strongly influenced by Tolkien and his notion that fantasy ought to entail a "eucatastrophe." Tolkien coined this term to describe an unexpected turn of events in which the protagonist is saved from certain doom. This idea was informed by Tolkien's Christianity and the theology of grace. In fact, he described the resurrection of Christ as "the Great Eucatastrophe" of the Gospels.[1] Of course, *D&D* games did not always end in eucatastrophe. But *D&D*, and particularly classic campaign settings like *Forgotten Realms* and *Dragonlance*, generally assumed fantastic worlds in which evil is powerful but never triumphant and the ability of the heroes to succeed is not only possible but likely. By contrast new, darker role-playing games like *Cyberpunk* (1988) and *Shadowrun* offered settings that not only retained the cynicism and anxieties of the modern world but enhanced and accentuated them.

White Wolf Publishing, founded in Stone Mountain, Georgia, in 1991, came to define this dark new generation of role-playing games. Beginning with its first game, *Vampire: The Masquerade*, White Wolf produced a series of games set in "the World of Darkness." As the authors of *Vampire* explained it,

> The world of *Vampire* is not our world—at least not quite. It is a Gothic-Punk vision of our world, a place of extremes—monolithic, majestic and altogether twisted. The government is corrupt, the culture is bankrupt, and the decadent mortals revel in the flames of the final days. It is a world where the forces of evil and entropy are even more powerful than they are in our world. It is a world of darkness.[2]

Players assumed the roles of supernatural beings who inhabit this world, keeping their existence a secret. Games like *Vampire: The Masquerade* and *Werewolf: The Apocalypse* offered characters who battled their inner-monsters as much as outer ones. As one reviewer stated,

> The Stone Mountain, Ga., company has reshaped the field with its stylish, moody RPGs that emphasize a sort of sullen Generation X glamour. . . . I like and respect both these games, but their basic conflicts admit no solutions. After playing them, sometimes you feel such contempt for humanity, you want to wash.[3]

White Wolf's games did reflect the experience of Generation X, just as *D&D* reflected the optimism and the rediscovery of myth experienced by baby boomers. A new generation had come of age with reasons to be cynical. Journalist Ethan Gilsdorf described growing up in the 1980s, where his love for *D&D* existed alongside "President Reagan's menacing apocalyptic age of Evil Empires and nuclear Armageddon."[4] The divorce rate doubled between 1965 and 1977, and by the age of sixteen 40 percent of Generation X had spent time in a single-parent household. This was also the generation of "latch-key children," who were more affected by mass media than previous generations. As adults, Generation X will probably bear the dubious distinction of being the first generation in US history to have lower lifetime earnings than their parents. As a result of these changes, Generation X developed hopes and dreams quite different from those of their parents. As Donald and Arpi Miller explained in *Gen X Religion,*

> Xers are not afraid of the truth, nor are they fooled into thinking they can change the world. They have by and large given up on large-scale utopian schemes and are working for practical change in their own lives, those of a few close friends, and, when feeling expansive, that of their neighborhood.[5]

This analysis was echoed by Michelle Belanger, who organized live-action games of *Vampire: The Masquerade* in the 1990s. On her podcast *Shadowdance,* she described how the World of Darkness reflected the concerns of Generation X: :

> The people who were gaming at that time were . . . We were not our parents' hippie generation who were trying to strive for a bright, shiny, sunshiny day. We weren't looking for a perfect world. We knew it was broken. It was probably broken beyond repair and mostly we were trying to just not be broken *by* it anymore than we already were.[6]

For Generation X, dark, atmosphere-heavy role-playing games were not just an escape into a fantasy world: they were a medium through which players and storytellers could explore their doubts and frustrations by creating stories that articulated the world's flaws by casting them into relief.

White Wolf's World of Darkness is significant to any analysis of role-playing games and religion for two reasons. First, darker and more realistic settings contributed to a fresh round of panic in the mid-1990s. The new panic resurrected fears first raised during the previous two decades and incorporated them into a narrative of rampant youth crime promoted by the media and the political right. Second, while *D&D* had only an indirect relationship with actual occultism, White Wolf's games often attracted subcultures that genuinely held magical worldviews. In particular, a community of self-identified vampires attracted the attention of the media during the 1990s, emboldening claims that role-playing games caused players to dissociate from reality. The so-called real vampire community was not entirely derivative of *Vampire: The Masquerade* but borrowed some ideas and vocabulary from the game. This was only one example of how the World of Darkness inspired and shaped emerging ideas about the supernatural, and this development suggests that the relationship between role-playing games and religious ideas is more complex than either moral entrepreneurs or game apologists suspected.

RUMORS OF SUPERPREDATORS

BADD was all but defunct by the 1990s, and while Satanic conspiracy theories were still discussed in certain churches and law enforcement circles, the media had begun to lose interest in these claims. Instead, a new folk devil had emerged in the myth of the juvenile "superpredator." In their book *Body Count: Moral Poverty and How to Win America's War against Crime and Drugs,* conservative pundits William J. Bennett, John J. DiLulio, and John P. Walters defined superpredators as "radically impulsive, brutally remorseless youngsters, including ever more preteenage boys, who murder, assault, rape, rob, burglarize, deal deadly drugs, join gun-toting gangs, and create serious communal disorders." They added, "They do not fear the stigma of arrest, the pains of imprisonment, or the pangs of conscience."[7] This language is eerily reminiscent of William Dear's discussion of the "shit-kickers" he allegedly rescued Dallas Egbert from in *The Dungeon Master.*

Body Count promoted a declension narrative in which the forces of secularization had reduced America to a state of "moral poverty" that had bred a generation of unprecedented brutality. The term "superpredator" is adapted from ecology and implies an animal rather than a person. Superpredators, it was claimed, could not be helped or reformed because they did not possess a conscience like normal human beings. The solution posed in *Body Count* was to simply imprison this lost generation. The authors explained: "A false premise has emasculated the criminal justice system: the notion that the first purpose of punishment is to rehabilitate criminals. We disagree. Strongly. The first purpose is *moral,* to exact a price for transgressing the rights of others."[8] *Body Count* closed with a call to promote "true religious faith" (a cypher for Christianity) in the hopes of breeding a new generation free from moral defects. The final paragraph explained that true faith can foster social virtue because it "allows the 'eyes of the heart' to see our fellow citizens not merely as distant body count statistics or as enemies or aliens or 'other' but as moral and spiritual beings, as children of God. For that is, in fact, what they are."[9] This is an improbable conclusion to a book claiming that impoverished young minorities are inhuman monsters.

The strangest aspect of the superpredator myth was that it occurred during an era of falling crime rates. In 1994, the FBI reported that crime of all types had fallen steadily by 7.7 percent since 1990, and violent crime had fallen by an average of 8 percent in the nine largest cities in the United States. By 1995, the rate of homicide had fallen as much as 12 percent in cities such as New York, Los Angeles, and Chicago.[10] However, advocates of the superpredator theory repeatedly claimed that the improved crime rate was merely "the calm before the storm," and pointed out that the rate of homicide committed by fourteen- to seventeen-year-olds was actually rising. Criminologist James Fox warned the press, "As long as we fool ourselves in thinking that we're winning the war against crime, we may be blindsided by this bloodbath of teenage violence lurking in the future."[11]

The superpredator narrative sometimes took fantastic and apocalyptic tones. Jack O'Malley, a state attorney, described the situation as "Lord of the Flies on a massive scale," adding, "We've become a nation being terrorized by our children."[12] The authors of *Body Count* suggested that the superpredators could ultimately lead to martial law and the collapse of democracy:

> Our democratic institutions cannot withstand much more crime without a terrible counterreaction. If violent crime continues to rise; if out-of-wedlock births continue to increase; if more children are thrown into moral poverty;

> if the human carnage continues to mount; the public will demand restored order at any cost—including a more-rapid-than-you-think rollback of civil liberties.[13]

These claims presented a new incarnation of a subversion narrative that had existed since the 1960s. In the 1990s, America's youth were still poised to destroy society. But now they were no longer good people who had been brainwashed by cult leaders or corrupted by Satanists until their values had been turned inside out. The superpredators were simply born evil, the wreckage of a decadent society. Books like *Body Count* suggested that by defeating them through an uncompromising campaign of urban warfare we might redeem ourselves as a nation.

Politicians responded to fears of superpredators with drastic policies intended to "get tough" on juvenile crime. Around the country, laws were passed to try juveniles as adults, incarcerate them in adult facilities, and impose the death penalty on younger offenders. "Three strikes" policies were imposed, leading to one of the largest prison expansions in US history. Approaching the presidential election of 1996, both Bill Clinton and Bob Dole postured as politicians who were tough on superpredators. Clinton urged cities to pass curfews for minors. Bob Dole vowed to fight a "real war" on juvenile crime. He also invoked the superpredators in his call for welfare reform, implying that government aid for the poor was somehow fueling the conditions of "moral poverty."[14]

Games like *Cyberpunk, Shadowrun,* and *Vampire* strangely mirrored these alarmist claims with their depictions of decadent societies and desperate criminals. The 1990s was a period in which both gamers and conservative pundits explored dark fantasies of urban decay. The chief difference was that books like *Body Count* presented an apocalyptic scenario in which the forces of evil would ultimately be defeated and American society would rediscover its moral center. By contrast, dark role-playing games offered no such hope of salvation. These games generally glamorized decadence and cynicism. Heroes were not individuals who could save the world but rather people who could, in spite of the world, preserve some iota of goodness within themselves.

The myth of the superpredator revolved around minority youth from low-income neighborhoods, while the stereotypical gamer was middle class and white. However, a number of high-profile murders committed by white youth allowed this narrative to shift. In 1996 and 1997, national news reported cases of suburbanites murdered in their homes by white youth who enjoyed role-playing games. Adolescent killers like Rod Ferrell, David Anderson, and Alex Baranyi became temporary celebrities. In 1999, Eric Harris and Dylan Klebold attacked Columbine High School with an arsenal of guns, killing thirteen and injuring twenty-one. These crimes both horrified and fascinated the public. As with Dallas Egbert's disappearance in 1979, true-crime paperbacks were written, and TV specials were produced. In an attempt to interpret acts of murder that were largely inexplicable, the media turned to both the superpredator narrative of a generation born without a conscience and the older narrative of young men lost in a fantasy game. These two narratives merged, and once again there was a call to censor role-playing games.

THE WEIRD OF WHITE WOLF

A new generation of game designers came of age in much the same way that the first had—namely, on a college campus in Minnesota. Mark Rein-Hagen and Jonathan Tweet were gamers at St. Olaf College. Both had played *D&D* in the 1970s. At a TED talk in 2013 on the educational value of games, Rein-Hagen confessed that he had been unable to read until the fourth grade and that before discovering *D&D* at age thirteen, he had been failing nearly every subject. By playing *D&D* with his father, he learned percentages, fractions, and other concepts that had not previously interested him. He created a fantasy kingdom that was so detailed it had a constitution. Creating a detailed fantasy required further study of history, government, and economics. Rein-Hagen explained: "I learned so much about the world that I became a learning machine. This game changed my life. Before this game, my parents were worried that I was going to become a criminal. After the game it was pretty clear I was going to college."[15]

At St. Olaf, Rein-Hagen and Tweet had progressed from TSR's *D&D* to Chaosium's somewhat darker *Runequest* and *Call of Cthulhu*. In 1987 they formed their own publishing company called Lion Rampant, named after the insignia of St. Olaf College. Their first real game was called *Ars Magica*. Their goal in designing the game, according to game reviewer Shannon Appelcline, was to "get wizards right" by creating a system of magic that seemed plausible.[16] Game referees had been reading texts on esotericism to make more "realistic" magic systems since the 1970s.[17] However, Rein-Hagen and Tweet presented an especially well-researched take on magic. *Ars Magica* is not set in a fantasy realm like

Middle Earth or Blackmoor but thirteenth-century Europe. Characters play learned mages who are members of the Order of Hermes. Mages produce spells by gaining control over five "techniques" and ten "forms." Each of these elements is described using Medieval Latin, creating a sense that the game could actually be a lost system of medieval magic.

Ars Magica also placed greater emphasis on narrative and role-playing instead of simulating combat. Gary Gygax had never really cared about the role-playing aspect of *D&D*. He once declared, "If I want to do that, I'll join an amateur theater group."[18] In *Ars Magica,* the creators encouraged what they called "troupe-style roleplaying" in which players can play multiple characters and take turns being the game master. The goal of the troupe was for the players to produce more compelling and exciting stories collaboratively.[19] Rein-Hagen's subsequent games also emphasized narrative, initiating a larger shift in role-playing games from simulation to narrative.

An early fan of *Ars Magica* was Stewart Wieck, who edited an amateur magazine about fantasy role-playing games. Wieck's publication began as a photocopied "fanzine" called *Arcanum.* However, there was already a published fantasy role-playing game called *Arcanum,* so Wieck changed the name to *White Wolf.* This was a reference to Michael Moorcock's novel *The Weird of the White Wolf,* about the albino anti-hero Elric of Melniboné. (*Weird* or *wyrd* is an Old English word meaning "fate.") In 1988 *White Wolf* magazine gave a glowing review of *Ars Magica* and began publishing articles about the game.

Although *Ars Magica* was well received, Lion Rampant was rapidly accumulating debt. Dan Fox, an independently wealthy man from Georgia, offered to fund the company if it would publish his medieval fantasy game *Hahlmabrea* (originally titled *Warriors, Wizards, and Witches*). The catch was that Fox wanted the company to relocate to Georgia. He even offered Lion Rampant a house to use as a physical plant. In 1990 Rein-Hagen and a few others accepted the offer and moved from Minnesota to Georgia. The arrangement with Fox soon disintegrated: he did not have as much money as he had led his business partners to believe. He also did not actually own the house where he had invited Lion Rampant to stay. The legal owners eventually arrived and evicted the company. This could have been the end of Rein-Hagen's career as a game designer, had it not been for Stewart Wieck. Wieck's magazine had become increasingly professional, and he had good credit with his printers. He was also located nearby, in Alabama. In 1991 the two companies merged and became White Wolf Publishing.[20]

White Wolf distinguished itself by emphasizing role-playing over rules. The company took deliberate steps to steer the role-playing game away from its origins in wargaming. The term "campaign" was replaced with the term "chronicle," and game masters were renamed "storytellers." White Wolf's "storyteller" games set in the World of Darkness were notoriously heavy on premise and light on combat rules. In fact, storytellers were encouraged to eschew dice entirely if they felt a particular outcome would make for a better story. Rein-Hagen conceived of *Vampire: The Masquerade* in 1990 while on a road trip with fellow game designers to Gen Con, the gaming convention founded by Gary Gygax. The game appeared in 1991 and was marketed as "a storytelling game of personal horror." The following year, it won the Origin award for best rules in a role-playing game.

The premise of *Vampire* is that immortal blood-drinkers live among us. These beings refer to each other as "Kindred" and claim to be the descendants of Cain, who became the first vampire when he was cursed for the murder of his brother and wandered into the land of Nod. Whether or not this legend is true, the Kindred have existed since the beginning of human civilization (which they may have started). While vampires are immensely powerful, they must sleep during the day and would be vulnerable if ordinary humans knew about their existence. And so they maintain a great "masquerade" in which they conceal their existence from the world. Posing as humans, vampires have assumed positions of power, adding worldly influence to their supernatural abilities. They are divided into rival clans and use their influence to engage in petty political feuding. These conflicts can last for centuries and often cause massive collateral damage for ordinary people. Each city is led by a powerful vampire known as a "prince," who has the power of life and death over his subjects. Only the most ruthless and manipulative princes are able to maintain their grip on power for long. One player described playing the game as "Machiavelli with training wheels."[21]

In most *Vampire* chronicles, players assume the role of young vampires who were recently human and are struggling to adapt to undead society. Vampires retain all of humanity's weaknesses and even a few of its virtues. They are still capable of feeling self-doubt, jealousy, remorse, and even love. However, vampirism enhances the darker aspects of the human psyche, empowering them to superhuman proportions. This aspect of the vampire is called "the Beast," and it drives each vampire toward lust, brutality, and violence. Each time a vampire succumbs to the Beast, she loses a piece of her humanity, becoming more and more of an inhuman animal. Characters who lose all of their humanity have become mindless monsters and must be retired from the game.

Vampire built on the popularity of Anne Rice's *Vampire Chronicles* and became an overnight sensation across college campuses. The game was also successful internationally and was translated into twenty languages. Like Middle Earth or Tékumel, the World of Darkness was highly detailed and offered an incredible degree of verisimilitude. White Wolf created an alternate human history in which vampires had secretly been behind the scenes of every war and political movement since the Bronze Age. One reviewer raved, "The history is so vividly imagined that I thought I was reading a textbook."[22] The game provided a detailed model of vampire society complete with rules and traditions. It also included extensive vocabulary so that players could speak as if they were members of a secret subculture. Across the country, groups of young adults could be seen gathered in Denny's at two in the morning, using odd terms like "obfuscate" and "Malkavian."[23]

Rein-Hagen had always envisioned a series of intersecting games in which different kinds of characters shared the same setting. The Kindred were not the only monsters lurking in the World of Darkness. White Wolf produced four more games over the next four years. This core of five games created a rich fabric of urban fantasy for storytellers to work with. In 1992, White Wolf released *Werewolf: The Apocalypse*. Like *Vampire,* this game focused on a race of supernatural beings posing as humans. However, Rein-Hagen had a very different take on the werewolf legend. Werewolves or "Garou" are not human beings cursed with lycanthropy but a separate species that can shape-shift and perpetuates itself by mating with both humans and wolves. Like the Kindred, the Garou have an elaborate culture and are divided into tribes fraught with political intrigue. Unlike the Kindred, the Garou do not suffer from existential angst but have a purpose: they were created as warriors by the spirit Gaia and tasked with defending the forces of creation. The "apocalypse" of the game's title refers to a coming battle that will be simultaneously environmental and spiritual. The Garou are a vanishing people, and their victory in this battle is far from certain. A reviewer for *Dragon* magazine opined:

> The designers do to the werewolf what Frank Miller and Tim Burton did to Batman: They thrust a familiar archetype into a bleak urban setting, drenching him in cynicism and despair. If role-playing games were people, *Werewolf* would be a brooding grad student with a stack of Sandman comics and Metallica albums.[24]

In creating this premise, Rein-Hagen devised an animistic religion for the Garou that was no less plausible than may real-world religions. In the creation myth of the Garou, the universe is divided into a triad of entities called the Wyld, the Weaver, and the Wyrm. The Wyld is associated with endless possibility, creation, and change. Gaia is a creation of the Wyld. It is a sort of nature goddess who created the Garou and other shape-shifters to help maintain the balance of nature. The Weaver is the personification of order. The Weaver selects elements produced by the Wyld and arranges them to produce pattern and meaning. The Wyrm is the force of decay and destruction. Its purpose is to clear away the creations of the Weaver so that the Wyld can continue to create.

The theodicy of the Garou religion came about when the Weaver attained consciousness. After becoming sentient, it attempted to spin the whole of the Wyld into its pattern, but the futility of this task drove the Weaver insane. The Wyrm became snared in the pattern, which drove it insane as well. Instead of a force of balance, the Wyrm became a malevolent entity bent on physical and spiritual destruction. Today the triad is sundered. The Weaver seeks to bring everything into its mad pattern, manifesting on the physical plane as the evils of modernity: mindless suburban sprawl, the brutal logic of capitalism, which subordinates all virtues to the forces of the market, and scientific rationalism, which undermines any sense of enchantment or wonder. Meanwhile, the Wyrm seeks to destroy all of creation from the inside out. Its sickness manifests as environmental devastation, epidemics, and humanity's deliberate inhumanity to man. The Wyld continues to weaken, represented by shrinking rain forests and the destruction of the last wild places on Earth. The warriors of the Garou seek to slay the Wyrm in a battle that is fought on many fronts, ranging from ecoterrorism to spiritual warfare against the Wyrm's demonic servants. The shamans of the Garou suggest that the Wyrm can be healed of its madness and that balance can be restored.

There is much in this mythology for a religion scholar to unpack. The triad of Wyld, Weaver, and Wyrm bears an obvious resemblance to the Hindu *trimurti* of Brahma, Vishnu, and Shiva, which are charged with the creation, preservation, and destruction of the cosmos, respectively. However, the notion of an apocalypse in which the fate of the universe will be resolved in a final battle is Western. The story of the Weaver's fall into madness is a retelling of the Gnostic myth of Sophia. Sophia (wisdom) was a powerful spirit who sought to comprehend all of the knowledge of the universe—a task that was beyond her abilities. Sophia became confused and separated from her fellow spirits. Her emotions of fear, anger, and confusion attained a kind of sentience and became spirits in their own right. It was these beings who created a world of matter. To keep Sophia from regaining her senses, they shattered her spirit and imprisoned the shards inside the fleshly bodies of ordinary people. For both the Gnostics and the Garou, the world was set into motion by a cosmic disaster. But perhaps what is so compelling about the Garou creation myth is not its creative repurposing of older ideas, but its capacity both to account for so many problems faced by humanity at the end of the twentieth century and to sacralize these problems as part of a cosmic battle between the spirits. Members of Generation X who played *Werewolf* often felt both pessimistic and helpless about the state of the world. The game's mythology validated these concerns and rendered them meaningful, at least within the context of the game.

White Wolf's third game presented an even richer model of metaphysics. In 1993, White Wolf published *Mage: The Ascension.* A team of designers, including Stewart Wieck, collaborated on the game, but *Mage* was really a modern version of Rein-Hagen's *Ars Magica* with its goal to "do wizards right." A three-page ad for the game that appeared in *Dragon* magazine seemed almost overtly religious:

> *Mage: The Ascension* is a hero's quest through modern twilight, winding through neon wastelands, high-tech towers, ancient ruins and magickal otherworlds. It's a game about doing something, about believing in something so strongly that faith can change reality.

Unlike vampires or werewolves, mages are "ordinary" humans who have "woken up." The truth to which they have awoken is that reality is not a fixed thing with an independent existence: it is the sum total of what sentient beings believe it to be. "Magic" is actually the ability of very strong-willed people to warp reality to their liking.

Mage's model of magic drew on modern-day occultists such as Aleister Crowley, whose axiom, "Magic is the Art and Science of causing change to occur in accordance with Will," is quoted in the rule book. It also appealed to popular understandings of quantum physics and the idea that at the subatomic level reality is determined by perception. In fact, within the premise of *Mage,* Western science is simply the dominant paradigm of magic. Television, the Internet, and other modern devices work only because billions of people believe that they ought to. In *Mage,* the apparent superiority of science over mysticism is actually a form of cultural hegemony.

Mages come from nine different traditions, ranging from Asian ascetics to Judaeo-Christian mystics to mad scientists. Each tradition has its own perspective on how it is able to achieve things that are normally thought to be impossible. However, these paradigms are simply culturally relative mythologies. The true source of magic is the human will. The goal of the traditions is to lead humanity toward "ascension," in which the human species will awaken to its true potential.

Despite this apparent celebration of humanity, *Mage* was mired in the same gloom as White Wolf's previous releases. A reviewer explained:

> Misfit characters struggle to survive in an urban squalor. Garbage chokes the streets, gangs compete for victims, death lurks around every corner. Stewart Wieck, Mark Rein-Hagen, and the rest of the White Wolf crew must have worn out a thesaurus looking up synonyms for "dreary" and "desperate."[25]

Like the Garou, mages are engaged in a losing battle against forces that personify the modern condition. To cast magic, mages must overcome the inertia created by billions of unenlightened humans and their quotidian notion of reality. For this reason, mages are often forced to use magic to create effects that a casual observer would dismiss as coincidence. Modern-day mages would have to use tremendous resources to smite their foes with a fireball but could easily cause a gas vein to conveniently detonate under their feet.

Mages are also hunted by "the Technocracy," a secret cabal that has taken it upon itself to enforce a universal and monolithic vision of reality in which materialism is triumphant and "magic" has no place. The mythology of the Technocracy drew heavily from a milieu of conspiracy theories circulating in the 1990s. One faction of the Technocracy is called the New World Order and has its headquarters in the United Nations building in New York City. The Technocracy operates a massive network of propaganda that keeps the populace mired in a false consciousness of consumption and television. They control "Men in Black," inhuman agents with supernatural abilities. They have access to secret technology unknown to the general public. These resources are used to hunt down and execute mages whom they regard as "reality deviants." Of course, the Technocracy are mages themselves, and their technology is actually a particular form of magic. Like the forces of the Weaver and the Wyrm, the Technocracy takes the abstract forces of modernity and disenchantment and presents them as a tangible threat that the heroes can confront and defeat.

In 1994, White Wolf released *Wraith: The Oblivion. Wraith* was regarded as the most atmospheric game of the World of Darkness series and also the darkest. (The game's subtitle was *A Storytelling Game of Death and Damnation.*) Rick Swan of *Dragon* magazine quoted a passage from the rule book: "The stench of Death taints everything we say and do. Life is so often pointless and devoid of meaning, little more than a journey into Oblivion. The pain just won't go away." He commented, "Somebody ought to send the Gloom Kings at White Wolf a box of cookies."[26]

In *Wraith,* characters play the ghosts of the recently departed dead. Wraiths inhabit a shadowy underworld realm from which they are able to observe the living and have limited interaction with them. The underworld is home to a society of wraiths, some of whom died thousands of years ago. Newly departed spirits must find their way in vast cities created by the dead where naive wraiths are often exploited or enslaved. Beneath these cities lurks a malevolent force called the Oblivion that seeks to destroy everything. The Oblivion is constantly expanding, consuming more and more of the underworld.

Before creating *Vampire,* Rein-Hagen had originally conceived of a game called *Inferno* in which the characters all played souls being tortured in hell. *Inferno* was abandoned, but *Wraith* renewed many of these themes. One goal for the game was to create an experience in which players were made uncomfortable. To this end, Rein-Hagen drew on elements from the "troupe-style" of play created for *Ars Magica.* Much as vampires struggle to control the Beast, wraiths have two sides: the Psyche and the Shadow. The Psyche is the ego and personality of the spirit, while the Shadow is self-destructive and seeks to lure the wraith into Oblivion. In a game of *Wraith* each player may play the shadow of another player's character—a sort of Mephistophelian double seeking to destroy the character from the inside.

Wraith is Sartrean in its existentialism. Mages search for ascension, Garou battle the Wyrm, and even Kindred can aspire to an enlightened state called "Golconda" in which they have made peace with their inner Beast. Only wraiths are confronted by the possibility of an eternity without purpose. Players must create goals for their characters known as Passions. Some spirits seek to protect loved ones still among the living or to avenge their deaths. Others become involved in the politics of the underworld. Still others seek a state called "Transcendence," which is achieved by reaching "the Far Shores," a distant region of the underworld that appears to correspond to the heavens and hells described in the world's religions. Without Passions, wraiths inevitably succumb to the forces of the Shadow and descend into Oblivion.

Characters in *Wraith* are dead to begin with, before a series of even worse things happens to them. This game consummates the theme of despair that defines the World of Darkness. This would seem to be as far as one could get from the clear struggle between good and evil presented in *D&D*. But it is the seeming assuredness of doom and Oblivion that makes a eucatastrophe possible. Tolkien wrote of the eucatastrophe:

> It does not deny the existence of dyscatastrophe, of sorrow and failure: the possibility of these is necessary to the joy of deliverance; it denies (in the face of much evidence if you will) universal final defeat and in so far is evangelium, giving a fleeting glimpse of Joy, Joy beyond the walls of the world, poignant as grief.[27]

Viewed from this perspective, the World of Darkness need not be a springboard for telling nihilistic stories. The very elements that make games like *Wraith* so depressing can also facilitate a vision of transcendence that, for Tolkien, is the true function of fantasy.

The last of the five major games created for the World of Darkness was *Changeling: The Dreaming,* published in 1995. Faeries first appeared in *Ars Magica* as creatures that thrived on the dreams of humanity. The premise of *Changeling* is that the fey are a magical species that owes its power to "glamour," a force generated by the dreams of humanity. Much like the mages, the power of the fey began to decline with the rise of scientific rationalism. Disenchantment and despair give rise to a force called "banality," which is toxic to fey. By the early modern period, fey with the power to do so left the world, retreating into a dimension of imagination called the Dreaming. Those fey who were left behind discovered a way for their spirits to inhabit human bodies. These beings became "changelings." Changelings are born to human parents but have fey souls. They may appear human but are truly fantastic creatures, such as elves, trolls, and satyrs. Changelings sustain themselves with glamour, which they derive by inspiring human dreams and desires or (in the case of evil changelings) destroying human dreams. Without glamour, their powers will fade, and they will eventually become ordinary people, forgetting their fey heritage completely.

Players assume the roles of changelings living in the modern world. In the 1990s, fey society is currently undergoing turmoil resulting from the 1969 Moonwalk. This event was so inspiring to millions of humans that it temporarily produced glamour in quantities that had not been seen since before the Industrial Revolution. The gates to the Dreaming were temporarily opened, and the nobility of the fey race were able to return. Unfortunately, this resulted in vicious feuding as the long-exiled nobility sought to reestablish their feudal dominance over the fey who had been left behind. In the World of Darkness, warring faeries are the true cause of much of the urban violence that followed the Summer of Love.

Changeling was not as popular as the previous releases but attracted a serious cult following. The tone and message of the game were ambiguous. On the one hand, it seemed that a game about faerie creatures who thrive on wonder and romance was completely at odds with the World of Darkness and its angst-ridden denizens. On the other hand, some regarded *Changeling* as the saddest and most tragic of the five games. The fey were dying because the modern world has crushed a part of what makes us human, our ability to dream. Had Joseph Campbell and Mircea Eliade lived another decade, they would likely have appreciated *Changeling* and regarded its message as a very serious one.

All of the five core games were eventually adapted to a live-action format that Rein-Hagen called "The Mind's Eye Theater." In LARP versions of *Vampire, Werewolf, Mage, Wraith,* and *Changeling,* players physically interacted as their characters. World of Darkness LARPs were especially popular on college campuses, often leading passersby to wonder who exactly these oddly dressed people were wandering about at night.

In 1996 White Wolf was affected by the same distribution problems that bankrupted TSR. Amid these hardships, Rein-Hagen left the company to Stewart Wieck. Under Wieck, the company produced more games for the World of Darkness with titles such as *Hunter: The Reckoning, Mummy: The Resurrection,* and *Demon: The Fallen.* Wieck served as president until 2002 when he stepped down and was replaced by Mike Tinny. Tinny felt that the World of Darkness series was in need of a housecleaning, and in 2003 White Wolf announced that the World of Darkness would reach its final denouement. A series of books called the Time of Judgment was published in which the apocalyptic scenarios and millennial expectations hinted at in the previous books all came to pass. Players could play characters who were witnessing and taking part in the final destruction of the world. After the release of these books, White Wolf stopped producing books for the World of Darkness. This was an unprecedented move in the history of role-playing games, the equivalent of Dave Arneson announcing that Blackmoor was being struck by a meteor or Gary Gygax declaring that Greyhawk had been sucked into a black hole. White Wolf went on to produce a new World of Darkness with a new line of games. These games featured many of the same creatures and themes as the previous world but had different conceptions and mythologies.

White Wolf was second only to TSR in its influence on role-playing games. Its mythology fueled a resurgence of vampires and werewolves in popular culture in the first decade of the twenty-first century. In 2001, Charlaine Harris wrote the first of her *Southern Vampire Mysteries* about an alternate America where vampires have revealed their existence to the world. The novels later became the basis of the wildly popular HBO series *True Blood*. While Harris created her own mythology of vampires, her stories borrow heavily from the social structure and traditions found in *Vampire: The Masquerade*. Beginning in 2003, the *Underworld* franchise of films depicted a war between vampires and werewolves fought in modern cities. White Wolf sued Sony Pictures, claiming that the plot of *Underworld* was stolen from a story called "Love of Monsters" written by Nancy Collins and set in the World of Darkness. Sony Pictures settled out of court and employed writers from White Wolf as consultants for the film's sequels.

White Wolf's more profound cultural significance lies in the metaphysical and philosophical themes explored through its games.The Wyld, the Weaver, and the Wyrm, the dominance of the Technocracy, the existential lure of Oblivion, and the death of glamour in the world were powerful ideas. Recalling Ian Barbour's idea of a model, players took these ideas "seriously but not literally." In her ethnography of gamers, Sarah Lynne Bowman interviewed a gamer who claimed *Mage* teaches "that there is no such thing as a single paradigm, that we're all really people with our individual ideas whether we like it or not and we're trying to find truth within our own perspective."[28] For some, the World of Darkness was a powerful metaphor that expressed complex feelings of frustration, alienation, and disenchantment. For others, games like *Werewolf* and *Mage* informed plausibility structures and suggested that if there are mysterious forces in the world, they might be something like the mythologies described in these games.

RENEWED PANIC

Patricia Pulling and Thomas Radecki were convinced that *D&D* induced violence and suicide. It is hard to imagine what they would have thought of games like *Vampire: The Masquerade* and *Wraith: The*

Oblivion. Although White Wolf did not market its games to schools and children, as TSR had, the company was prepared to weather the same attacks that had been made against *D&D* a decade before. In a TED talk, Rein-Hagen explained: "Games are either considered frivolous or dangerous. And the media frequently—when there's a tragedy—someone will come out and they'll say, 'Don't blame the guns. Don't blame the schools. Blame the games.'"[29] Many White Wolf books opened with disclaimers reminding the reader that vampires and werewolves are not real and that stories told in the game should have no corresponding reality outside of the game.

While this second generation of role-playing games met with far less resistance and criticism than did TSR's games, the trend toward darker, more realistic fantasy renewed confusion among outsiders about where the line between fantasy and reality should be drawn. This confusion was compounded by the fact that many role-playing games of the 1990s explored themes of moral decadence, criminality, and urban decay at the same time that politicians and the media were promoting a myth of moral poverty and an impending crime wave. This made it easy for moral entrepreneurs to repurpose role-playing games, incorporating the symbolism of these games into their own fantasies of a fallen society.

The Secret Service vs. Steve Jackson Games

In the summer of 1980, the FBI showed up at TSR's headquarters in Lake Geneva. TSR was developing a role-playing game about espionage entitled *Top Secret.* A concerned citizen had come across a memo describing an assassination plot and, not understanding the context, alerted the authorities.[30] The incident was a classic example of a failure to understand frames of metacommunication. A far more serious case occurred on March 1, 1990, when Steve Jackson Games in Austin, Texas, was raided by the Secret Service. Steve Jackson Games published GURPS (an acronym for generic universal role-playing system). GURPS had a simple system of game mechanics that could be adapted to any number of genres and settings. In 1990, the company was developing a game called *GURPS: Cyberpunk.*[31] "Cyberpunk" is a genre of science fiction that emphasizes information technology, cybernetics, and social decay. Science-fiction writer Bruce Sterling calls cyberpunk "an unholy alliance of the technical world with the underground of pop culture and street-level anarchy."[32] Hacking and cybercrime are the sine qua non of the genre. Steve Jackson Games developed game mechanics to represent hacking that were posted on the company's online bulletin board. Somehow the Secret Service discovered this material and misinterpreted it as a tutorial on cybercrime.

In a press release published on April 30, 1990, Steve Jackson described how Secret Service agents presented him with an unsigned photocopy of a warrant and then proceeded to confiscate every copy of *GURPS: Cyberpunk*. They also took the company's computers, a laser printer, computer cables, and even a plastic bag of screws and bolts used to repair computers. Jackson alleged that agents used bolt cutters to destroy locks, even while employees stood by with keys offering to open them. They also tried to pick locks on filing cabinets, using his letter openers (which were destroyed in the process). Adding insult to injury, the agents ate a breakfast from Whataburger, a local fast-food chain, as they ransacked the company, and left discarded wrappers on the floor.[33]

Tiny companies like Steve Jackson Games have razor-thin profits, and the raid nearly bankrupted the company. With its product held by federal authorities, the company was unable to generate revenue and lost an estimated $100,000 in sales.[34] In a letter to Pierre Savoie of CAR-Pga, Jackson wrote, "If I sold every single copy tomorrow, it wouldn't pay me back for the damage they've done."[35] The silver lining was that the incident served as free publicity for the game, much as the disappearance of Dallas Egbert had raised awareness of *D&D*. A number of magazines, including *Newsweek,* ran articles about the raid that were sympathetic to Steve Jackson Games.[36] The company was forced to recreate the game largely from scratch, as much of their computer data was destroyed. When the game was finally released, *GURPS: Cyberpunk* was promoted as "the book that was seized by the U.S. Secret Service!"

Before the raid, the Secret Service had investigated the game's author, Lloyd Blankenship, and decided that he had connections to the "computer underground." Jackson wrote Savoie, "Apparently the line they're taking now is that Lloyd, who wrote the book, is some kind of shadowy Secret Master of Hackers—though they haven't charged him with anything either."[37] In his press release, Jackson called the raid "a textbook example of heavy-handed enforcement directed at the 'little guy.'" He asked, "Had an IBM employee been suspected of data piracy, would federal agents have broken in, shut the staff out of the facility, and taken away carloads of hardware?"[38]

The following May, Steve Jackson filed a lawsuit against the government arguing that electronic bulletin boards are protected forms of speech and that the investigators did not meet the legal standards to seize instruments of speech. On March 12, 1993, Judge Sparks of the US District Court in Austin, Texas, ruled that the raid had violated the Privacy Protection Act and the Stored Wire and Electronic Communications and Transactional Records Access Act. Steve Jackson Games was awarded over $50,000 in economic damages and expenses.[39]

The incident is significant for two reasons. First, it demonstrated a fundamental failure by the Secret Service to discern the frame of the game from reality. Jackson described his desperate attempt to convince the agents that *Cyberpunk* was only a game: "I said, 'This is science-fiction.' They said, "No. This is real.'"[40] This scenario resembled the claims of Christian critics during the 1980s that *D&D* entailed actual rather than imaginary magic. However, the confusion had become greater as role-playing games had transitioned from clearly fantastic scenarios to increasingly realistic ones.

Second, the raid came about in part because the curiosity and interests of the Secret Service and the game designers intersected. Both parties were interested in emerging technology and its potential to destabilize society. But while Lloyd Blankenship used his imagination to envision a cybernetic dystopia, federal agents used their imaginations to predict dangerous scenarios that they could preempt. During the raid one agent allegedly told Jackson, "I think modems ought to be outlawed."[41] Two decades later, this seems an utterly absurd statement. However, it suggests that the agent was envisioning a future changed by communications technology just as much as the game designers were. Unfortunately, when these parallel lines of thinking intersected, authorities failed to understand the imaginary frame of Blankenship's ideas.

Jon C. Bush

White Wolf largely escaped the notice of antigaming claims makers for the first five years of its existence. This changed in 1996 when a series of strange cases proved too tempting for the media to resist. In January, Jon C. Bush of Virginia Beach attracted the attention of police with his "vampire family," which was loosely inspired by *Vampire: The Masquerade*. Bush, twenty-six, had been honorably discharged from the navy in 1992 after being diagnosed with a personality disorder. He worked as a heating and air-conditioning repairman and lived with his mother. But in his spare time he surrounded himself with a group of thirty to forty adolescents, who regarded him as the leader of a vampire clan.

Bush described himself as a vampire "elder" and referred to vampire "princes" who controlled nearby cities—all terminology purloined from Rein-Hagen's game. From reports, it seems that the "vampire family" was a kind of game that had become serious. A favorite activity of the vampire family was to parade through shopping malls in a phalanx of oddly dressed teenagers. Bush would position himself in the center of the group with his arms folded across his chest—a gesture adapted from the Mind's Eye Theater version of *Vampire*. Vampires who disrespected Bush could become the targets of "blood hunts"—another term borrowed from White Wolf. Despite the ominous name, blood hunts were essentially a form of hide-and-seek. The offending family member would flee into the woods at night, and the rest of the family would pursue. If the quarry could evade detection until dawn, he or she was forgiven. Otherwise, the person was banished.

Police became involved when two teenage girls reported that Bush was sexually assaulting his female family members, some of whom were as young as thirteen. An initiation ritual called "the embrace" (another *Vampire* term) involved female initiates being fondled or having sex with Bush. As the investigation proceeded, more teenage girls began to testify. One alleged that Bush had raped her after she joined the family. In the end, Bush was charged with thirty-five crimes, including rape, carnal knowledge, contributing to the delinquency of a minor, crimes against nature, and indecent liberties. Bush's attorney offered a variant of the *D&D* defense, claiming that Bush had multiple personalities that included Murbius, the vampire personality; Glandis, a violent personality; and Aladius, a personality preoccupied with partying and sex. Bush was convicted on thirty counts and received a twenty-six-year prison sentence.[42]

The story launched a media frenzy, and newspapers invariably mentioned *Vampire: The Masquerade* in connection with Bush. Paul LePree, a spokesman for White Wolf, told the *Washington Post:* "We didn't start the vampire mythology; we only played on something that has been in place for more than 100 years. Sure, the game could have enticed these young girls into going with a man, but I wouldn't raise my kid to go off with a stranger and interact with a bloodletting."[43] With Thomas Radecki avoiding public scrutiny, and Patricia Pulling suffering from terminal cancer, a new moral entrepreneur emerged in Don Rimer. Rimer was a detective from Virginia Beach and a friend of Pulling. As a self-declared "occult crime expert," he was first to investigate Bush and his family. Rimer obtained a warrant that allowed him to search Bush's residence for "any paraphernalia concerning vampirism, demonology, lycanthropy or witchcraft" as well as "costumes and any accessories related to the above topics." Sympathetic newspapers endorsed Rimer's persona as an occult crime expert and presented him as a heroic and skeptical foil to Bush's villainy and delusion. The *Virginian-Pilot* even described Rimer as a "top scholar." Following Bush's arrest, the paper quoted Rimer boasting, "That should be a lesson to all the kids who have an interest in the gothic side of things."[44] Rimer appeared on *Unsolved Mysteries* and the *700 Club* to discuss Bush. In a series of *700 Club* panels discussing Bush, Shawn Novak, and a recent double suicide in connection with role-playing games, Rimer declared:

> There are dozens of incidents, documented police investigations—more than a dozen, hundreds of cases, where children have participated in fantasy role-playing games, have either participated, have been the victims of those games and have died. . . . Many of these kids do not understand the difference between fantasy and reality. And they go out and get involved in the drugs. They get involved in these games. They get involved in following some of the practices in these occult books. They listen to the lyrics in some of the songs, which encourage this behavior. They take all of these elements together and create their own lifestyle and make up their own rules, and they're dying because of it.

Another panelist remarked:

> It's an incredible aberration in our society but Dungeons and Dragons, which sent some people over the edge, some kids committed suicide, was a very dangerous thing. We warned about it a long time ago and were criticized roundly and then all of a sudden it began to come out, the danger.[45]

At least in Virginia Beach, the panic over role-playing games was back from the dead.

Rod Ferrell

On November 25, 1996, only ten months after the discovery of Bush's underage vampire sex ring, Naomi Ruth Queen and Richard Wendorf of Eustis, Florida, were discovered murdered in their home. Their murderer was 16-year-old Roderick "Rod" Ferrell of Murray, Kentucky, who sometimes claimed to be a 400-year-old vampire named Vassago. Ferrell's case was similar to that of Bush: he was charismatic enough to attract a small group of teenage followers whom he initiated into vampirism. The teens would drink each other's blood and participate in rituals that Ferrell devised. Like Bush's "vampire family," Ferrell's "vampire clan" operated in a liminal state between a game and something else.

Ferrell had met Heather Wendorf at Eustis High School before he and his mother moved to Murray. There, he rapidly gained a reputation as the town delinquent. He was expelled from school and used psychedelic drugs. He briefly participated in a *Vampire: The Masquerade* LARP held at Murray State University, but lost interest in it. Ferrell remained in phone contact with Heather and her friend Jeanine in Florida. The two girls talked to Ferrell for hours over the phone. Heather complained that her parents were too controlling. Allegedly, their conversations also included running away and even killing Heather's parents, but this was likely a dark fantasy rather than a literal desire.

In November, Ferrell drove to Eustis in an old Buick to get Heather and start a new life in New Orleans. He brought three members of his teenage vampire clan: Dana Cooper, Charity Lynn Keesee, and Howard Scott Anderson. Ferrell met Heather on the side of the road near her home but decided to abandon the Buick and steal the Wendorf's Ford Explorer. While Heather, Dana, and Charity waited, Ferrell and Anderson entered through the garage. It is unclear when Ferrell made the decision to murder the Wendorfs, but once inside he killed Heather's parents using a crowbar he had found in the garage. Perhaps as an afterthought, Ferrell burned a *V* into Richard Wendorf's body. It was never determined whether the *V* stood for Vassago, for vampire, or had no meaning at all. Anderson was reportedly frozen and did not participate in the murder. It is possible that he never thought Ferrell was sincere about his plan to murder the Wendorfs.

After the murder, the teens transferred their belongings into the Wendorf's Explorer. Ferrell told Heather that he had murdered her parents, but she assumed this was simply another one of his outrageous claims. They were eventually arrested in New Orleans and sent to Florida to stand trial for murder. Ferrell, Anderson, Cooper, and Keesee all pleaded guilty. Only Heather was acquitted. Ferrell was initially given the death penalty, but his sentence was later commuted to life in prison. Anderson was given life in prison without parole. The two girls were found guilty of third-degree murder and were given lighter sentences.

The exploits of Ferrell and his vampire clan inspired a media frenzy, drawing reporters from as far away as Japan. Talk shows scrambled to feature anyone related to the case as guests. *Hard Copy* sent reporters to Eustis High in search of vampires. Anne Rice stated that she wanted nothing to do with the story and that it was unfortunate that some of her books were found in the stolen Explorer.[46] Two true-crime books were written about the case, and there was even a movie adaptation in 2002.

The murders revived concerns that role-playing games caused people to dissociate from reality. Newspapers ran headlines such as "For Some, Vampire Fantasy Can Be All Too Real." Several colleges capitulated to these fears and banned *Vampire: The Masquerade* LARPs from their campuses.[47] White Wolf's marketing director Greg Fountain responded in the *Orlando Sentinel:* "We feel strongly that if the allegations are true, there were pre-existing problems. The problems weren't derived from playing."[48]

While Ferrell had an elaborate fantasy life, the factors that contributed to the murders had surprisingly little to do with his interest in vampirism. Ferrell was young, immature, and used drugs heavily. He was raised by his mother, Sondra Gibson, a troubled woman who had worked as a prostitute and stripper. At his trial, an expert witness testified that Ferrell's mother had the emotional maturity of a twelve-year-old. Gibson dressed in gothic fashion like her son and told several investigators that she wanted to be initiated into Ferrell's coven. Gibson had also sent sexually explicit messages to the younger brother of one of Ferrell's friends. The boy's parents eventually found these messages, and Gibson was charged with soliciting rape and sodomy. These charges occurred only a few days before Ferrell left for Florida.[49] It is possible that taking his friends to New Orleans was a drastic way of escaping a socially humiliating situation created by his mother.

The murder of the Wendorfs appeared to have been an impulsive action committed while burglarizing a home and not an "occult crime" conducted as part of a belief system. Ferrell later commented: "I really don't understand it myself. There's really no reason. There never was."[50] While Ferrell did burn a *V* into Mr. Wendorf's body, this gesture did not seem to have any occult significance, as was later alleged. An early report on the murders cites a police statement that "there were no ritualistic signs connected with the deaths."[51] However, journalists and moral entrepreneurs remained determined to find the *meaning* behind these murders. The death of the Wendorfs became a sort of national Rorschach test onto which any number of narratives could be imposed.

The phrase "ontogeny recapitulates phylogeny" originally referred to an evolutionary theory that embryos develop in stages resembling the species' evolutionary ancestors. While this theory has been largely discredited in the field of biology, scholars in the humanities have found it useful to describe how ideas bear traces of their predecessors. The discourse about Ferrell incorporated several decades of social fears. Take, for example, Clifford Linedecker's true-crime book *The Vampire Killers* (1998). Linedecker discusses *D&D* and White Wolf at length. Although he specifies that role-playing games were not responsible for Ferrell's behavior, he connects the Ferrell case to the crimes of Jon C. Bush and Shawn Novak, which the media also attributed to role-playing games. More importantly, Linedecker's discussion of Ferrell and role-playing games is ensconced in a long chain of folk devils surrounding a generation ready to murder its elders.

Like many in media, Linedecker refers to Ferrell's small circle of teenagers as a "cult," even though it is not clear that members of the group shared any religious beliefs. He describes Ferrell as a cult leader who "sold his followers immortality," and compares him to Jim Jones, David Koresh, and Marshall Applewhite, one of the leaders of the Heaven's Gate group. Linedecker writes, "Failure to understand destructive cults—and that's exactly what Rod's followers were: the nucleus of a cult—strengthens their power and provides them with the lifeblood they need in order to feed."[52]

The Vampire Killers also implies that Ferrell was involved with organized Satanism. The book opens with a description of the Calloway County Animal Shelter. In October 1996, someone broke into the shelter's kennel and released most of the dogs. Police found several dead puppies in a nearby field. Linedecker writes that one of the puppies was found "stomped to death and its crushed body was lying at the center of a circle of tall grass that was flattened as if some strange ritualistic dance had been performed there."[53] Ferrell was never connected to this crime, and there is no real evidence that anyone killed the puppy as part of a ritual. But passages such as this leave the door open to the possibility that Ferrell was part of a larger network of criminal Satanists.

Finally, *The Vampire Killers* dwells on the fact that Ferrell was raised by a single mother who received welfare. The last chapter discusses other incidents of teenage gangs with a penchant for the dramatic. Linedecker asks:

> The savagery of the acts committed by bands of teenagers like the Vampire Clan . . . occurring in such rapid succession, has law enforcement professionals, social scientists and concerned parents asking themselves, "What in the world is going on in smalltown America?" . . . Are their violent acts a warning of worse to come; a peek into the future at a permanent slide into chaos and anarchy?[54]

Here we see evidence of the "superpredator" narrative and predictions of a coming wave of violent crime carried out by a generation without a conscience. With this passage, Linedecker's treatment of the Ferrell murders recapitulates three decades of subversion narratives including the brainwashing cult scare of the 1970s, the Satanic panic of the 1980s, and the superpredator narrative of the 1990s. Ferrell came to embody and validate all of these fears simultaneously. For decades, self-described occult crime experts pointed to the Ferrell murders as the one case that proved their claims that gothic culture, vampire fiction, and role-playing games were an entrée into a criminal subculture that celebrated murder and death.[55]

The Bellevue Massacre

Only a few months after the murder of the Wendorfs in New Orleans, David Anderson and Alex Baranyi, both seventeen, murdered a family of four in Bellevue, Washington. Once again a white, middle-class family had been murdered in the safety of their home by teenage dropouts with connections to an unusual subculture. The so-called Bellevue Massacre was the subject of another true-crime book and an episode of a crime show called *Wicked Attraction.* As with the Ferrell case, the country was equally fascinated and horrified and turned to facile explanations of the murder.

Unlike the murder of the Wendorfs, Anderson and Baranyi had planned their crime in advance. After his arrest, Baranyi initially told authorities that he had been "in a rut" and wanted to commit a murder. The two selected Kimberly Wilson, a former girlfriend of Anderson, as their victim. The pair met her at her home and lured her to a park where they strangled her and concealed her body. Then, realizing her family might be able to tell police who their daughter had left with, they returned to the house where they killed Bill and Rose Wilson and their daughter Julia using a knife and a baseball bat. Despite their effort to eliminate witnesses, Baranyi quickly confessed when police brought him in for questioning.

Both the trial and the media placed heavy weight on the pair's involvement in role-playing games. Baranyi was a fan of the TV series *Highlander* and owned a collection of swords. The two were known to have mock battles in the park using weapons made from PVC piping and foam. Baranyi and Anderson had been involved in a *Vampire* LARP but were thrown out after they violated a rule that players may not touch other players.[56]

The two were tried separately, and Baranyi's attorney attempted the *D&D* defense. Psychiatrist Karen Froming, who had previously served as an expert witness in the trial of Ted Kaczynski, testified that Baranyi demonstrated evidence of bipolar disorder. She claimed that Baranyi was unable to distinguish between reality and the exploits of his *D&D* character, "Slicer Thunderclap." This claim was discredited by prosecutors and ridiculed by law enforcement. Baranyi received a life sentence. In a prison interview, he later stated, "The mental defense that we used was basically a complete last resort."[57]

In 1997, an article in the British newspaper *The Times* covered the Bellevue Massacre and suggested that America was developing a new kind of murderer—one who was young, privileged, and white. The article suggested that the real superpredators were "preppie kids."[58] This seemed to be the one possibility Americans were unwilling to face. There was an increasing push to frame white murderers as "goths" or otherwise part of some strange subculture that made them fundamentally different from their white, suburban peers. A month before the shootings at Columbine High School, a school in Michigan banned any display of "vampire makeup," black nail polish, or pentagrams. Wearing such accessories was punishable by indefinite suspension. A district court declared the ban unlawful after Crystal Siefferly, a Wiccan student, filed a lawsuit supported by the ACLU.[59]

After Eric Harris and Dylan Klebold attacked Columbine High School in April 1998, killing thirteen and wounding twenty-one, commentators scrambled to find causal explanations for the massacre.[60] Much of the speculation focused on the deviant youth subculture that the shooters were allegedly involved in. The day after the shooting, a commentator for the *Washington Post* explained that the "Gothic" culture that produced Klebold and Harris was "inspired by fantasy games such as Dungeons and Dragons."[61] District Attorney Dave Thomas gave a speech about "the meaning" of Columbine, dragging out such familiar suspects as violent movies, video games, and *D&D*.[62] Pat Robertson also cited *D&D* alongside "occult video games" among the causes of Columbine.[63] In the weeks that followed, school authorities attempted to identify youth that might be plotting similar acts of violence. Frequently, this meant targeting students with unusual hobbies and interests. One student was told by his school counselor that he must either quit playing *D&D* or else seek therapy.[64] By June, a company called WordCHECK Systems had developed software to help schools profile potentially violent students. In an Orwellian turn, student writing assignments could be scanned in order to identify "key terms" associated with emotional turmoil. Along with "pain," "fury," and "lost," "dungeon" was among the words associated with potentially violent students.[65]

In 2001, Cambodian American journalist Putsata Reang wrote the true-crime book *Deadly Secrets.* The book was about the Bellevue Massacre but capitalized on interest in deviant subcultures brought about by the Columbine Massacre. In covering the details of Baranyi's insanity defense, *Deadly Secrets* demonstrated how claims about role-playing games could be resurrected and neatly folded into a more current fear of "gothic culture."[66] Reang included a description of the "Denny's gang" that Anderson and Baranyi associated with to create a portrait of gothic culture:

> Dressed in their combat boots and ubiquitous black pants and miniskirts over ripped stockings, the girls titter around, mussing the boys' hair and snatching their cigarettes. The boys wear black leather pants or jeans, and some have pierced tongues and wear spiked dog collars around their necks and wrists. They talk about movies, music, and sex, their conversations livened with vulgarities. Gently stroking the inner thigh of his girlfriend, one of the boys makes sexual jokes and discusses breast sizes while the girls gossip about who among the boys can boast the biggest penis.[67]

This tableau of a deviant orgy at Denny's is meant to inspire both revulsion and salacious fascination. The "Denny's crowd" with which Anderson and Baranyi associated are no longer ordinary people but an exotic and dangerous other.

Like *The Vampire Killers,* the book's epilogue warns of a coming surge of violence carried out by deviant teenagers. Reang writes:

> For the first time in more than a decade, according to FBI statistics, violent crime rates across the country are going down, but at the same time, a disturbing phenomenon is emerging: violent crime among youths is surging. . . . More and more youths like David Anderson and Alex Baranyi are getting swept into the current of crime. Their deviant behavior is sending an alarming message to society about how we are raising, or failing to raise, our children.[68]

But where Linedecker briefly exonerated role-playing games, Reang suggests that role-playing games may be a key factor in the coming violence:

> Many people, among them a renowned psychologist who evaluated Alex, believe that David and Alex perhaps blurred the lines between fantasy and reality. While it would be a stretch to say the boys' participation in these

> games led them to kill, it's likely that playing them enhanced the boys' propensity for violence.[69]

She then quotes Gary Alan Fine's *Shared Fantasy* out of context: "These games are centered on killing and death—the struggle between 'good' and 'evil,' in which evil must be wiped out without mercy or pity.... Within the context of the game, players are oriented toward murder and death without consideration of any moral niceties." Fine makes this comment as part of a larger discussion about whether fantasy violence is an index of actual violence. His conclusion is actually the opposite of Reang's. He goes on to write, "In large measure I think the barrier is impermeable."[70]

Deadly Secrets demonstrated just how enduring the myth of the mind-warping role-playing game is. In the same year that Peter Jackson's *The Fellowship of the Ring* was released in movie theaters, symbolically marking the arrival of fantasy in the American mainstream, books were still being published suggesting that participation in fantasy games contributes to criminal behavior and murder. Reang's conclusions are even odder considering that she saw firsthand how unpersuasive the *D&D* defense was in Baranyi's trial. Her theory about dangerous role-playing games somehow survived in the face of contradictory evidence. This suggests that there is something far more appealing about this idea than just a facile explanation when senseless tragedies arise. The myth of the delusional, violent gamer is a fantasy in its own right, and a powerful one. The panic over superpredators, gothic culture, and role-playing games would likely have continued to build momentum had it not been for the terrorist attacks of September 11, 2001. The attacks gave the United States a new enemy and an external threat toward which to direct its fear and anger. At least in the immediate aftermath, vampires and occult crime were hard pressed to compete for media coverage.

WHITE WOLF AND THE REENCHANTMENT OF THE WORLD

The 1990s was not only a decade in which fears about fantasy role-playing games blended with fears of goths and superpredators. It was also a decade in which fantasy role-playing exerted an influence on various emerging religious movements. A number of scholars have suggested that, in a secular age, fantasy role-playing games are a kind of substitute for the sense of enchantment once provided by religion. Daniel Mackay muses:

> The architectural reality of angels, demons, and saints—a presence in the lives of medieval citizens—has been replaced with flimsy renditions as represented in role-playing—elves, orcs, and demigods—wherein the only hope for efficacy is their transformation into the substance of shared social experience as an act of creation.[71]

Sociologist William Sims Bainbridge presents a similar idea in *eGods,* his study of online role-playing games. Bainbridge suggests that as secularization has enervated religious institutions, the fantasy gods and religions found in games like *World of Warcraft* have begun to assume functions once held by religion.[72] In these models, role-playing games are a sort of consolation prize through which modern people can experience, in a diminished way, the sense of a meaningful universe once provided by a religious worldview.

While Bainbridge's "consolation model" may account for some of the popular interest in fantasy, it has two weaknesses. First, it is dependent on the so-called secularization narrative: the hypothesis that religion is doomed to extinction in the face of scientific rationalism. While this idea remains persuasive to the general public, sociologists have increasingly claimed that the secularization narrative is an ideology not supported by the evidence.[73] Second, for some gamers, magic, vampires, and changelings are more than "flimsy renditions" of religious ideas. For these subcultures, White Wolf's World of Darkness, with its plausible models of the supernatural and its rich modern mythology, has facilitated a magical worldview that challenges the claims of scientific rationalism. These connections suggest that the relationship between fantasy games and religious ideas is potentially more substantial than mere nostalgia for a lost age of mythology. Fantasies—even while remaining fantasies—can provide models through which modern people can reassess notions of metaphysics and cosmology. A more detailed theoretical model of how this is possible appears in the next chapter. However, the response to White Wolf's World of Darkness during the 1990s is the most important case study for analyzing the convergence of magical subcultures and fantasy role-playing games.

Magic

Anthropologists have produced many definitions of "magic," but the term is most often used to circumscribe beliefs that are incompatible with either scientific rationalism or mainstream religious beliefs. Wouter Hanegraaff suggests that the key feature of a magical worldview is an idea of "participation"—a concept first used by the anthropologist Lucien Lévy-Bruhl. Whereas a scientific-rationalist worldview understands the world through a set of logical distinctions between things, a participationist worldview assumes a mystical union that is not reducible to primary reasoning. From such a perspective, magical effects are plausible. Unlike scientists, magicians believe that they can possess knowledge without empirical observation and affect the world in ways that cannot be reduced to causal explanations. Unlike many world religious traditions (certainly monotheistic ones), magicians feel that supernatural power is immanent rather than transcendent: the power to defy the laws of nature can be accessed by many people and is not the sole province of a transcendent deity. Lévy-Bruhl associated participation with the mind of "the primitive"; however, Hanegraaff argues that modern people still find the participationist view psychologically satisfying. For this reason, the modern world has not seen the death of magic. Instead, magic has been reimagined in a way that seems plausible to moderns. Modern magicians often speak of magic in terms of quantum physics and, especially, psychology.[74] White Wolf's urban fantasy games are both a reflection of and a resource for this process of adapting magic to the modern world.

It is not known what percentage of White Wolf's players had an interest in magic outside of the game. However, at least one scholar has noted that there appears to be a strong overlap between pagans and other groups that emphasize magical worldviews and some of the games developed by Mark Rein-Hagen.[75] In fact, some of the employees at White Wolf expressed magical worldviews. The rule book for *Wraith* concludes with an essay by Rein-Hagen entitled "Last Words" in which he states rather bluntly that "*Wraith* is cursed." Rein-Hagen describes an evening in Georgia when four friends had come to play test his game *Inferno,* about being tortured in hell. With a remorseful tone, Rein-Hagen describes running a game in which his friends's characters were first killed and then elaborately tortured and mocked by demons. As Rein-Hagen was playing the role of a particularly sadistic demon there was a crash, and all of the lights went out. Outside, a pizza delivery man had crashed his car into a transformer box, disrupting power. Rein-Hagen found him sitting in his car trying to turn the ignition while flames could be seen flickering beneath the vehicle. Rein-Hagen got the delivery man out of the car just before the gas tank exploded. When he tried to call 911, an electrical spike disabled all of the phones. Rein-Hagen felt this bizarre incident was somehow connected to *Inferno*. He wrote, "The next day I resolved that Mama Fate had given me a warning, and I packed away all of my notes and called it quits with Demons and Doom." He also felt that when *Wraith* incorporated elements originally designed for *Inferno* this set the curse loose again. Game production was stymied by numerous accidents and abnormally high tension between game designers. Rein-Hagen ends his missive, "Remember, I don't believe in curses, but if bad things start happening in your life . . . You've been warned."[76] This story does not mean that Rein-Hagen is irrational or even unusual. It is natural to find meaning in strange coincidences, and the story heightens the sense of fear that *Wraith* is meant to invoke. However, Gary Gygax would never have placed such a warning on one of his games. The story plays with frames to shift the nature of the game from "this is play" to "is this play?"

In another case, game designers from White Wolf not only interpreted events through a magical worldview but performed a magical working to help sell their games. I corresponded with Sam Chupp, a game designer who worked on *Mage, Wraith, Changeling,* and others. He described an informal ritual intended to aid the design of *Mage: The Ascension:*

> Although it was not an official White Wolf function, it involved many of the WW employees after work hours. The ceremony was held on Brigid's Night, February 2nd, to both mark and celebrate the start of work on the *Mage: the Ascension* rules design.
>
> I am reminded of the Shinto ceremonies Japanese companies conduct at the start of new endeavors.
>
> Lindy McKeeman and myself put it together. We built an altar of book boxes starting with the oldest books we had on hand and going until we got to the latest release, and put the design notes made for *Mage* so far in the middle of the altar as a focus for the energy. It was a neat thing, very appropriate for *Mage,* although whether or not it was efficacious I leave as an exercise for the observant. I do think that the Fundamentalist Christian church down the road a bit would have swallowed their gum had they known what we were doing![77]

This account should not be regarded as evidence that games like *Mage* are a tool for indoctrinating players into an occult religion. The ritual appears to have been improvisational, and Chupp was not particularly invested in its efficacy. He calls it "a neat thing." Instead, the story suggests that many of the game designers were thinking about plausible models of magic both within and without the frame of the games they designed. Just as *D&D* reflected Gygax and Arneson's Christianity, *Mage* reflects the designers' ideas about magic.

The second generation of role-playing games altered the portrayal of magic. *Ars Magica* and *Mage* were intended to portray magic in a way that seemed plausible to people living in a modern, Western society. There is evidence that some players found these models of magic applicable to actual occultism and magical practice. Consider the following post from the website occultforum.org:

> Have [*sic*] anyone here ever tried the RPG game Mage the Ascension. . . . I have gotten allot [*sic*] of my occult knowledge from playing this game as it really forces you to think about the nature of reality. . . . The creating of various paradigms and the nature of the game forces the player to really think about the nature of reality, and as such it is a great tool for self development and occult training.[78]

The poster is not claiming that the Technocracy or other aspects of the game's fictional mythology are real. Rather he or she is advocating *Mage* as a sort of training exercise that can prepare players for the practice of actual magic. This sort of convergence between alternative spiritualities and role-playing games is common.[79] It is not simply that players confused fantasy and reality as was claimed by moral entrepreneurs. Rather there is a form of intertextuality in which games facilitate a shift in plausibility structures.

Vampires

A more profound example of this process is the development of communities that, in some sense, self-identify as supernatural beings. The so-called real vampire community consists of individuals who feel they are living people but must feed on the blood or psychic energy of others in order to maintain their physical, mental, and spiritual health. Members of a related community call themselves therianthropes or "therians." Therianthropes feel that they have a special connection to a particular animal and identify with stories of lycanthropes and shape-shifters. Finally, the term "otherkin" has come to serve as a catchall label for people who feel that they are, in some sense, mythological creatures, such as faeries, elves, and dragons, who have become trapped in human bodies. While it is difficult to trace the historical origins of these communities, they seem to have existed in some form since the 1960s and 1970s, and their metaphysical ideas about psychic energy or nonhuman souls born into human bodies have precedents in occult literature from the nineteenth century.[80] However, these groups became far larger and more organized in the 1990s while White Wolf's World of Darkness games were being published.[81] It can hardly be considered a coincidence that vampires, therianthropes, and otherkin bear a strong resemblance to characters from *Vampire: The Masquerade; Werewolf: The Apocalypse;* and *Changeling: The Dreaming.*

Michelle Belanger identifies as a psychic vampire, or one who feeds on the psychic energy of others. She has written several books and is an intellectual leader of the community. She describes her condition as "vampirism," but this is really a homonym for the "vampire" of legend. Some psychic vampires have argued that the term "vampire" is only a form of cultural shorthand to describe the transfer of life force from one being to another. In her books, Belanger describes how she arrived at this understanding of herself gradually over years of introspection. Among vampires and otherkin this process of discovering one's identity is referred to as "awakening"—a term that appears in *Mage* and carries the same meaning.

Belanger became involved in *Vampire* LARPs and worked as a storyteller at national conventions. She suspected that some players were also psychic vampires undergoing a process of awakening, and used the game to seek such players out. She writes:

> While the game itself is based upon fiction and heavily influenced by the novels of Anne Rice, it still attracted many isolated psychic vampires. The live-action version provided them with a social outlet where they could openly adopt the identity of a vampire, even if this was only within the context of a game. More helpful than being able to play at being what they already were, was the fact that vampirism became an acceptable topic of conversation among players who met socially outside the game. . . . During the game, I would study the players, noting who wore jewelry or other symbols typically associated with occult practices and getting a feel for these people's energy. I learned to identify certain types of people by "feel" alone, and once the game was over, I would approach them and invite them to a closed-door discussion on beliefs, practices, and experiences. . . . It was through these closed-door discussions after games that my group was born.[82]

This networking eventually resulted in the creation of House Kheperu, a vampire new religious movement.

Vampire: The Masquerade was more than a venue through which self-identified vampires could seek each other out. In many cases, White Wolf's rich mythology, which included its own lexicon and structure of vampire society, served as a model for an emerging community. Some White Wolf supplements were so detailed that the real vampires sometimes failed to understand that they were works of fiction. A small-print vampire magazine called *The Midnight Sun* featured an article by a self-identified vampire who cited a game book called *The Book of the Damned* as if it were a nonfiction text. He wrote, "Principally, I relate to the sect known as Gangrel, with a string of Malkavian, destined to become Inconnu."[83] All of these terms were created by White Wolf and have no basis in actual vampire lore. In a subsequent article, the author wrote: "I was made aware . . . the book I made some references from, *The Book of the Damned,* was part of a role-playing game. I was not aware of this."[84]

More often, real vampires were aware that the vampire society depicted in White Wolf was fictional, but still used it as a basis for their own traditions and mythology. In New York City, the real vampires formed a community with elaborate titles inspired by White Wolf's vampire courts. An ethical code was created for vampire society called "the Black Veil," which covered such rules as how vampires are to respect community elders and how donors (those who willingly allow vampires to feed on their psychic energy or blood) should be treated. Particularly in its earlier versions, the Black Veil resembled "the Laws of the Masquerade" created by White Wolf.[85]

It became increasingly difficult to discern who considered him- or herself a "real vampire" and who was merely playing one in a role-playing game. An interesting artifact of this tension is a book called *Dhampir: Child of the Blood,* by a self-identified vampire named Viola Johnson. Johnson's book contains a mythology that seems highly derivative of *Vampire: The Masquerade:* the first vampire was Cain, vampires struggle against the Beast, and so on. However, Johnson reverses the situation and accuses the role-playing games of copying actual vampires. She writes: "Imitators and game players are simulating our ways and traditions often to unsafe ends. It is no longer easy to distinguish a true blood drinker from someone who emulates us because we are today's craze."[86] The tension between role-players and self-identified vampires was exacerbated by the media response to the Ferrell murders in 1996. Gamers wanted to make it clear that they did not think they were truly vampires, and the real vampire community was equally eager to prove that they were not delusional gamers. Both groups moved to distance themselves from one another, despite drawing on a shared milieu of vampire mythology and popular culture.

Otherkin

The otherkin are another group defined by their unusual identity claims. Otherkin feel that they are—in a spiritual or philosophical sense—not entirely human. Many otherkin feel as though they have the soul of a mythological creature that has become trapped in a human body. No finite list of otherkin types exists, but some of the most common include elves, faeries, and mythological creatures such as dragons. The term "otherkin" is sometimes used in a broader sense that would include vampires and therianthropes, although these groups have distinct subcultures.

Like vampires, otherkin describe a process of "awakening" in which they come to think about their identity in a new way. One otherkin described discovering that his "other self" was a dragon through a process of introspection and creative visualization:

> What I have figured out so far is that I'm a dragon of the Western variety, approximately 20 feet long (nose-tip to tail-tip) with what is likely a 7 to 10 foot wingspan, blue coloration, small scales, some gray markings, green or blue eyes (I think they change), and a bonecrown as well as maybe bone-spikes along the spine which are probably retractable.[87]

There is no consensus among the otherkin as to how their "otherness" is possible. Many otherkin believe in reincarnation and feel that in a previous life they were a mythological creature inhabiting a supernatural realm. A few have suggested that the condition is genetic, citing stories of angels mating with humans in the book of Genesis or Celtic lore about trysts between humans and faeries. Many more take a pragmatic view about their identity, framing it as a "personal mythology." For these individuals, identifying as an otherkin "feels right" and so does not need to be proved to others or supported with theoretical claims.[88]

The otherkin have a strong cultural association with role-playing games. Ethan Gilsdorf mentions otherkin in his book *Fantasy Freaks and Gaming Geeks,* and Mark Barrowcliffe, in his autobiography about *D&D*, describes how he briefly suspected he was a dragon that had been magically shape-shifted into a human.[89] Both discourses have developed together, sharing a common milieu of folklore, popular fiction, and magical ideas. The otherkin emerged from the 1960s and reflect the same fascination with Tolkien and mythology that also fueled the creation of *D&D* and the SCA. In the early 1970s—at almost the exact time that Gygax and Arneson were developing *D&D*—a pagan group called "the Elf Queen's Daughters" appeared in San Francisco. The Elf Queen's Daughters identified as Tolkienesque elves and are often regarded as the beginning of the otherkin community.[90]

In the 1980s and 1990s, the ideas that otherkin formed about their identities and the world they inhabited developed alongside fantasy role-playing games. For instance, some otherkin speak of "the Veil," a supernatural barrier separating magical and quotidian reality. Some believe that the Veil will soon fall, at which time magic will return to the world, and otherkin will be physically transformed into their mythological "true selves." Several otherkin (many of whom find this idea too fanciful) are quick to point out that the prophecy of the Veil falling is derivative of *Shadowrun* and its premise of magic returning to Earth.[91]

Much more common is the idea that otherkin have the souls of mythological creatures trapped in human bodies. This idea bears a strong resemblance to the premise of *Changeling*. Some otherkin even use the word "glamour" and claim that they require glamour to maintain their health. As with the vampires, arguments were raised over who was copying whom. An article about otherkin that appeared in the *Village Voice* in 2001 quoted an otherkin who praised how well *Changeling* explored mythological themes, but raised concerns that the game had convinced gamers that they might be otherkin when they were actually only ordinary, mundane humans. Rich Dansky, one of the designers for *Changeling,* described how he discovered otherkin shortly after the game came out. Exploring an online Listserv called "darkfae-l," Dansky found a heated debate over "how the folks at White Wolf had gotten so much of their existence right." "Finally," Dansky was quoted, "one of the list members came to the obvious conclusion that we'd gotten it right because we ourselves were in fact changelings."[92] This comment demonstrates the intertextual relationship between magical views and fantasy role-playing games: not only can role-playing games shape magical views, but magical worldviews can shape how role-playing games are interpreted.

Reenchantment without Delusion

How are we to account for White Wolf's strange relationship with "real" magicians, vampires, and faeries? How do fiction and reality begin to converge? Eliade suggested that humanity has a fundamental need for myth and that if scientific rationalism deprived humanity of sacred stories, popular fiction such as films and novels would arise to take their place.[93] However, the extent to which popular culture can adequately fill this role is debatable. In what I have called the "consolation model," secularization is triumphant, and role-playing games are a particularly potent mode of temporary escape into a realm of myth. However, there is now evidence that popular culture can reenchant the world by becoming "sacralized." The fictional worlds depicted in novels, films, and role-playing games serve as resources for the production of actual moral and metaphysical meaning.

As early as the 1980s, sociologist Nachman Ben-Yahuda noted that science fiction offers answers to "fundamental existential problems" in a way that (at least for the populations these genres attract) science and traditional religion cannot.[94] Many scholars found it significant that the first pagan group to obtain government recognition in the United States, the Church of All Worlds, derived its name from Robert Heinlein's science-fiction novel *Stranger in a Strange Land.*[95] In more recent decades, scholars such as Christopher Partridge have demonstrated how such popular media as *Buffy: The Vampire Slayer, The X-Files,* and the Harry Potter series have influenced metaphysical and theological questions.[96] A similar process has occurred in Japan where *anime* and *manga* have likewise contributed to new forms of religious belief and ritual.[97]

Danielle Kirby's research on otherkin has framed this movement as part of the sacralization of popular culture.[98] Lupa, a therianthrope, is the author of *A Field Guide to Otherkin,* which is currently the definitive text on this community from an emic perspective. Lupa cites an extensive list of popular media that otherkin can turn to in search of "inspiration for personal mythology." This includes the fantasy fiction of Lewis and Tolkien, a variety of comic books and fantasy films, as well as *D&D* and *Changeling.*[99]

Sociologist Adam Possamai coined the term "hyperreal religions" to describe new religions adapted from popular culture. He writes, "Religion and popular culture co-exist intimately, and cannot be seen simply as having a relationship of cause and effect."[100] The sacralization of role-playing games does not occur in the manner claimed by moral entrepreneurs, in which players simply forget that games are fiction, or, alternatively, the games were always religions and the pretense of a "game" was simply a ploy to indoctrinate children. Fantasy games do not affect what players believe so much as how they perceive the world. Vampires and otherkin do not regard game mythologies as religious truths, but rather engage in a creative process in which fictional media is approached alongside religious ideas. Lynn Schofield Clark, in her ethnography of the intersection of religion and popular culture, notes that the millennial generation has an especially strong "openness to possibility." Clark suggests that for many young people, urban fantasy and other fictional stories are viewed alongside the stories of religious traditions. In this free market of ideas, fiction and religious truth claims "may be viewed as equally possible and plausible—or equally fictional."[101]

While role-playing games are not necessary to the sacralization of popular culture, play is key to this process. Sacralization occurs when individuals are free to creatively reorder the symbols of religion and popular culture. It should also be noted that the ideas produced in this fashion rarely resemble religious dogmas so much as "meaningful possibilities." In her discussion of otherkin, Lupa seems uninterested in the distinction between imagination and objective reality in favor of pragmatism and spiritual health. She writes: "Sure we can explain it away as imagination, but repressing anything completely inevitably leads to ill health, whether the repression is physical or psychological. We need to play, and otherkin allows us to express that within safe boundaries." She cites Joseph Campbell to argue that imagination and play are essential for any religious ritual to be effective.[102]

From this perspective, the claims of moral entrepreneurs are turned on their heads. Pulling and others were preoccupied with the fact that some of the symbols and names in role-playing games were not imaginary but drawn from real occultism. However, categories such as real and imaginary are not particularly helpful for understanding groups like the otherkin. For pragmatists like Lupa, it is not the case that playing a game becomes a form of religion, but rather that religion is simply another form of play.

Jon C. Bush and Rod Ferrell were engaged in a similar, albeit more dangerous, form of play. These individuals were not isolated loners but were charismatic and had coteries of friends. Collaboration is an important distinction between madness and imaginative play. In this state of serious play, when Ferrell claimed he was a 400-year-old vampire named Vassago, his friends did not regard his statement as literally true or mere imagination but something in between. In keeping with Ikuya Sato's model of deviance, irrevocable action caused the frame of play to become permanent. In Roger Caillois's terms, the play became corrupted when it became entangled in the details of the profane world. Once crimes had been committed and a criminal investigation was under way, it was impossible for Bush and Ferrell to abandon their assumed roles as vampires. What had begun as imaginative play was now interpreted by society as either collective insanity or a cult.

In the 1990s both claims makers and spiritual seekers turned to role-playing games for reenchantment. The claims of occult investigators such as Rimer and true-crime authors such as Linedecker and Reang saw role-playing games as tangible evidence of hidden forces that had infiltrated America, turning ordinary youth into gang members, murderers, and cultists. While these theories were frightening, they were also clearly a source of excitement and pleasure. Meanwhile, figures such as Michelle Belanger and Lupa employed White Wolf's games as a theoretical tool with which to think about the supernatural as well as personal narratives. While understanding that games are "just games," they used the models these games provided to formulate ideas about reality, meaning, and identity. All of these figures approached fantasy role-playing games in new and unprecedented ways that were both a source of pleasure and a way of ordering the world. Part 2 examines these processes more closely and considers their significance for the sociology of knowledge.

PART II

Interpreting the Panic

CHAPTER 6

How Role-Playing Games Create Meaning

We all know that Art is not truth. Art is a lie that makes us realize truth, at least the truth that is given us to understand.

—Pablo Picasso, "Statement to Marius de Zayas"

Life imitates Art far more than Art imitates Life.

—Oscar Wilde, "The Decay of Lying"

Fantasy role-playing games have functions in common with religion that moral entrepreneurs have misunderstood and that gamer apologists have historically had to overlook in order to refute the claims of their opponents. While the narratives changed over time, moral entrepreneurs claimed that role-playing games cause young people to dissociate from reality and to reject traditional values. Gamer apologists countered that their hobbies were "just games" and "harmless escapism." Both of these positions are polemical and fail to account for the subtle ways that these games inform questions of meaning, identity, and morality. On the one hand, it is patently false that games like *D&D* are actually a religion or are engaged in some sort of proselytizing. On the other hand, there is ample evidence that role-playing games *do* shape how players see the world and themselves. Furthermore, as seen in the previous chapter, there is a substantial subset of gamers who have magical worldviews that have developed alongside fantasy role-playing games. This evidence suggests that the alternate worlds imagined during these games have consequences for how players make sense of the real world.

Tolkien wrote that one of the functions of fairy stories is "escapism." He felt the term "escapism" was frequently misused and regarded with scorn because it had become associated with the "Flight of the Deserter," which is selfish and cowardly, instead of the "Escape of the Prisoner," which is noble and ingenious. He wrote: "Why should a man be scorned, if, finding himself in a prison, he tries to get out and go home? Or if, when he cannot do so, he thinks about and talks about other topics than jailers and prison-walls? The world outside has not become less real because the prisoner cannot see it."[1] In contrast to moral entrepreneurs and gamer apologists, for Tolkien "escapism" is not the opposite of religion. Tolkien's image of a man finding freedom in another world that is hidden but no less real is undeniably a religious image.

This chapter presents a theoretical framework that explains how these games not only allow players to escape, in the sense that Tolkien describes, but potentially to return to the world of "the prison" and repurpose it. The keys to this process are imagination and play. The mechanism through which fantasy worlds are created and rendered meaningful conforms closely to sociological models of how cultures work to construct an idea of a sacred order. While I am not claiming that fantasy role-playing games are a religion, there is evidence that both religious worldviews and the worlds of fantasy role-playing games are products of a single faculty through which human beings create meaning together.

The ability and the need to construct worlds of meaning is a product of human biology. Peter Berger writes:

> Each animal lives in an environment that is specific to its particular species. There is a mouse-world, a dog-world, a horse-world, and so forth. . . . There is no man-world in the above sense. . . . Man must *make* a world for himself. The world-building activity of man, therefore, is not a biologically extraneous phenomenon, but the direct consequence of man's biological constitution.[2]

This process of creating meaning out of chaos or "world-building" is a religious one. Clifford Geertz articulated the function of religion as creating a "general order of existence."[3] Creating a general order of existence (Berger's "man-world") makes up for our lack of biological instincts; it allows us to function, gives us purpose, and sets us on the same footing as the animals. However, this does not make us fully human. As world-makers, human beings are capable of creating and maintaining multiple worlds at once.

Cognitive scientists have now discovered that as soon as babies are able to talk they begin to talk about things that are possible as well as things that are real.[4] In *Principles of Psychology* William James described how multiple worlds of meaning can exist simultaneously. He described these as "sub-universes" and noted that "each world whilst it is attended to is real after its own fashion; only the reality lapses with the attention."[5] Alfred Schutz expanded on this work, explaining:

> All these worlds—the world of dreams, of imageries and phantasms, especially the world of art, the world of religious experience, the world of scientific contemplation, the play world of the child, and the world of the insane—are finite provinces of meaning.[6]

In general, these finite provinces of meaning are neither completely overlapping nor hermetically sealed from each other. Instead, one world can provide a reflection of another. In fact, Robert Bellah suggested that this ability to see reality from the perspective of a secondary world is necessary for human happiness. He writes, "It is through pointing to other realities, through beyonding, that religion and poetry, and science too in its own way, break the dreadful fatalities of this world of appearances."[7] This is a sociological model of Tolkien's argument that fairy stories are important because they facilitate escape.

In order to escape, humanity must have a world to escape to. There must be a world that is meaningful but also an alternative to what Schutz calls "the world of daily life." Where do these alternative worlds come from, and how are they rendered meaningful? To describe this process, I draw on the theories of Émile Durkheim, Johan Huizinga, and Victor Turner. Although they use different terminology, each of these theorists outlines a mechanism through which human beings produce "a general order of existence." In each model the production of new meaning is always a collective process, and it is always carried out within a special mode of activity during which ordinary social norms are suspended. These models are attempts to explain the genesis of ritual, culture, and religion, but they apply equally well to the genesis of alternate realities in role-playing games. Players often struggle to articulate exactly *why* role-playing games are so engrossing and the feeling they have while playing them. If role-playing games utilize the same process that human beings have always used to order the world and construct meaning, then the appeal of these games may be hardwired. Playing them is pleasurable because the ability to create worlds is our birthright as human beings.

MODELS AND MEANING-MAKING

For theorists such as Eliade and Durkheim, religion entails a dichotomy between the profane—equivalent to Schutz's "world of daily life"—and the sacred, an alternate order defined by virtue of being separate and distinct from the profane. While Eliade regarded the sacred as a sui generis category, Durkheim assumed there was a naturalistic explanation for the sacred. He wrote: "Nothing comes from nothing. The feelings the physical world evokes in us cannot, by definition, contain anything that transcends this world. From the tangible, we can make only the tangible; we cannot make something unlimited from something limited."[8] Using ethnographies of Aboriginal totemism, Durkheim formed his thesis that the dichotomy between sacred and profane has its origin in two different modes of social interaction. The profane corresponds to the reality experienced by individual Aborigines as they went about the concerns of daily life: gathering food, securing shelter, and so on. The experience of the sacred arises from collective rituals, in which Aborigines cease to pursue material necessities and enter an ecstatic state of "collective effervescence." Durkheim theorized that the feelings of excitement and euphoria generated by collective effervescence are attributed to symbols, imbuing them with a "sacred" status. To defile certain objects, such as tribal totems or national flags, is blasphemous because these objects have become symbols of collective identity. In fact, Durkheim's chief criterion of the sacred is that it is something "set apart and forbidden," something that can be defiled. For Durkheim, this process of collective meaning-making was the origin not only of religion, but of all "social facts"—the values, cultural norms, and social structures that transcend the individual.

Durkheim's theory that special social contexts facilitate the creation of new social realities shows important similarities to Huizinga's model of play. Huizinga too theorized that culture is created through a particular mode of social interaction. Like the sacred, play is something "set apart" and subject to defilement. Huizinga explained: "The play-mood is *labile* in its very nature. At any moment 'ordinary life' may reassert its rights either by an impact from without, which interrupts the game, or by an offense against the rules, or else from within, by a collapse of the play spirit, a sobering, a disenchantment." Play also creates order. Even spontaneous play quickly leads to the development of rules, and the play can continue only if the players abide by them. Huizinga's theory that culture has its genesis in play is now supported by developmental psychologists such as Alison Gopnik, who argues that play contains the seeds of culture, history, morality, science, and literature.[9]

Alongside collective effervescence and play, the concept of "liminality" provides a third model of how new realities are produced collectively. Arnold van Gennep first developed this term to describe tribal initiation rituals in which adolescents entered a temporary phase of "betwixt and between," being no longer juveniles and not yet adults. Victor Turner greatly expanded the idea of liminality, theorizing that special "liminal" modes of interaction allow old patterns of meaning to be dissolved and new ones to be created. Like collective effervescence and play, liminality can occur only in certain prescribed contexts that Turner described as "sacred space-time."[10] Liminal events such as religious pilgrimages and initiation rituals are regarded as sacred and also present the opportunity for a change in status. During conditions of liminality, social norms and status are temporarily dissolved, opening the door to what Turner calls "anti-structure." This is not a reversal of the ordinary social structure but rather a way of making room for new possibilities. Turner described antistructure as "the liberation of human capacities of cognition, affect volition, creativity, etc." from the constraints of the social roles produced by being affiliated with one's class, family, nation, and so on.[11] In antistructure, the world of daily life is dismantled and rearranged. Turner wrote, "It is the analysis of culture into factors and their free or 'ludic' recombination in any and every possible pattern, however weird, that is of the essence of liminality, liminality *par excellence.*"[12]

Each of these models posits an alternative mode of human interaction (collective effervescence, play, liminality) that exists in contrast to the ordinary mode of interaction, which is goal oriented and structured. It is through this alternative mode that the human ability to create new worlds of meaning is activated. The normally fixed order of things becomes fluid, and symbols and people can be infused with new meaning.

Fantasy role-playing games are another manifestation of this faculty. The apparatus by which it produces uniquely realistic shared fantasies has much in common with religious ritual. As a leisure activity, role-playing serves no material interest and exists outside the normal mode and structure of daily life. Consistent with Huizinga's and Turner's characterization of ritual, gaming is "serious play." Dungeon masters and storytellers may spend hours preparing for games. Also as in ritual, a particular atmosphere must be maintained for most players to enjoy the game. Anyone who has ever seen teenagers engaged in role-playing has probably heard a frustrated player's call to "be serious."

Within this state of ritualized play, players are able to achieve a form of liminality. As their characters, players have temporarily escaped the structure of their ordinary social roles. Within the small body of scholarly literature on role-playing games, it now goes almost without saying that role-playing games are a form of liminal experience.[13] Turner would probably agree with this assessment. As he continued to develop his concept of liminality, he arrived at the related concept of "the liminoid." Liminoid phenomena share many features with liminal phenomena, but unlike the rites of passage studied by van Gennep, participation in liminoid phenomena is optional, and they are more often found in modern societies. Turner cites leisure, pastimes, and games as important liminoid activities that allow people to temporarily escape the confines of structure.[14]

Finally, there is a phenomenological aspect to role-playing that likewise resembles the models outlined above. Gary Alan Fine noted that the object of role-playing is not to "win" but "engrossment"—to become absorbed in the game. Daniel Mackay describes a "presence of emotion" during game play that is ephemeral and irreproducible. This presence can be produced only through collective play and bears a family resemblance to Durkheim's notion of collective effervescence. In describing it, Mackay employs the concept of "flow" put forth by Hungarian psychologist Mihaly Csikszentmihalyi. Flow is a mental state in which human beings lose themselves in a task. Csikszentmihalyi described it as

> the merging of action and awareness. A person in flow has no dualistic perspective: he is aware of his actions but not the awareness itself. . . . The steps for experiencing flow . . . involve the . . . process of delimiting reality, controlling some aspect of it, and responding to the feedback with a concentration that excludes anything else as irrelevant.[15]

Much like Huizinga's concept of "play," flow is autotelic. Someone in a state of flow is happy because he or she is interested in the task itself rather than an end result. Turner also refers to Csikszentmihalyi's "flow" in attempting to describe the fleeting experience that occurs during liminal states.[16]

To summarize, role-playing resembles not only religious ritual but broader models of how human beings produce meaning. It is collective; it is autotelic; it is "set apart and forbidden" in that it must be performed in a certain way and will be spoiled if it is not "taken seriously"; it provides a "liminoid" state in which ordinary social norms are suspended; and it produces a unique experience of flow or engrossment. It is through this mode of "serious play" that humans are able to temporarily suspend the ordinary world in order to imagine alternative worlds together.

In addition to the mechanism by which role-playing produces singularly realistic fantasies, some attention should be paid to the product of this mechanism—namely, narrative. During collective liminal states, symbols are rearranged and acquire new meaning. An important product of this semiotic undertaking is narrative. For Bellah and Huizinga, play is relevant to the study of religion because it gives rise to myth. In role-playing games, the narrative is what is left over when the players go home, the liminoid state ends, and the presence of emotion fades.

Narrative is perhaps the oldest form of world-making. We are narrative creatures, and stories render the world apprehensible. Narrative tells us about the world we live in and our place within it. Charles Taylor wrote, "In order to have a sense of who we are, we have to have a notion of how we have become, and of where we are going."[17] In fact, narrative is required to apprehend not only our individual identities, but also those of our families, cultures, and nations. Stories are also uniquely engrossing. Listening to an exciting story or watching a film can elicit physical responses—audiences cringe, grip their seats, futilely yell advice at the characters, and so on. In light of James's idea that a world is "real" so long as it is attended to, this quality of engrossment gives narrative a form of reality not found in paintings or sculpture. For this reason, sacred narrative, in the form of myth, has always been a means by which human beings achieve a sense of propinquity with sacred times and places. Levi-Strauss described narrative as "an instrument for the obliteration of time."[18]

Fantasy role-playing games, then, can be thought of as modern forms of ritual and myth. Although they do not have the same status as ritual and myth in world religions, these games are powerful because they utilize humanity's most primal faculties of meaning production. On a small scale, games invoke the very mechanisms through which all human culture is created. By doing so, they create a unique mental space in which players rethink their world and their selves in order to create new worlds and new selves.

I suspect that statements like "*D&D* is a cult" are in part an attempt to articulate this religious function. In *The Truth about Dungeons and Dragons,* Joan Robie warned, "D&D requires each player to make philosophical, religious, and moral decisions, whereas ordinary games do not."[19] Here, the critique of *D&D* is not that it is a catechism of the occult or causes dissociation from reality (although Robie goes on to make these claims). Rather it is that *D&D* is a reflection of the moral world of the players and provides the players with an opportunity to reflect on morality. From an ideological perspective, such moments of reflection are dangerous because they cannot be controlled. Once players are able to mentally step into the realm of play and antistructure, there is no way to predict what new structure they might conceive.

FANTASY WORLDS AND THE WORLD OF DAILY LIFE

There is no such thing as "sheer fantasy" because fantasy is inherently derivative. Sartre wrote that all imaginary objects are "a melange of past impressions and recent knowledge."[20] Howard and Tolkien created imaginary worlds by drawing on myth, poetry, and history. Arneson and Gygax then drew on these works along with a wide variety of science fiction and pulp fantasy to create *D&D*. All of the worlds of fantasy role-playing, no matter how fantastic, are constructed by rearranging and repurposing familiar elements. Mackay describes how he took pictures of the Arizona desert so that they could later be used to describe a fantasy desert in his *D&D* campaign.[21] An even more striking example of this comes from Stephen Colbert. As a child, Colbert wanted to play a published adventure called *The Thieves of Fortress Badabaskor* but had no one to play with. And so he played the adventure with himself, assuming the roles of the dungeon master and all the players. Each character he created was based on a member of his nuclear family, including his eleven brothers and sisters (only one of whom survived the adventure).[22] This anecdote demonstrates how fantasy is always a repurposing of the familiar. Colbert was candid about basing his characters on his family, but all imaginary characters are based on either real people or other characters. Furthermore, according to Turner, *bricolage* is exactly what liminality is for. He writes: "In liminality people 'play' with the elements of the familiar and defamiliarize them. Novelty emerges from unprecedented combinations of familiar elements."[23]

This means that fantasy worlds are not separate from the world of daily life but have a relationship with it. Because fantasy worlds are ultimately derivative of the world of daily life, they are reflections *of* this world and enable a reflection *on* this world. In his essay "Religion as a Cultural System," Geertz described religion as a system of symbols. Symbols are not reality, but "models" of reality. Furthermore, they are models in two senses: they are models *of* reality in that they attempt to accurately reflect the real world and to make sense of it. But they are also models *for* reality in that they create a symbol system through which the world can be analyzed and manipulated. Geertz regarded this dual use of symbols as a uniquely human faculty, writing, "The intertransposability of models *for* and models *of* which symbolic formulation makes possible is the distinctive characteristic of our mentality."[24] In other words, the world can be apprehended only through models, and models make further analysis an inherent possibility. The two functions cannot be separated. Applied to role-playing games, this means that the relationship between fantasy and reality is necessarily a two-way street. When they look into the mirror of fantasy, gamers can either affirm and reinforce their assumptions or call them into question.

Analyzing fantasy worlds as both a reflection *of* the world of daily life and a reflection *on* the world of daily life informs many of the controversies and claims surrounding role-playing games. As a reflection of the player's world, game fantasies often articulate experiences that are otherwise inexpressible, and render them apprehensible. Games are amenable to psychoanalysis precisely because they often reflect the player's view of the world in ways that the player himself is unable to express. This function accounts for much of the violence and misogyny prevalent in certain gaming groups.

As a reflection on the world of daily life, role-playing games create the possibility of seeing the world in a new way. Many of the models and game mechanics devised to create a realistic fantasy can be used to analyze and interpret the real world. Many gamers describe occasionally thinking about the real world in terms of their favorite game. Players have also described thinking about themselves differently as a result of gameplay. Thus there is a natural progression from articulation to analysis, as imaginary worlds created as a form of personal expression give players newfound agency with which to interpret the real world. In some cases, players may come to think about the social order and plausibility structures in new ways. This process is also the key to understanding how role-playing games sometimes lead to reenchantment and the sacralization of popular culture.

Games as a Reflection of the World of Daily Life

In his essay "Deep Play: Notes on the Balinese Cockfight," Geertz attempts to theorize how a seemingly violent and irrational form of leisure can have value to the people of Bali. His findings are applicable to fantasy role-playing games that have also been regarded as deviant and unwholesome.[25] The term "deep play" was coined by Jeremy Bentham, the father of utilitarianism, and refers to gambling situations in which the stakes have been raised to a ruinous level. Bentham regarded such situations as irrational because they lead to a net loss of resources for those involved. As such, he argued that deep play should be illegal. Some fantasy role-playing games can certainly resemble deep play. The fear perpetuated by Patricia Pulling and others was that young players would identify too closely with their characters, committing suicide if the character died. While I have found no confirmed cases of players killing themselves following the death of a character, it is true that beloved characters die and that this is often quite painful for the players. John Eric Holmes remarked, "When one of these alter egos gets killed, the game player sometimes suffers psychic shock and may go into depression."[26] Mark Barrowcliffe said of this experience, "At fourteen years old it [a character's death] can be the first real grief you've known in your life."[27] Bentham might argue that any pleasure found in imaginary adventures is not worth the risk if the loss of a character induces actual depression and grief. Why then are Holmes and Barrowcliffe compelled to play such games?

Geertz took on a similar question in his study of Balinese cockfighting, an illegal activity in which the Balinese would likewise place ruinously high bets. His conclusion was that the "deep play" of the cockfight is not about acquiring money, but is a performance of status. An entire network of relationships that forms the structure of Balinese society is vicariously represented through the cocks (the Balinese word for "cock" having the same double entendre as in English). The cocks are stand-ins for their owners, just as characters are stand-ins for the players. Geertz notes that "the cockfight is 'really real' only to the cocks—it does not kill anyone, castrate anyone, reduce anyone to animal status, alter the hierarchical relations among people, or refashion the hierarchy; it does not even redistribute income in any significant way." The cockfight (of which irrationally high bets are a part) matters because it functions as a reflection of the world. Geertz writes:

> What it does is what, for other peoples with other temperaments and other conventions, *Lear* and *Crime and Punishment* do; it catches up these themes—death, masculinity, rage, pride, loss, beneficence, chance—and, ordering them into an encompassing structure, presents them in such a way as to throw into relief a particular view of their essential nature.

For the Balinese who enjoy this sport, it is engrossing because it is part of the process of world-making. As Picasso observed, art is a lie that allows us to see the truth, or at least "the truth that is given us to understand." As an art form, the cockfight

> renders ordinary, everyday experience comprehensible by presenting it in terms of acts and objects which have had their practical consequences removed and been reduced (or, if you prefer, raised) to the level of sheer appearances, where their meaning can be more powerfully articulated and more exactly perceived.[28]

Like the Balinese cockfight, role-playing games allow players to simultaneously articulate and perceive the world precisely because they are an externalized alternate reality.[29] One of the experiences that players are often seeking to render comprehensible is their own sense of self. By being someone else, players simultaneously express and discover who they are. Actor Vin Diesel said of his love of *D&D,* "What kept us hooked was the search for the character that represented our higher self."[30] Similarly, a subject from Sarah Lynne Bowman's ethnography of gamers explained, "All my characters teach me something about myself because I get to externalize a part of me and really look at how it interacts and plays with other people."[31] Mackay takes this line of analysis even further, suggesting that role-playing games help players to define a sense of self over and against the alienating conditions of modern, bureaucratized life:

> This process of fabricating a character can, in turn, render the players' own subjectivity and sense of self-identity intelligible in a world in which people are archived according to credit ratings, income tax returns, IQ tests, student exams, job evaluations, consumer habits, and so forth. After going through the process of creating a cohesive character from various fragments and bits, players can carry this experience over to their own life.[32]

This may be why role-playing games are particularly appealing to adolescents, who are actively engaged in constructing a sense of self. David Waldron compares role-playing games to Erik Erikson's model of a "psychosocial moratorium."[33] Erikson defined this term as "a period that is characterized by a selective permissiveness on the part of society and of provocative playfulness on the part of the youth." He puts a wide range of cultural practices into this category from tribal coming-of-age rites to modern juvenile delinquency. Erikson argues that such periods are "of the utmost importance for the process of identity formation."[34] As with the cockfight and the role-playing game, the psychosocial moratorium facilitates meaning-making because behavior conducted in this state has diminished consequences and is not "really real." Like collective effervescence, play, and liminality, Erikson is describing an alternative mode of interaction in which the ordinary social order is suspended and new meaning can be produced.

As reflections of the world, role-playing games are also amenable to psychotherapy. In his theory of frames, Gregory Bateson noted that play and therapy both entail a space where signs are divorced from their ordinary meaning and new forms of expression and communication become possible.[35] Fine described role-playing games as "collective Rorschach tests" and "communal TAT cards."[36] As early as 1979, physician and game designer Leonard H. Kanterman wrote an article for the gaming magazine *Different Worlds* suggesting that role-playing can help people to better understand themselves. He explained:

> I see role-playing as an opportunity for people to learn more about themselves. By exploring the possibilities of different courses of actions, even to the point of different morality systems, through the "safe" medium of fantasy, people can learn who they are and why they think and act the way they do.[37]

Kanterman's idea was later supported in an article in the *American Journal of Psychotherapy* about the therapeutic uses of *D&D*. The article described a patient named "Fred," a nineteen-year-old, single, white college student who had cut both his wrists in an attempted suicide. Fred made his first friends outside of his therapy circle through a game of *D&D*. He described his fellow gamers as "fringe people like myself." Fred's therapist argued that the narrative constructed through Fred's role-playing was both an insight into the nature of his problems and a tool for working through his problems.

Fred's character was lawful evil. He described to his therapist how his character took a job working for the wealthiest man in town. He then proceeded to kill his employer's sons, conspired to marry his daughter, and ultimately seize his fortune. When Fred's therapist discussed the motivations of the character in doing such things, Fred expressed that his brother had always gotten the family "treasures" of love and attention and that he wanted to murder him much of the time. By inflicting evil on an imaginary family, Fred was able to work through his rage and come to terms with it.[38] The game became a tool through which Fred could construct a model of his own feelings.

Moral entrepreneurs claimed that playing evil characters makes players evil. However, Fred's case suggests that the decision to play an evil character is an expression of something already present in the player. It should also be noted that Fred could not have confronted these parts of his personality playing a game like *Dragonraid* in which characters do not have the option of being evil. Players cannot make sense of evil if it remains taboo even in the context of play.

This is not to say that instances of immorality and sadism in role-playing games are inherently therapeutic. However, this understanding of games as a reflection of the world can help to interpret games that become juvenile, cruel, misogynistic, and scatological. Anyone who has ever watched a group of middle-school boys playing *D&D* has probably seen this sort of nastiness. Moral entrepreneurs cite such behavior as evidence that role-playing games are inherently amoral, while gamer apologists tend to dismiss them as either bad examples of the game or catharsis. Distasteful elements are better understood as an attempt to articulate and think about a world that appears threatening and cruel.

Arduin Grimoire was frequently cited as an example of the inherent cruelty and violence of role-playing games. Created by David Hargrave in 1977, the game was one of the first competitors of *D&D*. One of the game's innovations was a "critical hit table." If players struck a particularly deadly blow, they could roll two ten-sided dice to determine a number between 1 and 100. This number could then be applied to a table to determine the nature of the injury. Several moral entrepreneurs quoted selections from the following passage from the game's critical hit table:

> Dice roll: 37–38; hit location: crotch/chest; results: genitals/breast torn off, shock. . . .
> Dice roll: 95; hit location: guts ripped out; results: 20 percent chance of tangling feet, die in one to ten minutes. . . .
> Dice roll: 100; hit location: head; results: entire head pulped and spread over a wide area.[39]

Arduin Grimoire featured similar tables to determine the dimensions of a female character's hips, waist, and bust. Certain combinations were ruled unattractive and imposed penalties on the character's charisma attribute.[40]

These violent and sexist elements reflected Hargrave's experience of the world. He had served in Vietnam as a combat photographer and seen firsthand what weapons do to the human body. The critical hit table was a reflection of these experiences and an attempt to share them with others. In an interview with Moira Johnston, Hargrave defended the depiction of violence in his game:

> It's deliberately gruesome. You have to blow a hole through that video shell the kids are encased in. They're little zombies. They don't know what pain is. They've never seen a friend taken out in a body bag in bitty pieces. They've got to understand that what they do has consequences. The world *is* sex. It

> *is* violence. It's going to destroy most of these kids when they leave TV land. . . . Arduin is a reflection of what my life has been—90 percent of what I've seen has been human garbage. War, death, intrigue, back-stabbing. I'm trying to show that 10 percent of hope.

Johnston countered, "Perhaps, but the mother in me rebels at my kids playing in the garbage dump of Hargrave's unhappy life."[41] Her response is valid, and, indeed, *Arduin Grimoire* was always an obscure game. However, I find it significant that Hargrave defended his game as an attempt to give young players an understanding of the world. He presents the game as a sort of rite of passage for young men, similar to those studied by Turner and Erikson.[42]

Fine also describes cases of disturbing and distasteful behavior during games. As game master, he conducted an experiment in which he told the players that their party had come across a group of twenty unarmed children in the wilderness. He writes:

> I decided that these children would give no information to the party, nor would they harm the players' characters in any way. Despite this lack of harm, there was serious talk of killing the entire party of children for fear of what they might do. Eventually the consensus was that the children should be forced to leave immediately with the warning that if they were spotted by the party they would be summarily executed. Unfortunately because of the structure of the game I could not bring the party of children in contact with the players again, but that outcome would likely have been the children's death. Frequently male nonplayer characters who have not hurt the party are executed and female nonplayer characters raped for sport.[43]

Fine also encountered disturbing examples of rape and misogyny such as the following:

> In a game of EPT [Empire of the Petal Throne] our party comes across six Avanthe worshippers [female warrior-priestesses, enemies of our party] in their refectory. Their leader (a nonplayer character, played by the referee) places a spell on us, but I remove the spell before it can work. Tom says, laughing loudly: "I will dive over and grab their turdy necks." (He really looks as if he is eager to kill). Tom yells: "I'm screaming at them, 'Stop and be raped, you goddamn women!'" After all six are killed, Tom, still excited, suggests: "Let's get gems and jewels and panties." Later in the game when we meet another group of Avanthe priestess-warriors, Tom comments: "No fucking women in a blue dress are going to scare me . . . I'll fight. They'll all be dead men."[44]

Fine even found himself engaged in vicarious acts of sadism. He recalled, "More than just participating, I enjoyed the murderous actions of our party, although reflecting upon my actions and those of my friends, I felt chagrined."[45]

This sort of behavior is often explained as the venting of antisocial impulses. Holmes described *D&D* as "a vicarious release of unacceptable behavior."[46] Fine noted that the players he studied appeared to have a high level of aggression that needed to be expressed. One of his interviewees explained: "Relief for your frustrations is a big [value of gaming], 'cause when you've gone all day and you've put up with as much crap as you have, and you walk into a fantasy game and go beat somebody up. It makes you feel good, it really does."[47]

Catharsis may be an important function of role-playing violence, and the idea of release conforms to Turner's notion of "liminoid" leisure, in which the constraints of societal structure are temporarily loosened. However, like Hargrave expressing his experience of Vietnam through simulated violence, these incidents of sadism and misogyny also appear to be a process of meaning-making in which players negotiate the tensions and anxieties of adolescence. Any number of behaviors can serve as an outlet for negative impulses: listening to antisocial music, breaking things, cursing, and so on. Violent role-playing games are enjoyable because negative ideas are expressed in such a way that they can be articulated and shared.

Child psychologists Dorothy and Jerome Singer suggest that violent fantasy is most likely to translate into overt action when the fantasy comes with no sense of consequences or moral implications and when there is no possibility of suffering for the victim or punishment for the fantasizer. Singer and Singer also cite several studies suggesting that children with a natural tendency to fantasize were generally more aware of the implications of violence and therefore less likely to act out. In one study conducted by Ephraim Biblow using Rorschach tests and interviews, nine- and ten-year-olds were tested to see how imaginative they were. Two groups of children—one more imaginative and one less so—were then placed in a frustrating situation, after which they were shown either an aggressive film or a nonaggressive film. The less imaginative children demonstrated an increase in aggression after watching the aggressive film. The imaginative children showed less aggression after watching either film. However, the imaginative children responded to the aggressive film with increases in fearfulness, sadness, and shame. This experiment challenged conventional wisdom that aggressive fantasy serves a cathartic function. More importantly, Biblow suggested that rich fantasy lives prepare children to think about different options for dealing with frustration and allow them to consider the possible consequences of these options.[48] Role-playing games are fun exactly because the decisions one's character makes have consequences: if characters are violent and cruel they will be hunted by authorities, outraged communities will retaliate, and so on. This suggests that violent fantasies and role-playing games are a tool for analyzing violence and its consequences and not necessarily a rehearsal for actual violence.

If adolescent games of *D&D* suffer from a preponderance of misogyny and sadism, this is probably because adolescents are still forming their understanding of sexuality and social interaction. Fine noted that games often reflected concerns about male sexual potency and the fear of impotence. When Fine played *Chivalry and Sorcery*, the players assumed that their physical constitution score (ranging from 1 to 20) represented the number of times their characters could have sexual intercourse during a night.[49] Similarly, the sadism that players often direct toward each other is an articulation of social status, much as Geertz's cockfights were "a mock war of symbolical selves" and "a formal simulation of status tensions."[50] Kevin Schut has suggested that fantasy role-playing games are appealing to young men not merely as catharsis but as an opportunity to negotiate the often-conflicting cultural expectations of manhood: to be simultaneously respectable, rough, and playful.[51]

This interpretation suggests that the most shocking and distasteful aspects of role-playing games are a reflection of the struggles and conflicts experienced by the players, who during the decades of the panic over role-playing games were predominantly adolescent males. Barrowcliffe reflects on his own experiences of sadism and misogyny in *D&D:* "It wasn't really D&D that had caused us to behave so vilely to each other but masculinity itself. Shutting ourselves away in male-only company for our entire youths was like distilling that maleness, taking all other influences away and just leaving us with our dark selves."[52] In one sense the implications of this reading are more disturbing than the claims of the moral entrepreneurs. It is naive to assume that adolescent males would be devoid of negative impulses were it not for a violent fantasy game. In reality, outsiders are horrified by the contents of these fantasies because they reflect the horror of being an adolescent male—an experience of cruelty and inner turmoil that adults could ignore if role-playing games did not give it artistic expression.

Child psychologist Bruno Bettelheim makes a similar point in *The Uses of Enchantment*, defending the darker aspects of fairy tales. He writes:

> Fairy tales underwent severe criticism when the new discoveries of psychoanalysis and child psychology revealed just how violent, anxious, destructive, and even sadistic a child's imagination is. . . . Parents who wish to deny that their child has murderous wishes and wants to tear things and even people into pieces believe that their child must be prevented from engaging in such thoughts (as if this were possible). By denying access to stories which implicitly tell the child that others have the same fantasies, he is left to feel that he is the only one who imagines such things. This makes his fantasies really scary. On the other hand, learning that others have the same or similar fantasies makes us feel that we are a part of humanity, and allays our fear that having such destructive ideas has put us beyond the common pale.[53]

Bettelheim's defense of violence in children's stories need not be extended into tolerance of rape fantasies in role-playing games. Rather, just as fairy tales reflect rather than cause a child's negative impulses, when players perform monstrous acts in role-playing games they are reflecting on their own monstrosity. This suggests that while sadism and misogyny in role-playing games may be an index of emotional turmoil outside of the game, these fantasies are not likely to contribute to violent behavior.

Games as a Reflection on the World of Daily Life

Fine described role-playing as a collective Rorschach test. However, looking at an inkblot and seeing a butterfly is not likely to change the way we think about butterflies. By contrast, the symbolic models created through role-playing games often do change the ways that players interpret the world. Dennis Waskul writes of role-playing:

> Realms of fantasy, imagination, and reality are notoriously porous; experience, knowledge, and understanding routinely slips from one to another. In the lived experience of everyday life—just as in play and games—fantasy, imagination, and reality are not so easily compartmentalized; they necessarily blend and blur to such an extent they are often difficult to convincingly separate into mutually distinct categories.[54]

The blurring of the object and its reflection is not unique to role-playing games but occurs in many forms of play and art. Peter Stromberg explains that many forms of play can induce experiences in which

> we feel the potency of certain ideas and symbols and physical objects in ways that are not typical of our lives in the day-to-day world. We may as a result form convictions about the capacity of these ideas and symbols and physical objects to change us noticeably. This knowledge is carried into the day-to-day world.[55]

Oscar Wilde observed that art not only imitates life, but that life also imitates art. Richard Schechner compared life and theater to a Möbius strip in which each turns into the other.[56] Geertz said that religion is sociologically interesting not because it describes the social order but because it shapes it.[57] This is so because any attempt to articulate a model of the world affects the way that we view the world.

One way that role-playing games facilitate a reflection on the world is through game mechanics. Fine referred to game mechanics as "frame two" because they serve to translate between the frame of daily life (frame one) and the content of the fantasy (frame three). In order to carry out this translation, game mechanics must be able to accommodate models of everything. Paul La Farge described his initiation into *D&D:*

> In fact, as I wandered farther into the cave, and acquired the rulebooks for Advanced Dungeons & Dragons, I found that there were rules for *everything:* what kind of monsters you could meet in fresh water, what kind you could meet in salt water, what wise men knew, what happened when you mixed two magic potions together. If you happened to meet a harlot in the game, you could roll two twenty-sided dice and consult a table which told you what kind of harlot it was.[58]

Not only combat, but psychological reactions, social encounters, and economic exchanges are rendered as systems of factors with numerical values. Even the supernatural is translated into a mathematical model. An optional rule in the first edition of *D&D* stated that if a character prays to his deity for aid, there is a 1 percent chance that a divine intervention will occur. (Christian critics found this rule particularly objectionable.)[59] Of course these models cannot literally represent everything. But, at least in theory, any scenario that can be imagined must be translatable into game mechanics. Fine writes of these game mechanics, "Absolute logic is not necessary; what is required is consistency and the belief that the game is logical."[60] This project of modeling requires players to formulate complex ideas about how these phenomena work. As in an aphorism attributed to Albert Einstein, "Games are the most elevated forms of investigation."

Along with Geertz, Ian Barbour also argued that models both render the world apprehensible and shape how we interpret it. Barbour argued that in both religious and scientific thought, models are created as tools for thinking about a particular concept but produce "surplus meaning" that can be applied to other problems and inspire new discoveries. He concludes, "A model is a continuing source of plausible hypotheses."[61]

The models used in game mechanics are no exception. Players who use these models to translate ideas into the game often find the models are applicable to phenomena outside of the game. It is not uncommon for players to describe actual events in terms of game mechanics. As one player explained, "It's [the rules of *D&D*] a good shorthand vocabulary. If I say someone has 18 charisma plus bonuses, a D&D player knows I'm talking about someone like Sean Connery. And if I say someone has 3 dexterity, you know he drops things all the time."[62] Barrowcliffe confessed that after playing *D&D* he began to think of himself as a character, and people he met as monsters he was encountering. He recalled an incident in which he crashed his bicycle into a car and somehow landed on his feet, damaging the car in the process. From this he concluded that his dexterity was low but that he had a high constitution score as well as sufficient hit points to walk away from the crash unscathed.[63] This sort of thinking is not a case of confusing fantasy and reality. Instead it is using a game model as the lens through which one interprets reality.

Most people do not require such an interpretive lens to make sense of a physical event such as a car crash. However, role-playing games also employ models of metaphysical, philosophical, and moral realities. For some players these models have had a more profound influence on how they see the world. Jon Cogburn describes how the *D&D* alignment system exerted a serious moral influence on players:

> The D&D alignment system was central to a generation of adolescents whose educations and upbringing provided very little reflection on the foundations of morality. Role-playing in the *Dungeons and Dragons* universe helped us make concrete sense of the people we were and the people we wanted to become. We thought about *Dungeons and Dragons* law and chaos and good and evil in an attempt to be more virtuous people ourselves.[64]

Of course, many other players concluded that this model was flawed and that real morality is nothing like the system created by Gygax and Arneson. Paul Cardwell, of the Committee for the Advancement of Role-Playing Games (CAR-PGa), argued:

> I have always felt alignment a rather absurd aspect of gaming anyway. What is your alignment? Lawful Good, you say? What would your reaction be when good and law conflict? Would you follow the Nuremberg Edicts and help kill your neighbors, or shelter them and risk both of you going to Dachau? Or have a nervous breakdown over the conflict since your alignment is impossible? No one has alignment. A real person's actions are determined by a mass of conflicting loyalties: family, nation, religion, occupation,

> friends, hobbies, political party, etc. The characters in a game should be just as complex as real people. D&D is one of the few RPGs which has not realized this.[65]

Regardless of whether gamers think alignment is an accurate model, it is impossible to think about alignment without reflecting on its corresponding reality in the real world. Anyone who critiques the alignment system is ipso facto an amateur moral philosopher.

Another way that role-playing games shape how players see the world is by effecting shifts in attitude.[66] By stepping outside of themselves through role-playing gamers are able to reflect on their own attitudes toward the world and potentially reassess them. Several gamers have described how this process has changed their lives for the better. One gamer wrote in a letter to *Dragon:*

> What became of my group? The paladin is now a professional Army officer and veteran of the Panama invasion. The fighter/magic-user owns his own business. The ranger is now a successful attorney. We're well-adjusted adults who learned that nothing is impossible once you've kicked the snot out of the demi-lich Acererak.[67]

In this case, the experience of simulated challenges affected the players' attitudes toward obstacles, resulting in personal growth.

A similar example was presented at a medical anthropology conference. A paper described a gamer named "Malori," a twenty-seven-year-old woman who suffered from crippling depression that had lasted for over a year. Malori attributed her recovery to playing *Call of Cthulhu* in the role of a young Englishman named John "Jack" Hargreaves. Malori was quoted as saying: "Often, very often, I find myself imagining how Jack would handle a situation that I find difficult. Sometimes that helps. Just thinking of him, I gain energy. The character has a certain power."[68]

In 2004, Heather L. Mello conducted a study at Dragon Con, an annual science-fiction and fantasy convention held in Atlanta, Georgia. She surveyed seventy-four gamers about how their characters affected their lives outside of the game. Twelve reported that they sometimes invoked aspects of their character during social interactions or else thought about social interactions in terms of the game, much in the way that Malori described invoking Jack. One gamer described how she used to be shy and reluctant to approach strangers. She explained: "When I tried seeing the situation as a (gaming) encounter, I could often negotiate the situation with more ease and confidence. This has eventually internalized itself so that I can now handle these situations with confidence." Several respondents admitted to using characters to meet the opposite sex. One described how she would draw on her character from *Vampire: The Masquerade* during dates in order to enjoy the character's uninhibited personality.[69]

Of course the characters these gamers invoke have an existence independent of the player. Malori constructed Jack in her imagination, probably drawing on any number of heroic English gentleman from fiction or people she had met in real life. But this process of assembling new symbols from old ones has consequences. Jack proved useful not only as a model *of* a hero but also as a model *for* a hero, allowing him to exert a measurable impact on Malori's life.

ROLE-PLAYING GAMES AND MAGICAL WORLDVIEWS

In some cases players may experience shifts in plausibility structures as the mental freedom provided by role-playing games allows them to think differently about what kinds of ideas might be accepted as real. Moral entrepreneurs contended that *D&D* "leads to occultism" and that casting imaginary spells in the context of a game naturally progresses to a corresponding use of magic outside of the game. This is, of course, inaccurate. No amount of fantasy role-playing will cause a materialist to believe in magic. However, there is a subset of gamers that is engaged in magical practices or otherwise subscribes to a worldview that mainstream culture regards as deviant. This subset raises the question, Do fantasy role-playing games cause some people to believe in magic, or does a belief in magic cause one to gravitate toward fantasy role-playing games? It is a difficult question to answer, but the problem is worth exploring if only to lay to rest decades of claims about role-playing games and occultism. I argue that for a subset of "magical gamers," role-playing games do play an important role in making magical ideas seem plausible. Like the other examples considered here, the reinforcement of a magical worldview is a product of the liminoid state experienced during play and the dual relationship between fantasy and the world of daily life.

The Magical Gamers

Much of what is known about the relationship between role-playing games and magical worldviews is anecdotal. We have already discussed how the real vampire and otherkin communities employed some of the models and vocabulary of role-playing games to think about metaphysical and esoteric problems. Several ethnographies of contemporary magicians and pagans indicate that many people in these communities enjoy *D&D*.[70] Moral entrepreneurs attempting to prove a correlation between fantasy role-playing games and actual occultism sometimes cite the case of Isaac Bonewitz (1949–2010), who was both a gamer and a magician. In the spring of 1968, when Bonewitz was a seventeen-year-old student at UC Berkeley, he decided to satirize evangelical proselytizing on campus by standing on top of a black soapbox with a sign that read, "The Devil's Advocate." He then proceeded to deliver a sermon in praise of the devil while speaking in an affected Southern accent. These antics got him recruited into Anton LaVey's Church of Satan, but he had a falling out with this group and was asked to leave. Bonewitz went on to join the Reformed Druids of North America and became a lifelong pagan.[71] In the 1970s, he became interested in *D&D* but felt Gygax's model of magic was "absurd."[72] So in 1978 he published a book called *Authentic Thaumaturgy: A Professional Occultist on Improving the Realism of Magic Systems in Fantasy Simulating Games*. The book went into two printings, first with Chaosium, and then with Steve Jackson Games. As early as 1980, Christian critics of *D&D* homed in on Bonewitz's book as the "smoking gun" that proved the game was not about imaginary magic but "real occultism."[73]

Details such as this demonstrate a degree of correlation but offer few clues as to causation. Gareth Medway, in his study of Satanic panic, argues that the relationship is entirely coincidental. He interviewed Debbie Gallagher, who won the award of "top role-player in Europe" during a convention in 1994. Gallagher also had an avid interest in esotericism. She got her first Tarot deck at age eleven and played her first game of *D&D* at seventeen. Gallagher explained:

> Occultists I know tend to look at fantasy role-players and see them as failures who can't face reality. The role-players say exactly the same thing about the occultists. Both sides see each other as washed out losers who cannot cope with the real world.[74]

Medway regards this testimony as evidence that moral entrepreneurs are wrong and that there is no causal link between role-playing games and occultism. I am not convinced. Gallagher's description of how occultists and role-players each regard the other as "losers who can't face reality" parallels the way the real vampire community and vampire role-players spoke of each other after the Ferrell murders. No one wants to be regarded as delusional or derivative. Role-players have a vested interest in distancing themselves from occultists in response to the claims of moral entrepreneurs, while occultists desire to be taken seriously and not associated with a game of fantasy.

Barrowcliffe was also interested in both *D&D* and the occult. In his autobiography, he speaks candidly about how his interest in *D&D* was followed by experimentation with psychedelic mushrooms and even experiments with magical rituals based on the writings of Aleister Crowley. Barrowcliffe offers a somewhat different take on the relationship between role-playing games and magic:

> It was hotly debated in the 1980s whether D&D led people to an interest in the occult. It doesn't seem unreasonable to suppose that, if you spend your entire imaginative life caught up with magic, then sooner or later you're going to end up wondering what it might be like to try it out for real.
>
> The opponents of D&D—overwhelmingly American—failed to see that an interest in the occult doesn't arrive out of the blue for most people. I'd been fascinated by tales of witches and wizards from early childhood. From the age of nine I'd been taking out books from the library with titles such as *The History of Witchcraft in England* and *Dion Fortune's Psychic Self Defence* or *Astral Projection.*[75]

In Barrowcliffe's case, fantasy role-playing games seem to have nurtured an interest in magic that was already there. Similarly, Sarah Pike suggested that for some of the pagans she interviewed role-playing games had intensified their interest in magic. She explained:

> If fantasy books introduce children to Neopagan beliefs, then interest in medieval reenactment and popular role-playing games (RPG) such as Dungeons and Dragons carries potential Neopagans deeper into the fold. . . . Neopagan ritual groups seem for some individuals the next logical step from fiction to reality. Both rituals and role-playing games are theatrical and encourage improvisation.

In this account, play—the elements of theatricality and improvisation—serves as an intermediate link between passively consuming popular culture and magical ritual. As a liminoid state, play creates a space in which the possibility of magic can be reassessed. One of Pike's informants explained: "From my childhood experiences, I knew there was something to the occult. I just needed to find WHAT I believed in. For a while I thought I believed in RPG-style magic. Now I know that's not how it works, but it was a starting point for my spiritual journey."[76]

Here again role-playing games provide a context in which plausibility structures can be tested and experimented with.

Role-Playing Games and Interpretive Drift

In the 1980s, anthropologist Tanya Luhrmann conducted a study of modern-day magicians living around London (many of whom enjoyed *D&D*). Luhrmann builds on Huizinga to describe magic as a kind of play in which "belief and make-believe are intertwined," and the magician "plays at magic and understands the play is serious, and the truth of magical theory hovers in limbo between reality and fantasy." She concludes that while modern Western people are generally taught that magic is not real, magicians undergo a series of gradual changes in the way they see the world such that magic comes to seem plausible. She calls this process "interpretive drift" and defines it as "the slow shift in someone's manner of interpreting events, making sense of experience, and responding to the world."[77] Interpretive drift involves "three loosely interlocked transformations" of interpretation, experience, and rationalization. By studying magical traditions, Luhrmann's subjects learned new ways of interpreting the world. While practicing magic, the magicians had phenomenologically significant experiences that the interpretive shifts had prepared them for. These experiences, in turn, inspired greater investment in magical theory and further interpretive shifts. At the same time, magicians also shifted their intellectual habits such that their magical worldview seemed objectively reasonable. Like notes in a chord, the three shifts work together to create a worldview in which the reality of magic comes to seem not only possible but almost self-evident.

Fantasy role-playing games are uniquely suited for facilitating two of these shifts—the interpretive and the rational. Interpretive shifts are facilitated by the dual nature of role-playing games as models of and for the world. Shifts in rationalization are facilitated by the imagination and play. As a liminoid state that exists outside of the ordinary social structure, play entails its own epistemology, which, in some cases, can serve to shelter magical worldviews from rationalist critiques.

Most fantasy role-playing games feature some form of magic. Anyone designing or playing a game must therefore create a model of what magic is and how it works. For players who assume magic exists only in fantasy, these models do not need to be very plausible (thus Gygax's "absurd" presentation of magic). But for those who believe that magic is real (or suspect that it might be), role-playing games provide a kind of mental laboratory in which increasingly plausible models of magic can be developed. Games like *Ars Magica, Mage: The Ascension,* and the writings of Isaac Bonewitz represent attempts at "realistic" models of magic. Like all models, these ideas of magic serve as "continual sources of plausible hypotheses." Realistic models of magic make it possible to interpret events outside the game through a magical worldview.

An example of this appears in the writings of Glenn J. Morris (1944–2006), a self-described energy worker and ninja master. Morris encouraged his students to play *D&D* because it would allow them to understand metaphysics. In his books on martial arts, Morris described elaborate visions he experienced during meditation. He felt his visions were not subjective but represented contact with an alternate reality. Morris suggested that the frames of *D&D* provided a sort of analogue to mystical experiences that might render them understandable. He writes, "Entering the inner world of consciousness is a lot like playing Dungeons and Dragons."[78] Elsewhere he explains: "It would seem D&D is more useful than an easy way to teach kids achievement motivation, strategy, role-playing, and how to use their imaginations. Playing magic users and clerics can be more useful than thieves and fighters for developing survival skills for the Void. Study on that."[79] Here *D&D* provides a way of interpreting the subjective experiences that occur during meditation, ultimately facilitating an esoteric worldview.

Luhrmann suggested that being a magician in the modern world also requires the development of new forms of rationalization. Otherwise, magical worldviews cannot remain plausible in the face of rationalist criticism. For modern magicians, magic is plausible because it operates in an interstitial realm between the imaginary and the real—a state of play. Luhrmann explains:

> Magic gives magicians the opportunity to play—a serious play, but nevertheless a rule-defined separate context in which they identify with their imaginative conceptions, and act out the fantasies and visions of another world. They find their increased capacity for play a great resource, and indeed through the play there are psychotherapeutic benefits from the practice. And there is a remarkable extension of this play structure into the realm of belief. The ideas and theories of magical practice are for magicians both assertions about the real world and "let's pretend" fantasies about strange powers, wizards, and even dragons.[80]

In this model, magic cannot exist unless it is supported by the kind of rich, imaginary worlds depicted in fantasy novels and role-playing games. The magicians Luhrmann studied referred to these imaginary worlds frequently in order to discuss magical ideas in ways that were protected from rational criticism because they were simultaneously literal and metaphorical. She writes:

> Anthropologists have paid relatively little attention to the imagination. This is a mistake, because the neither-true-nor-false status of an imaginative, fiction-laden language can serve a vital role in making culturally peculiar remarks believable, by providing a way in which one can know of the terms and their reference without ever committing oneself to their truth or falsity.[81]

The statement "I am a vampire" is a perfect example the sort of language Luhrmann is describing. On the one hand, this statement invokes all of the associations from *Vampire: The Masquerade* and a hundred other imaginary vampires: a being with supernatural powers, a romantic outsider, a predator, and so on. But the statement "I am a vampire" is meant in neither a strictly literal nor a strictly metaphorical sense. Real vampires know that they are not immortal and, if pressed by rationalist critics, will often say that "vampirism" refers to a health condition not yet recognized by medical science.

This alternative mode of rationalization that Luhrmann describes, in which the difference between fiction and reality is no longer important, is another form of "serious play." However, the type of magical play described by Luhrmann is different from that of fantasy role-playing games. Role-playing games may provide the shared vocabulary, but the frames of reality and fantasy are never blurred. In magical play, these frames are creatively confused.

White Wolf games in particular, with their incredibly detailed mythology, are amenable to this type of magical play. In *A Field Guide to Otherkin*, Lupa recalls:

> Sometimes roleplaying game material gets dragged, piecemeal or wholesale into the bargain. As mentioned earlier, my early explorations into otherkin were all tangled up with RPGs. At the tender young age of seventeen, stuck in a small town with hardly any resources beyond Montague Summers' *The Werewolf*, I was fully convinced that I was a Child of Gaia Philodox straight out of White Wolf's *Werewolf: The Apocalypse*. I counted as friends another were, a vampire, and a faerie-blooded vampire hunter (who somehow never attacked our vampire friend). And, of course, we were at war with a rival group of local vampires and werewolves who never seemed to manifest physically, though we seemed to experience an awful lot of psychic attacks, complete with Salem-witch-trial-style convulsions and panic attacks. Thankfully, I grew out of it pretty quickly.[82]

This testimony is a fascinating account of the sacralization of popular culture, and I am grateful that Lupa has shared it so candidly. White Wolf games gained a sort of reality because they provided the vocabulary through which a magical worldview could be expressed, discussed, and developed.

Lupa was probably never "fully convinced" that she was a creature described in *Werewolf: The Apocalypse*. Instead this belief appears to have been a form of serious play that was meaningful within its own symbolic frame. In the nineteenth century, advocates of the so-called animist theory of religion claimed that human beings have an inherent tendency to assume spirits reside in inanimate objects, and cited the way that children play with dolls as evidence of this claim. Durkheim rejected this argument, pointing out that children's games of imagination are not understood to be "true" in the same manner as religious truth claims. He used the example of a boy playing with a puppet, writing, "So little is he the dupe of his own fiction, that if it suddenly became reality and his puppet bit him, he would be the first astonished."[83] By the same token, if Lupa and her teenage friends had actually encountered an eight-foot-tall werewolf they would probably not have regarded it as a fellow supernatural being but rather as a terrifying alien entity the existence of which could not be reconciled with their understanding of the world.

At the same time, the frame in which Lupa was a Child of Gaia Philodox (a particular type of character from *Werewolf*) was more than a game and real enough to induce panic attacks. It apparently had a level of reality somewhere between that of imagination and the world of daily life. Furthermore, Lupa's point in telling this story is that this sort of "serious play" is quite common. Jon C. Bush and Rod Ferrell drew media attention because they committed crimes while performing their vampire personas, but every high school in America may be home to a teenage vampire or werewolf engaged in this sort of play.[84]

It should be noted that while role-playing games can be powerful tools of meaning-making and shape the way that gamers interpret the world, there is no predetermined end point toward which these shifts are directed. While there is a demonstrable connection between fantasy role-playing games and belief in magic, a player might just as easily conclude that no model of the supernatural seems plausible and become a materialist (a possibility that antigaming crusaders feared as much as occultism). Fantasy role-playing can also support traditional religious views by causing ideas such as a benevolent deity or divine grace to seem more plausible. Michael J. Young of the Christian Gamers Guild argued that magic in fantasy role-playing games is not a catechism of the occult but a kind of "apologetics to the heart" and "a way of undermining disbelief, of subtly suggesting that there is a greater reality undreamt by most."[85] Role-playing games are not sociologically significant because they inculcate a player with a particular worldview but because they can expand the player's worldview in radical and unpredictable ways.

A BRIEF CODA ON COMPUTER GAMES

Almost from the moment role-playing games were developed in the 1970s, programmers began making computer versions of role-playing games. Computer games allow players to experience a form of role-playing without finding a group of players. They also feature increasingly impressive graphics, leading some to suggest that these games now blur the lines between fantasy and reality.[86] Today, far more people play computerized role-playing games than traditional role-playing games. Blizzard Entertainment's *World of Warcraft* is an MMO (massively multiplayer online) role-playing game in which millions of players can create characters and interact with each other, embarking on quests and defeating monsters controlled by a computer. The game introduced many people who had never played *D&D* to game mechanics originally devised by Gygax and Arneson, such as character level, hit points, and armor ratings. When Gygax died, a new software patch of the game was dedicated to him. At its peak, *World of Warcraft* was played by more than 10 million people.[87] Some have suggested that online role-playing games will completely replace traditional role-playing games.[88] David Ewalt suggests the relationship may be cyclical, as computer games introduce new players to traditional role-playing. He writes, "D&D helped create video games; video games almost destroyed D&D; and now video games were leading people back to Dungeons and Dragons."[89]

In his book *eGods,* Bainbridge argues that games like *World of Warcraft* perform a religious function by providing an experience of an enchanted world and inviting players to think about such phenomena as gods, souls, and the afterlife.[90] There is also evidence that some players use online games to explore aspects of their own identity, particularly gender and sexuality. Players can create characters of either gender and sometimes form romantic and sexual relationships with other characters. However, I find it unlikely that computer games can carry the same sociological significance as traditional role-playing games. Computer games do not give players the same sort of mental autonomy or effect the same sort of shifts in plausibility structures.

In 1990, TSR's Harold Johnson said of computer games:

> I think there'll always be a market for computer D&D. Because we're such a mobile society, it's hard to find someone to play with. But it won't supplant the paper game because it's a totally different experience. When you have a living, human Dungeon Master, the game is different every time you play. It's a unique experience that's worth sharing and retelling to other people.[91]

Gygax compared computer games to home movies, and traditional role-playing to Broadway theater. Playing *D&D* with friends was "the finest experience, but relatively small."[92] While serious communities of role-players have formed around online games, more often "role-playing" in a computer game is only a homonym for "role-playing" in the traditional sense. In *World of Warcraft,* it is not uncommon to find characters with names like "UDieNow." These are not characters in any narrative sense, but collections of attributes and numbers. "Role-playing" these characters simply means completing game objectives so as to make them more powerful than some other character. Nothing resembling Malori's transformative experience in creating Jack Hargraves is possible here.

Computer games also limit the agency of the player because, even in the most elaborate games, only a very finite number of actions are possible.[93] One irate gamer wrote, "The whole point of pen-and-paper games, especially D&D, was that you had an open world where you could be almost anyone you wanted to be." Computerized games, he argued, "strip players of this joy."[94] For these reasons, in most computerized role-playing games, playing a character does not entail articulating and reflecting on the world, but is really an exercise in arithmetic as the player seeks to advance through a prewritten narrative by manipulating the mathematical representations of fantasy elements provided within the game.

It is also significant that computer games relieve players of the burden of designing and adjudicating models. The game calculates the results of any action, often using algorithms that are totally unknown to the player. This is convenient because it eliminates the need to roll dice and consult tables. The downside is that if a computer game seems implausible or unfair, the algorithm cannot be negotiated with or revised. To enjoy computer games, players generally accept the alternate reality that is offered and do not compare it with the world of daily life. This effectively sunders the dual relationship between reality and fantasy, eliminating one of the most intellectually satisfying aspects of role-playing games. Pete Wolfendale and Tim Franklin describe the pleasure of revising and negotiating models of reality in role-playing games:

> The real world is real because it *resists* our attempts to understand it. It can always throw something up that forces us to rethink how we look at it. The models we build of it are often incomplete and frequently just wrong. This means that we must constantly *revise* our picture of the world: filling in specific details, tweaking general principles, and resolving inconsistencies. It's this back and forth that makes the process of understanding the world a dynamic one. The fictional worlds we encounter in novels, movies, and similar art-forms activate our capacity to construct a picture of the real world, but only role-playing mimics the *friction* we encounter in bumping up against an autonomous reality. Role-playing presents us with our own power not just to construct a consistent world, but to do so in response to external constraints. The experience of depth is pleasurable because it demonstrates our ability to cope with the *reality* of the world. Deliciously ironic for a medium occasionally accused of escapism.[95]

In computer games this friction between reality and its models is absent. Without it, role-playing games have far less ability to shape the way players think about the world.

Finally, computer games severely reduce the liminoid aspect of role-playing games that is conducive to meaning-making. The conjunctive function of role-playing games is largely absent from computer games, which are often played alone. Online games do feature various modes of interaction, including associations of players or "guilds" that can be socially significant for players. But many online games place heavy emphasis on "player-versus-player" events, the object of which is for players to assert their superiority over others. This is the disjunctive function that Levi-Strauss associated with games, not the conjunctive function of ritual.

In fact, it is not clear that online role-playing games represent true play in the manner described by Huizinga. These games are "persistent" in that time continues to pass in the games whether one is playing them or not. They do not have the same quality of timelessness experienced in ritual and narrative. Instead of occurring outside the ordinary concerns and structure of daily life, games like *World of Warcraft* demand the same rational management of time and other resources as the real world. In his ethnography of *World of Warcraft* players, Ethan Gilsdorf commented that unlike traditional role-players, the online gamers would never "fly their freak flag."[96] That is, online gamers appear far less deviant and more "normal" than their in-person counterparts. This is to be expected from a form of role-playing that has severely compromised the mechanisms by which reality is questioned and new meaning is produced. All of this is not to say that computer games like *World of Warcraft* are not fun or should not be played. In fact, they bring joy to millions of people. However, these games do not have the same ability to challenge worldviews, create meaning, or alter plausibility structures as traditional role-playing games. For the most part, these games truly are "just escapism."

If I were going to be a storyteller for a game of *Mage: The Ascension,* I might design a story in which the players discover that online role-playing games are actually a plot created by the Technocracy. In this story the Technocracy has discovered the potential of role-playing games to challenge traditional paradigms and promote magical worldviews—a potential that threatens their goal of stamping out any rival paradigms of reality. Instead of using BADD's strategy of attempting to censor role-playing games, the Technocracy is craftier and invents a saccharine technological substitute for these games that is easier to play, has impressive graphics, and does not fuel the imagination. Instead of bringing misfits and free spirits together to engage in intellectual colloquy, the online games inspire them to stay at their computers, where they are isolated and more susceptible to the Technocracy's constant propaganda. Of course, the Technocracy is not real, and computer games are not a conspiracy intended to suppress deviance and constrain the interpretation of reality. This is not a serious thesis but an example of the creative arrangement of elements facilitated by a mind at play. However, the fact that I can imagine this scenario demonstrates how the models provided by role-playing games enable us to think about real-world problems in new ways.

CHAPTER 7

How the Imagination Became Dangerous

> Liminality may be for many the acme of insecurity, the break-through of chaos into cosmos, of disorder into order, rather than the milieu of creative interhuman or transhuman satisfactions and achievements.
>
> —Victor Turner, "Liminal to Liminoid in Play, Flow, and Ritual"

> As a society, we have become more and more fascinated with wild fantasy and less and less disciplined about responsibility. We are on a mindless trip created by our unbridled imaginations. Barney is an excellent gauge of where we are headed.
>
> —Dr. Joseph R. Chambers, "Barney: The Purple Messiah"

In May 2013, as I was writing this book, a news story began circulating about a preschool that had allegedly forbidden children to pretend to be superheroes. The story first circulated when a parent posted a letter from the preschool on the website Reddit. The letter began with the headline "Parents We Need Your Help" and contained a picture of the Justice League (Superman, Batman, Wonder Woman, etc.) framed in a red circle with a slash through it. Beneath this image was the following message:

> Recently it has been brought to our attention that the imaginations of our preschool children are becoming dangerously overactive causing injuries within our pre-k community. Although we encourage creative thinking and imaginary play, we do not promote out [*sic*] children hurting one another. Wrestling, Super Hero play, and Monster games will not be permitted here. . . . In addition please monitor the different media that your children may view. The re-enactment of televisions [*sic*] shows/movies are being done during active paly [*sic*] times in school.[1]

Children can be disruptive when they pretend to be superheroes, and there is a small body of literature by child psychologists on superhero play. More than two decades before this incident, Dorothy and Jerome Singer wrote:

> Children like to imitate superheroes they see on television. If they do so, elaborating on the themes they have seen, some imaginative play may result. But in many instances, we see children wearing their Superman or Batman capes (usually a towel fastened by a safety pin) simply running around the nursery school or day-care center knocking down other children's block constructions, bumping into other children, and even hitting some. This kind of perseverative play and subsequent aggression is usually found among our heavier TV watchers.
>
> It is understandable that children want to play Superman, Batman, Spiderman, Wonder Woman or He-Man. Most of the time they feel small, helpless, and dependent on the adults in their lives. A superhero game affords children power and makes them feel magical and strong. [2]

The solution, for Singer and Singer, is not to ban superhero play but to channel the energy into socially acceptable and imaginative games. The parent who posted the letter on Reddit used superhero fantasy to model a moral universe for his son in much the way that Singer and Singer prescribe. In his post, he explained why he was so upset by the preschool:

> It is this constant dialogue of ours [son and parent] regarding superheroes that has allowed us to address concepts such as right and wrong, good and bad, justice and injustice. You can therefore well imagine my anger when my son showed me the flyer with superheroes crossed out. I was livid! It was akin to a religious person (which we are not) finding their deity of choice called into question and ridiculed. . . . This is nothing more than a bully who has her own issues with superheroes and is trying to force her views down the throat of others.[3]

Significantly, the parent is raising his child in a secular household and giving superheroes a deliberately religious function. The situation at the preschool demonstrates two starkly different responses to imaginative play: what for some is an exploration of the self and values is for others a danger that must be stamped out.

The media was sympathetic to the parent's characterization of the day-care providers as bullies. One site ran the headline "Preschool Bans Superhero Play, Imagination, Fun."[4] And yet similar cases were occurring all over the country. In Loveland, Colorado, second-grader Alex Evans was suspended for tossing an imaginary grenade into an imaginary box. Alex was playing a game of make-believe called "Rescue the World." The box contained a terrible evil that his grenade destroyed before it could contaminate the world. The school was concerned that this game violated its policy prohibiting weapons, whether "real or play." In a television interview Alex told reporters, "I can't believe I got dispended!" Not only could he not pronounce his punishment, but he could not understand why he was being disciplined for something that was only imaginary. In Pennsylvania a five-year-old was suspended for talking about a toy gun that fired soap bubbles, and a fifth grader was searched in front of her classmates for bringing a piece of paper that resembled a gun. In Maryland, a boy received a two-day suspension for biting a Pop-Tart into the shape of a gun. (Upon hearing of this, the NRA awarded the boy a lifetime membership.)[5]

Much of this irrational behavior can be attributed to the massacre at Sandy Hook Elementary School in December 2012, in which a lone gunman shot twenty children and six educators. This was followed by an additional five school shootings between December 2012 and February 2013. But these tragedies alone are not sufficient to explain a crackdown on symbolic representations of weapons that exist only in the form of paper or Pop-Tarts or entirely in the imagination. These shootings seem to have a triggered a deeply embedded fear that the imaginative play is somehow threatening and must be controlled.

Psychoanalysts such as Freud and Jean Piaget claimed that make-believe was a sign that young children are unable to discern between fiction and truth. By the early twentieth century, some parents suggested that fairy tales not be read to children because fiction was a form of "lying" that would hinder their understanding of the world.[6] These concerns were always unfounded. Durkheim pointed out that children can discern fantasy from reality, with his hypothetical example of a child being bitten by his puppet. Similarly, Tolkien argued that children approach fantasy with an "appetite for wonder" that is often mistaken for belief. For instance, if a child asks whether a fantastic story is "true," this may be an attempt to ask what genre of story it is and not evidence of an inability to determine what is plausible.[7] Durkheim and Tolkien are now supported by cognitive scientists, who have found that children as young as two can discern fantasy from reality quite well. In fact, this is obvious upon empirical observation. When children are playing make-believe they give visible cues such as giggles and dramatic exaggerations indicating that the make-believe is not real. Alison Gopnik explained:

> For young children, however, the imaginary worlds seem just as important and appealing as the real ones. It's not, as scientists used to think, that chil-

> dren can't tell the difference between the real world and the imaginary world. It's just that they don't see any particular reason for preferring to live in the real one.[8]

Conversely, adults are not entirely able to divorce imagination from reality. Psychologist Paul Rozin conducted an experiment in which adults were asked to fill a bottle with tap water and then apply a label that read "cyanide." Adults refused to drink from the bottle, even though they had positive knowledge it was not really cyanide.[9] This experiment points to the heart of the matter: in the alarm over imaginary weapons, as with the panic over role-playing games, it was not the children but the *adults* whose response indicated a failure (or perhaps a refusal) to differentiate between imagination and reality. Freud described thought as a form of "trial action" that allows people to explore different possible courses of action without suffering any consequences. Imagining actions empowers us to make better decisions. However, on playgrounds across America, the imagination is not privileged as a separate frame of reality. In the era of school shootings, there has been an attempt to impose consequences on what children imagine.

Seven-year-old Alex expressed complete bewilderment that grown-ups could not distinguish between a real and imaginary grenade, just as many young *D&D* enthusiasts could not understand why parents thought *D&D* magic was "real." Of course, if Alex's grenade had been real, the response would not have been a suspension but a SWAT team. Still, the suspension indicates that the imaginary grenade was real to school officials in a way that it was not for Alex. Somehow, banishing imaginary weapons was expected to mitigate the danger of real weapons.

The panic over role-playing games was an extreme example of a larger pattern in which moral entrepreneurs ignore the frame of fiction and treat imaginary symbols and narratives as reality. In his investigation, William Dear obsessed over the contents of Dallas Egbert's fantasy life to the exclusion of numerous, more tangible factors. Occult crime experts such as Patricia Pulling insisted that the occultism depicted in role-playing games was not fiction but "real." However, it was conservative evangelical critics who brought this line of thought to its ultimate conclusion, arguing that when players imagine monsters, they are actually having a supernatural encounter with literal demons. Making this claim sundered any meaningful distinction between imagination and reality.

Several observers have noted that there appears to be a form of projection at work here. As with Alex and his imaginary grenade, it is the critics and not the players who seem to be struggling to negotiate between frames of reality. In *Lure of the Sinister* Gareth Medway writes of the panic over role-playing games:

> Do children who play monopoly grow up to be property speculators? Does chess foster racial disharmony by setting up white against black? Because anti-Satanists cannot distinguish fantasy from reality, does that mean the rest of the population are similarly afflicted?[10]

The question Medway does not ask is *why* the anti-Satanists appear to confuse fantasy and reality. This is not a simple case of confusion over frames. Moral entrepreneurs understand that objectionable material is *intended* as fiction. Instead, they refuse to regard the imaginary as imaginary. How did this suspicion of the imagination arise?

I offer three insights into this question. First, the critics of role-playing games demonstrate a general lack of competence when it comes to understanding and interpreting the metacommunicative frames of meanings employed in fantasy and play. Anti-role-playing-game literature generally resists any notion of context and implies that everything must be "true" in the same way. The premises of fiction and games are not regarded as distinct from claims made about the world of everyday life, particularly if this fiction contains any trace of magic or the supernatural. From this perspective, nothing can ever be "just pretend."

This refusal to let fiction be fiction is closely linked to the idea of biblical literalism promoted by the New Christian Right. According to a Gallup poll, in 1980—the year in which Dallas Egbert committed suicide—40 percent of the American public claimed to believe that the Bible is "the actual reported word of God, and is to be taken literally, word for word."[11] Biblical literalism assumes that narratives are either literally true or else they are lies, heresy, or otherwise without value. This way of thinking is not a return to a pre-Enlightenment worldview, as some might imagine, but a thoroughly *modern* perspective. Biblical literalism emerged as a response to modernist claims that the Bible is "a myth." It collapsed the multiplicity of meanings that the Bible had traditionally held in order to argue that the scripture is "true" in the same way as scientific theories. By conceding to the modernist assumption that stories are only worthwhile if they are true in a historical and scientific sense, biblical literalists were left poorly equipped to analyze the significance of fantasy, which contains symbolic significance despite being imaginary.

Second, fantasy worlds are threatening because they are meaningful despite being invented, and therefore imply that other meaningful worldviews might be similarly factitious. Beneath the religious attack on role-playing games there lurks a fear that Christianity could also be a socially constructed fantasy world. This fear is directly connected to the intolerance for multiple forms of truth. From the literalist perspective, if biblical narratives are not true in a literal, modernist sense, then no other meaning they may have is of value.

The third insight is more general. It is in the interest of any hegemonic institution, religious or otherwise, to discourage imagination. Hegemony can be resisted only if we can imagine new possibilities. In this sense, fantasy role-playing games, along with novels, film, and other imaginary worlds, provide mental agency. Moral entrepreneurs interpreted this agency as subversion and a deliberate attempt to undermine traditional values. While fantasy is not an inherent threat to tradition, as long as humans possess imagination, tradition will never be secure. It is for this reason that fiction and fantasy have been regarded as especially dangerous in the hands of those members of society deemed most important to control, such as children, women, and adolescents.

THE IMAGINATION AND THE DEMONIC

In order to examine deeper structural issues behind the New Christian Right's attack on the imagination and fantasy, it is necessary to first examine the stated reasons that imaginary worlds are objectionable and dangerous. Imaginary narratives have long been regarded with suspicion. In *The Republic* Plato explained why playwrights and poets would be banished from his ideal society. While he conceded that mimetic arts are needed for purposes of education, he claimed that poetry and especially drama pervert the audience. Moral people should strive to control their passions, and poetry and drama only foster them.[12] Plato's concerns were not so different from those raised by Thomas Radecki, who claimed that television and *D&D* corrupt audiences by "desensitizing" them to violence. However, religious critics of fantasy role-playing games made a claim that Plato never made: that fantasy games are not, in fact, fantasy. Many religious critics even claimed that playing fantasy role-playing games led to possession and other supernatural consequences. The claim that the fictitious magic and demons in role-playing games are somehow "real" frequently develops into a discussion of whether Christians can tolerate any form of fantasy or fiction. In an essay arguing that *D&D* is unbiblical, Elliot Miller writes:

> When we look hard at the implications of this question, we find that the root issue we are dealing with is whether it is justifiable for us to create imaginary worlds where some things are different than (and thus, inevitably, sometimes contrary to) the real world which has been created by God. Do the likes of C.S. Lewis, J.R.R. Tolkien, Charles Williams, and contemporary authors such as Robert Siegel, have the right (on the level of imagination) to create a universe to some extent different than the one in which we live?[13]

Many Christian critics claim that the fantasy worlds of Lewis and Tolkien are acceptable but that other forms of fantasy are dangerous. However, their explanations as to why this is so are inconsistent, suggesting that their true concerns remain unstated.

In *Stairway to Hell: The Well-Planned Destruction of Teens,* published by Chick Publications, author Rick Jones describes a study on *D&D* conducted by the Christian Broadcasting Network. This "study" was actually an episode of *The 700 Club* in which game designer Gali Sanchez explained that the *D&D* villain Moloch is also a biblical personage. Jones writes:

> They concluded that D&D does contain authentic occult materials. Rituals, magic spells, charms, names of demons, etc. were all **authentic.** They said a list of names of demons and devils that were in a new D&D book kept showing up in the Bible.
>
> The conclusion of the study should send shivers up and down the spine of every D&D playing teenager. They found that D&D is **"not fantasy."**[14]

Several evangelical writers went even further to argue that there is no distinction between merely imagining demons and literal encounters with demons. Bob Larson explains:

> The truth is that Dungeons and Dragons guides participants into a world of nonmaterial entities, forces, and spirits. Obviously, if such beings exist, the line of demarcation between fantasy and reality can easily be blurred. . . . There is no assurance that conjuring an imagined entity will prevent a real spirit from responding![15]

Rebecca Brown, whose books are also published by Chick Publications, argues that the imagination is an inherently supernatural and dangerous faculty:

> What people don't realize at first, is that these monsters are actually real demons. The deities they serve are also demons. What they think they are visualizing in their minds, they are in actuality beginning to see in the spirit world. The better they become at "seeing" the game, the more in-tune they are with the spirit world. Imagination is a key stepping stone to contact with the spirit world.[16]

The suspicion of the imagination expressed by these critics is rooted in their understanding of the New Testament. Christian critics of fantasy role-playing games often cite 2 Corinthians 10:4–5, "We destroy arguments and every proud obstacle raised up against the knowledge of God, and we take every thought captive to obey Christ."[17] The Greek word *logismous* is more accurately translated as "arguments" or "speculations." However, these critics typically prefer the King James Bible and its translation "imaginations."[18] For Larson and Brown, Paul calls on Christians to destroy imaginations.

These arguments also draw support from the antitheses in the Sermon on the Mount. When Bob Larson read the pamphlet "Games Don't Kill," which argued that imagining immorality does not lead to actual immorality, he countered that this was "an unreserved denial of the teachings of Jesus Christ" and cited Jesus's teaching in Matthew that whoever looks at a woman with lust is guilty of adultery in his heart.[19] Larson does not quite connect the Gospels to the pamphlet's argument. Jesus did not say that someone who looks at a woman with lust is going to commit adultery. Instead he said that a fantasy of adultery is just as sinful as the real thing. However, Larson's use of the antitheses does demonstrate that Christian tradition has long assumed that there are moral consequences to what we imagine.

William Schnoebelen also cites Matthew in explaining why he crusades against role-playing games. He writes:

> I am frequently told to "get a life" or write about something more important than D&D, like social justice or world hunger. The devil would sure like that.
>
> It needs to be emphasized that a spiritual deception which draws people away from Jesus Christ is **much** more dangerous than . . . people of dying of starvation. . . . But remember what the Lord Jesus said:
>
> "*And fear not them which kill the body, but are not able to kill the soul: but rather fear him which is able to destroy both body and soul in hell.*"–*Matt. 10:28.*[20]

If we accept Schnoebelen's premises, then his argument is logical. If saving people from eternal damnation is infinitely more important than worldly suffering, and if *D&D* leads people to damnation, then crusading against *D&D* should take priority over social justice. This is a classic example of what Max Weber called an otherworldly attitude toward salvation.

But while the idea that merely imagining evil is as bad as committing evil has a precedent in the New Testament, in application this becomes untenable almost immediately. Brandon Cooke explains the problem in his essay "It's OK to Be Evil in Your Head":

> It's highly doubtful that any half-sensible religion will condemn the mere *imagining* of certain things, since, it seems the imagination is active in the process of language comprehension. For instance, the Old Testament condemns the practice of certain kinds of magic. But in understanding those passages, we can't help but imagine what's being described. Indeed, we must if we are to genuinely comprehend the passage at all! Imagine, then, how absurd it would be to say "Practicing magic is strictly forbidden. So is thinking about practicing magic." I'm afraid you've probably just violated that second rule.[21]

As Cooke points out, any model or symbolic order by which one might make sense of the world—including language—begins with the imagination. There can be no mental concept of evil unless it is first imagined. This is a problem for authors like Larson, Brown, and Schnoebelen whose theology and politics are firmly located in "the religion of fear." Religious literature attacking role-playing games is often festooned with pentagrams and descriptions of human sacrifice. By the theology these critics employ, the artist who created the comic strip *Dark Dungeons* was actively engaged in Satanic occultism. An artist could draw the evil Ms. Frost—the teacher, dungeon master, and priestess of Diana—only if he encountered a demonic force in the spiritual realm, visualizing it well enough to give it material form through his art.[22]

For this reason, more mainstream Christian critics of *D&D* concede that it is acceptable to imagine evil in at least some circumstances. In a more nuanced Christian critique of *D&D*, Presbyterian theologians Peter Leithart and George Grant ask whether a Christian actor can play Iago or Mephistopheles.[23] Much like Plato, they conclude that mimicking evil is acceptable for educational purposes, but discourage fictional narratives that appear to celebrate corruption. This leads to a more sensible discussion of what kinds of fantastic narratives might be acceptable. Most, but not all, Christians who oppose fantasy role-playing games approve of Lewis, Tolkien, and even traditional fairy tales. The original version of Jack Chick's tract *Dark Dungeons* contained a footnote to the text in which the preacher urges the congregation to go home and burn *D&D* books and any other occult books. The footnote read: "Including C. S. Lewis and Tolkien, both of which can be found in occult bookstores." However, current versions of the tract contain no such reference. It is easy to see how a conservative evangelical like Jack Chick would assume that if *D&D* is Satanic, then Lewis and Tolkien must be Satanic as well. And yet most anti-*D&D* crusaders praise these writers. Leithart and Grant urge their readers to fill their homes with Lewis and Tolkien as well as Shakespeare, Milton, and Chaucer. The arguments of the moderates, who advocate Tolkien and Lewis while condemning fantasy role-playing games, are more revealing than those of religious critics who condemn all fantasy as demonic. Moderate religious critics struggle to articulate why wizards, magic, and demonic antagonists are acceptable in some fantasy narratives but not in others. The reasons they cite are inconsistent, suggesting the presence of hidden fears and desires underlying their suspicion of the imagination.

Christian critics John Ankerberg and John Weldon claim the difference between Tolkien and *D&D* is a moral one: that in the narratives of Tolkien and Lewis good wins, while in fantasy role-playing games "good does not triumph over evil."[24] There are two problems with this argument. First, in games like *D&D* good does win the majority of the time. While players have the freedom to run games where evil triumphs, TSR's Code of Ethics stated explicitly that evil is not be portrayed in a positive light. Furthermore, the innocent children that writers like Ankerberg and Weldon claim to protect would presumably not enjoy a game where the good guys always lose. Second, this argument ignores the fact that The Chronicles of Narnia and the Lord of the Rings are finished narratives, whereas role-playing games are methods of producing narratives. Tolkien's eucatastrophe is possible only if evil is a credible threat at the beginning of the story. To claim that role-playing games are bad because evil always wins is a bit like claiming that a typewriter is bad because it can be used only to write evil stories.

Another argument addresses why magic is acceptable in Lewis and Tolkien but is considered dangerous "occultism" in other fiction. Critics sometimes claim Tolkien and Lewis portray magic being wielded only by supernatural beings and not by human protagonists. Leithart and Grant explain:

> As Lewis' and Tolkien's mentor, G.K. Chesterton pointed out, the genius of fairy tales lies in the fact that the hero is a normal person in an abnormal world, an innocent among ravaging nether beasts. Make the hero abnormal and you destroy the tension and interest (not to mention the moral focus) of the entire narrative. There's all the difference in the world between Hansel and a dwarf cleric who casts spells. Both may meet a witch, but they react differently. The dwarf covets the witch's power; Hansel just wants a chance to shove her into the oven.[25]

I find this moral praise for Hansel remorselessly burning his enemies in an oven disturbing. It certainly contradicts Leithart and Grant's argument that fairy-tale protagonists must be innocents. More importantly, the claim about abnormal heroes is a strange one for a Christian writer to make. Jesus and the apostles—the model on which the cleric character class is based—wielded superhuman powers. Jesus is a highly "abnormal" protagonist, but no Christian can claim this destroys the moral focus of the New Testament.

This argument was used again in response to J.K. Rowling's Harry Potter series. In his book *Harry Potter and the Bible: The Menace behind the Magick* Richard Abanes demonstrates a detailed knowledge of Middle Earth in arguing why Gandalf is a good role model for children but Harry Potter is not. First, Abanes argues that Narnia and Middle Earth are fantasy worlds, while Hogwarts is in contemporary England. Thus, Rowling suggests that magic is "real" in a way that Lewis and Tolkien do not. Second, Abanes explains that in the Lord of the Rings, magic is not a series of rituals that human beings can learn but rather a power wielded only by supernatural beings such as elves. Gandalf and the other wizards are not actually learned mortals but angelic beings called the Maiar.[26]

Lewis and Tolkien shared Abanes's religious objection to magic and would not have wanted their readers to believe in the efficacy of magical rituals. However, in making these arguments, Abanes distorts his data. In Rowling's novels, wizards and witches are a special race of superhumans not unlike Tolkien's elves and Maiar. Just as in Middle Earth, ordinary human beings (Muggles) cannot learn magic through any amount of study. Furthermore, Lewis's Narnia is not a separate world but a parallel one that can be accessed not only through a magical wardrobe but by any number of methods. An impressionable child is just as likely to seek the entrance to Narnia as to Hogwarts.[27]

These arguments are a cover for what is actually at stake. The true reason that these critics regard the fantasy and magic of Lewis and Tolkien as acceptable is not that their stories are inherently more moral than other forms of fantasy or that their portrayal of magic can somehow be divorced from the negative associations of occultism for evangelicals. These critics accept Lewis and Tolkien because these writers were avowed Christians and their faith is reflected in their stories. Why, then, do Christian critics of *D&D* not just say this?

The erotics of fear are apparent in these critiques. Leithart and Grant as well as Abanes clearly *enjoy* fantasy. In fact, all of these critics must be drawn to fantasy at some level or they would direct their energy toward other issues. And yet fantasy is somehow inherently threatening. The real threat of fantasy is not that it depicts evil as triumphant or that slight variations in the portrayal of magic will lure audiences into demonic occultism. Fantasy is threatening because it provides a means of "beyonding." The imaginary worlds of fantasy novels and role-playing games allow audiences to mentally step outside their own worldview and look back on it. Not only does this kind of agency threaten the power of hegemonic movements; it also inspires doubts in the moral entrepreneurs themselves. As Jason Bivins wrote, "The religions of fear's most pressing concern is that the monster may lurk within as well as without."[28] For these reasons, the door to fantasy can be safely opened only if it is certain that the other side is still thoroughly Christian. However, to simply state that fantasy is dangerous because it leads to critical thinking would reveal the presence of hegemony and thereby undermine it. The arguments presented by Ankerberg, Weldon, Leithart, Grant, and Abanes serve as a cover to conceal the mechanisms of hegemony as well as their own doubts about how indulging their love of fantasy might challenge their faith.

To truly prevent the beyonding effect of fiction, it is necessary to claim that the imaginary worlds are not, in fact, imaginary but another part of reality. The moral panic over role-playing games employed a hermeneutic of fantasy that framed imaginary worlds not only as real but as part of a demonic threat. This hermeneutic has a long genealogy in the West dating back at least to the Puritans.

HOW FICTION CEASED TO BE FICTION

The New Christian Right has always been suspicious that popular culture may be a form of subversion. In the 1980s Christian critics of role-playing games often discussed even the most banal aspects of popular culture as evidence of a surge of occultism. Mike Warnke objected to such films as *Ghost* starring Patrick Swayze and *Ghost Dad* starring Bill Cosby as glorifying the occult.[29] Leithart and Grant indicted children's cartoons such as *The Smurfs* and *Carebears* as part of the "same mentality" as fantasy role-playing games.[30] Frequently this material was portrayed as not only immoral but part of a subversive conspiracy or demonic inspiration. Rus Walton explains:

> Values clarification, "sensitivity training," and role-playing, have been going on in the United States for decades. Evidence continues to suggest that it is part of a program to remold American traditions and values through

> generational-revision (Judges 2:10). The seemingly innocuous games of "fantasy" would seem to be a part of that strategy.[31]

Nicky Cruz, an evangelical who believes that *D&D* is part of a conspiracy of criminal Satanism, objected to the film *E.T.* because it evoked affection for a creature that Cruz regarded as a hideous demon:

> I also believe that Spielberg is being manipulated by evil forces that he cannot begin to understand to *condition* human minds to blindly accept some terrible things: That terrible ugliness is beautiful. . . . Satan desires to pervert beauty and majesty so that we will accept mediocre and lousy. I believe the artist Picasso was used in this same way. Just look at his effect on the world of art. Suddenly, silly scrawls and misshapen hideousness was extremely "sophisticated" and impressive.[32]

Significantly these critiques do not regard it as relevant that *Ghost Dad, The Smurfs, E.T.,* and *D&D* are works of fiction and are interpreted as such by their audiences. In fact, Walton encloses the term "fantasy" in scare quotes.

The imagination is a universal human faculty, and very young children create imaginary worlds to supplement their own. Yet the Christian critics of role-playing games developed a hermeneutic that sunders the distinction between real and imaginary.[33] This hermeneutic collapses metacommunicative frames and flattens the symbolic order into a single realm wherein symbolic expression, imaginative play, and trial action become almost impossible. The development of this hermeneutic, in which fiction can no longer be fiction, has a long history in the West. It began in the early modern period with the Protestant Reformation and its notion that the Bible is "clear as well as truthful." The Puritans desired "solidness" and expressed suspicion of the imaginary when it came to Christianity. The Enlightenment severely aggravated the problem with its insistence that valid truth could be gained only through reason and empirical observation. While the romantics rejected the Enlightenment's exaltation of reason, many theologians accepted it and sought to frame the Bible as a set of empirical data. In the nineteenth century, the attack on the imagination received further support from capitalism. Victorians regarded make-believe as unproductive and sought to discourage it in their children. Finally, the early twentieth century saw the rise of fundamentalism. By the end of the century the idea of biblical inerrancy was widespread. Christians who subscribed to this view had few resources for thinking about fiction and fantasy as anything other than delusion, heresy, or demonic machinations.

Programs of Truth

Karen Armstrong frames religious fundamentalism as a confusion between two types of truth: *mythos* and *logos*. *Logos* is logical, discursive, and scientific reasoning. *Mythos*, according to Armstrong, consists of sacred stories that are regarded as true but are not taken literally. She argues that they serve as "an ancient form of psychology." The two are meant to be complimentary. *Mythos* cannot cure diseases, develop new technologies, or help human beings adapt to their environment, while *logos* cannot answer existential questions or discover meaning in human suffering. Fundamentalism, in Armstrong's model, represents a failure to distinguish between *mythos* and *logos*. The claim that the creation stories of Genesis are comparable to the findings of geologists, evolutionary biologists, and astrophysicists is an attempt to use *mythos* as if it were *logos*.[34] Some critics have objected to Armstrong's formulation, noting that there are numerous cases of ancient peoples taking action as if their myths are literally true.[35] Likewise, the claim that ancient people regarded their sacred stories as psychoanalysis is anachronistic. However, the language of *mythos* and *logos* is useful because it acknowledges that most cultures have multiple criteria of "truth" and employ different strategies for negotiating between different kinds of truth. Armstrong is correct that fundamentalism represents a collapse of two different frames of meaning.

In his book *Did the Greeks Believe Their Myths?* classics scholar Paul Veyne outlines what he calls "programs of truth." These are the socially constructed criteria by which every culture, from epoch to epoch, negotiates ideas of truth and falsehood. This is a more nuanced approach for thinking about how such categories as "reality," "imagination," and "illusion" change over time. Veyne argues that while most Greeks did not doubt their myths, they were not regarded as "real" in the same way as ordinary reality. He writes, "A Greek put the gods 'in heaven,' but he would have been astounded to see them in the sky."[36] Thus, myth was originally understood to be "true" within its own context, which was situated beyond the alternatives of truth and falsehood.

Veyne concludes that people understand the world through a "plurality of modalities of belief." People hold different kinds of beliefs, supported by different criteria of how they can be known. These can often be conflicting. Veyne cites the example of the Dorze people of Ethiopia who believe the leopard is a Christian and observes the fast days of the Coptic Church. But on fast days the Dorze are still wary of leopards. In one sense they believe the leopard is a Christian, and in a different sense they believe leopards are always dangerous predators.[37] To confound these two types of belief could potentially result in being mauled.

While Greek historians and philosophers did not necessarily regard myth as psychoanalysis, they developed programs of truth to explore in what sense myths are "true." Several interpretations were developed: myths occurred in a fantastic epoch that cannot be judged by modern criteria; they contain historical truths that have been distorted over the centuries; they contain allegorical and moral lessons, and so on. The ancient Greeks never assumed that myths had no value because they were not literally true.

Christian tradition has developed different programs of truth over its 2,000-year history. Many of the truth claims of Christianity, such as the divinity of Christ, are taken literally. Only a minority of modern Christians assume metaphorical interpretations of such claims. However, the imaginary—that which is true only symbolically—has traditionally held a place of importance in Christianity. There are several examples of this from medieval and early modern Europe. In the *Divine Comedy*, Dante suggests the imagination comes from God:

> O fantasy (*imaginativa*), that reav'st us oft away
> So from ourselves that we remain distraught
> Deaf though a thousand trumpets round us bray,
>
> What moves thee when the senses show thee naught?
> Light moves thee, formed in Heaven, by will maybe
> Of Him who sends it down, or else self-wrought.[38]

In the sixteenth century, Saint Ignatius of Loyola wrote *Spiritual Exercises* as a course for Christians to cultivate a closer relationship with God. The imagination plays an important role in the exercises, and participants are encouraged to cultivate a vivid imagination. At times, Ignatius even prescribes a kind of role-playing. For instance, in an exercise intended to cultivate a greater awareness of sin, he describes imagining himself as a prisoner in chains or that he is "a knight who stands before his king and his whole court, shamed and humiliated because he has grievously offended him from whom he received numerous gifts and favors."[39] Ignatius also finds value in imagining the demonic. At one point in the exercises, participants are instructed to "imagine the leader of all the enemy in that great plain of Babylon. He is seated on a throne of fire and smoke, in aspect horrible and terrifying."[40]

For Ignatius, there are consequences to the mental realities of the imagination, but they are not the same as action. Entertaining evil thoughts is not a sin, but deriving pleasure from such thoughts is. Planning to act on evil thoughts is a mortal sin, and actually acting on evil thoughts is an even graver mortal sin.[41] The purpose of these mental exercises is not to achieve some sort of literal contact with the spirit realm but to cultivate discernment (*discretio*). Like Dante, Ignatius regards the imagination as a sacred faculty to be used for constructing a cognitive map of a moral universe. Imagination leads to discernment, with which Christians can align their thoughts and actions more closely to the will of God. In this program of truth, imaginary things are not the same as real things, and yet they have spiritual value.

The Puritans may have been the first Christians to raise doubts that the imagination holds any spiritual value. Puritans repeatedly attacked the theater, leading to bans on theaters in both England and the American colonies. The suspicion of anything that lacked "solidness" extended even to metaphor. John Bunyan responded to these concerns in his apology for *Pilgrim's Progress*, in which he defends the use of metaphor to preach Christian truths. Bunyan justifies the imagination by pointing out that parables and metaphors were used by Jesus as well as by the Hebrew prophets:

> Some men with feigned words, as dark as mine,
> Make truth to spangle, and its Rays to shine.
> But they want solidness; speak man thy mind;
> They drown'd the weak. Metaphors make us blind.
> ....
> By Metaphors I speak? Were not God's Laws
> His Gospel-Laws in olden times held forth
> By Types, Shadows and Metaphors?[42]

The Enlightenment and the Need for Evidence

Bunyan could defend the imagination using scripture. However, the Enlightenment brought about an entirely new program of truth that held serious consequences for the Christian West. Veyne cites the treatise "Des Origin des Fables" (1724) by Bernard Fontenelle as a watershed moment in how the West negotiated truth and falsehood. For the Greeks, criticizing myth had never been about proving myths were false but discovering their truthful basis. Fontenelle was the first to assert that myths have no value whatsoever, not even as allegory. He wrote,

"Let us not seek anything else in fable but the history of the errors of the human spirit."[43] "Fable" became a serious slur among Enlightenment thinkers who were suspicious of anyone willfully indulging in fiction.

With the Enlightenment came the Deists, who generally rejected the authority of scripture or any form of "revealed religion." Thomas Paine's publication of *An Age of Reason* in 1795 persuaded many that the authority of scripture was under attack. In *A Brief Retrospect of the Eighteenth Century* (1803), Princeton theologian Samuel Miller wrote, "There was never an age in which so many deliberate and systematic attacks were made on Revealed Religion, through the medium of pretended science, as in the last."[44] Although the Deists were small in number, they had a disproportionate influence because their attack on biblical revelation forced Christian theologians to frame their beliefs in terms of evidence.[45]

Like the ancient Greeks, some theologians responded that Christian stories are true allegorically if not historically. The English theologian Thomas Woolston offered such an interpretation in his *Discourses on the Miracles of our Savior* (1727–29). Woolston claimed that his goal was not to deny Christianity but to restore the ancient "mystical" way of reading biblical text. In Armstrong's terms, he sought to present the Gospels as *mythos* rather than *logos*. For doing so, he was convicted of blasphemy and died in prison. Far more theologians responded by claiming that the authority of scripture could be proven empirically. As early as 1702, Cotton Mather published *A Discourse Proving that the Christian Religion is the Only True Religion,* directed at Deists. In 1759 Ezra Stiles, who would go on to become president of Yale, wrote, "The evidences of Revelation in my opinion are nearly as demonstrative as Newton's Principia."[46]

Such claims represented a new program of truth for Christian theology. In the second century, Tertullian wrote of the resurrection of Christ, "Certum est, quia impossible est" (It is certain, because it is impossible). In doing so, Tertullian refused to apply the discursive reasoning of *logos* to the Gospels. By contrast, eighteenth-century theologians, in attempting to show that the Bible could be proven empirically, tacitly consented to the epistemology of the Enlightenment. By fighting the Deists on their own terms, they further entrenched the idea that only empirical data holds spiritual value.

The Suspicion of Novels

By the eighteenth century the contempt for "fable" had extended to the arts. Some of the most educated minds of the day warned of the corrupting influence of a new form of fictional narrative—the novel. This move engendered contempt for those who read novels as well as concerns that indulgence in fantasy could impair the mind. Samuel Johnson, the first president of King's College (now Columbia University), renewed Plato's concerns about the arts. He argued that if readers mentally participate in the adventures of morally questionable people, they will gradually adopt questionable morals themselves.[47] Samuel Miller wrote an essay entitled "On Novel Reading" in which he warned, "The rage for novel reading, so extensively prevalent, cannot fail of being regarded with deep concern by every well informed and reflecting Christian philanthropist." Many of BADD's arguments against *D&D* are present in this essay. Like Plato, Miller warned that novels encourage immoral behavior. He described them as seductive, immoral, and "ingenious apologists for the most atrocious crimes." But most significantly, he warned that novels overstimulate the imagination and erode the capacity for reason. In his words they "excite a greater fondness for the production of imagination and fancy than for sober reasoning and the practical investigations of wisdom."[48]

A decade later, Thomas Jefferson, who once stated, "I cannot live without books," called novels "a mass of trash." For Jefferson, the purpose of reading was to gain a better understanding of reality, and attending to the fictional worlds of novels was at best a distraction from this goal. In a letter from 1818, he described novels as a poison that infects the mind, producing "a bloated imagination, sickly judgment, and disgust toward all the real business of life."[49]

Female novel readers were believed to be especially susceptible to this sort of poison. In 1798 the editor of *Weekly Magazine* opined:

> Novels not only pollute the imaginations of young women, but likewise give them false ideas of life, which too often make them act improperly; owing to the romantic turn of thinking they imbibe from their favorite studies. They read of characters which never existed, and never can exist . . . it requires more discernment than is to be found in youth to separate the evil from the good . . . the evil steals imperceptibly into her heart, while she thinks she is reading sterling morality.[50]

It is significant that these opponents of fiction were not afraid that *they* might confuse fantasy and reality. This was always framed as a danger for some other class of people.

One eighteenth-century novel became the focus of a panic that anticipated twentieth-century claims about the dangers of popular culture. In 1774, Goethe published *The Sorrows of Young Werther* about a young man who commits suicide when he can no longer bear the pain of unrequited love. The novel was quite popular in Europe, and it was soon rumored that young men were imitating Werther's suicide. In one of his letters, Goethe wrote, "My friends . . . thought that they must transform poetry into reality, imitate a novel like this in real life and, in any case, shoot themselves; and what occurred at first among a few took place later among the general public." Goethe's novel was banned in Italy, Leipzig, and Copenhagen out of fear that it would inspire further deaths. Today there is a body of psychological literature on the so-called Werther effect, a theory that the depiction of suicides (either real or fictional) through mass media will inspire further suicides. Larson endorsed the Werther effect in his book *Extreme Evil: Kids Killing Kids,* which attributes the Columbine Massacre to violent movies, rock music, and *D&D*. However, modern research on suicide suggests that suicide comes about through a complex matrix of factors that often confounds the public's desire for a simple causal explanation.[51]

Three years after *The Sorrows of Young Werther,* Goethe wrote a play entitled *Lila* to honor the birthday of a Weimar duchess. The play revolves around a baroness named Lila who suffers from pathological melancholy. She has retreated into a fantasy world and no longer recognizes her own family or husband. A doctor cures her madness by recruiting family members to dress as beings from Lila's fantasy, including faeries, ogres, and a demon. By playing along with her delusions her family is able to lead her through a heroic quest, at the end of which she is restored to sanity. *Lila* anticipated nineteenth-century claims that women are inherently prone to confusing fantasy and reality. It also presents an early form of psychoanalysis that anticipates Rona Jaffe's *Mazes and Monsters.*

The Imagination as Unproductive

In the Victorian era, the suspicion of the imagination merged with the philosophy of capitalism and its assumption that only tangible resources have value. In *The Protestant Ethic and the Spirit of Capitalism* Max Weber famously argued that capitalist ideology has its roots in Calvinist theology. The Puritans shunned such activities as singing, dancing, and games because they were unproductive. Echoes of the Puritans often appeared in religious critiques of fantasy role-playing games. One such critic called *D&D* "a time-eating monster."[52] The religious emphasis on productivity was carried into a capitalist critique of the imagination.

Some Victorians felt it was necessary to teach children not to indulge in make-believe so that they might become productive adults. The history of this attack on the imagination was recorded by Victorians who rebelled against it. In *Hard Times,* Charles Dickens presented Mr. Gradgrind as a caricature of utilitarianism. A school headmaster, he encourages his pupils to be practical and profitable, even naming his own sons Malthus and Adam Smith. Gradgrind and his associate explain to a child: "But you mustn't fancy. That's it! You are never to fancy. . . . Fact, fact, fact!"[53]

We find a similar account of Victorian pedagogy in an 1866 article by E. B. Tylor, a founder of the anthropology of religion. Tylor begins his essay on "primitive religion" by describing an article in a children's magazine in which a teacher tells his pupils a story about a broomstick. In the story, it is Christmas Eve, and a family is gathered around their hearth for tea and mirth. Outside on the porch is a broomstick that someone has forgotten to bring in. The teacher describes in great detail the merriness and warmth of the party while outside night sets in and the poor broomstick is left to freeze on the porch, alone and forgotten. The story goes on until the children are near tears in sympathy for the broomstick. It is precisely at this point that the teacher exclaims: "You silly children! Don't you know that a broomstick is a bit of wood with no sense, and can't feel the cold, and doesn't know or care whether it is left out or taken indoors? Now remember for the future that you must keep your sympathy for creatures that can really feel pleasure and pain, and not waste it on insensible broomsticks."

Tylor takes the side of the children and describes the teacher as "a Philistine." Like Dickens, he posits a link between utilitarianism and an attack on the natural human tendency toward imagination. He writes that the chief feature of the Philistine is that "the exertion and development of the mind for its own sake, where they cannot be estimated by a material equivalent in money or position or comfort, are things lying out of his regular track, and are therefore the objects of his scarcely tolerant contempt."[54]

The belief that the imagination is unproductive continued into the moral panic over role-playing games. While Christian critics of role-playing games emphasized the psychological and spiritual dangers of the games, they never failed to claim that the games are also a waste of time and energy. Patricia Pulling invokes a bit of the Victorian attitude toward childhood make-believe in *The Devil's Web.* She writes of gamers: "Sadly, there are those who, for a variety of reasons, do not have a solid grasp on reality. Some of these individuals find the fantasies of childhood far more rewarding than the day-to-day details of their lives."[55] Mr. Gradgrind would concur with this assessment.

Fundamentalism and Biblical Literalism

The Deists of the eighteenth century were followed in the nineteenth century by the "higher criticism" school of biblical scholarship. These scholars, most of whom were German, developed new techniques for analyzing how biblical texts were compiled and copied over time that revealed new conclusions about the authorship and historicity of the Bible. Between the circulation of these new ideas and Charles Darwin's *The Descent of Man* (1871), the truth claims of the Bible appeared to be under heavy attack. Some Christians responded by reiterating that the Bible is true in a historical and scientific sense. In 1910 Milton and Lyman Stewart, brothers who had made their fortune in the California oil business, sponsored a series of pamphlets entitled The Fundamentals: A Testimony of Truth. Written by prominent theologians, the pamphlets defended the Bible as inerrant. They focused their defense around "fundamental" tenets of Christianity such as the creation of the world ex nihilo, the virgin birth of Jesus, and his imminent return to judge the world. In 1920 conservative Baptist editor Curtis Lee Laws coined the term "Fundamentalist" to describe "those who were ready to do battle royal for the Fundamentals."[56]

The Fundamentals series marked the beginning of a culture of biblical literalism. Biblical literalism does not mean that the Bible can be interpreted only in a literal sense. As John Bunyan pointed out, the Bible clearly contains parables, metaphors, and poetic expression. Rather biblical literalism is the position that the Bible is inerrant. James Barr described biblical literalism as the position that the Bible contains "no error of any kind" and that "not only theological error, but error in any sort of historical, geographical or scientific fact is completely absent from the Bible."[57] As with the writings of Cotton Mather and Ezra Styles, there was a concession hidden in fundamentalism. By "doing battle" to prove the inerrancy of the Bible, fundamentalists confirmed that if scripture is not true in an empirical sense, then it is without value. For this reason, some scholars have noted that fundamentalism is a mirror image of the post-Enlightenment outlook that it opposes. By valuing only literal truth, it bleaches out the multifaceted ways in which sacred stories appeal to different aspects of human experience.[58] In an essay for *Christian Century*, Conrad Hyers, a professor of comparative mythology, condemned biblical literalism as a modernist approach to the Bible that impoverishes Christian tradition. In describing the truth of the Bible, he recounted a story in which the dancer Anna Pavlova was asked about the meaning of her dance. Pavlova responded, "If I could say it, do you think I should have danced it?" Hyers claims that biblical literalism empties symbols of their meaning and power, "reducing the cosmic dance to a calibrated discussion."[59] Armstrong concurs, opining that "a God who cannot appeal to the imagination is in trouble."[60]

Of course, twentieth-century Christians developed more than one program of truth. At the same time that fundamentalism was gathering strength, theologians like Rudolf Bultmann were attempting to "demythologize" Christianity by devising nonliteral interpretations of biblical miracles. Still other Christians preserved a sense of *mythos* by regarding fantasy and imagination as valuable and even sacred. A notable proponent of this view was Tolkien who wrote: "Fantasy is a natural human activity. It certainly does not destroy or even insult Reason."[61] On the contrary he argued that keen reason facilitated richer and more pleasurable fantasy. Tolkien described the imagination as an act of "sub-creation," an earthly reflection of God's ability to create the world ex nihilo.

Tolkien used this understanding of Christianity as *mythos* as well as *logos* to convert C. S. Lewis, who was originally a materialist. Lewis had always enjoyed myths and fairy tales but, much like Fontenelle, regarded them as "lies." He described them to Tolkien as "breathing a lie through silver." Tolkien countered that the Gospels have an imaginative and intellectual appeal and demand a response from the whole person. He later composed a poem for Lewis entitled "Mythopoeia," in which he wrote:

> Man, Sub-creator, the refracted Light
> Through whom is splintered from a single White
> To many hues, and endlessly combined
> In living shapes that move from mind to mind
> Though all the crannies of the world we filled
> With Elves and Goblins, though we dared to build
> Gods and their houses out of dark and light,
> And sowed the seed of dragons—'twas our right
> (Used or misused). That right has not decayed:
> We may make still by the law in which we're made.[62]

Here, Tolkien has returned to the Christian idea of imagination put forth by Dante and Saint Ignatius—namely, a divine faculty bestowed on humanity by God.

Yet the Christians who took aim at fantasy role-playing games, as much as they might enjoy Tolkien, could not share his understanding of the imagination. While they believed fervently in the reality of the supernatural, they were also influenced by centuries of rationalist epistemology in which the imagination is tantamount to delusion. Their program of truth left them ill equipped to think about how an idea could be both fictional and meaningful. The meaning worlds created through imagination and fantasy, unless explicitly framed as Christian, appeared threatening. Lacking any sense of *mythos,* these critics were predisposed to interpret fantasy as pathology, propaganda, or the demonic. Because fantasy could never be fantasy and had always to be interpreted as something else, it was easy for fantasy role-playing games to be folded into subversion narratives such as the cult scare, Satanic panic, and the superpredator myth.

THE FEAR OF THE FACTITIOUS

A peculiarity of the Christian critique of fantasy role-playing games is that while the critics claim that gamers will mistake fantasy for reality, they are equally concerned that gamers will mistake "real" aspects of the supernatural for fantasy. This is especially true of supernatural evil and the demonic. Mike Warnke, in his writings on role-playing games and Satanism, quotes Cotton Mather's *Discourse on the Wonders of the Invisible World:* "That there is a Devil is a thing that is doubted by none but such as are under the influences of the Devil. For any to deny the being of Devil must be from an ignorance or profaneness worse than diabolical."[63] Mather's phrasing raises the question, What profaneness is *worse* than the diabolical?

Since Mather, other Christian writers have interpreted doubts about the existence of demons as itself being a demonic plot. Lindy Beam of Focus on the Family cautioned against fantasy role-playing games because "any time the dark side of the supernatural world is presented as harmless or even imaginary, there is the danger that children will become curious and find too late that witchcraft is neither harmless nor imaginary."[64] Lewis was an important early advocate of this view. In *The Screwtape Letters* (1942), a demon writes a letter to his nephew explaining how rationalist materialism and demonic occultism appear to be at odds but can actually be used in concert to damn mankind. The demons dream of creating a "materialist magician" who denies the existence of God while worshipping such idols as psychoanalysis and "life force."[65] The idea of a "materialist magician" is expanded on in *That Hideous Strength* (1945), in which England is threatened by a coalition of scientists that is secretly directed by a fallen angel. Lewis's conspiracy theory of demonic materialism influenced religious critics of fantasy role-playing games. Gary North, one of the first evangelicals to write about the dangers of *D&D*, quotes *The Screwtape Letters* in his book *Unholy Spirits: Occultism and New Age Humanism*.[66]

This demonic conspiracy theory forms a bookend to medical claims about fantasy role-playing games and brainwashing: if players believe magic is real, they are delusional and have been deceived by the game, but if they believe magic is not real, they are in spiritual danger and have been deceived by Satan. This rhetoric strikes me as a bit too convenient. Mather's comment that there is something "worse than diabolical" suggests that materialism presents a more fundamental kind of threat to modern Christians than the demonic. To regard the demonic as fantasy casts doubt on all religious truth claims, at least where the supernatural is concerned. The unnameable threat that is worse than diabolical is that taken-for-granted realities can be called into question: that one might be confronted with a vision of a meaningless universe devoid of angels or demons. This fear, I argue, is the primary reason why some Christians found fantasy role-playing games so intolerable. If players can construct a shared fantasy complete with gods and demons, what assurance is there that Christianity is not itself a kind of game? What if Christian tradition is simply a great fantasy campaign, played by billions of players, that has run for thousands of years? Such fears would probably not trouble Christians like Bultmann or Tolkien who appreciated the Gospels on multiple levels. But for Christians who have accepted a modernist epistemology and value only literal truth, the implications of fantasy role-playing games are uniquely threatening.

Fantasy Role-Playing as Grenzsituation

Peter Berger argues that human beings require socially constructed worlds in order to function. These worlds are needed to render experience comprehensible, and serve as "a shield against terror." The ultimate danger that society protects us from is that of meaninglessness, in which existence is without order or purpose. Berger refers to this state as *anomie*. He writes: "This danger is the nightmare *par excellence*, in which the individual is submerged in a world of disorder, senselessness and madness. Reality and identity are malignantly transformed into meaningless figures of horror. To be in society is to be 'sane' precisely in the sense of being shielded from the ultimate 'insanity' of such anomic terror."[67]

Most of the time, the socially constructed worlds we inhabit are accepted without question. They do not seem arbitrary or factitious but appear, in Geertz's words, as "uniquely realistic." However, certain situations challenge our confidence in the meaningfulness of the world. Berger describes such moments as "marginal situations," a term he adapts from Karl Jaspers's *Grenzsituationen.* Berger explains:

> Such marginal situations commonly occur in dreams and fantasy. They may appear on the horizon of consciousness as haunting suspicions that the world may have another aspect than its "normal" one, that is, that the previously accepted definitions of reality may be fragile or even fraudulent. . . . In other words, the marginal situations of human existence reveal the innate precariousness of all social worlds. Every socially defined reality remains threatened by lurking "irrealities." . . . In other words, the marginal situations of human existence reveal the innate precariousness of all social worlds.[68]

Tellingly, Berger lists "fantasy" as a potential *Grenzsituation* that threatens to throw our world into chaos. Because fantasy role-playing games are a reflection on the world, they are perfect vehicles for the "lurking irrealities" described by Berger. Fantasy role-playing games have the power to make fantasies seem real and to make social realities appear as fantasies. What for gamers is a door to a world of imagination is for others a dangerous portal to a realm of insanity that quite literally threatens reality as we know it.

Fantasy role-playing games require players to deconstruct social realities in order to create plausible models of imaginary societies. Governments, religions, and entire cultures are created by disassembling and reassembling actual social institutions. This project often reveals the arbitrariness of these systems. Sarah Lynne Bowman explains, "Because players must keep game systems and meta-plots in mind when they make decisions, many gamers start to adopt a view of reality that looks beyond the surface and identifies the inherent structures underlying all things."[69] Gamers do not experience this as a frightening *Grenzsituation* but rather as the pleasure of liminality. In a 1979 article for the fantasy magazine *Different Worlds,* game designer Stephen L. Lortz explained:

> What do people do in life, other than play roles? We are the people we are because we selected roles when we were children. We know how to behave in

> most situations because we practiced playing our roles in childhood games. . . . Apart from the fact that RPGs can be just plain fun, they can help us survive in our shifting cultural environment by restoring our childish ability to vary the number of roles we can play in "real" life, and by allowing us to explore the nature of that "reality" through engaging in fantasy. RPGs can perform an invaluable service by preparing us to face the unexpected with equanimity and to search for truth in spite of manifest meaninglessness.[70]

It is highly significant that Lortz places scare quotes around the word "reality," while religious critics of fantasy role-playing games place scare quotes around the word "fantasy." Lortz is able to appreciate this reflexive aspect of fantasy role-playing because he is already looking "manifest meaninglessness" in the eye. For those trying to defend their socially constructed worldview against *anomie,* fantasy role-playing games are threatening. Berger writes that "to go against the order of society as religiously legitimated . . . is to make a compact with the primeval forces of darkness."[71] For Christian moral entrepreneurs, it would be far preferable if gamers really did believe in and worship Satan. If they did, then fantasy role-playing games would confirm what the moral entrepreneurs already believed: that Christian culture is opposed by Satan and the deluded individuals who worship him. Instead, role-playing games imply that the entire pageant of God and Satan could be factitious. The move made by Lewis, North, and Beam—to claim that demons want to be understood as a fantasy—takes a step back from this *Grenzsituation* and restores the sense of a self-contained world. When doubt itself is demonic, there is no longer a way to step outside to the paradigm of angels and demons to question how it was constructed.

Conservative evangelicals cannot express that fantasy role-playing games cause them to doubt their religious convictions, so the fear of *anomie* can be detected only by applying the hermeneutics of suspicion. However, there are several instances in which they appear to show their hand. Their critiques of role-playing games can also be applied to religious worldviews and imply that, in some sense, they are aware that both may be factitious.

Robie writes of *D&D:* "Since this is a shared fantasy, the more players that share the fantasy, the more blurred becomes the line between that and reality. . . . The game can become an almost mystical experience, consuming, addictive, and potentially dangerous."[72] The realization that fantasies become "real" as more and more people believe them shows an awareness that reality is socially constructed. Robie's comparison of

D&D to an addictive mystical experience implies that religion may likewise be a socially constructed fantasy. From these insights, Robie is not far from deconstructing her own faith.

The connection between fantasy and Christianity is made more explicit by critics such as William Schnoebelen in his objection to the cleric character class. He writes: "The cleric is the general religionist of 'any myth.' In other words, religions are myths. Christianity is a myth; Judaism is a myth, etc."[73] Leithart and Grant reach a similar point in their indictment of *Deities and Demigods,* a *D&D* supplement about world mythology. They write:

> Not only are gods, devils, and demons treated as fantasy, Jesus Himself is included as one of the deities. Note carefully the logic here: "It's just a game. The monsters aren't real. The magical powers aren't real. Jesus is one of the gods." Christ is reduced to the level of fantastic monsters, halflings, dwarves, and elves. We can give this no less a label than blasphemy.[74]

Deities and Demigods featured rules for such deities as Zeus, Thor, Isis, and even Cthulhu, but no edition of this book ever contained an entry for Jesus or any other biblical personage. While one could, in theory, create a set of attributes to represent Jesus in the context of a fantasy role-playing game, to my knowledge no published game has ever attempted to do so. What is significant is that Leithart and Grant (or perhaps some evangelical informant they relied on) realized *on their own* that Jesus could be included as a set of statistics in a *D&D* book. They understood that their religious truth claims could be translated into a model in a game just as easily as those of pagan religions. Then, by claiming that *Deities and Demigods* listed Jesus among the gods, they effectively projected their realization onto their opponent rather than acknowledging that it had occurred to them. The "blasphemy" condemned by Leithart and Grant was not committed by TSR but in their own minds.

Finally, in an interview for *Newsweek* Patricia Pulling cited children's belief in God to argue that child gamers cannot distinguish fantasy from reality. She remarked, "If kids can believe in a god they can't see then it's very easy for them to believe in occult deities they can't see."[75] By "occult deities" she meant the mythological and imaginary deities used in *D&D* pantheons. This argument, made to a journalist, is a concession that traditional monotheistic religion exists on the same level of plausibility as the fantasy religions of *D&D*. The converse of Pulling's rhetoric is that if children are delusional for believing in *D&D*

gods then Christians are also delusional for believing in God without empirical evidence.

"Bad Faith"

Christian critics of role-playing games are motivated by a repressed fear and unwillingness to face the possibility that the world might not operate as they imagine it does. This act of repressing doubts resembles Sartre's notion of "bad faith" (*mauvaise foi*). Sartre argued that people, by virtue of being conscious beings, are free and resent their own freedom. Bad faith refers to the natural tendency of people to flee from the fact that they are free to be whatever they wish. It is a form of self-deception by which people seek to constrain the possibilities presented to them.[76] Sartre's notion that we are "condemned to be free" is a corollary to Berger's idea that we must first construct worlds for ourselves and then conceal the apparatus by which these worlds are constructed.

Bad faith was first hinted at in Mather's vague reference to "a profaneness worse than diabolical." The religious attacks on role-playing games reveal both a discomfort with intellectual freedom and an attempt to deny the existence of this freedom. In their conclusion, Leithart and Grant claim that fantasy role-playing games "take modernity to its logical conclusion," writing:

> Since Descartes, modern man has retreated from the bright light of God's creation into the dark world of his own mind and imagination. Though his world is a dungeon populated by dragons, demons, and monsters, he says with Milton's Satan, "Better to rule in hell than to serve in heaven!"[77]

Sartre and Berger would say that we have no choice but to inhabit worlds of our own mind and creation and that the worldview of Leithart and Grant is but one such imaginary world. In fact, Sartre's axiom that "existence precedes essence" implies that ultimately we are all role-players, whether we want to be or not.[78]

I would further argue that bad faith is the reason that Christian critics of *D&D* appear alienated from their own tradition when regarding *D&D*. The alignment system, which presents good and evil in absolute terms, is regarded as an attempt to pervert traditional values. Cleric spells and other game elements with an obvious biblical provenance are not recognized as Christian but lambasted as "occultism." When Christian terminology appears in *D&D*, it is dismissed as blasphemy without argument or analysis. The most ironic claim of all may be that *D&D*

encourages suicide because characters can be resurrected by powerful clerics: if the idea of resurrection contributes to suicide, then Christianity is responsible for far more suicides than *D&D*.[79] By refusing to acknowledge the Christian elements of *D&D*, religious critics seek to protect themselves from the unsettling thought that their worldview, which they desire to be solid and beyond question, resembles the constructed fantasy of a role-playing game.

THE IMAGINATION VS. HEGEMONY

Hegemony is an ideological system by which the interests and worldviews of a particular social group are expressed so as to pass for the interests and worldview of the whole of society. The power of hegemony is that it cannot be detected. As Slavoj Žižek explains, "We feel 'free' because we lack the very language to articulate our unfreedom."[80] One of the most important theorists of hegemony was Antonio Gramsci, the Italian Marxist intellectual who was arrested under Mussolini. Gramsci was interested in creating culture as a form of resistance to Fascist hegemony. In his *Prison Notebooks,* Gramsci wrote about the importance of teaching Latin in secondary schools. He argued that students should learn Latin not because it is "practical" but because learning a dead language carries with it an understanding that the world was once ordered in a different way and could be reordered again in the future. In this sense, immersion in history, or what Gramsci called "the myth" of ancient Rome, could inoculate the populace against Fascist propaganda.[81] In fact, all of the secondary worlds of art, religion, science, and role-playing games present the means to step outside of hegemony and look at it critically.

The project of fundamentalist Christianity can be read as an attempt to preserve Christian hegemony in the face of challenges from various secondary worlds. Scientific rationalism presented a challenge to biblical truth claims, and so biblical literalism was developed as an attempt to conflate religion and science into a single discourse. Fiction represented another secondary world, and so novels were interpreted as either mentally unwholesome or a demonic plot. The goal of all of these maneuvers is to collapse any and all secondary worlds back into a single frame of meaning, leaving no space to stand outside of an ideological worldview.

As the keepers of hegemony, moral entrepreneurs are threatened by fantasy role-playing games and the intellectual autonomy that they foster. Christian critics have sometimes taken the position that the imagination is inherently heretical because "reality" is an expression of God's will, and therefore imagining any alternative to reality is an attempt to rebel against God's plan. In the 1980s, moral entrepreneurs were fond of quoting "John," the gamer interviewed for an article in *New West.* John was quoted as saying: "The more I play D&D, the more I want to get away from this world. The whole thing is getting very bad." Leithart and Grant commented on this quote: "In a very dramatic way, D&D reinforced John's hatred for life as ordered and given by God."[82] This is a peculiar comment for Christian theologians to make. Longing for a better world is arguably the essence of Christianity. Traditionally, Christianity has regarded the world as fallen to sin and fundamentally flawed. What is really at stake here is not proper reverence for God but control. Or rather, submission to hegemony has become synonymous with submission to God.

Leithart and Grant go on to write:

> In summary, Scripture *encourages* leisure, play, and even role-playing, though always within the limits of the moral Law. In the context of these standards, however, our imaginations find true freedom. Like the sheep to which Scripture so often compares us, our freest play is within the fold. Outside, there is only the bondage of fear that allows for no real leisure.[83]

For all their condemnation of modernity, the claim that reality is ipso facto God's plan for us is a modernist theology. It has far more in common with the Enlightenment philosophy of Gottfried Leibniz, who argued that this must be "the best of all possible worlds," than with the theodicy of Augustine, who believed that evil exists because while God is incorruptible, his creation is not. The strange theology suggested here appears to be simply a means of attacking the autonomy that role-playing provides. Here role-playing is condemned precisely because it entails a kind of freedom that Leithart and Grant regard as heretical. Anyone who has read George Orwell's *1984* will recognize their claim that freedom is actually bondage. Hegemonic rhetoric often presents propositions that are logical contradictions.

Others who have analyzed the panic over role-playing games have reached similar conclusions. Daniel Mackay, drawing on the work of Roland Barthes, notes that role-playing games are potentially threatening to the social order:

> Perhaps this is why much of the hostility and aggression against role-playing games in the United States has come from the religious right, which accuses

> role-playing games of being avenues to satanic worship and occult practices. The religious right is really at war with an alternative social world in which "men give meaning to things."[84]

Isaac Bonewitz in the preface to *Authentic Thaumaturgy*, his book on realistic occultism in fantasy role-playing games, identifies role-playing as a dire threat to hegemony and the religious right:

> Obviously, a hobby that teaches young people how "reality" is a socially constructed concept, that many people have had different religious and magical ideas over the millennia, that one faith's demons are another faith's deities, and that anyone can easily invent their own religion (complete with "infallible" scriptures), is going to be a direct threat to wealthy and powerful men who would rather not let such "dangerous" knowledge spread.
>
> The preachers' kids and their friends will, of course, continue to read and play fantasy games whenever their parents aren't looking. Perhaps when enough young people have learned the tolerance, flexibility and creativity that becoming good game players requires, the Greyfaces who've built their empires of anger, hatred, and fear, will finally fall—and the real Illuminati will be able to rejoice![85]

Bonewitz's tone is gleeful and almost messianic. However, his advocacy of playing role-playing games as a form of resistance to hegemony is not very different from Gramsci's advocacy of learning Latin.

As the font of new possibilities, the imagination is inherently threatening to those who seek to preserve order and the status quo—whether they are kindergarten teachers, Victorian pedagogues, the religious right, or a Fascist government. However, maintaining order by closing off the secondary worlds of fiction and fantasy comes at a terrible price. Cognitive scientists now know that the imagination does not weaken children's grasp on the real world but is actually the mechanism through which the world is rendered sensible. If we abandon our capacity to create new worlds, other capacities are diminished as well. Our facilities for reason, art, and abstract thought of all kinds begin with our ability to step outside of the world as it is given to us and discover it anew. A Christian like Tolkien would argue that this is not a heretical faculty but our divine right as subcreators.

CHAPTER 8

Rival Fantasies

We live in a fantasy world, a world of illusion. The great task in life is to find reality.

—Iris Murdoch

That a group playing a fantasy RPG will lose touch with reality, or become "mind-controlled" is completely fatuous. This is obvious to any observer of or participant in RPG activity. Those who claim such an effect is possible are the ones who have lost touch with reality.

—Gary Gygax

In an essay for the Christian Research Institute on the dangers of role-playing games, Elliot Miller writes:

> There are certain needs and desires which draw people to FRP in the first place. Many sensitive teenagers and adults continually bombarded with evolutionary theories and naturalistic philosophies, seek through FRP an escape from the cold, mechanistic view of the universe which they've been led to believe is "reality." Who wouldn't prefer an adventurous existence in a magical, purposeful world over the complex, impersonal "real world" being pushed on young people by our educational institutions and the media?[1]

This paragraph is a rare expression of empathy for gamers. Miller concedes that he understands the desire to live a life of purpose in a world filled with mysterious forces. Indeed, he implies that both fantasy role-playing games and Christianity represent alternatives to the modernist worldview with its "mechanistic" understanding of the universe. The difference, from Miller's perspective, is that while he knows that secularism is a lie promoted by a culture hostile to Christianity, gamers prefer to escape this lie into another lie of their own creation.

Daniel Martin and Gary Alan Fine were the first to suggest that both gamers and moral entrepreneurs are engaged in a project of reenchantment.[2] Both get to experience being heroes who battle to save the world from the forces of darkness. In this sense, fantasy role-playing games and antigaming subversion narratives represent rival fantasies. In Freudian terms, the hostility of the claims makers toward gamers represents "the narcissism of minor differences." That is, moral entrepreneurs are antagonistic toward fantasy role-playing games precisely because the games mirror their own heroic fantasies.

There are at least three ways that fantasy role-playing games and the narratives presented by moral entrepreneurs resemble each other. First, fantasy role-playing games and Satanic conspiracy theories draw elements from the same milieu of monsters and evil rituals found in popular culture. The horror movies and television of the 1960s and 1970s were the inspiration for both *D&D* and Satanic panic. Second, the mechanisms through which these narratives are constructed are collective. Claims makers do not invent theories about subversive threats in isolation but build off of one another. The collaborative construction of these narratives often resembles a form of imaginative play in which ordinary standards of evidence are ignored and elements can be creatively arranged. Finally, most anti-*D&D* crusaders were associated with the New Christian Right. This movement has been defined by figures such as Jerry Falwell and Pat Robertson and emphasizes biblical inerrancy as well as charismatic preachers who present themselves as postbiblical characters whose lives are part of a biblically framed drama. The self-narratives constructed by Pulling and others as heroes battling an evil conspiracy can be read as an extreme example of the way that moral leaders presented stories about themselves in mainstream evangelical culture. In the 1970s both gamers and evangelicals were developing narrative strategies through which new personas could be constructed. These narrative strategies allowed individuals to reimagine themselves in a way that connected their lives with sacred times, places, and stories. Where gamers battle demons such as wizards and warriors, moral entrepreneurs battle the imagined forces of evil as occult crime investigators and exorcists.

The key difference between fantasy role-playing games and evil conspiracy theories is one of framing. Games are set in the context of the game, firmly separated from the world of play. Moral entrepreneurs, however, are generally suspicious of imaginary worlds. For them, the world of daily life is the only one in which they may become a hero.

With nowhere to go, their heroic fantasies are imposed on the real world as conspiracy theories.

Furthermore, claims makers constructed their subversion narratives by repurposing the fantasies of others. They developed a hermeneutic that allowed them to shift the metacommunicative frame of fantasy role-playing games from an imaginary frame to a more literal one. The symbols and narratives of an imaginary game were reinterpreted as actual brainwashing, occultism, and actual contact with demons in order to create an opponent for the moral entrepreneurs to crusade against. In this sense, the relationship between these two fantasies was not just one of rivalry but one of cannibalism. Claims makers consumed and repurposed the heroic fantasies of gamers to construct heroic fantasies for themselves.

Human beings need play and fantasy to be psychologically well. Play provides a mental space through which we can order our world. However, by confounding the world of heroic fantasies and narrative tropes with the world of daily life, figures like Mike Warnke, William Schnoebelen, William Dear, and Patricia Pulling engaged in a form of corrupted play. This became dangerous when the performance of their personas became entangled with the sphere of practical realities. The Satanic panic that these moral entrepreneurs helped to produce resulted in hundreds of innocent people being accused. In some cases, accused Satanists received lengthy prison sentences for crimes that never occurred. Robert Hicks noted that the concomitant attack on role-playing games posed a potential threat to civil liberties as moral entrepreneurs called to ban books, place warning labels on game products, and require libraries to track the lending habits of patrons.[3] By sundering the barriers between fantasy and reality, the way that moral entrepreneurs and their audiences constructed heroic narratives ironically resembled the dangerous play of deviant teenagers such as Jon C. Bush and Rod Ferrell.

THE FANTASY OF EVIL RITUAL

Gamers and their critics share a desire to construct a moral universe to mentally inhabit. This project requires antagonists to personify the forces of evil. In *Evil Incarnate: Rumors of Demonic Conspiracy and Ritual Abuse in History* David Frankfurter argues that "evil" functions as a discourse—a way of interpreting and ordering the world. Throughout history, societies have attributed ordinary misfortune to the malevolence of evil conspiracies: Satanists, witches, Jews, and even early Christians have all been accused of working in secret to undermine the public good. In fact these groups have been accused of engaging in "cosmic evil" or the very antithesis of goodness. They are invariably said to murder children because they are in conspiracy against all that is holy and innocent. Paradoxically, belief in these conspiracies inspires a sense of security. The perpetrators of these crimes are never unorganized but always have a detailed hierarchy that is known to the conspiracy theorist. This vision of cosmic evil serves as a shadow of the culture that opposes the conspiracy, reinforcing its sense of an ordered universe and bestowing a sense of righteous purpose.

Frankfurter notes that in each case the alleged evildoers are accused of engaging in obscene, nocturnal rituals. Across the centuries the evil ritual always features the same taboo elements, such as incest, cannibalism, coprophagia, and human sacrifice. There has never been any material evidence to suggest that such rituals actually occurred, and it can be assumed that the descriptions of these awful rituals are not historical realities but fantasies that reveal the needs and desires of the claims makers. The imagined atrocities at these rituals provide a "tableau of evil" that serves to assemble and organize various frightening elements. While the particular elements may change slightly, the tableau of evil always involves a reversal of the established order: Mass is said backwards, babies are killed instead of nurtured, feces are eaten instead of excreted, and so on. The function of these horrible inversions is to organize the world in a stark dichotomy of good and evil. There is something oddly comforting about the way the abominations are performed in a prescribed and orderly manner. These fantasies allow claims makers to perceive evil as manageable and ultimately controllable.

Frankfurter's insights into the fantasy of the evil ritual are the key to understanding literature about the dangers of fantasy role-playing games. Games like *D&D* proved to be ideal material from which a tableau of ritual evil could be constructed. By the 1980s, moral entrepreneurs were describing *D&D* in elaborate, albeit inaccurate, detail meant to evoke exactly the same feelings of fascination and revulsion as descriptions of witches' Sabbaths or Satanic orgies. Stanley Semrau, a psychologist associated with BADD, said of *D&D:*

> Attacks and counter-attacks are continuous, and they may include assassinations, poisonings, spying, theft, injury, disablement, self-mutilation, cannibalism, torture, curses and mental attacks. . . . Any number of monsters can appear, including demons and devils, and sub-human soldiers, who are less expensive than humans, but "expect to loot, pillage, rape freely at every chance, and kill (and probably eat) captives."[4]

Thomas Radecki's description is the same: "The game is full of human sacrifice, eating babies, drinking blood, rape, murder of every variety, curses of insanity."[5] At the height of the panic, this discourse became almost entirely dissociated from the reality of fantasy role-playing games. Columnist Paul Harvey describes "monsters [in *D&D*] capable of infecting flesh, poisoning, whipping, immolation. They can cast insanity curses on one another. But as excesses inevitably eventually are their own undoing, dare one hope that the interest in video games—including this one—is phasing out?"[6] Harvey provides a detailed description of the horrors of *D&D,* even though he refers to it as a "video game" and is apparently unaware of the entire premise of fantasy role-playing games.

There was, in fact, a kind of litany of the abominations associated with *D&D* that was recycled from claims maker to claims maker. The earliest iteration I have found appeared in a 1983 pamphlet created by the Otero County Coalition of Women Aware. According to this pamphlet, *D&D* promotes "demonology, witchcraft, voodoo, murder, rape, blasphemy, suicide, assassination, insanity, sex perversion, homosexuality, prostitution, Satan worship, gambling, and Jungian psychology."[7] The Coalition of Women Aware did not create this list and attributed its information to Christian Life Ministries. Almost like DNA, the litany of atrocities was reproduced by one moral entrepreneur after another, with each iteration grafting new elements onto the list. A decade later, Joan Hake Robie's *The Truth about Dungeons and Dragons* presented the objectionable elements of *D&D* as an itemized list that included the following:

demonology
witchcraft
voodoo
murder
rape
blasphemy
suicide
assassination
insanity
sex perversion
homosexuality

prostitution
Satan worship
gambling
Jungian psychology
barbarism
cannibalism
sadism
desecration
demon summoning
necromantics
divination[8]

Robie's list is longer, but its provenance in the older materials is obvious.

Of course, most of these elements *could* appear in a fantasy role-playing game, and *D&D* books did contain rules to represent many of these elements. However, the litany does not represent an objective evaluation of the game. Rather it represents the construction of a fantasy from the raw material of another fantasy. Moral entrepreneurs simply picked through gaming material in search of objectionable elements to assemble into a tableau of evil. Gareth Medway points out that this same process can be applied to the Bible. He asks:

> Why, then, it could be asked, do responsible parents permit teenagers to read the Bible, which contains scenes of adultery, murder, infanticide, necromancy, demonic possession, suicide, assassination, harlotry, coprophagy (feeding on excrement), human sacrifice, rape, cannibalism, and incest, with instructions on how to carry out blood sacrifices and cursing rituals?[9]

Consistent with the erotics of fear, the claims makers demonstrate a kind of delight in pouring over *D&D* books to discover new material for this litany. Schnoebelen found obscure references to venereal disease and satyriasis—details that many lifelong gamers were probably unaware of.[10] This project of discovering, cataloging, and organizing evil also explains why some moral entrepreneurs appear preoccupied with numbers. For instance, Robie writes:

> Players can arm their characters with any of 62 different types of weapons. There are 39 different tools that players can use in their torture chambers, 11 types of mercenary soldiers that players can hire who have tendencies to pil-

> lage and rape, and 11 types of prostitutes possible in the game. . . . The word "demon" appears 106 times in pages 16–19 of the Monster Manual. . . . The word "evil" appears 94 times and the word "hell" appears 25 times in pages 20–23 of the Monster Manual.[11]

A religious tract claims that *Deities and Demigods* uses the word "devil" 94 times and hell 25 times, and remarks, "It is into this world of evil, ugliness and brutality that the player has voluntarily descended."[12]

Applying Frankfurter's theory of evil as a discourse, the purpose of keeping these litanies and counts is obvious. They serve to arm the claims maker with a vision of cosmic evil. *D&D* becomes the hidden link through which everything horrible and threatening is united. As an abominable ritual, *D&D* offers the hope that all the problems of the modern condition—the inevitable conflicts between children and their parents, the compromising of the domestic sphere by market forces, youth suicide, and so on—are not complex and multifaceted problems but are actually orchestrated by a force of subversive evil that can be rooted out and destroyed once it has been successfully identified. In this sense, the attacks on fantasy role-playing games actually present a message of hope.

Several features of fantasy role-playing games make them amenable to this fantasy of evil ritual. While fantasy role-playing is not a "religion" in the sense that its opponents claimed it does contain elements of ritual. This is key as ritual is the sine qua non for any fantasy of an evil conspiracy. Frankfurter explains:

> Religion and ritual are inevitable cultural components of the Other, however monstrous. Yet religion and ritual are also horrific things to uncover. The very notion that witches, foreigners, or Satanists are in thrall to an ancient cult, in whose ceremonies they foreswear humanity for a sequence of perverse and bloody acts, renders the conspiracy more resilient (as religions are purported to be), more dangerous (as religious motivations are thought to be unassailable), and more enthusiastic (as the Other's rites invariably bring him to addictive states of ecstasy) than, say, conspiracies of a more political or racial character.[13]

Additionally, in the 1980s fantasy role-playing games were presented as a pastime for children, which appealed to ideas of evil conspiracies as parasitical and preying on innocence. Finally, *D&D* was amenable to the fantasy of evil ritual because of its liminal quality: fantasy role-playing games occur in both physical space and the imagination, and to outside observers they appear both familiar and other, tangible and unknowable. This made fantasy role-playing games ideal for bridging the gap between fantasies of evil conspiracies and observable evidence. Unlike Satanic rituals, which were always said to have occurred in hidden locations and left no physical evidence afterward, *D&D* was demonstrably present in schools and living rooms. But *D&D* also occurs in the imagination, and so claims made about it are unburdened by plausibility. Moral entrepreneurs were free to imagine the most nasty and evil game possible, and players were hard pressed to prove that they had not performed this evil ritual in their imaginations.

D&D was so amenable to these fantasies that it became part of a larger tableau of evil within evangelical culture. *D&D* is often found in "hell houses," a variation on the haunted house usually sponsored at Halloween by conservative churches. Visitors are shown tableaux of sin, demons tempting teenagers to evil, and sinners suffering in hell. Scenes of teenagers dabbling in occultism generally feature *D&D*, *Harry Potter*, and Ouija boards.[14] In 1990, evangelical singer Carman produced a music video for his song "Witch's Invitation." In a strange reversal of evangelism, the video portrays a warlock who invites Carman to his home so that he can proselytize to him about the powers of Satanism. As the Christian hero, Carman hears the warlock's pitch before triumphantly rebuking him in the name of Jesus. Carman sings about the warlock's house, "His house was filled with every occultic symbol you could fathom; hanging pentagrams and horoscope signs, a Ouija board, and dungeons and dragons game set on the table." The warlock's name—Isaac Horowitz—is an apparent reference to Isaac Bonewitz, whose writings evangelicals often presented as proof that fantasy role-playing games are linked to actual occultism. The description of Isaac's house serves the same function of organizing and consolidating evil. *D&D* is assigned a place alongside various occult and heretical paraphernalia, all of which serves as a menacing backdrop for Carman's adventure.

Ironically, the principles of the fantasy of evil ritual are also at work within fantasy role-playing games, especially *D&D*. The covers of early *D&D* books frequently depicted the same scenes of demonic evil. A supplement called *Eldritch Wizardry* (1976) featured a nude woman on an altar. The first edition *Dungeon Master's Guide* (1979) featured an enormous devil clutching a scantily clad woman as two heroes attempt to battle it. Gamers found pleasure within these fantasies for the same reason that moral entrepreneurs did. In fact, the cover art of first edition *D&D* books and of Christian publications condemning *D&D* is nearly identical. Both employ images suggestive of combat and peril, biblical monsters such as demons and dragons, and medieval symbols such as warriors and swords. In poring through *D&D* books in search of vile elements to add to their litany, moral entrepreneurs were vicariously enjoying an especially nasty game of *D&D* and participating in the very pleasures they claimed to condemn.

PLAYING THE HERO

The fantasy of evil ritual serves to organize the universe into a Manichaean battle between good and evil. Once this moral landscape is established, those who participate in this discourse of evil can assume the roles of heroes and villains. In conspiracy theories as in fantasy role-playing games, most people prefer to play the role of the hero. Moral entrepreneurs who claim to oppose evil conspiracies invariably construct larger-than-life personas for themselves. They present themselves as adventurers whose ability to discern evil has also made them a target of it. In the narratives they tell about themselves they are heroic because they have either survived or defeated the aggression of the conspirators. Moral entrepreneurs can also reinforce the discourse of evil by playing the role of villains. This happens in two ways. Some claims makers, such as Warnke and Schnoebelen, simply claim to have been evil conspirators before converting to Christianity. They can claim to have positive knowledge of evil rituals because they orchestrated them. Less often, convicted criminals will join the moral entrepreneurs by claiming that their crimes were caused by their involvement with Satanism and role-playing games. Such individuals are not regarded as treacherous by moral entrepreneurs but rather as valuable allies and informants.

To play a hero in this fashion it is necessary to present one's audience with a vision of cosmic evil. Frankfurter describes the role of "the expert in evil":

> In his ability to show the evil system behind inchoate misfortune, he offers his audiences the tangible hope of purging it. And in conjuring a counter-realm of demons, witches, or subversives (whose activities only he can identify), the expert in evil grows into a heroic, solitary warrior against evil.[15]

Within the sphere of Satanic conspiracy theories, some people are willing to lie outrageously to present themselves as this "lone warrior" figure. An extreme example was Mark Rizzo of Freedom Flyer Ministries. Rizzo attended national law enforcement conferences on gangs where he falsely claimed to be an FBI agent and gave lectures on Satanic ritual abuse. In 2004, actual FBI agents arrived at a conference and arrested him for impersonating an agent.[16] Anti-role-playing-game crusaders were especially willing to invent details. Jerry Johnston, an evangelical pastor who attacked *D&D* in such books as *Why Suicide? What Parents & Teachers Must Know to Save Our Kids* and *The Edge of Evil*, presents this nominally true story about a teenager named "Ellen":

> Ellen got into Dungeons and Dragons when she was fourteen. "It's the most exciting thing I've ever done," she told several friends.
>
> By the time she turned fifteen, Ellen spent every weekend playing D&D. Occasionally, it left her so fatigued by Monday morning she would stay home from school. Her parents became understandably concerned about her obsession, but she wouldn't quit playing. "Just leave me alone," she insisted. "After all, it's only a game."
>
> Ellen never celebrated her sixteenth birthday. In Dungeons and Dragons she received the punishment of banishment from her kingdom and could never return. Ellen was so distraught she took an ornate sword she purchased from an antique store months earlier and thrust it through her body.
>
> "After all, it's only a game," she had said. The words would ring hauntingly in the memory of her grieving parents.[17]

This story is clearly the product of Johnston's imagination. Johnston does not relate how he knows this story, and the extensive lists of suicides kept by BADD and others contain no mention of such a case. It is not clear what Johnston means when he says Ellen was "punished with banishment," and this detail would be cogent only to someone with no idea of how *D&D* is played. Finally, the prospect of a teenage girl purchasing a functional sword at an antique store and successfully committing suicide by stabbing it through her own body is so unlikely as to border on the impossible. But Johnston's goal is not to provide his readers with accurate information about suicide. It is instead to present a vision of monstrous evil that preys on innocent girls and, in doing so, to present himself as a heroic expert in evil.[18]

When Dallas Egbert disappeared in 1979, William Dear became the first expert in evil to utilize fantasy role-playing games as a foil in a heroic self-narrative. Dear persuaded the public that there was an invisible and systematic danger behind the seemingly random misfortune of a missing college student. In outlining this danger, he presented himself as a kind of superhero, describing himself to a reporter as "the real-life James Bond." Like Johnston, Dear was not above inventing details such as his story in *The Dungeon Master* about rescuing a girl from an armed cult in a helicopter raid. While Dear never claimed that *D&D* had anything to do with Satanism (Satanic panic had not yet swept the nation), the beginnings of a fantasy of evil ritual are clearly present in *The Dun-*

geon Master, with its discussion of strange cults and hints of secret meetings in steam tunnels.

Patricia Pulling became the quintessential expert in evil of the panic over role-playing games. She also took steps to build up her image as a lone warrior fighting against evil. She even visited Matamoros, Mexico, to pose for pictures next to ritual implements found at a crime scene. As with Johnston and Dear, some of Pulling's claims were entirely invented, such as her claim that 8 percent of the population of Richmond, Virginia, are Satanists or that she played *D&D* several hours a day every day for a month. It is possible that these statements are simply calculated lies intended to advance Pulling's agenda. However, it is also possible that the experts in evil do not think of these statements as lies. Rather, moral entrepreneurs and their audiences seem to employ a narrative strategy in which these statements are tacitly understood to be beyond the categories of truth and falsehood. If pushed, Johnston might well defend his story of "Ellen" as a story that *could* happen and therefore ought to be told, even if it is the product of his imagination. Moral entrepreneurs generate narratives of evil and heroism together within their own metacommunicative frame. This special frame closely resembles a form of imaginative play in which ordinary standards of evidence are suspended and creativity reigns. It is only when these narratives are investigated by outsiders or legal action is taken that they come to be understood as false statements.

After *Michelle Remembers* became a best seller in 1980 there was a booming market for experts in evil. As evangelical publishers rushed to print new books about Satanic threats, even the most fringe individuals were able to publish their heroic narratives. A key example was Rebecca Brown, whose stories of battling cultists, demons, and Satanic role-playing games were published by Jack Chick. Rebecca Brown was born Ruth Irene Bailey in Shelbyville, Indiana. She received her degree as a doctor of medicine in 1979 and began her internship and residency at Ball State Hospital in Indianapolis. After several years of good service, Bailey's behavior became erratic. She began diagnosing patients as suffering from the influence of demons and curses and took to performing exorcisms in the intensive care unit, often involving candles and other paraphernalia. She allegedly claimed that she was chosen by God as the only doctor who could diagnose spiritual ailments. It was during this period that Bailey treated Edna Elaine Moses. Moses later claimed to have been a Satanic high priestess and to have married Satan before meeting Bailey and becoming a Christian. The two formed a partnership and moved in together. When Bailey was dismissed from Ball

Memorial Hospital for her erratic behavior, the pair moved to Lapel, Indiana, where Bailey set up a private practice.

In 1983, Moses was admitted to St. Vincent's Hospital in Indianapolis. Her body was covered with lesions, and she was nearly dead from an overdose of Demerol, a prescription painkiller. An investigation by the medical board revealed that Bailey had written over 100 prescriptions for Demerol to four different pharmacies in six months, acquiring 330 vials of the drug. Numerous patients had become addicted to Demerol under Bailey's care and now required detoxification. She had misdiagnosed Moses with leukemia and various other blood diseases and had been treating her with massive quantities of Demerol to the point where Moses could tolerate what would normally be four times a lethal dose. Moses also had a fifteen-year-old daughter, Claudia, who was mentally challenged. Claudia had been prescribed Demerol for nausea and had even been allowed to inject herself. Finally, Bailey had announced that Jesus had given her the ability to "share" Moses's leukemia and to take on some of her suffering. As such, Bailey had been injecting herself with Demerol as well. Bailey refused to appear before the medical board and instead fled to California, where she changed her name to Rebecca Brown. Her medical license was revoked in an emergency suspension.

It was in California that Bailey (now Brown) and Moses met Jack Chick. Moses's story became the basis of a tract entitled "Poor Little Witch." Through Chick, Brown and Moses (called simply "Elaine") published a series of tapes entitled "Closet Witches 1" and "Closet Witches 2," in which they outlined an international conspiracy carried out by witches, Freemasons, and the Roman Catholic Church, all of whom were working together. The tapes were followed by two books, *He Came to Set the Captives Free* and *Prepare for War.* Brown was endorsed by other experts in evil, including Jerry Johnston, and was featured on Geraldo Rivera. She was also invited to speak at police training seminars about fantasy role-playing games and other aspects of the Satanic conspiracy.[19]

What is significant about Brown's claims is their collaborative nature. A board psychiatrist diagnosed Brown with acute personality disorders, including delusions and/or paranoid schizophrenia. But schizophrenics do not normally publish books. It seems that much of her strange worldview developed through her relationship with Moses as the two constructed a narrative of themselves as spiritual warriors battling a vast conspiracy. Brown continued to work with others to construct these fantasies. She eventually married Daniel Michael Yoder, who claims that he was raised by Jewish international bankers before converting to Christianity. The two currently run a ministry called Harvest Warriors and continue to publish books together outlining dark conspiracies.[20] Brown's project of constructing and inhabiting paracosms with like-minded people is strikingly similar to the fantasy role-playing games she condemns.

PLAYING THE VILLAIN

Stories of evil conspiracies and abominable rituals, however vivid, are not enough to sustain the discursive function of evil. In order to be an effective element for organizing the world and energizing social movements, evil must be encountered in a more direct and tangible form. Because child-murdering witches and Satanists exist only in fantasy, evil must be performed by others. Frankfurter explains, "When historical and social circumstances decree, roles for the mimetic performance of evil open up and invite actors."[21] Many of the opponents of role-playing games were involved in performing evil, casting themselves as villains rather than heroes.

In constructing a threat of Satanism and role-playing games, moral entrepreneurs performed evil in three ways. First, evil could be performed indirectly through narratives of alleged Satanic ritual abuse (SRA). A number of people came forward to claim that evil Satanic rituals truly occurred because they had been forced to witness and participate in them. Second, evil could be performed indirectly by moral entrepreneurs who claimed to have been the leaders of Satanic organizations before converting to Christianity. Third, evil was sometimes performed directly by convicted criminals, especially those who committed violent crimes as teenagers. These individuals supported the claims makers by insisting that they were the pawns of demonic forces. Such individuals often form strong alliances with moral entrepreneurs and are even praised as saint-like figures. Each of these methods of performing evil is a creative act requiring imagination on the part of the claims maker. These performances are also an inherently social process, as the claims of evil are meant to be shared.

Satanic Ritual Abuse Narratives

Michelle Remembers (1980) spawned an entire industry of experts who promised to help "victims" recover memories of SRA and, in some cases, prosecute the alleged perpetrators. Books like *Michelle Remembers* were frequently cited by Pulling and other moral entrepreneurs as evidence that Satanic cults existed and used numerous devices to ensnare children. Precedents for SRA narratives were provided by stories told by apostates from groups such as the Unification Church (Moonies) and the International Society for Krishna Consciousness (Hare Krishnas). Former members of these religious movements, some of whom had been abducted and "deprogrammed," told lurid tales of their abuse and humiliation at the hands of "cults." The year before *Michelle Remembers* was published, an article in the *Journal of Communication* coined the term "atrocity tales" to describe such narratives. The authors argued that atrocity tales have a discursive function of defining evil and mobilizing resources against a particular group. Atrocity tales always focus on the entire group as a force for evil rather than individuals, and they are often effective whether or not the details are true.[22] Like the atrocity tales of the 1970s cult scare, the alleged survivors of SRA claimed to have participated in awful religious ceremonies either as unwilling participants or while under the influence of brainwashing. Their testimony helped to bridge the gap between observable reality and the fantasy of evil ritual. SRA narratives had a liminal quality as both real and imaginary that was useful to claims makers in much the same way as fantasy role-playing games.

SRA narratives were frequently constructed by two people, the patient and an expert, usually a pastor or therapist. Hypnosis and similar techniques were often used to induce the recovery of memory. Many psychologists argue that hypnosis is essentially a performance in which the hypnotized plays a role for the hypnotist. In this model, the hypnotized is not necessarily pretending to be hypnotized, but his or her altered state of consciousness is an entirely social event.[23] Like role-playing games, SRA narratives are fantasies that seem uniquely real because they are formed in a collaborative and ritual context. In fact, one psychiatrist described SRA as "a shared fantasy."[24] The experts were not so different from dungeon masters or storytellers, as they took the lead role in a process of collective storytelling.

Ex-Satanist Narratives

In another genre of narrative, moral entrepreneurs did not claim to have been unwilling witnesses but the leaders of Satanic organizations before their conversion to Christianity. In *The Paranoid Style in American*

Politics, Richard Hofstadter notes that paranoid worldviews attach a specific significance to "the figure of the renegade from the enemy cause."[25] Some antigaming crusaders discovered the easiest way to "prove" the existence of an evil conspiracy was to simply claim to be a former leader of the conspiracy. While BADD struggled to produce evidence that *D&D* contained "real" occultism, self-proclaimed ex-Satanists could claim they had firsthand experience using *D&D* to spread teenage Satanism. In his 1993 book *Lucifer Dethroned,* William Schnoebelen claimed to be a former Satanic high priest, Wiccan, Old Catholic bishop, Mormon elder, and a literal blood-drinking vampire. He also claimed that he had personally used *D&D* to recruit college students into Satanic worship. By 2001, Schnoebelen was claiming to have helped design *D&D*. He explained, "In the late 1970's, a couple of game writers actually came to my wife and I as prominent 'sorcerers' in the community. **They wanted to make certain the rituals were authentic.** For the most part, they are."[26]

Ex-Satanist narratives became surprisingly common. A pastor wrote to *Dragon* and explained how compelling these narratives were to Christians like his parishioners: "As a preacher, I am concerned not so much about D&D games as I am about the willingness of Christians to accept all this kookishness about Satan. Someone who claims to be an ex-satanist priest has an automatic audience in some Christian circles."[27] Ex-Satanist narratives appear to be a source of pleasure for those who tell them. Within the landscape of the evil conspiracy theories, playing a villain has richer opportunities for fantasy than playing a hero. Satanic conspiracy theories usually postulate small armies of people disposing of bodies, fabricating medical records, undermining police investigations, and so on. But moral entrepreneurs never claim to have been mere foot soldiers in this network. They invariably claim to have been leaders who wielded vast secular and supernatural powers. Consider the account of Edna Moses (in print as "Elaine"), whose ex-Satanist narrative served as a foil to Rebecca Brown's persona as a spiritual warrior. Elaine describes being taken to a "witch camp" where she was crowned as a "top witch":

> A crown of gold was placed upon my head and my fellow cult members bowed down and gave homage to me. . . . I was treated like a queen . . . I was given all the beautiful clothes to wear that I could possibly want. I was bathed, my hair fixed and I was waited on hand and foot by servants. There were parties and I always had a handsome escort who was also my body guard.[28]

After becoming a top witch, Elaine married Satan himself. The ceremony was held in a Presbyterian church, and Satan wore a white tuxedo. Satan then took her to their honeymoon in California in his private jet. Afterward, Elaine was employed as Satan's emissary on Earth. She was given the demonic ability to speak any language, which she used to negotiate arms sales with foreign emissaries. While not all ex-Satanist fantasies are quite as over the top as this, it is easy to discern elements of wish fulfillment in this narrative: as the bride of Satan, Edna/Elaine was glamorous, powerful, and beloved. Her existence as a socially isolated woman in Indiana was not a matter of circumstance, but the result of her decision to renounce Satan, her jilted lover. Like role-playing games, ex-Satanist narratives reflect individual fears and desires as well as those of their audiences. Those who tell these narratives acquire celebrity as others build on their stories, ultimately constructing a rich mythology.

Mike Warnke's *The Satan Seller* (1972) was the seminal ex-Satanist text. *The Satan Seller* describes how Warnke dropped out of college, became a drug dealer, and was recruited as a Satanist. He ascended the ranks of a Satanic conspiracy overseen by the Illuminati, eventually becoming the leader of 1,500 Satanists, who carried out abductions, rapes, and human sacrifice. His empire crumbled when his two female sex slaves, whom the Satanists had provided him, attempted to kill him with an overdose of heroin. Hunted by his own organization, Warnke joined the navy, where he converted to Christianity.

Warnke's book followed closely on the heels of Hal Lindsey's *The Late, Great Planet Earth* (1970), which offered readers a vivid depiction of a Christian end-time scenario from a literalist perspective. Lindsey's book proved there was a sizable market for prophecy books. In 1973 it was picked up by Bantam, a secular publisher, and in 1979 it was adapted into a film starring Orson Welles. In 1972 Warnke's manuscript was picked up by Bridge/Logos, one of the largest Christian publishing houses. Logos was scrambling to take advantage of the market created by *The Late, Great Planet Earth* and never questioned the details of Warnke's story. The same year Logos published *Michael, Michael, Why Do You Hate Me?*, a fabricated account of a Jewish rabbi who converted to Christianity. *The Satan Seller* became a religious best seller almost immediately and received positive reviews in *Moody Monthly* and *The Christian Century*. Warnke became a celebrity on the charismatic and evangelical circuit. With Morris Cerullo World Evangelism Ministries, Warnke set up a "Witchmobile." This was a trailer full of occult artifacts that served as a sort of mobile museum. Now anyone who was interested could visit the Witchmobile to experience a sense of propinquity with evil ritual. In 1985 Warnke appeared on ABC's *20/20* to discuss Satanism. His claims were then used as further evidence of Satanic conspiracy by such figures as Bob Larson and Jack Chick.[29]

In 1991, the evangelical magazine *Cornerstone* wrote an article debunking *The Satan Seller.* Investigators interviewed acquaintances who had known Warnke in college and confirmed that he had been an active evangelical—not a Satanist or a drug dealer. That same year, Warnke published a new book, *Schemes of Satan,* which placed heavy emphasis on the Satanic threat posed by fantasy role-playing games. Ironically, in the introduction to this book, Warnke wrote: "The greatest weapon we have at our disposal is truth. . . . The sword of truth always gives us victory over Satan and all his works."[30]

More ex-Satanist narratives followed *The Satan Seller.* In 1974, Herschel Smith and Dave Hunt published the ex-Satanist narrative *The Devil and Mr. Smith* in an apparent imitation of Warnke. When Warnke formed his own ministry, Smith even purchased the Witchmobile and continued to take it on tour. Another imitator was John Todd, who claimed to have been born into a witchcraft family. Todd told his followers he had been a member of "the council of thirteen," a group that secretly rules the world on behalf of the Rothschild family—who are actually demons. Pastors across the country embraced some or all of Todd's narrative and even supplied him with money to found a support center for ex-witches. Todd also formed an alliance with Jack Chick, whose tracts he claimed helped him decide to abandon witchcraft for Christianity. Todd is likely the basis for the witch-turned-pastor who orders his congregation to burn *D&D* books in *Dark Dungeons.* The character physically resembles Todd with his mustache and cleft chin. Todd's conspiracy theory was unique in that he accused prominent Christians from C. S. Lewis to Pat Robertson and Jerry Falwell of being secret members of the conspiracy. This is likely the source of the claim in the original version of *Dark Dungeons* that the works of Lewis and Tolkien are sold in occult bookstores. A 1979 article in *Christianity Today* debunked Todd's claims much as *Cornerstone* had Warnke's.[31]

Schnoebelen's latest book, *Romancing Death,* may hold the dubious honor of being the most fantastic ex-Satanist narrative of all time. Presented as a warning about the dangers of the Twilight series of teen fiction, *Romancing Death* expands on Schnoebelen's previous claims to have been a literal vampire. Schnoebelen describes how his Satanist friends told him that he could become either a vampire or a werewolf through Satanic magic. He chose to become a vampire because he did not want to endure the pain of transforming into an eight-foot-tall, furry humanoid. He prepared for this ritual by taking certain herbs and vitamins as well as large quantities of cocaine, and sleeping in a silk-lined coffin filled with soil from a Catholic graveyard. After these preparations, he was taken to a Russian Orthodox Church in Chicago to be initiated into the "Nosferatic mysteries." (A footnote to this story adds: "Please understand, I am certainly not saying that all Russian Orthodox churches of any sort are citadels of vampirism. For all I know, this one may have been a freaky aberration.") He exchanged blood with a Satanic priest while chanting in Old Slavonic and praying to Dracula, "the dark christ of the vampiric current."[32] He was then placed inside a coffin. When he emerged, he found that he had superhuman senses, could not tolerate daylight, and could eat nothing but human blood. Fortunately, as an Old Catholic bishop, he could create blood from wine through transubstantiation. He sustained himself on communion wine and blood taken from priestesses from his Wiccan circle. Schnoebelen's life as a vampire ended when he sent in his annual check to the Church of Satan, and the carbon copy was returned with a note from a bank teller stating, "I'll be praying for you in Jesus' name." As a result of this prayer, all of his vampire powers vanished, and he was restored to humanity.

Romancing Death is a difficult text to interpret. Details such as speaking Old Slavonic during his initiation as a vampire suggest Schnoebelen put research into his story. The narrative demonstrates a creative process more akin to that of a fiction writer than someone suffering from paranoid delusion. Is it meant as a calculated lie, a hoax, or something else entirely? Schnoebelen's book reads like a fantasy novel, and it is difficult to imagine that anyone would accept it as true. However, at least some of Schnoebelen's readers appear to take this story literally. Several reviewers on Amazon.com praised *Romancing Death* for speaking the truth about the occult. One reviewer said the best information in the book was Schnoebelen's step-by-step description of how werewolves transform from human beings into monsters. Schnoebelen and his audience may simply not be concerned with the categories of real and imagined.

Testimony from Criminals

Evil is also performed by criminals who enact the roles set for them by moral entrepreneurs. Gary Alan Fine and Jeffrey Victor describe the phenomenon of "teenage Satanism" as a self-fulfilling prophecy. They write:

> It is ironic that most of the vigorous spreaders of Satanic beliefs and rituals are not the tiny band of religious Satanists themselves, but the tireless local police, social workers, school administrators, and members of the clergy, all of whom ostensibly desire the elimination of any vestiges of criminal Satanism. Only a cynic would note that, if these opponents succeeded, they themselves would be out of the public spotlight. In a form of self-fulfilling prophecy, though, a society often creates its own "folk devils," thereby managing to find the kinds of deviants that it fears and condemns most.[33]

By warning the public about Satanism, figures like Pulling, Larson, and Schnoebelen effectively transmitted a "script" for how adolescent Satanists ought to behave. There is an almost symbiotic relationship at work in which claims makers give rebellious teenagers the means to act out their defiance and teenagers provide claims makers with justification for their crusades. Like the construction of narratives about Satanism, this relationship between deviant teenager and moral entrepreneur often resembles a form of imaginative play in which each player assumes a role. Consider the following exchange from Bob Larson's radio show *Talk-Back,* in which a caller identifying himself as "Number One" claimed to be a practicing Satanist.

> *Number One:* "I called your talk show to discuss your topic—crimes for the devil."
>
> *Larson:* "Have you killed or would you kill for Satan?" I wanted to know.
>
> *Number One:* "I'd kill instantly. It doesn't have to be for any reason. Not even the devil. Remember, I'm Number One." . . .
>
> *Larson:* "Do you have any morals?"
>
> *Number One:* "My only moral is that I'm Number One. If what I do is wrong, why do I feel so great when I kill? Why do I smile?"
>
> . . .
>
> Number One went on to explain that he sacrifices various animals, drinks their blood, and is currently teaching his six-year-old daughter to engage in these activities.[34]

Both parties appear to enjoy this exchange, which supplies Larson with evidence of criminal Satanism and allows "Number One" to experience the pleasure of shocking and horrifying Larson's Christian audience. This narrative of Number One, the murderous Satanist, is a collaboration constructed through Larson's questions and the caller's responses.

While they appear to be adversaries, they are actually cooperating to imagine a story together.

Convicted criminals sometimes cooperated with moral entrepreneurs in a similar fashion. Criminals such as Darren Molitor and Sean Sellers found that moral entrepreneurs were more sympathetic to them than the penal system and were happy to provide gruesome details of their former lives as misguided Satanists. Darren Molitor was convicted of murder in 1984 after strangling his friend in a poorly executed prank while under the influence of alcohol and marijuana. Pulling corresponded with Molitor in prison, and he eventually supplied BADD with a letter explaining how *D&D* had led him to murder his friend. This letter was disseminated widely by BADD and appeared in their document "A Law Enforcement Primer on Fantasy Role-Playing Games." It read in part:

> It [*D&D*] may seem to be harmless and very entertaining and it is entertaining, but far from harmless. I have had the experience of the game for more than 3 years now and I know the effects of the game. For the majority of those that play it becomes a way to escape reality. It is a way of letting tension and anxieties loose. And that is good. But subjecting the mind to the amounts of violence involved isn't. It is far more bad than it is good. Especially to a young mind. And an 18 or 20 year old still has a young mind. Its effects are both mental and physical. It is in comparison to drugs, alcohol or tobacco. It is very possessive, addictive and evil. Evil may sound wrong or peculiar to explain a game, but there is no other way to describe it. It is a device of Satan to lure us away from God. It is an occult.
>
> An occult you say? What is an occult? Defined in *American Family and School Dictionary,* a publication based on the *American College Dictionary,* prepared by Random House, Inc, it is: beyond the bounds of ordinary knowledge, secret. And *Webster's Dictionary* defines it as: secret; mysterious; magical; supernatural; mystical. Staying on the same subject let's define occultism; the doctrine or study of the supernatural, magical, imaginary, etc. Stated concisely it is the participation or involvement in *anyway* with fortune telling, magic practices, spiritism, or false religions cults and teachings. Within that category is using a ouija board, ESP, telepathy, horoscope, a seance, yoga, remote influence of the subconscious mind of others, self-hypnosis, following astrology and Dungeons and Dragons. . . .
>
> So, please for your own safety and salvation and the safety of others don't play the game anymore. If you don't play it now, don't even start. It is more dangerous than I can fully explain. Don't play with your physical life that way and don't condemn your soul to hell by participating in the game.
>
> A very concerned ex-player,
> Darren Molitor[35]

There is no way of knowing whether Molitor sincerely came to believe that his drunken decision to tie a bandage around his friend's neck was the result of playing *D&D* or if he hoped that by cooperating with BADD his sentence might somehow be commuted. However, the process of collaboration is apparent. Molitor makes the same medical and religious claims as Pulling. But as an actual murderer, Molitor gives these claims a sense of authenticity that Pulling cannot.

In 1986, sixteen-year-old Sean Sellers of Oklahoma City murdered his mother and stepfather. Sellers had been a self-styled Satanist prior to the murders. He too attempted the *D&D* defense and gained the attention of moral entrepreneurs. In prison, he founded a ministry called "Radical Teens for Christ" and cooperated extensively with anti-role-playing-game crusaders, gaining endorsements from Pulling, Warnke, Larson, and others. Sellers was executed by lethal injection in 1999, becoming the first person since the reinstatement of the death penalty to be executed for crimes committed while a minor. The combination of Seller's gruesome crimes, conversion to Christianity, and youth gained him celebrity. He appeared on numerous talk shows and television documentaries to talk about the destructive influence of Satanism. He became a regular call-in guest on Larson's radio show and published a book, *Web of Darkness*. His execution on February 4, 1999, was condemned by such figures as Archbishop Desmond Tutu and celebrity Bianca Jagger.[36] In the thirteen years that Sellers spent on death row, he constructed and revised a narrative in which his crimes were due to either *D&D*, multiple personalities resulting from childhood abuse, or demonic possession. In the end, moral entrepreneurs felt free to construct almost any narrative they wanted around Sellers's crimes. His performance of evil became a sort of anchor to which claims of evil conspiracies could be tethered.

By all accounts Sellers was playing the role of a teenage Satanist prior to his first murder. He would flash his copy of Anton LaVey's *Satanic Bible* at his classmates. He would also carry vials of his own blood that he drank in front of other students. He even canvassed the school with posters to recruit new Satanists.[37] While Satanic conspiracies were said to operate perfectly without detection, Sellers was anything but secretive about his interest in Satanism. Instead, his odd behavior was a public performance.

Accounts of Sellers's early experiences with adolescent Satanism resemble the sort of corrupted play engaged in by Jon C. Bush and Rod Ferrell. He formed a coterie of teenage Satanists who engaged in mischief and regarded Sellers as their leader. He visited occult bookstores and was a regular at *The Rocky Horror Picture Show.* At some point the performance of Satanism crossed the line into murder.[38] Sellers committed his first homicide with the help of a friend, Richard Howard. Howard stole a .357 Magnum handgun from his grandfather, a police officer. The two visited a Circle-K convenience store where clerk Robert Bower had previously refused to sell them beer. Sellers waited until there were no witnesses and then shot and killed Bower.

Six months later, Sellers shot his mother and stepfather as they slept using his stepfather's .44 Smith and Wesson revolver. He then changed clothes, showered, and opened all of the drawers in his house so as to suggest a robbery. He visited Howard, who disposed of the revolver and agreed to tell authorities that Sellers had spent the entire night at his house. In the morning, Sellers returned home and feigned shock as he pretended to "discover" his parents' corpses. Howard was questioned by police and gave Sellers up, becoming a key witness in his trial. After his arrest, Sellers claimed that he had no memory of killing his parents and that his involvement with Satanism had left him with no control over his actions. While moral entrepreneurs supported this claim, law enforcement found it unpersuasive. Detective Robert Jones remarked: "Satanism was not the cause. That was just another symptom of his twisted little mind. He was a pseudo-Satan worshipper. . . . He was full of bull."[39]

Sellers's attorney, a young public defender, attempted the *D&D* defense and contacted Patricia Pulling. Pulling was happy to help and quickly added Sellers to her "trophy list" of violent crimes related to role-playing games. Sellers initially supported the narrative provided by BADD, commenting: "Dungeons and Dragons got me started. I wanted to learn more about it, so I went to the library and stole some books about dragons, witches, wizards, and Satanism."[40]

In time, a different narrative emerged in which Sellers had been possessed by a separate personality (possibly a demon) named Ezurate. He claimed it was Ezurate who had actually murdered his parents. In explaining this he appealed to the theories of recovered memories used by the SRA panic: "I kept meditating and thinking, going back in time and then forward again. When I hit a blank spot, I forced myself to remember. I think now I was two people—Sean and Ezurate."[41] Sellers's statements about what exactly he remembered were not consistent. In his book he wrote: "I drove home, did some homework, performed a ritual, and slept. My next clear memory is a jail cell two days later. Without realizing it, I had taken my father's .44 revolver and shot both my parents in the head as they slept!"[42] In other accounts his memories are not dim and forced but vivid and obsessing. An antigaming critic quotes him as saying: "I watched blood pour from the hole in my mother's face and I laughed. . . . It haunts me that I could have been the person that did that."[43] The narrative of how and why Sellers murdered his parents continued to change in part as a result of interaction with his audience.

Sellers was so willing to collaborate with moral entrepreneurs that his crimes became amenable to any narrative of evil. The interpretations promoted by moral entrepreneurs resembled a state of play in which the murders were one more symbol to be repurposed into new patterns of meaning. Pulling reported that *D&D* had been Sellers's first step toward murder. Warnke emphasized one of Sellers's claims that a witch had initiated him into black magic prior to his first murder. After Sellers was executed, Larson claimed that Sellers had learned about witchcraft through a school-sponsored convocation where a witch was invited to speak to students about witchcraft. He writes:

> Sean Sellers would be alive today, and so would his three victims, if he hadn't heard that witch. The blood of these crimes is not only on Sellers's hands. The school officials who permitted the witch to speak to his school bear responsibility; their decision started the chain of events leading to Sellers's demonic activity.[44]

There is no corroboration for this account, and the likelihood that a public high school in Oklahoma City featured a lecture on witchcraft in 1985 borders on the absurd. The New Christian Right has repeatedly argued that the presence of fantasy role-playing games and novels such as *Harry Potter* in public schools amounts to a government endorsement of witchcraft. Larson's claim demonstrates how Sellers's cooperation with moral entrepreneurs could be repurposed into a variety of claims about subversive threats.

Sellers occasionally attempted to exert autonomy over his own narrative and gave some resistance to Pulling. In 1989, game designer Michael Stackpole telephoned Sellers in prison as part of a report he was preparing on Patricia Pulling. Sellers allegedly commented, "Patricia has an aptitude for going beyond moderation." In a subsequent letter to Stackpole, Sellers explained:

> I do have objections to some of the material TSR releases for their role playing games. I think their excessive use of paganism and occultism is unnecessary and can lead to idealistic problems among some players; however, to be fair to TSR and in the spirit of honesty I must concede that D&D contributed to my involvement in Satanism like an interest in electronics can

> contribute to building a bomb. Like the decision to build a bomb, I had already made decisions of a destructive nature before I incorporated D&D material into my coven projects, and it was Satanism not D&D that had a decisive role in my crimes.
>
> Personally, for reasons I publish myself, I don't think kids need to be playing D&D, but using my past as a common example of the effects of the game is either irrational or fanatical.[45]

Sellers reiterated this point in *Web of Darkness,* where he wrote, "Although I must disagree with some of Patricia's conclusions and state that D&D has not had quite the decisive role the National Coalition on Television Violence maintains, there is enough honest concern to give their declarations space."[46]

This resistance indicates that moral entrepreneurs needed Sellers more than he needed them. In the end, Pulling, Warnke, and Larson could do nothing to save Sellers from lethal injection. But Sellers's performance of being both the perpetrator and the victim of evil was invaluable for propping up a conspiratorial worldview. Ironically, Sellers wrestles with the same problems of evidence as the other claims makers. He writes of Satanic criminal networks:

> People who do not have much experience with the occult often cannot believe such a network exists. Their reasoning is logical. There is no proof. We don't have reports from people who have ever talked to someone who has been a part of such an organization. These points are true. There is no proof. However, that does not negate the network's existence.[47]

A further irony is that the opponents of *D&D* came to praise a murderer in hagiographic tones. *Web of Darkness* begins with a forward by Larson in which he writes, "Sean Sellers deserves admiration and respect, not for his past crimes, but for his current commitment to reaching teens."[48] Richard Abanes, in *Harry Potter and the Bible,* also recounts the tale of Sean Sellers and praises what are supposedly Sellers's last words before execution:

> All of the people who are hating me right now and are here waiting to see me die, when you wake up in the morning you aren't going to feel any different. You are going to hate me just as much tomorrow as you do tonight. When you wake up and nothing has changed inside, reach out to God. . . . He will heal you. Let Him touch your hearts. Don't hate all your lives.[49]

It is particularly interesting to compare the response of moral entrepreneurs to Sellers to their response to the McMartin Preschool trial. After the defendants were finally exonerated of being Satanists who ritually tortured children, Pulling remarked, "It saddens me that, when the general public reads in a newspaper article that 'charges were dismissed,' they assume this means that the defendants were innocent."[50] The desire to maintain a worldview in which ritual evil occurs leads to a strange inversion of reality wherein the guilty are praised as martyrs and the innocent are condemned as guilty.

I myself had to contend with the authority created by a performance in evil in 2010 when I was interviewed for a documentary on MSNBC about Rod Ferrell. The double homicide committed by Ferrell in 1996 effected a repeat of the sensationalism over Sellers the decade before. In both cases the media homed in on the apparent evil of a sixteen-year-old murderer. A new wave of moral entrepreneurs, including Pulling's associate Don Rimer, mobilized to incorporate Ferrell's crimes into a larger narrative about role-playing games and a dangerous youth subculture. When the Twilight series became popular, figures such as Rimer and Schnoebelen again claimed that young readers were being lured into occultism, and cited the Ferrell murders as evidence that vampire fiction is inherently dangerous. It was in the wake of the Twilight craze that MSNBC decided to produce a special on the murders that included prison interviews with Ferrell. I was asked to comment because of my research on the Ferrell case and the culture of self-identified vampires.

I did many interviews in 2010 as the country went through a heavy obsession with vampires. Being a vampire expert is its own sort of performance. At one point I was asked to sit next to an ornate candelabra, apparently to suggest that I came from another century. MSNBC interviewed me in an office that was not actually mine. The production crew taped black plastic over the windows to make the room appear suitably macabre. I was shown footage of Ferrell's prison interview in a dark room while the crew filmed my reactions. Much like Sellers, Ferrell had revised the narrative of his crimes while in prison. He told the producers that he had become ensnared in a vast network of criminal Satanism as a child and described how he had witnessed human sacrifices conducted in the woods of Kentucky. Ferrell gave them a classic fantasy of an evil ritual.

The producers asked me what I thought of this story. I tried to explain that Ferrell is a charismatic individual and a gifted storyteller, that he once convinced a group of teenagers to regard him as 400-year-old vampire, and that now he was duping the producers. I stated that there is no network of criminal Satanists and that Ferrell had absolutely not witnessed a human sacrifice. The producers were obstinate. They wanted to know how I could prove that Ferrell was not telling the truth or that there were no Satanic cults abducting and murdering people in Kentucky. They countered that authorities had once denied the existence of the Mafia as well. I was not prepared for these questions. I had come to talk about my ethnography of self-identified vampires, not to debate claims of Satanism that had been discredited two decades ago. I finally told them that it is impossible to prove a negative and that the burden of proof is on Ferrell, who—like all people who tell such stories—is unable to provide names, dates, locations, or precise details of any kind. In the edited interview, I was presented as saying that there is no evidence to support stories of Satanism, but the documentary generally suggested that Ferrell's story was plausible.

I found this experience disturbing for two reasons. First, the producers seemed entirely unaware of the Satanic panic of the 1980s or that the media had played a role in disseminating claims that led to the arrest of innocent people. Second, I was astonished at how much authority was invested in the word of a convicted criminal who claimed to be a vampire. As far as persuading the producers, I felt that my research and training were in no way a match for Ferrell's charisma or the popular allure of his dark fantasy. This suggests that we may be doomed to repeat history and that our need to play the roles of heroes and villains will continue to undermine reason and justice.

THE BUILDING BLOCKS OF FANTASY

The worlds of fantasy role-playing games and evil conspiracy theories are assembled in a similar way: storytellers and conspiracy theorists mine the tropes of popular culture and mythology to create a world of monsters and heroes. These *bricolage* worlds seem uniquely real because they are created and inhabited collectively. Moral entrepreneurs are, in fact, fascinated by the same milieu of occultism and the monstrous as the gamers they condemn. However, unlike gamers, they cannot indulge this fascination within an imaginary context. Instead they reverse fact and fiction to claim that Satanic cults, monsters, and global conspiracy theories have an actual existence beyond the frame of fictional media. This process is also applied to role-playing games through claims that games like *D&D* are not "really" fantasy but actually part of an occult conspiracy. This means that the relationship between the claims makers and role-playing games is quite complex. Moral entrepreneurs condemn these games because this is the only way that they can enjoy them.

Fantasies of Evil as Bricolage

Pulling claimed that stories of Satanic rituals must be true because no one could have invented such details without a detailed knowledge of the occult.[51] This argument directly contradicts another of BADD's claims—that *D&D*, movies, and almost any form of popular culture serve to introduce the audience to occultism. In reality, inventing narratives about Satanism was quite easy for anyone raised in a culture saturated with fictional media of evil cults.[52] The origins of Satanic panic lie in pulp fiction and especially the horror films of the 1960s and 1970s. In this sense, Satanic panic and *D&D* share a common ancestry. In the 1970s, both *D&D* and Satanic conspiracy theories drew from a milieu of a fictional media and occult lore in order to transform this material into worlds that could be inhabited more directly. In a moment of honesty, Mike Warnke wrote: "Like so many others have reported, my fascination with the dark world of the occult began in my childhood. I loved ghost stories, for example, and I wanted to learn all I could about things in the supernatural realm."[53] Warnke describes being a fan of the television show *Bewitched* as well as *Creature Feature*. Significantly, *Creature Feature* is one of the sources cited by Dave Arneson as the inspiration for *Blackmoor*, the forerunner to *D&D*. Warnke's ex-Satanist narrative draws directly from the same mass media as the monsters and villains of *D&D*.

BADD misinterpreted this connection as evidence that *D&D* contains authentic occultism. A BADD pamphlet challenged the reader to compare Warnke's description of Satanic rituals in *The Satan Seller* with the description of the spell "cacodemon" found in the first edition *D&D Player's Handbook*.[54] Cacodemon (Greek for "evil spirit") was a wizard spell that summons a powerful demon. The rules specify that the demon, being evil, will kill the wizard who summoned it unless properly controlled. Although the rules do not contain a complete description of the ritual, the cacodemon spell has far more details than other *D&D* wizard spells. The rules specify that the wizard must stand within a symbol called the thaumaturgic triangle inscribed on the floor while the demon must be conjured within a circled pentacle. There is also a description of the materials necessary to conduct the ritual:

> The components of this spell are 5 flaming black candles; a brazier of hot coals upon which must be burned sulphur, bat hairs, lard, soot, mercuric-nitric acid crystals, mandrake root, alcohol, and a piece of parchment with the demon's name inscribed in runes inside a pentacle; and a dish of blood from some mammal (preferably a human, of course) placed inside the area where the cacodemon is to be held.[55]

Despite this detail, no one could ever actually cast the cacodemon spell. Even if all of the components could be obtained, mercuric-nitric acid crystals (otherwise known as mercury fulminate) is an explosive, and burning it in a brazier would likely kill any would-be conjurer. These details were included for storytelling purposes. If heroes enter a room to find a thaumaturgic triangle and a pentacle on the floor, alongside a slaughtered wizard, they will know that there is probably an escaped demon on the loose. Or, while searching for a missing child, the heroes might notice that someone in town has been purchasing these ingredients and conclude that they have abducted the child as a demonic sacrifice. Claims makers from BADD compared this description to claims of human sacrifice in *The Satan Seller* and concluded that the accounts were similar because they were true. In reality, they resemble each other because both are derivative of a common milieu of horror movie tropes and occult lore.

Warnke's successors also drew on popular culture to construct ex-Satanist narratives. John Todd claimed that he was born into a witchcraft family and that his witch name was "Lance Collins." In a series of tapes, Todd explained how the Collins family had come from Scotland to Massachusetts where they masqueraded as Puritans. He claimed that "Collins Bay" near Salem is named after his family. (The inlet in Salem is actually called Collins Cove.) Todd's story was derived from the soap opera *Dark Shadows,* which revolved around the Collins family of Collinsport, Maine, and aired on ABC from 1966 to 1971. Todd accounted for the obvious provenance of his claim by explaining that during his witchcraft days he flew to Hollywood and supplied producers with a copy of his family diary, which became the basis for the show.[56] He claimed that the television show was derivative of his story and not the other way around. Along with *Creature Feature, Dark Shadows* was another one of Arneson's influences.[57]

In the 1980s, SRA narratives continued this pattern of turning popular culture into conspiracy theories. The atrocities described in *Michelle Remembers* are a pastiche of tropes from 1970s horror films. For instance, at one point Smith describes being locked inside a giant wicker effigy of Satan. This detail is taken directly from the film *The Wicker Man* (1974) about modern-day pagans who practice human sacrifice. After *Michelle Remembers,* Laurel Rose Wilson (also known as Lauren Stratford) produced *Satan's Underground* (1988), another SRA narrative. An article for *Cornerstone* debunking Wilson found that the details of abuse in her story were taken from the book *Sybil,* which had been adapted into a made-for-television movie in 1976.[58]

More recent moral entrepreneurs have also admitted to being interested in the supernatural, conspiracy theories, and heroic fantasies from a young age. Schnoebelen confesses that as a child he was fascinated by the supernatural and UFOs. *Romancing Death* not only draws on horror films featuring Satanic cults but claims that the monsters of the Universal and Hammer studios—vampires and werewolves—have a literal existence. Similarly, Don Rimer explained to the *Virginian-Pilot,* "I've always had an interest in studying the occult, mainly from the literary side." The *Virginian-Pilot* added: "As a kid, Rimer often dressed up as Roy Rogers with a six-gun slinging from his hip. He was playing a role then just as the vampire followers play a role now."[59] Tellingly, Rimer's law enforcement primer "Ritual Crime and the Occult (The New Youth Subculture)" advises investigators examining the scene of an occult crime to "look for painted rocks, symmetrically placed rocks, bones, feathers, or symbols that would indicate traps."[60] The advice to always check for traps has far more relevance in a *D&D* adventure than in actual law enforcement.

Paracosms vs. Fact-Fiction Reversals

While both gamers and claims makers reassemble elements of popular culture to construct worlds of fantasy, these fantasies are presented in different frames. Arneson's Blackmoor incorporated the contents of horror movies and fantasy novels into a paracosm. Blackmoor, like all worlds of fantasy role-playing games, exists only within a separate and imaginary frame of reality. Claims makers do not employ an alternative frame of reality. Instead of assembling fictional elements into a paracosm, they use a conspiratorial worldview to attack the frames of fiction and fantasy and claim that fictional elements are real. In *A Culture of Conspiracy,* Michael Barkun describes "fact-fiction reversals" in which conspiracy theorists claim that "fact" is actually the fictional production of a conspiracy, and manifestly fictional narratives are asserted to be representations of reality.[61] John Todd's claim that *Dark Shadows* was based on his family diary is a classic example of fact-fiction reversal. More often, the proponents of Satanic conspiracy theories claim that evil rituals are *like* those depicted in popular culture. For instance, Bill Lightfoot, a police officer from Richmond, Virginia, told attendees at an occult crime seminar that *Rosemary's Baby* is an accurate depiction of Satanism, and that *The Believers,* another horror film, is an accurate depiction of Santeria.[62]

The most obstinate example of fact-fiction reversal concerns *The Necronomicon,* a fictional book on the occult created by pulp horror writer H. P. Lovecraft. Lovecraft's idea of a forbidden book penned by "the mad Arab," Abdul Alhazred, and kept secretly in Ivy League libraries has fascinated gamers and moral entrepreneurs alike. TSR's *Deities and Demigods* (1980) contained rules for including *The Necronomicon* in *D&D*. The following year, Chaosium published *Call of Cthulhu* in which players could role-play Lovecraftian investigators. By contrast, moral entrepreneurs insisted that *The Necronomicon* was an actual book and that law enforcement must be alerted to its existence. Both John Todd and William Schnoebelen claimed that they had seen *The Necronomicon* or parts of it with their own eyes. Schnoebelen claimed to have wielded dark Lovecraftian magic during his days as a Satanist, writing, "Contrary to the ramblings of D&D defenders . . . the Necronomicon and the Cthulhu mythos are quite real."[63] Todd was also fascinated by Lovecraft and described the Lovecraftian horror film *The Dunwich Horror* (1970) as a "truthful" film about witchcraft. He told an audience in Chicago that *The Necronomicon* was written by Nimrod and was actually a manual of Baal worship. One one occasion, he claimed *The Necronomicon* was the basis for the Book of Mormon.[64] Other moral entrepreneurs used more roundabout methods to argue that *The Necronomicon* should not be treated as simply the product of Lovecraft's imagination. Sean Sellers wrote:

> There is evidence to support the contention that the *Necronomicon* is a hoax—an imaginative book put together by H. P. Lovecraft enthusiasts. However, the book's ideals are completely evil and people, especially teenagers, have taken the book seriously enough that its rituals and practices are being performed in many places. Thus, hoax or not, Marduk is being worshiped, and Satan uses this false worship to accomplish his goals.[65]

Carl Raschke acknowledged that *The Necronomicon* is fantasy, but wrote: "The snug relationship between occult fantasy and the actual practice of the occult is well established in history. Writers such as H. P. Lovecraft and Edgar Rice Burroughs, progenitor of the Tarzan and Jane tales, were practicing occultists."[66] In reality, while Lovecraft may have been fascinated by stories of occultism, he was a professed materialist and certainly not a practicing occultist.

Of course, modern occultists, including Church of Satan founder Anton LaVey, did develop rituals and traditions based on Lovecraft's stories.[67] In 1977 an individual using the pseudonym "Simon" published a version of *The Necronomicon* as an apparent hoax. The so-called Simon Necronomicon was published by Avon Books and then by Bantam and sold in bookstores across the country. It became an important prop for both moral entrepreneurs and adolescent performances of evil. Patricia Pulling included this text in the bibliography to *The Devil's Web* and urged police officers to ask gamers whether they had read it. A copy was also found in the Ford Explorer that Ferrell stole from the Wendorfs. However, this means only that modern occultists sometimes serve as accomplices to moral entrepreneurs in reversing fact and fiction. By claiming *The Necronomicon* as real, the claims makers have more in common with Simon and Ferrell than gamers who incorporate this text into their paracosms.

The same mechanism that turns Lovecraft stories into the subject of occult crime seminars is also applied to fantasy role-playing games. The paracosms created for fantasy role-playing are simply more raw material with which conspiracy theorists can reenchant the world. Like the horror movies that were declared real during Satanic panic, fantasy role-playing games provide a rich source of imagery and tropes useful for constructing a potent tableau of evil.

Becoming Engrossed in Evil

There is an inherent irony in the project of the moral entrepreneur in that moral entrepreneurs must devote their time and energy to researching and discussing the very things that they claim to find objectionable and upsetting. Pat Robertson advised the audience of the *700 Club* to avoid *D&D* or any game dealing with magic, arguing simply, "I think we should flee from evil." But moral entrepreneurs do not flee from evil. Instead they enjoy becoming engrossed in the discourse of evil much as gamers enjoy becoming engrossed in their paracosms. In fact, moral entrepreneurs are often more fascinated by the occult than gamers. Books that condemn *D&D,* such as *The Devil's Web, Satanism: The Seduction of America's Youth,* and *The Edge of Evil,* contain lengthy appendixes filled with pentagrams, runes, and other occult symbols as well as lengthy glossaries with superficial information about tarot cards, the *I Ching*, and other forms of divination. This information has been nominally included to help readers identify dangerous occult activity around them. But the barely disguised purpose of this material is to shore up the authors' authority as experts in evil and to provide readers with occult lore that they find fascinating. This occult knowledge is probably all the more tantalizing for evangelical audiences who regard this information as dangerous and forbidden. Ironically, it is the claims makers who are actually supplying the public with a "catechism of the occult."

This means that there are actually two forms of alienation at work in the moral panic over fantasy role-playing games. Christian critics are alienated from the Christian elements of games like *D&D,* recognizing biblical references as "occultism." In fact, in a list of "symptoms of Satanic involvement" prepared by Sean Sellers, the first item is "an unusual interest in the Bible."[68] But moral entrepreneurs are also alienated from their own fascination with the demonic. By condemning fantasy role-playing games, moral entrepreneurs and occult crime investigators can allow themselves to become engrossed in the arcane and the macabre.

FANTASTIC CLAIMS AND EVANGELICAL NARRATIVE STRATEGIES

One might well ask *why* so many of the figures who attack fantasy role-playing games engage in fact-fiction reversal or otherwise blend fiction with reality. It is a difficult question to answer, and one that gamer apologists never really asked. It is facile to simply dismiss figures like John Todd, Rebecca Brown, and William Schnoebelen as mentally ill. The delusions of paranoid schizophrenics tend to be simplistic and directed toward the here and now.[69] The narratives presented by these figures have a richness and complexity more akin to a fantasy novel. Mentally ill people generally do not write books, nor are their delusions read and accepted by others. It is also not sufficient to claim, as some gamer apologists have, that Christians are inherently irrational because their truth claims concern the supernatural.[70] Many Christians believe in the reality of angels and demons but do not regard fantasy as inherently dangerous. Furthermore, evangelical publications such as *Cornerstone* and *Christianity Today* have done more than any other media outlet to investigate and debunk the fantastic claims of SRA and ex-Satanist narratives.

Instead, the roots of these fantasies appear to lie within a particular approach to narrative that developed within the New Christian Right. In *The Book of Jerry Falwell: Fundamentalist Language and Politics,* cultural anthropologist Susan Harding examines how biblical literalists like Falwell make sense of their own lives in light of their relationship with the Bible. She points out that the seemingly rigid position of biblical inerrancy paradoxically entails a great deal of creativity, as the inerrantist is constantly rediscovering the meaning of the Bible and creating new truth. This same process of "generative" interpretation is also applied to the personal narratives of Christian leaders who regard their lives as a "third testament" and a continuation of the themes and tropes of the Bible. The televangelists of the 1980s gained their authority through their ability to construct self-narratives as postbiblical characters acting within an unfolding biblically framed drama. Constructing such narratives often involved the same sort of "generativity" associated with biblical inerrancy.

Falwell occasionally invented details in order to present the sort of self-narrative expected by his followers. He had been a segregationist during the 1950s and 1960s, and when public schools were required to integrate, he created a Christian day school that accepted only white students. However, in the 1980s he presented himself as the victim of a racist regime. Harding relates an anecdote Falwell told about "Lewis," an elderly black man who shined his shoes. Lewis told Falwell he loved his preaching and wanted to know when he could join his church. Lewis's request became Falwell's call to join the side of right and take an integrationist stance. Harding expresses skepticism that this conversation with Lewis actually occurred—at least in a literal historical sense. She points out that Falwell never told this story until after Lewis had died. Falwell also specified that Lewis spoke in "soft tones" that no one else would have been able to hear. This story then was not a historical truth but a narrative that makes sense of Falwell's shifting position toward racial integration.

In one instance Falwell was caught lying about an exchange between himself and Jimmy Carter concerning homosexuality at a White House breakfast. An audiotape of the breakfast revealed that this exchange had never actually occurred. Falwell responded that he had not meant this story as a literal truth, but rather as a "parable" or an "allegory." These sorts of distortions inspired scorn from Falwell's critics, but his followers afforded him a kind of leeway to construct his own narrative. Harding explains:

> Falwell's speech is not like secular speech. He inhabits a world generated by Bible-based stories and, as a "man of God," his speech partakes of the generative quality of the Bible itself. He incessantly frames his life, if only lightly, in biblical terms, and his faithful followers read him as they read the Bible—not as already true, but as always coming true.[71]

Within Falwell's evangelical culture, authority is the product of a particular narrative strategy wherein biblical narrative and biography stream together.

The ex-Satanist narratives of Warnke, Todd, and Schnoebelen can be read as an extreme example of the sort of narrative strategy employed by Falwell. These narratives do reveal something about the characters of the tellers, but they also reveal something about their audiences and their approach to narrative. Conspiracy theories involving Satanists and the Illuminati offer an even more urgent sense of being part of an unfolding biblical drama. *Cornerstone* framed the desire to accept John Todd's claims uncritically as a form of pride, writing: "There are those Christians who simply want to believe what Todd says. There is something inside all of us that desires to be exalted while seeing those we just don't like put down. This is called pride or sin. Our sinful nature loves to gain the 'inside' knowledge on things."[72]

The narrative strategy described by Harding is particularly interesting because the New Christian Right emerged at almost the exact time that activities like *D&D* and the SCA were developing. These new cultural forms also sought to use personal narratives to form a connection to sacred times and places. Historical reenactment and fantasy role-playing allow players to construct personas together in a manner that is not unlike that of televangelists. Gygax and Arneson were themselves evangelical Christians, and it is even possible that their approach to personal narrative was shaped by evangelical culture.

Harding argues that many of Falwell's followers were aware of the way that Falwell rewrote his personal narrative. Older followers could remember when Falwell had been a committed segregationist. But their narrative strategy allowed them to overlook these biographical inconsistencies, either ignoring them or turning them into a source of meaning. Still there seems to be some cognitive dissonance inherent in this narrative strategy. Biblical narratives and personal biographies are regarded as literally true and inerrant, but they are simultaneously the subject of an unstated process of interpretation in which new truth is produced. This cognitive dissonance may be what motivates moral entrepreneurs such as Schnoebelen—who take extreme liberties in constructing their personal narratives—to accuse gamers of losing their ability to distinguish fantasy from reality.

Alan Dundes coined the term "projective inversion" to describe the process in which a claims maker accuses another of seeking to carry out an action that the claims maker would actually like to carry out himself.

Dundes adapted this theory from Freud's theory of myth but found that it also applied to conspiracy theories, such as the medieval "blood libel" in which Jews were accused of murdering Christian children for their blood. Jews were an oppressed minority in Europe, but the claim that Jews required Christian blood reversed this dynamic, casting the oppressors as the victims of Jewish aggression.[73] If we apply this theory to claims about fantasy role-playing games, it seems that claims makers object to the fantasies of others because on some level they know that their claims are also the product of imagination. The fantasy paracosms in which gamers construct new personas for themselves remind claims makers that their personas are also constructed. Accusing gamers of becoming lost in fantasy distracts claims makers from the realization that they are engaged in a form of self-deception.

THE LESSON OF GMORK

Many gamer apologists, including Gary Gygax, responded to the attacks against role-playing by arguing that it is the claims makers who are delusional. This defensive rhetoric ignores the remarkable similarities between gamers and their critics. It is not a coincidence that the turn in evangelical culture toward demonic conspiracy theories emerged at the same time as fantasy role-playing games. Both movements developed narrative strategies in order to escape the constraints of modernity by creatively invoking other times and places. Both movements were resourceful in using tropes and symbols from diverse sources to create an alternative to the mechanistic worldview offered by scientific rationalism. Both movements were collaborative and found strategies to generate meaningful narratives together.

The difference between gamers and their critics was not in their longing for adventure or their sense of morality but in their attitude toward the imagination. The New Christian Right inherited a tradition of biblical literalism that had developed in response to the Enlightenment. Were it not for this suspicion of the imagination, the 1970s and 1980s might have produced a renaissance of evangelical fiction—an American equivalent to Lewis and Tolkien. But removed from the realm of imagination, heroic fantasies became destructive in the form of conspiracy theories.

In the same year that Dallas Egbert disappeared, Michael Ende published his fantasy novel *Die unendliche Geschichte* (*The Neverending Story*). Ende's father had been a surrealist painter in Germany before his art was declared degenerate by the Nazis. Ende attended a Waldorf school founded on the ideas of esoteric philosopher Rudolf Steiner. The Waldorf school emphasized the values of spirituality and intuition.[74] *The Neverending Story* explores how imagination and reality inspire and define each other and how the imagination must be healthy to resist ideological movements such as the Nazis. The narrative has been described as "a profoundly religious text" in that it is meant to shape how the reader thinks about the world.[75] The premise of Ende's story is that there are two interconnected worlds—Reality and Fantastica. Fantastica, a realm composed of human dreams and fantasy, is being destroyed by a mysterious void called the Nothing. Atreyu, a young Fantastican warrior, embarks on a quest to save his world from the Nothing. On his adventure, he encounters a werewolf named Gmork. Gmork exists in Reality as a man and in Fantastica as a great wolf. Being an outsider in both worlds has made him a nihilist, but he also has a unique insight into the relationship between Reality and Fantastica. He engages in a dialogue with Atreyu that contains much of Ende's philosophy.

Gmork explains to Atreyu that the boundaries between Reality and Fantastica must be preserved. The Nothing that has invaded Fantastica is actually a manifestation of lies in the human world. When the people of Fantastica are sucked into the Nothing, they enter Reality, where they become lies, delusions, and propaganda. Removed from their proper home in the imagination, Fantasticans are transformed into "fears where there is nothing to fear, desires for vain, hurtful things, despairing thoughts where there is no reason to despair." Gmork gloats to Atreyu about his immanent capture by the Nothing, telling him:

> When you get to the human world, the Nothing will cling to you. You'll be like a contagious disease that makes humans blind, so they can no longer distinguish between reality and illusion. . . . Maybe you'll persuade people to buy things they don't need, or hate things they know nothing about, or hold beliefs that make them easy to handle, or doubt the truths that might save them. Yes, you little Fantastican, big things will be done in the human world with your help, wars started, empires founded.

Furthermore, humans falsely believe they can destroy lies and delusion by attacking the imagination. But this only aggravates the problem. As Fantastica shrinks, more healthy fantasies are shifted into the human world as lies. Gmork explains:

> That's why humans hate Fantastica and everything that comes from here. They want to destroy it. And they don't realize that by trying to destroy it they multiply the lies that keep flooding the human world. For these lies

> are nothing other than creatures of Fantastica who have ceased to be themselves and survive only as living corpses, poisoning the souls of men with their fetid smell. But humans don't know it. Isn't that a good joke? . . . . The human world is full of weak-minded people, who think they're as clever as can be and are convinced that it's terribly important to persuade even the children that Fantastica doesn't exist.

Gmork rejoices in the destruction of Fantastica and the spread of delusion throughout the world because he desires power and understands that a poisoned imagination is the most powerful form of hegemony. He explains his decision to aid the Nothing: "When it comes to controlling human beings there is no better instrument than lies. Because, you see, humans live by beliefs. And beliefs can be manipulated. The power to manipulate beliefs is the only thing that counts. That's why I sided with the powerful and served them—because I wanted to share their power."[76]

Gmork's lesson in metaphysics is not simply the premise of a fantasy novel but a model of the complex relationship human beings have with their imaginations. Gmork represents hegemonic regimes that seek to control the imagination, including that of the Nazis, who banned surrealist art as degenerate even as their propaganda invoked powerful mythic tropes. Ende's fable of Fantasticans that turn to delusions when taken out of their proper environment is a powerful metaphor for the two kinds of truth that Karen Armstrong calls *mythos* and *logos*. Both forms of truth are necessary, but confounding them is dangerous. Writing in 1979, Ende foresaw the panic over fantasy role-playing games. While claiming to fight against delusion, moral entrepreneurs refused to let the imagination be imaginary. They condemned the fantasy worlds of others while using them to forge waking fantasies in the form of a conspiracy theory. By confounding the worlds of fantasy and reality, the heroic impulses of people like Pulling and Warnke manifested as lies, fear, and the very real danger of moral panic.

CONCLUSION

Walking between Worlds

At this point, it may be of interest to ask what becomes of games when the sharp line dividing their ideal rules from the diffuse and insidious laws of daily life is blurred. . . . They will necessarily have to take quite different, and on occasion doubtlessly unexpected, forms.

—Roger Caillois, *Man, Play, and Games*

I have seen incredible things in fearful worlds. As it is your imagination that takes you there, so it is only by your imagination that you can get back.

—Lord Dunsany, "The Hashish Man"

Like Lord Dunsany's "hashish man," we have undertaken mental journeys to fearful worlds, examining moral panic, madness, and murder. By exploring the strange history of religious opposition to fantasy role-playing games, it is now possible to bring new perspective to some old questions. If reality is socially constructed, then all of our realms of constructed meaning—from paracosms to conspiracy theories to the sacred canopy of religious polities—may be regarded as so many "games" created through imaginative play. These worlds are able to coexist because they each occur within their own frame of meaning. By navigating these frames of metacommunication we are able to participate in different games and "walk between worlds." It is when these frames break down and worlds collide that the potential for confusion and danger arises.

The ability to define these frames of meaning is perhaps the greatest form of political power. Censorship allows authorities to restrict what we say, but controlling the frames of metacommunication allows authorities to restrict the kind of meanings we can convey. The panic over fantasy role-playing games and the imagination reflects an attempt to secure hegemony by reordering these frames of meaning. By controlling how messages are framed, it is possible to claim that fantasies are actually real, that realities are in fact only fantasies, or that discussion of fantasy or reality is actually evidence of madness. For this reason, it is especially important to study the mechanisms through which these discrete worlds of meaning are created and maintained. There is evidence that the imagination functions similarly to a muscle that allows us to shift frames of metacommunication. As such, a healthy imagination may be our best mode of resistance against epistemic confusion and hegemonic attempts to define reality for us.

THE SACRED CANOPY AS A FANTASY ROLE-PLAYING GAME

In *The Sacred Canopy,* Peter Berger outlines a model of how reality is socially constructed. He argues that human beings and the realities they create mold each other through a three-part process of externalization, objectivation, and internalization. In "externalization" human beings impose meaning onto the world through mental and physical effort. In "objectivation" the order that people have created ceases to appear arbitrary or invented and becomes taken for granted. Berger writes that the social order attains "a reality that confronts its original producers as a facticity external to and other than themselves. . . . It is through objectivation that society becomes a reality *sui generis.*"[1] Finally, this social order is "internalized" as human beings allow themselves to be shaped by it. Through socialization, they assume the roles and behaviors that the social order assigns to them. Religion has historically been the primary method through which this three-part process is achieved. After exploring how imaginary worlds are called into being through fantasy role-playing, as well as the complex fears and desires that motivate the attacks on role-playing games, a new reading of Berger's theory is in order.

First, an aspect of Berger's theory that is often forgotten is that human beings do not create a single world in which to exist, but *multiple* worlds. The world that has been rendered "real" through objectivation must share its existence with the worlds of art, science, paracosms, dreams, and so on. Berger wrote that everyday reality exists alongside "a penumbra of vastly different realities."[2] Religions—in order to maintain their authority—must be able to account for these other spheres.

The religious crusade against the imagination in general and fantasy role-playing games in particular is a manifestation of this imperative to account for other worlds. (We might note that Tolkien's idea of humanity as subcreator and conservative evangelical claims that the imagination is demonic are both effective religious accounts of the imaginary realm.)

Second, the tangible effects that fantasy role-playing games have on players demonstrate that it is possible to be transformed by a created world without accepting it as "real." In Bergerian terms, it is possible to create an imaginary order in the mind (externalization), skip over the step of objectivation, and (with the full understanding that it is only a fantasy) internalize this created order. This is evident in numerous accounts from gamers who describe changes in attitude or discovering new confidence from their experiences in the imaginary frame of fantasy. "Malori" knew that Jack Hargreaves was a character she had created, but was nevertheless able to overcome her depression by imagining herself as Jack.

In *The Sacred Canopy* Berger—along with other sociologists of that era—predicts the inevitability of secularization. He argues that religious pluralism will undermine the process of objectivation, causing socially constructed realities to seem invented rather than taken for granted. Since the 1960s, Berger has recanted the secularization hypothesis. One factor in the failure of the secularization hypothesis is that objectivation is desirable but not required in order for religious worlds to be meaningful. While encounters with alternative socially constructed realities may challenge the taken-for-granted status of a religious worldview, people also engage in something akin to what William James called "the will to believe." Frequently, they are able to simply screen out contradictory evidence or nagging doubts because doing so provides happiness, moral certainty, or other tangible rewards.

Finally, analysis of the New Christian Right's opposition to fantasy role-playing games suggests that Berger's model of objectivation is flawed or (perhaps more likely) that he has been misread. Berger explains that while reality is socially constructed, it is nevertheless real. He writes, "Once produced these worlds cannot simply be wished away."[3] This is sometimes interpreted to mean that objectivation is simply a process of *forgetting* that the symbolic order was created. But we never truly forget that the symbolic order is constructed. If we did, there would be no need for the techniques of "world maintenance" that

Berger describes. For instance, if I come to a red light, my foot will automatically move to break. Even though traffic laws are socially constructed, I cannot wish them away. Furthermore, I have internalized this social reality to the point where my body responds to the red light unconsciously. But in spite of this, I can still conceive of running the light. In thinking about running the light, I can further imagine an anomic situation in which the social reality of traffic laws has collapsed and every intersection has become a dangerous situation. Thus, it is not enough that everyone has internalized the social reality of the traffic light. The significance of the red light is never really taken for granted, and resources must be invested in punishing anyone who would challenge its meaning.

We might argue that religious claims backed by a transcendent authority are more difficult for believers to question than traffic laws. Berger describes religion as cloaking human productions in a "veil of mystification" that prevents human beings from comprehending them.[4] But if I am right that religious attacks on role-playing games were motivated by nagging doubts about religious truth claims, then this veil can be peeked through even by ardent believers. Perhaps objectivation is a not a matter of forgetting or a "veil of mystification" so much as an ongoing process in which we try to convince ourselves that the symbolic order cannot be questioned when we know that it can. Berger actually uses Sartre's term "bad faith" in describing this process. He describes bad faith as a "false consciousness" in which "the dialectic between the socialized self and the self in its totality is lost to consciousness."[5] The trouble is (as Sartre would argue) that this dialectic is never *really* lost to consciousness. In fact, the very methods used to mystify social reality and shore up its plausibility demonstrate an awareness that the social order is *not* taken for granted but must be defended. For instance, Berger cites historic situations such as the Spanish Inquisition or the millet system of the Ottoman Empire in which religious minorities were banished because their existence challenged the taken-for-granted status of the dominant religion. But if authorities were truly not conscious of the fact that the symbolic order of their religion could be weakened, there would be no need to banish dissenters. While a religious society may persecute infidels, there is no need to banish people who insist that two and two make five, because there is no danger that their strange ideas could undermine the taken-for-granted order of arithmetic. Behind the campaigns of BADD, the narrative strategies of Jerry Falwell and the New Christian Right, and Cotton Mather's allusion to something "worse than diabolical," there is a kernel of awareness that religious realities are socially constructed and that strategies must be developed to bury this realization as much as possible.

This means that the religious "veil of mystification" is really a kind of serious game in which the players are always trying to forget that there is a reality beyond the game. Johan Huizinga observes that while cheating may sometimes be allowed, spoilsports—those who simply ignore the game and its premise—cannot never be tolerated because they rob the game of its illusion.[6] Banishing religious dissenters in order to maintain the illusion of a sacred order is not so different from a *D&D* group banishing a player who refuses to "be serious."

Furthermore, Berger suggests that the idea of God functions to anchor the socially constructed "game" by serving as a steadfast player who will never be a spoilsport and who will always affirm the roles of the other players. Berger writes:

> An Arabic proverb puts it succinctly: "Men forget, God remembers." What men forget, among other things, is their reciprocal identifications in the game of playing society. Social identities and their corresponding roles are assigned to the individual by others, but others are also quite liable to change or withdraw the assignments. They "forget" who the individual was and, because of the inherent dialectic of recognition and self-recognition, thus powerfully threaten his own recollections of identity. If he can assume that, at any rate, God remembers, his tenuous self-identifications are given a foundation seemingly secure from the shifting reactions of other men. God then becomes the most reliable and ultimately significant other.[7]

Berger's analyis turns on its head the characterization that the dungeon master "acts as God." As an omnipotent and invisible player who makes the roles of all the other players possible, it could be argued that God serves the social function of a dungeon master!

By comparing religion to a role-playing game, I do not mean to slight religion or dismiss its significance. Human beings must have such socially constructed worlds to function, and there is ultimately no "objective" reality beyond these imagined worlds. Furthermore, these are games with real consequences: laws are formed, wars are fought, and values are created as a result of the shared reality of religious traditions. Rather than dismissing religion, I am suggesting that we take play more seriously. In particular we should pay attention to the frames of meaning in which these constructed realities occur. It is not the content of the game but its frame that determines whether it will translate into action.

DISCERNING FRAMES OF MEANING

The "penumbra of vastly different realities" has grown exponentially since the 1960s when Berger first addressed the problem of multiple symbolic orders coexisting. This has come about primarily through communications technology, which has led to an unprecedented amount of information being exchanged across the planet. In addition to the worlds of television and film, new forms of discourse have produced an entire ecosystem of interrelated frames of meaning. Social networking sites, virtual communities, and massively multiplayer online (MMO) games all provide the opportunity to perform a new identity in a different frame of reality.

Gregory Bateson notes that there are forms of play that revolve around the question "Is this play?" Emerging cultural forms increasingly play with the frames of reality and fiction. "Viral marketing" campaigns for films attempt to create confusion as to which elements of the film are real and which are invented. The assumption is that people will generate excitement for the film as they debate its reality. Similarly, the new genre of "live-record horror," spearheaded by films like *The Blair Witch Project* (1999), attempts to confuse the audience as to whether they are watching fiction or a documentary. "Parody religions" such as the Church of the Flying Spaghetti Monster employ the same principle: they advance public discourse around a political issue by confusing the public as to whether they are sincerely a religious movement or a form of play.[8]

So-called alternate reality games may be the starkest example of deliberate distortion of frames. These games, which evolved out of viral marketing, feature a narrative set within the fictional frame of the game. However, they attempt to disguise the fact that a game is being played at all. Rather than announcing a game and inviting players to participate, people are lured into the game through a deliberate clue sometimes called a "rabbit hole." The first such game is generally considered to be *The Beast,* created in 2001 to promote Steven Spielberg's film *A.I.* Advertisements for the film included a credit listing for someone named Jeanine Salla, who served as a "Sentient Machine Therapist." A certain number of viewers were shrewd enough to realize that there are no sentient machines and curious enough to investigate who Jeanine Salla was. An Internet search for "Jeanine Salla" led to websites that were also part of the game. Further searching led to a an interactive murder mystery set in the year 2142. *The Beast* was not limited to online interaction and involved phone calls with actors playing characters. Eventually a certain number of "players" participated in rallies in New York, Chicago, and Los Angeles.[9]

In his 2005 book *This Is Not a Game,* alternate reality game designer David Szulborski writes:

> In an alternate reality game, the goal is not to immerse the player in the artificial world of the game; instead, a successful game immerses the world of the game into the everyday existence and life of the player. . . . The ultimate goal is to have the player believe that the events take place and characters of the game exist in his world, not an alternate reality. In a strange but very real way, the ARG creator is trying not to create an alternate reality, but change the player's existing world into an alternate reality.[10]

There is anecdotal data of alternate reality gamers experiencing lingering uncertainty as to whether or not they are playing a game or seeing "rabbit holes" where none actually exist. However, Szulborski expresses doubt that the games could actually induce delusion. He explains that while the goal may be to erase the frames of game and reality, the ability to distinguish reality from game never really goes away. Roger Caillois describes "vertigo," or the attempt to blur perceptions, as one of the four basic forms of play. In this sense, the attempt to hide the line between reality and game in alternate reality games could be regarded as a kind of "metaplay"—a very sophisticated version of children finding pleasure in spinning until they collapse.

The fact that there is a community of people who understands, designs, and enjoys alternate reality games suggests that we are becoming more facile at shifting between different frames of meaning. However, confusion and controversies regarding discrete frames of meaning still arise. When they do, they frequently invoke the past thirty years of discourse over the alleged dangers of fantasy. Taking an opponent's statements "out of context" has always been a tactic in the political arena, and the emergence of new frames of meaning has made this tactic more versatile. The political attacks on Colleen Lachowicz and Jake Rush for comments made in the context of role-playing games represented a calculated refusal to acknowledge the frame of a fantasy game.

The courts are another sphere in which the borders of fantasy and reality are contested. The *D&D* defense was attempted as recently as 2005. In Ireland Robert Boyd robbed a lingerie store at knifepoint, stealing a number of women's undergarments. Boyd, who was regularly seeing a psychiatrist before the robbery, claimed that he believed he was his character, a criminal female elf from the fantasy role-playing game

Shadowrun.[11] However, since the panic, *D&D* is most likely to be invoked in trials involving conspiracy charges. For instance, white supremacist Brit "Hawke" Greenbaum was a college student who founded an online group called "the Knights of Freedom." In attempting to assess whether Greenbaum was a threat, a representative of the Southern Poverty Law Center commented, "In some ways, it's like 'Dungeons and Dragons.' But he has the potential to become a real leader."[12] In other words, it was difficult to discern whether Greenbaum's statements about killing blacks and Jews in a national uprising were simply fantasies or a sign that he was preparing for literal acts of violence.

This situation repeated itself in 2012 when members of a Christian militia called "the Hutaree" were tried for seditious conspiracy. Informants reported that members of the militia had discussed a number of plans to incite an uprising against the government, one of which involved murdering a police officer and then attacking the funeral procession using weapons of mass destruction. Instead of the *D&D* defense, wherein defendants claim they committed crimes while lost in fantasy, members of the Hutaree claimed that authorities had mistaken their fantasies for a literal plan of action. The trial revolved around the question of whether the discussion of killing police officers represented coherent plans that might actually be carried out or merely dark fantasies. In the end, a judge decided that while the discussion of the Hutaree members was "vile," the group's plans were too vague to be deemed conspiracy. The Hutaree were acquitted of sedition, and their discussion was declared free speech protected under the First Amendment.[13] There is no way to know if the dark imagination of the Hutaree would have resulted in action had law enforcement not intervened. It is likely that the Hutaree themselves were uncertain where their discussions of violent revolution might ultimately lead.

Huizinga writes that "the most fundamental characteristic of true play, whether it be a cult, a performance, a contest, or a festivity, is that at a certain moment it is *over.*"[14] Both Huizinga and Caillois understand that play is a mechanism through which human beings construct new frames of meaning. At a certain point the frame of the game ceases to be play. It assumes an independent existence and becomes something else entirely. As Caillois points out, it is difficult to predict what happens to games once they cease to be games. For a culture, the shared meanings constructed in play can become the paradigms through which it understands the world. For an individual, the roles adopted during play can become a permanent identity. Disturbingly, the transition from play to something else can happen gradually such that the players are unaware of it. It *is* possible for the lines between imaginative play and reality to become blurred, and this does sometimes lead to dangerous consequences. However, this does not happen in the manner suggested by the critics of role-playing games. When sufficient energy is invested into imaginative play, the play can assume one of three levels of reality ranging from the purely imaginary to paradigms that are, for all intents and purposes, real. These are (1) paracosms, (2) socially constructed realities, and (3) corrupted play.

Imaginative play can develop into paracosms such as the worlds of fantasy role-playing games. Fantasy role-playing games represent a highly stable form of imaginative play because while they have demonstrable impact on the way players think about the world beyond the game, they are clearly demarcated as imaginary rather than real. In other cases, a culture may come to accept the products of play as reality. This process can occur over a long period of time as described in the theories of Huizinga and Robert Bellah. However, this transformation also occurs in the "liminal" situations described by Victor Turner. Initiation rituals can be regarded as a form of play in that symbols are taken out of their ordinary context and repurposed. At the end of this process, the initiates have a new role. They are not "pretending" to be initiated; their change in status is accepted as reality by the entire society.

Rarely, imaginative play can develop into corrupted play. This is an interstitial frame in which the premise of the game and the roles of the players are simultaneously real and unreal. Such frames are inherently unstable. Corrupted play is no longer clearly a game, but it is also not yet accepted as reality. Eventually corrupted play either ends and is dismissed as only a game or else it continues and is regarded as reality. Corrupted play is significant because it is a sort of crossroads between fantasy and reality. It is a necessary state through which the ideas generated in play must pass in order to become socially constructed reality. This makes corrupted play a site of strategic importance for anyone seeking to define what reality is. For the "magical gamers," the language of play helps to rationalize and sustain ideas that are at odds with scientific rationalism. In the interstitial space between play and objective claims making it is possible to introduce new ideas such as "otherkin" into the established order. Conversely, hegemony is threatened by corrupted play. Institutions seeking to preserve the status quo have an interest in suppressing and stigmatizing the emergence of new ideas and cultural forms from play. Corrupted play is also threatening because it displays the mechanisms through which reality is socially constructed. The awareness that fantasies can become reality implies that our own taken-for-granted realities may actually be fantasies. For some, the best way to stave off a sense of *anomie* and secure the taken-for-granted status of their worldview is to attack the other products of play by condemning corrupted play and even paracosms as madness and heresy.

In the long run, Huizinga and Caillois regard the emergence of new cultural forms from play as a natural cultural process. However, within their own times and cultures, they regard the corruption of play with great suspicion. The liminal roles between play and reality are most often assumed by adolescents. The "psychosocial moratoriums" studied by Erik Erikson, in which certain cultures allow youth to temporarily deviate from societal norms, are a sort of corrupted play. In cultures where these periods are institutionalized, youth eventually transition into their new roles as adults. However, in other contexts, the corrupted play of adolescents can become dangerous. Youth like the *bosozoku* studied by Ikuya Sato, as well as adolescent murderers such as Sean Sellers and Rod Ferrell, found themselves in situations where their respective roles as dangerous bikers, Satanist, and vampire could no longer be abandoned.

Corrupted play is also dangerous when adults engage in it. Huizinga expresses concerns that modern society has increasingly come to blur play and reality. He describes this outlook as "puerilism" because of its association with adolescence. Huizinga feels that America, in particular, is a nation in which play and reality are confounded:

> The country where a national puerilism could be studied most thoroughly in all its aspects from the innocent and even attractive to the criminal, is the United States. . . . The modern puerilism shows itself in two ways. One the one hand, activities of a professedly serious nature and universally regarded as serious, like those mentioned above, come to be permeated with the spirit of play and to bear all the characteristics of play; on the other, activities admittedly of a play-character come to lose the true quality of play because of the manner in which they are carried on.[15]

This characterization is, of course, sheer opinion, and Huizinga presents virtually no evidence that Americans have a less healthy relationship with play than do people of other nations. However, there are certainly examples of adults engaging in corrupted play in the United States. The plans of violence discussed by groups like the Knights of Freedom and the Hutaree fall into this category. During the decades of the panic, moral entrepreneurs also engaged in a form of corrupted play not unlike that of the adolescent criminals whom they held up as examples of the dangers of fantasy role-playing. Like teenage Satanists and vampires, figures like Warnke, Dear, Pulling, Brown, and Schnoebelen combined their imaginary roles and narratives with empirical claims, seemingly without realizing they were doing it.

Danger arises not from the realm of sheer fantasy or socially constructed reality, but from the liminal space between these frames. How might we prevent dangerous games from resulting in tragedy? In his study of the *bosozoku,* Sato observes that the transformation from playing the role of a dangerous biker to becoming a criminal occurred when play resulted in irrevocable consequences. He notes that certain dangers, such as AIDS, drugs, and guns, greatly increase the chance that actions taken during play will result in such consequences. Almost all the cases of juvenile violence cited by BADD and other antigaming crusaders involved either minors who had unsupervised access to firearms or who were engaging in dangerous activities while under the influence of drugs and alcohol. It is possible that without these factors, in many cases the play would have ended before irrevocable consequences ensued.

This is not to suggest that legislation can prevent the consequences of corrupted play. Furthermore the factors cited by Sato are applicable to juveniles who engage in dangerous actions while performing heroic roles. Adults also play dangerous games. How can we ensure the dark fantasies of groups like the Hutaree will not result in irrevocable action? How can conspiracy theorists be prevented from inciting moral panic when they present their fantasies? There are no simple solutions to these problems because there will always be outlets for people to present their imaginative play as reality.

However, the worst response would be to blame fantasy itself. Since the Enlightenment, there has been a long tradition of associating the imagination with delusion. Like the preschools that banned imaginary weapons and superhero play, there is a recurring assumption that we can somehow foster security by restricting imaginative play. This, I would argue, is the most dangerous path of all. Far from encouraging delusion, the imagination allows us to analyze models of reality and enhances our powers of discernment. There is evidence that by switching back and forth between different frames, we become more adept at distinguishing fantasy and reality. Studies in developmental psychology have suggested that children with a high "fantasy orientation"—that is, children who are more imaginative—are better at discerning fantasy from reality.[16] It is possible that the more we intentionally engage in fantasy the less likely we are to engage in it unintentionally. By using the imagination deliberately, we learn to master frames of metacommunication instead of allowing them to master us. The moral panic over role-playing games developed out of a religious culture that shuns imaginary realms as demonic. It is possible that figures like Warnke and Schnoebelen were predisposed to blend fantasy with reality because they never had any practice at negotiating these frames.

To avoid the dangers of corrupted play, we must learn to walk between worlds. Robert Bellah writes, "Possible worlds, multiple realities, have consequences we could not live without."[17] The alternate worlds presented by art, science, fantasy, and religion make it possible for us to interpret our world. The ability to imagine other worlds means that change is always possible, including the rise of deviance and challenges to the social order. However, when we attempt to secure the status quo by blocking access to these worlds, we do so at great peril. Like Michael Ende's Fantasticans, who are transformed into lies when their native realm is destroyed, the attempt to stamp out dangerous fantasy only produces more insidious forms of delusion. In order to navigate the multiple realities that are our birthright as human beings, we must first become comfortable with their existence. Only by becoming conscious of these other worlds and thinking about them deliberately can we stop ourselves from playing dangerous games.

Notes

PREFACE. "YOU WORSHIP GODS FROM BOOKS!"

Epigraph: Christopher Robichaud, "Remarks on the Occasion of Harvard's Reenactment of the Black Mass," https://medium.com/p/ea2c0bae79e5 (accessed May 13, 2014). A group called the Satanic Temple organized a reenactment of a Satanic black mass through the Harvard Extension Cultural Studies Club, originally to be held on May 12, 2014, in the pub beneath Memorial Hall. In response to the announced event 1,500 outraged Catholics marched from MIT to Harvard in a Eucharistic procession. The event was relocated off campus, but a private venue ultimately refused to host it. Dr. Robichaud was never able to deliver his speech.

1. T. Michael Anthony, *Suicide: Knowing When Your Teen Is at Risk* (Ventura, Calif.: Regal Books, 1991), 54.

2. Joan Hake Robie, *The Truth about Dungeons and Dragons* (Lancaster, Pa.: Starburst Publishers, 1991), 23.

INTRODUCTION. FANTASY AND REALITY

Epigraphs: Sigmund Freud, *A General Introduction to Psychoanalysis* (New York: Washington Square Press, 1960), 92; George Santayana, *The Life of Reason: The Phases of Human Progress* (Auckland, New Zealand: The Floating Press, 2009), 547.

1. Daniel Mackay (*The Fantasy Role-Playing Game: A New Performing Art* [Jefferson, N.C.: McFarland, 2001], 4–5) provides a more rigorous definition: "An *episodic* and *participatory* story-creation *system* that includes a set of quantified *rules* that assist a group of *players* and a *gamemaster* in determining how their fictional *characters'* spontaneous interactions are resolved." Jennifer Grouling Cover (*The Creation of Narrative in Tabletop Role-Playing Games*

[Jefferson, N.C.: McFarland, 2010], 168) expands this definition to "a type of game/game system that involves collaboration between a small group of players and a gamemaster through face-to-face social activity with the purpose of creating a narrative experience."

2. Alison Gopnik, *The Philosophical Baby* (New York: Farrar, Straus and Giroux, 2009).

3. Marjorie J. Kostelnik et al., "Living with He-Man: Managing Superhero Fantasy Play," *Young Children* 4:4 (May 1986): 3–9.

4. Sarah Lynne Bowman, *The Functions of Role-Playing Games* (Jefferson, N.C.: McFarland, 2010), 95–103.

5. Michael Tresca, *The Evolution of the Fantasy Role-Playing Game* (Jefferson, N.C.: McFarland, 2011), 14.

6. David M. Ewalt, *Of Dice and Men: The Story of Dungeons & Dragons and the People Who Play It* (New York: Scribner, 2013), 30.

7. Wizards of the Coast, *30 Years of Adventure: A Celebration of Dungeons & Dragons* (Renton, Wash.: Wizards of the Coast, 2006); Liam Lacey, "Dungeons and Dragons: An Underground Game Is Ready to Surface," *Globe and Mail,* November 29, 1978; Ethan Gilsdorf, *Fantasy Freaks and Gaming Geeks: An Epic Quest for Reality among Role Players, Online Gamers, and Other Dwellers of Imaginary Realms* (Guilford, Conn.: The Lyons Press, 2009), 52.

8. Jerry Adler and Shawn Doherty, "Kids: The Deadliest Game?," *Newsweek,* September 9, 1985, 93.

9. Quoted in Lawrence Schick, *Heroic Worlds: A History and Guide to Role-Playing Games* (Buffalo, N.Y.: Prometheus Books, 1991), 14.

10. Mackay, *The Fantasy Role-Playing Game,* 118.

11. Schick, *Heroic Worlds,* 15.

12. John Eric Holmes, "Confessions of a Dungeon Master," *Psychology Today,* November 1980, 84–88.

13. Ibid., 93.

14. Peter Berger, *The Sacred Canopy: Elements of a Sociological Theory of Religion* (New York: Anchor Books, 1969), 5.

15. Stanley Cohen, *Folk Devils and Moral Panic* (New York: Routledge, 2002), 1.

16. Christopher B. Strain, *Reload: Rethinking Violence in American Life* (Nashville: Vanderbilt University Press, 2010), 56–57.

17. David Frankfurter, *Evil Incarnate: Rumors of Demonic Conspiracy and Ritual Abuse in History* (Princeton, N.J.: Princeton University Press, 2006), 108.

18. Gilsdorf, *Fantasy Freaks and Gaming Geeks,* 143. For other examples of this genre, see Mark Barrowcliffe, *The Elfish Gene: Dungeons and Dragons and Growing Up Strange* (New York: Soho Press, 2007); Ewalt, *Of Dice and Men.*

19. Richard White, "Dungeons and Dragons: Adventure or Abomination?," *The Baptist Challenge* LI:7 (July 2011): 5–19.

20. Alison T. Williams, "Ritual Crime, Occults on the Rise," *Newport News Daily Press,* January 15, 2011.

21. Gilsdorf, *Fantasy Freaks and Gaming Geeks,* 180.

22. Maine Republican Party, "Colleen's World" (2012), http://www.colleensworld.com/ (accessed November 24, 2012).

23. Mike Krumboltz, "Wow Fan Colleen Lachowicz Victorious in State Senate Bid," *The Ticket,* November 8, 2012, http://news.yahoo.com/blogs/ticket/wow-fan-colleen-lachowicz-victorious-state-senate-bid-170734118—election.html (accessed November 24, 2012).

24. Hunter Walker, "Florida House Candidate Defends His 'Hobby Activities,' Sends Out This Picture of Himself in a Costume," *Business Insider,* April 1, 2014, http://www.businessinsider.com/florida-house-candidate-defends-his-hobby-activities-2014-4 (accessed April 29, 2014).

25. Johan Huizinga, *Homo Ludens: A Study of the Play-Element in Culture* (Boston: Beacon Press, 1955), 5.

26. Gary Alan Fine, *Shared Fantasy: Role-Playing Games as Social Worlds* (Chicago: University of Chicago Press, 1983), 3–5.

27. William James, *Principles of Psychology,* vol. 2 (New York: Cosimo, 2007); Alfred Schutz, "On Multiple Realities," *Philosophy and Phenomenological Research* 5:4 (June 1945): 533–76; Gregory Bateson, *Steps to an Ecology of Mind* (New York: Ballantine Books, 1972); Erving Goffman, *Frame Analysis: An Essay on the Organization of Experience* (Cambridge, Mass.: Harvard University Press, 1974).

28. Fine, *Shared Fantasy,* 3.

29. For a more detailed exegesis of discourse regarding multiple frames of reality in role-playing games, see Sean Q. Hendricks, "Incorporative Discourse Strategies in Tabletop Fantasy Role-Playing Gaming," in *Gaming as Culture: Essays on Reality, Identity, and Experience in Fantasy Games,* ed. J. Patrick Williams, Sean Q. Hendricks, and W. Keith Winkler (Jefferson, N.C.: McFarland, 2006), 39–56.

30. Wizards of the Coast, *Dungeon Master's Guide, Core Rulebook II,* 3.5 (Renton, Wash.: Wizards of the Coast, 2003), 11–12.

31. Fine, *Shared Fantasy,* 242.

32. Mackay, *The Fantasy Role-Playing Game,* 156.

33. Bob Mackey, "Letter," *Dragon* 181 (May 1992): 80.

34. Stuart M. Leeds, "Personality, Belief in the Paranormal, and Involvement with Satanic Practices among Young Adult Males: Dabblers versus Gamers," *Cultic Studies Journal* 12:2 (1995): 148–65. This study depended on rather dubious surveys with titles such as the "Satanic and Fantasy Envelopment" (SAFE) survey. A comment by Paul Cardwell challenged the study's methodology; see Paul Cardwell, Jr. "Comment on Leeds (1995)," *Cultic Studies Journal* 16:2 (1999): 197–202.

35. See, for example, Sarah M. Pike, *Earthly Bodies, Magical Selves: Contemporary Pagans and the Search for Community* (Berkeley: University of California Press, 2001), 171; Martin Ramstedt, "Metaphor of Invocation? The Convergence of Ritual between Modern Paganism and Fantasy Fiction," *Journal of Ritual Studies* 21:1 (2007): 1–15.

36. Berger, *The Sacred Canopy,* 45.

37. Christopher Partridge, "Alternative Spiritualities, New Religions, and the Re-Enchantment of the West," in *The Oxford Handbook of New*

Religious Movements, ed. James R. Lewis (New York: Oxford University Press, 2004), 56.

38. Bateson, *Steps to an Ecology of Mind,* 181.

39. Lev Vygotsky, *Mind in Society* (Cambridge, Mass.: Harvard University Press, 1978).

40. Gopnik, *The Philosophical Baby,* 21.

41. C.S. Lewis, *Surprised by Joy: The Shape of My Early Life* (New York: Harcourt, Brace, 1956).

42. Dorothy Singer and Jerome Singer, *The House of Make-Believe: Children's Play and the Developing Imagination* (Cambridge, Mass.: Harvard University Press, 1990), 115.

43. Huizinga, *Homo Ludens,* 13. Calliois builds on Huizinga's work to establish six formal criteria of play. He argues that for anything to be classified as play it must be free, separate, uncertain, unproductive, regulated, and fictive. See Roger Caillois, *Man, Play, and Games* (New York: Free Press of Glencoe, 1961).

44. Roger Caillois, *Man and the Sacred* (Glencoe, Ill.: Free Press of Glencoe, 1959).

45. Robert Bellah, *Religion in Human Evolution: From the Paleolithic to the Axial Age* (Cambridge, Mass.: Harvard University Press, 2011), 77–80.

46. Bateson, *Steps to an Ecology of Mind,* 182.

47. Johan Huizinga, *In the Shadow of Tomorrow* (New York: W.W. Norton, 1936), 177.

48. Ikuya Sato, *Kamikaze Biker: Parody and Anomy in Affluent Japan* (Chicago: University of Chicago Press, 1991), 221.

49. Daniel Martin and Gary Alan Fine, "Satanic Cults, Satanic Play: Is 'Dungeons and Dragons' a Breeding Ground for the Devil?," in *The Satanism Scare,* ed. James T. Richardson, Joel Best, and David G. Bromley (Hawthorne, N.Y.: Aldine De Gruyter, 1991), 121.

50. Gareth J. Medway, *Lure of the Sinister: The Unnatural History of Satanism* (New York: New York University Press, 2001), 369; Kurt Lancaster, "Do Role-Playing Games Promote Crime, Satanism and Suicide among Players as Critics Claim?" *Journal of Popular Culture* 28:2 (1994): 77–78.

51. Huizinga, *In the Shadow of Tomorrow,* 23.

52. In 1992, Daniel and Francine Keller of Oak Hill, Texas, were accused of using their day-care center as a front to conduct ritual abuse. Even after the alleged victim, a three-year-old girl, testified in court that she had invented the allegations, the Kellers were found guilty and sentenced to forty-eight years in prison. They were finally exonerated and released in 2013. See Jordan Smith, "Believing the Children," *Austin Chronicle,* March 27, 2009. In 1994, a survey by the National Center on Child Abuse and Neglect investigated 12,000 accusations of SRA but did not find evidence to support a single accusation. Daniel Goleman, "Proof Lacking for Ritual Abuse by Satanists," *New York Times,* October 31, 1994.

53. See Susan Friend Harding, *The Book of Jerry Falwell: Fundamentalist Language and Politics* (Princeton, N.J.: Princeton University Press, 2000).

54. Steven Starker, *Evil Influences: Crusades against the Mass Media* (New Brunswick, N.J.: Transaction Publishers, 1989), 143.

55. Cohen, *Folk Devils and Moral Panic,* xii.

56. Joan Robie, *The Truth about Dungeons and Dragons* (Lancaster, Pa.: Starburst Publishers, 1991), 9.

57. Ibid., 61.

58. Rus Walton, *Biblical Solutions to Contemporary Problems: A Handbook* (Brentwood, Tenn.: Wolgemuth & Hyatt Publishers, 1988), 341.

59. Vince Londini, "Escaping Reality: The Dangers of Role-Playing Games," Way of Life Literature, Inc. (March 22, 2005), http://www.wayoflife.org/database/roleplaying.html (accessed November 24, 2012).

60. Peter Leithart and George Grant, *A Christian Response to Dungeons and Dragons: The Catechism of the New Age* (Fort Worth, Tex.: Dominion Press, 1988), 14.

61. Jason Bivins, *Religion of Fear: The Politics of Horror in Conservative Evangelicalism* (New York: Oxford University Press, 2008), 18.

62. Schmuel Eisenstadt, *The Origins and Diversity of Axial Age Civilizations* (Albany: State University of New York Press, 1986).

1. THE BIRTH OF FANTASY ROLE-PLAYING GAMES

Epigraphs: Edgar Rice Burroughs, *Jungle Tales of Tarzan* (New York: Grosset and Dunlap, 1919), 120; T.E. Lawrence, *Seven Pillars of Wisdom: A Triumph; The Complete 1922 Text* (Charleston, S.C.: CreateSpace, 2011), 7.

1. Several books have appeared recently outlining the development of role-playing games. Of these, the most comprehensive is Jon Peterson's *Playing at the World: A History of Simulating Wars, People, and Fantastic Adventure from Chess to Role-Playing Games* (San Diego: Unreason Press, 2012). At nearly 700 pages, Peterson's work is astoundingly detailed and draws on dozens of interviews and hobby magazines from the early days of recreational wargaming.

2. Quoted in Peter Perla, *The Art of Wargaming: A Guide for Professionals and Hobbyists* (Annapolis: Naval Institute Press, 1990), 17.

3. European cartographers were just discovering how to make accurate topographical maps in the century that *Kriegspiel* was created. A complete topographical map of France first appeared in 1789. See Peterson, *Playing at the World,* 219.

4. Gary Alan Fine, *Shared Fantasy: Role-Playing Games as Social Worlds* (Chicago: University of Chicago Press, 1983), 8–9. In his biography of Steve Jobs, Walter Isaacson describes the founder of Apple playing *Kriegspiel* in college while under the influence of LSD. See Walter Isaacson, *Steve Jobs* (New York: Simon & Schuster, 2011), 35.

5. Charles R. Shrader, *History of Operations Research in the United States Army,* vol. 1, *1942–1962* (Washington, D.C.: Office of the Deputy Under Secretary of the Army for Operations Research, U.S. Army, 2006), 113–14.

6. Charles Adiel Lewis Totten, *Strategos: A Series of American Games of War* (New York: D. Appleton, 1880). *Strategos* should not be confused with *Stratego,* created by Milton Bradley in 1961.

7. H.G. Wells, *Little Wars: A Game for Boys* (London: Frank Palmer, 1913).

8. "Life Visits the Planet Atzor," *Life,* May 3, 1941, 102–5.

9. Daniel Mackay, *The Fantasy Role-Playing Game: A New Performing Art* (Jefferson, N.C.: McFarland, 2001), 153.

10. Michael J. Tresca, *The Evolution of Fantasy Role-Playing Games* (Jefferson, N.C.: McFarland, 2011), 48–49.

11. Although Wesley was a regular visitor to the University of Minnesota, he was enrolled at Hamline University, where he was a physics major. See David M. Ewalt, *Of Dice and Men: The Story of Dungeons & Dragons and the People Who Play It* (New York: Scribner, 2013), 57.

12. Lawrence Schick, *Heroic Worlds: A History and Guide to Role-Playing Games* (Buffalo, N.Y.: Prometheus Books, 1991), 17.

13. Yehuda Berlinger, "The History of the New Games Foundation" (February 14, 2008), http://jergames.blogspot.com/2008/02/history-of-new-games-foundation.html (accessed December 17, 2012).

14. Tresca, *The Evolution of Fantasy Role-Playing Games,* 60–61.

15. Quoted in Peterson, *Playing at the World,* 62.

16. Claude Levi-Strauss, *The Savage Mind* (Chicago: University of Chicago Press, 1966), 30–32.

17. While the group had only about a hundred members, it claimed to be "international" because a handful of players lived in Puerto Rico and at least one in Germany. Peterson, *Playing at the World,* 10.

18. "What Is the SCA?," http://www.sca.org/officers/chatelain/sca-intro.html (accessed December 19, 2012).

19. Nick Montfort, *Twisty Little Passages: An Approach to Interactive Fiction* (Cambridge, Mass.: MIT Press, 2003), 74. Mackay, *The Fantasy Role-Playing Game,* 15. To represent these fantastic units, Gygax reportedly created an early dragon miniature from a plastic dinosaur. A giant was created by affixing doll's hair and a matchstick "club" to an Elastolin Viking figure. Ethan Gilsdorf, *Fantasy Freaks and Gaming Geekss: An Epic Quest for Reality among Role Players, Online Gamers, and Other Dwellers of Imaginary Realms* (Guilford, Conn.: The Lyons Press, 2009), 70.

20. Gilsdorf, *Fantasy Freaks and Gaming Geeks,* 8.

21. Peterson, *Playing at the World,* 429.

22. Barrowcliffe, *The Elfish Gene,* 18.

23. Quoted in Fine, *Shared Fantasy,* 13–14.

24. Moira Johnston, "It's Only a Game—Or Is It?," *New West,* August 25, 1980, 37.

25. Quoted in Schick, *Heroic Worlds,* 166.

26. Schick, *Heroic Worlds,* 18.

27. Quoted in David Kushner, "Dungeon Master: The Life and Legacy of Gary Gygax," *Wired,* March 10, 2008, http://www.wired.com/gaming/virtualworlds/news/2008/03/ff_gygax (accessed January 1, 2013).

28. Tresca, *The Evolution of Fantasy Role-Playing Games,* 50.

29. Steward Alsop, "TSR Hobbies Mixes Fact and Fantasy," *Inc.,* February 1982, 68.

30. Quoted in Kushner, "The Dungeon Master."

31. Liam Lacey, "Dungeons and Dragons: An Underground Game Is Ready to Surface," *Globe and Mail,* November 29, 1978.

32. In some versions of the story, Gygax would credit the name to his wife, Mary, rather than to Cindy. Peterson, *Playing at the World,* 75.

33. Patricia Pulling, "A Law Enforcement Primer on Fantasy Role Playing Games" (Richmond, Va.: B.A.D.D., n.d.), 11.

34. Richard White, *Dungeons and Dragons: Adventure or Abomination?* (Virginia Beach: Christian Broadcasting Network, 2007), 1.

35. Quoted in Kushner, "The Dungeon Master."

36. Alsop, "TSR Hobbies Mixes Fact and Fantasy," 68.

37. Wizards of the Coast, *30 Years of Adventure: A Celebration of Dungeons & Dragons* (Renton, Wash.: Wizards of the Coast, 2006), n.p.

38. Lacey, "Dungeons and Dragons," n.p.

39. Wizards of the Coast, *30 Years of Adventure,* n.p.

40. Ewalt, *Of Dice and Men,* 73–98.

41. "Dungeons and Dollars," *New York Times,* November 2, 1980, 19.

42. Fine, *Shared Fantasy,* 15.

43. La Farge, "Destroy All Monsters," *The Believer,* September 2006, http://www.believermag.com/issues/200609/?read = article_lafarge (accessed December 17, 2012).

44. Fine, *Shared Fantasy,* 38.

45. *Enter the Dragon* was released in 1973 and became exceedingly popular. Ewalt (*Of Dice and Men,* 73) interviewed a former member of Arneson's gaming group who claimed the monk class was created because one player enjoyed the song "Kung Fu Fighting" by Carl Douglas (1974).

46. Tresca, *The Evolution of Fantasy Role-Playing Games,* 62.

47. Johnston, "It's Only a Game," 37.

48. Michael A. Stackpole, "Game Hysteria and the Truth: Part 1" (1989), http://www.featherlessbiped.com/6696/RPGSATAN/rpgsatan.htm (accessed December 17, 2012).

49. Schick, *Heroic Worlds,* 31.

50. Quoted in Peterson, *Playing at the World,* 551.

51. Ewart, *Of Dice and Men,* 140–41.

52. Ibid., 151.

53. La Farge, "Destroy All Monsters"; Ewalt, *Of Dice and Men,* 162.

54. Ewalt, *Of Dice and Men,* 162–63.

55. Kushner, "The Dungeon Master."

56. Kathleen Ostrander, "Dungeons and Dragons—A Big Soap Opera," United Press International, August 2, 1986.

57. Wizards of the Coast, *30 Years of Adventure,* n.p.

58. Ostrander, "Dungeons and Dragons."

59. Mackay, *The Fantasy Role-Playing Game,* 20.

60. Wizards of the Coast, *30 Years of Adventure,* n.p.

61. Gen Con Staff, "Gary Gygax Remembered" (2012), http://www.gencon.com/pm/events/ligoh/Gygaxrem.aspx (accessed December 17, 2012).

62. Ewalt, *Of Dice and Men,* 231–32.

63. "Gygax Memorial Fund," http://www.gygaxmemorialfund.org/ (accessed July 3, 2012).

64. An online obituary for Dave Arneson can be found at http://www.legacy.com/guestbooks/guestbook.aspx?n = dave-arneson&pid = 125981485 (accessed December 17, 2012).

2. *DUNGEONS & DRAGONS* AS RELIGIOUS PHENOMENON

Epigraphs: Mark Barrowcliffe, *The Elfish Gene: Dungeons and Dragons and Growing Up Strange* (New York: Soho Press, 2007), 146; Mircea Eliade, *The Quest: History and Meaning in Religion* (Chicago: University of Chicago Press, 1969), iv.

1. Liam Lacey, "Dungeons and Dragons: An Underground Game Is Ready to Surface," *Globe and Mail,* November 29, 1978.

2. Phil Taylor Hanover, "It's an Evil Cult," *The Record,* May 25, 1992, A7.

3. Jon Peterson, *Playing at the World: A History of Simulating Wars, People, and Fantastic Adventure from Chess to Role-Playing Games* (San Diego: Unreason Press, 2012), 112.

4. Christian Lindke, "Advanced Dungeons and Parenting" (April 18, 2013), http://www.advanceddungeonsandparenting.com/2013/04/pat-robertson-still-getting-d-wrong.html (accessed August 5, 2013).

5. Quoted in Lawrence Schick, *Heroic Worlds: A History and Guide to Role-Playing Games* (Buffalo, N.Y.: Prometheus Books, 1991), 223–24.

6. Quoted in Gary Alan Fine, *Shared Fantasy: Role-Playing Games as Social Worlds* (Chicago: University of Chicago Press, 1983), 77.

7. Wizards of the Coast, *Player's Handbook, Core Rulebook I, 3.5* (Renton, Wash.: Wizards of the Coast, 2003), 103.

8. J.R.R. Tolkien, *The Two Towers* (New York: Del Rey, 2012), 249.

9. This notion of evil was loyally depicted in a Lord of the Rings role-playing game, published by Decipher Inc. The game states that orcs are evil by nature, explaining, "They aren't misunderstood, the victims of non-nurturing cultures, downtrodden and oppressed members of the lower class, or anything like that." Quoted in Michael J. Tresca, *The Evolution of Fantasy Role-Playing Games* (Jefferson, N.C.: McFarland, 2011), 26.

10. Tresca, *The Evolution of Fantasy Role-Playing Games,* 89.

11. Poul Anderson, *Three Hearts and Three Lions* (Garden City, N.Y.: Doubleday, 1961), 82,

12. Ibid., 190.

13. Michael Moorcock, *Elric at the End of Time* (New York: Daw Books, 1984), 86.

14. Ibid., 87.

15. Bob Larson, *Satanism: The Seduction of America's Youth* (Nashville: Thomas Nelson Publishers, 1989), 198–99.

16. Larson, *Satanism,* 54.

17. Peter Leithart and George Grant, *A Christian Response to Dungeons and Dragons: The Catechism of the New Age* (Fort Worth, Tex.: Dominion Press, 1988), 10.

18. Carl A. Raschke, *Painted Black* (New York: Harper and Row, 1990), 187.
19. Fine, *Shared Fantasy,* 210.
20. Barrowcliffe, *The Elfish Gene,* 30.
21. "Review of Dragonraid Adventure Learning Center," RPG.net, http://www.rpg.net/reviews/archive/11/11723.phtml (accessed December 17, 2012).
22. One of the strangest features of the cleric class is their choice of weaponry. In the original rules, clerics could use only blunt weapons such as maces. A possible influence on this rule is the Bayeux Tapestry, depicting the Battle of Hastings. Odo, the bishop of Bayeax, is portrayed wielding a mace rather than a sword. This detail reflects an idea that clergy were not allowed to "shed blood," and that blunt weapons represented a sort of legal loophole around this restriction. Tresca, *The Evolution of Fantasy Role-Playing Games,* 86.
23. Gary Gygax, "Jack Vance and the D&D Game" (2001), http://www.dyingearth.com/files/GARY%20GYGAX%20JACK%20VANCE.pdf (accessed December 17, 2012).
24. David M. Ewalt, *Of Dice and Men: The Story of Dungeons & Dragons and the People Who Play It* (New York: Scribner, 2013), 68–69.
25. Leithart and Grant, *A Christian Response to Dungeons and Dragons,* 9.
26. Raschke, *Painted Black,* 186.
27. Albert James Dager, "Dungeons and Dragons: A Look at Fantasy Role-Playing Games," *Media Spotlight,* 1980, n.p.
28. Robert Shroeck, "The City beyond the Gate," *Dragon* 100 (August 1985): 45–68.
29. C.S. Lewis, *The Discarded Image* (New York: Cambridge University Press, 1994), 39–40.
30. Fine, *Shared Fantasy,* 129.
31. Quoted in Fine, *Shared Fantasy,* 131.
32. Schick, *Heroic Worlds,* 151.
33. Quoted in Fine, *Shared Fantasy,* 125.
34. Quoted in Fine, *Shared Fantasy,* 125.
35. Quoted in Fine, *Shared Fantasy,* 261.
36. Fine, *Shared Fantasy,* 127.
37. In the sixth grade, my English teacher assigned a crossword puzzle on mythology as homework. Some of the answers drew from Egyptian mythology, which was not part of the curriculum. It was impossible to solve the puzzle using our textbook. I discovered what "The Great Ennead" was because I owned a copy of *Deities and Demigods.* I was the only person who completed the assignment, to the great irritation of my classmates.
38. John Ankerberg and John Weldon, "Dungeons and Dragons and Fantasy Role-Playing Games" in *Encyclopedia of New Age Beliefs,* ed. John Ankerberg and John Weldon (Eugene, Ore.: Harvest House Publishers, 1996), 159.
39. Phyllis Ten Elshof, "D&D: A Fantasy Fad or Dabbling in the Demonic?," *Christianity Today,* September 4, 1981, 56.
40. Andrew Bartness, "Letter," *Dragon* 162 (October 1990): 36–37.
41. Quoted in John Walliss, "The Road to Hell Is Paved with D20s: Evangelical Christianity and Role-Playing Gaming," in *The Handbook of Hyperreal Religions,* ed. Adam Possamai (Boston: Brill, 2012), 221.

42. Hans Penner, "Is Phenomenology a Method for the Study of Religion?," *Bucknell Review* 18:1 (1970): 29.

43. Russell McCutcheon, *Critics not Caretakers: Redescribing the Public Study of Religion* (Albany: State University of New York Press, 2001), xv.

44. Timothy Fitzgerald, *The Ideology of Religious Studies* (Oxford: Oxford University Press, 2000), 6.

45. Jason N. Bum, "Retrieving Phenomenology of Religion as a Method for Religious Studies," *Journal of the American Academy of Religion* 80:4 (December 2012): 1025–48.

46. Kushner, "The Dungeon Master."

47. Robert Ellwood, *The Politics of Myth: A Study of C. G. Jung, Mircea Eliade, and Joseph Campbell* (Albany: State University of New York Press, 1999), 1.

48. Quoted in Peterson, *Playing at the World,* 115.

49. Wizards of the Coast. *30 Years of Adventure: A Celebration of Dungeons & Dragons* (Renton, Wash.: Wizards of the Coast, 2006), n.p.

50. Graeme Davis et al., *Vampire: The Masquerade,* 2nd ed. (Stone Mountain, Ga.: White Wolf, 1992), 188.

51. Mircea Eliade, *Myth and Reality* (New York: Harperbooks, 1963), 192.

52. Ellwood, *The Politics of Myth,* 1.

53. Quoted in Fine, *Shared Fantasy,* 55.

54. Moira Johnston, "It's Only a Game—Or Is It?," *New West,* August 25, 1980, 38.

55. Eliade, *Myth and Reality,* 136.

56. Dean MacCannell, *The Tourist: A New Theory of the Leisure Class* (Berkeley: University of California Press, 1999), 3.

57. Richard Mathews, *Fantasy: The Liberation of Imagination* (New York: Twayne Publishers, 1997), 1.

58. Wouter Hanegraaff, "Fiction in the Desert of the Real: Lovecraft's Cthulhu Mythos," *Aries* 7 (2007): 86.

59. G.K. Chesterton, *The Ballad of the White Horse* (New York: John Lane, 1916), vi.

60. Rusty Burke, "A Short Biography of Robert E. Howard," in Robert E. Howard, *The Savage Tales of Solomon Kane* (New York: Del Rey, 1998), 393–406.

61. Eliade, *Myth and Reality,* 137.

62. Allen Varney, "ProFiles: Ed Greenwood," *Dragon* 244 (February 1998): 112.

63. Peterson, *Playing at the World,* 124.

64. Barrowcliffe, *The Elfish Gene,* 140 (italics mine).

65. Eliade, *Myth and Reality,* 193.

66. S.N. Eisenstadt, *The Origins and Diversity of Axial Age Civilizations* (Albany: State University of New York Press, 1986).

67. Benjamin Schwartz, "The Age of Transcendence," *Daedalus* 104:2 (Spring 1975): 3.

68. Kenneth Burke, *Language as Symbolic Action: Essays on Life, Literature, and Method* (Berkeley: University of California Press, 1966), 298–99.

69. Eisenstadt, *The Origins and Diversity of Axial Age Civilizations,* 1–6.

70. Ian G. Barbour, *Myths, Models, and Paradigms: A Comparative Study in Science and Religion* (New York: Harper & Row, 1974), 7.

71. Wizards of the Coast, *Dungeon Master's Guide, Core Rulebook II, 3.5* (Renton, Wash.: Wizards of the Coast, 2003), 6.

72. Barbour, *Myths, Models, and Paradigms,* 69.

73. Ibid., 33.

3. PATHWAYS INTO MADNESS: 1979–1982

Epigraphs: Jerry Johnston, *Why Suicide? What Parents & Teachers Must Know to Save Our Kids* (New York: Oliver Nelson, 1987), 90; The Dead Alewives, "Dungeons and Dragons" sketch, *Take Down the Grand Master.*

1. Francis Wheen, *Strange Days Indeed: The 1970s, the Golden Age of Paranoia* (New York: BBS/PublicAffairs, 2010), 9.

2. Kathleen Eleanor Taylor, *Brainwashing: The Science of Thought Control* (New York: Oxford University Press, 2004), 4–5.

3. Robert Jay Lifton, "Protean Man," *Archives of General Psychiatry* 24:4 (1971): 298–304.

4. Quoted in James T. Richardson, *Regulating Religion: Case Studies from Around the Globe,* Critical Issues in Social Justice (New York: Kluwer Academic/Plenum Publishers, 2004), 512.

5. "Pseudo Prison Turns into Brutal Reality," *Lodi News Sentinel,* August 21, 1971, 7.

6. For a review of this literature, see David H. Gleaves, "The Sociocognitive Model of Dissociative Identity Disorder: A Reexamination of the Evidence," *Psychological Bulletin* 120:1 (1996): 42–59.

7. A previous film about multiple personality disorder, *Three Faces of Eve* (1958), was based on psychiatrist Corbett Thigpen's book about his work with Chris Costner Sizemore. Joanne Woodward won an Academy Award for Best Actress for portraying "Eve White," a character based on Sizemore. In 1977, Sizemore published her book *I'm Eve,* revealing her identity as the basis for the book and film.

8. Dominic Streatfeild, *Brainwash: The Secret History of Mind Control* (New York: Macmillan, 2007), 159–60.

9. Moira Johnston, "It's Only a Game—Or Is It?," *New West,* August 25, 1980, 34.

10. Louise Shanahan, "Games Unsuspecting People Play: Dungeons and Dragons" (Boston: Daughters of St. Paul, n.d.), 2.

11. Beatrice Sparks, *Jay's Journal* (New York: Pocket Books, 1979).

12. Beth Ann Krier, "Dungeons and Dragons," reprinted with permission in *Gifted Child Quarterly,* Winter 1979, 858–60.

13. William Dear, *The Dungeon Master* (Boston: Houghton Mifflin, 1984), 13.

14. Jennifer Gavin, Associated Press, September 7, 1979.

15. After writing *The Dungeon Master,* Dear went on to appear on the Fox documentary *Alien Autopsy: Fact or Fiction.* In 2012, he published another book, *O.J. Is Innocent and I Can Prove It.* See David M. Ewalt, *Of Dice and*

Men: The Story of Dungeons & Dragons and the People Who Play It (New York: Scribner, 2013), 156.

16. Dear, *The Dungeon Master,* 12, 22, 87.

17. Ibid., 45.

18. Associated Press, August 17, 1980, n.p.

19. Dear, *The Dungeon Master,* 132.

20. "Game Cultist Still Missing," *Edmonton Journal,* September 8, 1979, C6; Chris Parks, "Dungeons and Dragons Cult May Lead to Missing Boy," *Sarasota Tribune,* September 7, 1979, 10A; "Fantasy Turned Real Life May Have Killed Student," *Boca Raton News,* September 7, 1979, 2A.

21. Jennifer Gavin, Associated Press, September 11, 1979.

22. "Computer Whiz Kid's Life a Puzzle, Even after Death," *Lakeland Ledger,* August 18, 1980, 2A.

23. Carla Hall, "Into the Dragon's Lair: Detective William Dear's Story of a Student Suicide," *Washington Post,* November 28, 1984, F1.

24. Ibid.

25. Dear, *The Dungeon Master,* 5.

26. This detail is plausible. George Ivanovich Gurdjieff was a Russian philosopher who developed a system of "esoteric Christianity" in the first half of the twentieth century. By 1979, there were several groups in the United States dedicated to Gurdjieff's ideas; some of these groups merged with encounter groups.

27. Dear, *The Dungeon Master,* 175.

28. T.J. Kask, "Rumblings," *Dragon* 30 (October 1979): 2, 41.

29. Dear, *The Dungeon Master,* 314.

30. Ibid., 62.

31. Ibid., 151 (italics in the original). Citing his own interviews with people who have entered the Michigan State steam tunnels, Paul Cardwell has challenged the accuracy of Dear's account of the steam tunnels.

32. Dear, *The Dungeon Master,* 314.

33. Ibid., 96.

34. Johnston, "It's Only a Game," 37.

35. Paul Cardwell, "The Attacks on Role-Playing Games," *Skeptical Inquirer* 18:2 (Winter 1994): 157–65. Cardwell has also pointed out that this was the same year that TSR entered a distribution agreement with Random House. See Paul Cardwell, Bruce Gulke, and William J. Walton, "Dungeons & Dragons: Adventure or Abomination? by Richard White: An Examination" (CAR-PGa Publications Committee, 1996), 2.

36. Dear, *The Dungeon Master,* 236.

37. Stanley Semrau and Judy Gale, *Murderous Minds on Trial: Terrifying Tales from a Forensic Psychiatrist's Casebook* (Toronto: The Dundurn Group, 2002), 292.

38. "Fundamentalist Christians Fear 'Dungeons and Dragons,'," United Press International, June 12, 1981.

39. Carl A. Raschke, *Painted Black* (New York: Harper and Row, 1990), 188.

40. This rumor originated with Darren Molitor, who was convicted of manslaughter after claiming that *Dungeons & Dragons* left him mentally incompe-

tent. In prison, Molitor became an ally and informant for BADD. See Darren Molitor, "Dungeons and Dragons" (March 22, 1985), http://www.theescapist.com/archive-molitorletter.htm (accessed May 2, 2013).

41. Reverend James R. Cotter, "Dungeons and Dragons Lecture" (September 16, 1980), http://www.theescapist.com/archive-cotter.htm (accessed February 1, 2013).

42. Shanahan, "Games Unsuspecting People Play," 1–21.

43. Gary Alan Fine, *Shared Fantasy: Role-Playing Games as Social Worlds* (Chicago: University of Chicago Press, 1983), 107. Christopher Lehrich goes further and suggests that attempts at hegemonic control during role-playing games actually inspire increasing resistance from players. See Christopher Lehrich, "Ritual Discourse in Role-Playing Games," *The Forge*, October 2005, http://www.indie-rpgs.com/_articles/ritual_discourse_in_RPGs.html (accessed April 27, 2012).

44. Kenneth R. Clark, "Entertainment," United Press International, January 19, 1982.

45. Christopher Lasch, "From the Culture of Narcissism," in *The Eighties: A Reader,* ed. Gilbert T. Sewall (New York: Perseus Books, 1998), 4.

46. Rona Jaffe, *Monsters and Mazes* (New York: Delacorte Press, 1981), 39.

47. Clark, "Entertainment."

48. Jaffe, *Monsters and Mazes,* 199.

49. Ibid., 275.

50. Ibid., 279.

51. Ibid., 287

52. Ibid., 328.

53. Ibid., 41.

54. Ibid., 81.

55. Ibid., 176.

56. Ibid., 200.

57. Ibid., 188.

58. Ibid., 246.

59. Robert Jay Lifton, *Thought Reform and the Psychology of Totalism: A Study of "Brainwashing" in China* (Chapel Hill: University of North Carolina Press, 1989), 423.

60. William Schnoebelen, "Straight Talk on Dungeons and Dragons," http://www.chick.com/articles/dnd.asp (accessed February 2, 2013).

61. Jaffe, *Monsters and Mazes,* 201.

62. Ibid., 271.

63. Ibid., 194.

64. See, for example, Wayne D. Blackmon, "Dungeons and Dragons: The Use of a Fantasy Game in the Psychotherapeutic Treatment of a Young Adult," *American Journal of Psychotherapy* 48:4 (Fall 1994): 624–32; John Hughes, "Therapy Is Fantasy: Roleplaying, Healing and the Construction of Symbolic Order" (paper presented in Anthropology IV Honours, Medical Anthropology Seminar, Australian National University, 1988), http://www.rpgstudies.net/hughes/therapy_is_fantasy.html (accessed February 2, 2013).

65. Lorne Dawson, *Cults in Context* (New Brunswick, N.J.: Transaction Publishers, 1998), 93–95.

66. Robert Hicks, "None Dare Call It Reason: Kids, Cults, and Common Sense" (talk prepared for the Virginia Department for Children's Twelfth Annual Legislative Forum, Roanoke, Virginia, September 22, 1989).

67. Dear, *The Dungeon Master,* 34.

68. Matthew Kirschenbaum, "How Reading Is Being Re-imagined," *Chronicle of Higher Education*, December 7, 2007, B20.

69. Sheryl C. Wilson and Theodore X. Barber, "The Fantasy-Prone Personality: Implications for Understanding Imagery, Hypnosis, and Parapsychological Phenomena," in *Imagery: Current Theory, Research, and Applications,* ed. Anees A. Sheikh (New York: Wiley, 1983), 209–39.

70. Raschke, *Painted Black,* 184.

71. Rebecca Brown, *Prepare for War* (Chino, Calif.: Chick Publications, 1987), 133.

72. Stanley Cohen, *Folk Devils and Moral Panic* (New York: Routledge, 2002), 56.

73. Joel Paris, *The Fall of an Icon: Psychoanalysis and Academic Psychiatry* (Toronto: University of Toronto Press, 2005), 67.

74. Dear, *The Dungeon Master,* 64.

75. Fine, *Shared Fantasy,* 42.

76. Joan Hake Robie, *The Truth about Dungeons and Dragons* (Lancaster, Pa.: Starburst Publishers, 1991), 11.

77. Dorothy Singer and Jerome Singer, *The House of Make-Believe: Children's Play and the Developing Imagination* (Cambridge, Mass.: Harvard University Press, 1990), 115, 143.

78. Helen L. Mitternight, "Groups Blame Fantasy Game for Several Deaths," Associated Press, March 22, 1985.

79. Jerry Adler and Shawn Doherty, "Kids: The Deadliest Game?," *Newsweek,* September 9, 1985, 93.

80. Johnston, "It's Only a Game," 38.

81. Ewalt, *Of Dice and Men,* 126.

82. Quoted in Lawrence Schick, *Heroic Worlds: A History and Guide to Role-Playing Games* (Buffalo, N.Y.: Prometheus Books, 1991), 142.

83. Lisa A. DeRenard and Linda Mannik Kline, "Alienation and the Game Dungeons and Dragons," *Psychological Reports* 66 (1990): 1219–22; Gary T. Rosenthal and Barlow Soper, "Role-Play Gamers and National Guardsmen Compared," *Psychological Reports* 92 (1998): 169–70; Suzanne Abyeta and James Forest, "Relationship of Role-Playing Games to Self-Reported Criminal Behaviour," *Psychological Reports* 69 (1991): 1187–92; Armando Simon, "Emotional Stability Pertaining to the Game of Dungeons and Dragons," *Psychology in the Schools* 24 (October 1987): 329–32; Simon, "Emotional Stability Pertaining to the Game *Vampire: The Masquerade.*" *Psychological Reports* 83 (1998): 732–34; James L. Carroll and Paul M. Carolin, "Relationship between Game Playing and Personality," *Psychological Reports* 64 (1989): 705–6; Stuart M. Leeds, "Personality, Belief in the Paranormal, and Involvement with Satanic Practices among Young Adult Males: Dabblers versus Gamers," *Cultic Studies Journal* 12:2 (1995): 148–65.

84. DeRenard and Kline, "Alienation and the Game Dungeon and Dragons," 122.

4. SATANIC PANIC: 1982–1991

Epigraphs: Rus Walton, *Biblical Solutions to Contemporary Problems: A Handbook* (Brentwood, Tenn.: Wolgemuth & Hyatt Publishers, 1988), 339; Paul La Farge, "Destroy All Monsters," *The Believer,* September 2006, http://www.believermag.com/issues/200609/?read = article_lafarge (accessed December 17, 2012).

1. Mike Warnke, *Schemes of Satan* (Tulsa, Okla.: Victory House, 1991), 155; William Robbins, "Brilliant Computer Student Dies from Gun Wound," *New York Times,* August 18, 1980, B8.

2. Mike Warnke, *The Satan Seller* (South Plainfield, N.J.: Bridge Publishing, 1972); Jon Trott and Mike Hertenstein, "Selling Satan: The Tragic History of Mike Warnke," *Cornerstone* 98 (1992), http://web.archive.org/web/20110629063019/http://www.cornerstonemag.com/features/iss098/sellingsatan.htm (accessed May 19, 2013).

3. Joan Hake Robie, *The Truth about Dungeons and Dragons* (Lancaster, Pa.: Starburst Publishers, 1991), 55; Roger Sutton, "A D&D Phenomenon," *School Library Journal,* November 1984, 82.

4. David G. Bromley, "Satanism: The New Cult Scare," in *The Satanism Scare,* ed. James T. Richardson, Joel Best, and David G. Bromley (Hawthorne, N.Y.: Aldine De Gruyter, 1991), 49.

5. In a study of cases conducted in 2012, researchers found 66 legal cases alleging Satanic activity in the 1970s, 168 cases in the 1980s, 361 cases in the 1990s, and 201 cases in the first decade of the twenty-first century. This data suggests that public belief in Satanism has declined little. Instead, the media and the legal system have become more critical of claims of Satanism. See Jenny Reichert and James T. Richardson, "Decline of a Moral Panic: A Social Psychological and Socio-Legal Examination of the Current Status of Satanism," *Nova Religio* 16:2 (2012): 47–63.

6. Natchez Police Department, Criminal Justice Task Force on Organized Occult Crime & Gang Violence, "Warning Signs of Occult Involvement," http://natchezpd.com/warsigns.html (accessed February 10, 2013).

7. Philip Jenkins, "Weird Tales: The Story of a Delusion," in *The Last Pentacle of the Sun: Writings in Support of the West Memphis Three,* ed. M.W. Anderson and Brett Alexander (Vancouver: Arsenal Pulp Press, 2004), 35–41.

8. Bill Ellis, *Raising the Devil: Satanism, New Religions, and the Media* (Lexington: University Press of Kentucky, 2000), 178.

9. Harry L. Kuhlmeyer, "Letter to McMartin Preschool Parents from Police Chief Kuhlmeyer" (September 8, 1983), http://www.law.umkc.edu/faculty/projects/ftrials/mcmartin/lettertoparents.html (acccessed December 8, 2009); Paul Eberle, *The Abuse of Innocence: The McMartin Preschool Trial* (New York: Prometheus Books, 1993), 172–73; Robert Reinhold, "The Longest Trial—A Post-Mortem: Collapse of Child-Abuse Case; So Much Agony for So Little," *New York Times,* January 24, 1990, http://www.nytimes.com/1990/01/24/us/longest-trial-post-mortem-collapse-child-abuse-case-so-much-agony-for-so-little.html (accessed December 8, 2009); Debbie Nathan and Michael Snedecker, *Satan's Silence: Ritual Abuse and the Making of a Modern American Witch Hunt* (New York: Basic Books, 1994), 127.

10. Kenneth V. Lanning, "FBI Report: Satanic Ritual Abuse" (1992), http://www.rickross.com/reference/satanism/satanism1.html (accessed November 21, 2012).

11. Wendy Kaminer, *Sleeping with Extra-Terrestrials: The Rise of Irrationalism and Perils of Piety* (New York: Vintage Books, 1999), 193.

12. Nathan and Snedecker, *Satan's Silence,* 3.

13. Bromley, "Satanism," 67.

14. Ibid., 68.

15. Peter Leithart and George Grant, *A Christian Response to Dungeons and Dragons: The Catechism of the New Age* (Fort Worth, Tex.: Dominion Press, 1988), 1.

16. Louise Shanahan, "Games Unsuspecting People Play: Dungeons and Dragons" (Boston: Daughters of St. Paul, n.d.), 19.

17. Molly Ivins, "Utah Parents Exorcise 'Devilish' Game," *New York Times,* May 3, 1980, 8.

18. Judy Gibbs, "School Discontinues Use of 'Dungeons and Dragons' Game," Associated Press, April 29, 1980.

19. Moira Johnston, "It's Only a Game—Or Is It?," *New West,* August 25, 1980, 32–40.

20. Quoted in Walton, *Biblical Solutions to Contemporary Problems,* 340.

21. Lizzie Stark, *Leaving Mundania: Inside the Transformative World of Live-Action Role Playing Games* (Chicago: Chicago Review Press, 2012), 92.

22. Phyllis Ten Elshof, "D&D: A Fantasy Fad or Dabbling in the Demonic?," *Christianity Today,* September 4, 1981, 56.

23. Rebecca Brown, *Prepare for War* (Chino, Calif.: Chick Publications, 1987), 136.

24. "Evangelist Wants to Burn 'Dungeons and Dragons,'" United Press International, June 23, 1981.

25. Nels Bruckner, "Forum Letter," *Dragon* 65 (September 1982): 3; Michael Shigatani, "Forum Letter," *Dragon* 161 (September 1990): 77.

26. Jack Chick is a cartoonist based in California. When he heard that Maoists had successfully used comic books to sow Communist propaganda, he came to believe that similar tactics could be used to spread conservative evangelicalism. Chick Publications produces tiny comics or "Chick tracts" that can be found at bus stops, pay phones, and men's room urinals throughout America. The tracts are theologically heavy-handed and visually gory. Many of them end with sinners burning in hell for various transgressions. In addition to such topics as the dangers of Catholicism, "cults," and liberal Christianity, many Chick tracts discuss the hidden occult influences of popular culture. See Jack Bivins, *The Religion of Fear: The Politics of Horror in Conservative Evangelicalism* (New York: Oxford University Press, 2008).

27. In 1984, Health and Human Services Secretary Margaret Heckler commissioned a Task Force on Youth Suicide. *Newsweek* reported that the incident of teenage suicide tripled between 1960 and 1985. See Jerry Adler and Shawn Doherty, "Kids: The Deadliest Game?," *Newsweek,* September 9, 1985, 93.

28. Patricia Pulling, *The Devil's Web: Who Is Stalking Your Children for Satan?* (Lafayette, La.: Huntington House, 1989), 2–5. Although Pulling was

nominally Jewish, the appendix of "occult signs" in her book includes a Star of David. The text explains that this symbol is actually a symbol of Egyptian occultism that the Jews did not adopt until the Babylonian exile.

29. Michael Isikoff, "Parents Sue School Principal: Game Cited in Youth's Suicide," *Washington Post,* August 13, 1983, A1.

30. Pulling, *The Devil's Web,* 5.

31. Stanley Cohen, *Folk Devils and Moral Panic* (New York: Routledge, 2002), 44–46.

32. Jeff Freeman, "Concerns Christians Should Have about Dungeons and Dragons" (1995), http://www.theescapist.com/archive-davidfisher.htm (accessed May 7, 2013).

33. Pulling, *The Devil's Web,* 9.

34. Richard White, *Dungeons and Dragons: Adventure or Abomination?* (Virginia Beach: Christian Broadcasting Network, 2007), 4.

35. Pat A. Pulling, Mary Dempsey, and Pat Dempsey, *Dungeons and Dragons: Witchcraft, Suicide, and Violence* (Richmond, Va.: B.A.D.D. Inc, n.d.), 34.

36. Isikoff, "Parents Sue School Principal," A1.

37. Paul Cardwell, who provided me with these resources, concluded independently that "Narthöl" was Bink's character.

38. Quoted in David Alexander, "Giving the Devil More Than His Due," *The Humanist,* March 1, 1990, 8–9.

39. "Suit Filed over Suicide Following 'Dungeons and Dragons' Game," Associated Press, August 14, 1983; "Fantasy Game Lawsuit against Principal Dismissed," Associated Press, October 26, 1983.

40. John Weldon and James Bjornstad, *Playing with Fire* (Chicago: Moody Press, 1984), 19. In 1989, Sheila Watters also attempted to sue TSR after her son committed suicide. This case was also dismissed. Judge Edward Johnstone explained, "The theories of liability sought to be imposed upon the manufacturer of a role-playing fantasy game would have a devastatingly broad chilling effect on expression of all forms." See Sheila Waters v. TSR Inc. Civil Action No. C88–0298 P(J) (May 31, 1989).

41. Christopher B. Strain, *Reload: Rethinking Violence in American Life* (Nashville: Vanderbilt University Press, 2010), 54.

42. Gareth J. Medway, *Lure of the Sinister: The Unnatural History of Satanism* (New York: New York University Press, 2001), 285; Kathryn May, "Experts Link Fantasy Play to Violence," *Ottawa Citizen,* March 25, 1985, D1.

43. David Waldron, "Role-Playing Games and the Christian Right: Community Formation in Response to a Moral Panic," *Journal of Religion and Popular Culture* 9 (Spring 2005), http://utpjournals.metapress.com/content/v3503x532wxjoq28/.

44. Tipper Gore, *Raising PG Kids in an X-Rated Society* (Nashville: Abingdon Press, 1987), 88.

45. Michael A. Stackpole, "Game Hysteria and the Truth," http://www.skeptictank.org/files/religion/d-and-d.htm (accessed May 7, 2013).

46. Pulling, *The Devil's Web,* 9.

47. Robert Hicks, *In Pursuit of Satan: The Police and the Occult* (Buffalo, N.Y.: Prometheus Books, 199), 288–89. Hicks notes that in a radio interview

that aired that month Pulling stated she had been a private investigator for the past six years—a date that preceded her son's death.

48. Pulling, *The Devil's Web,* 11.

49. Hicks, *In Pursuit of Satan,* 288.

50. Pulling, *The Devil's Web,* 4.

51. Anthony T. Michael, *Suicide: Knowing When Your Teen Is at Risk* (Ventura, Calif.: Regal Books, 1991); Jerry Johnston, *Why Suicide? What Parents & Teachers Must Know to Save Our Kids* (New York: Oliver Nelson, 1987); Charles Ewing, *Kids Who Kill* (Lexington, Mass.: Lexington Books, 1990), 83.

52. William G. Shuster, "Critics Link a Fantasy Game to 29 Deaths," *Christianity Today,* May 17, 1985, 64–65.

53. David Gelman, "The Mind of a Rapist," *Newsweek,* July 23, 1990, 46.

54. David Frankfurter, *Evil Incarnate: Rumors of Demonic Conspiracy and Ritual Abuse in History* (Princeton, N.J.: Princeton University Press, 2006), 32.

55. Christian Broadcasting Network, *Dungeons and Dragons: Adventure or Abomination* (Virginia Beach: CBN, 2007), 5–6; William Schnoebelen, "Straight Talk on Dungeons and Dragons," http://www.chick.com/articles/dnd.asp (accessed May 7, 2013).

56. Paul Cardwell has expressed suspicions about these two suicides. A search of newspapers archives turned up no obituary or article for Steven Loyacano. Cardwell also notes that Dempsey was the only witness to his son's suicide. Dempsey was armed and, by his own admission, had been arguing with his son before he was shot. Paul Cardwell, e-mail correspondence with author, December 6, 2013.

57. Hicks, *In Pursuit of Satan,* 292.

58. Gore, *Raising PG Kids in an X-Rated Society,* 88.

59. Hicks, *In Pursuit of Satan,* 288; Greg Stafford, Loren Wiseman, and Michael A. Stackpole, *Games Don't Kill* (Plano, Tex.: Game Manufacturer's Association, 1988), 5. A document by BADD psychiatrist Thomas Radecki cited *Monsters and Mazes* as fact, so Paul Cardwell sent a copy to Rona Jaffe for comment. She wrote back, "I don't think these people can even read!!!" Paul Cardwell, personal communication, November 22, 2003.

60. John Allen Paulos, *Innumeracy: Mathematical Illiteracy and Its Consequences* (New York: Hill and Wang, 1988), 126.

61. Suzanne Abyeta and James Forest, "Relationship of Role-Playing Games to Self-Reported Criminal Behaviour," *Psychological Reports* 69 (1991): 1192.

62. Stuart Hall et al., *Policing the Crisis: Mugging, the State, and Law and Order* (London: Macmillan, 1978), 226.

63. Paul Cardwell, "The Attacks on Role-Playing Games," *Skeptical Inquirer* 18:2 (Winter 1994): 157; La Farge, "Destroy All Monsters"; White, *Dungeons and Dragons,* 2.

64. Ewing, *Kids Who Kill,* 84.

65. Federal Trade Commission to Patricia Pulling, May 13, 1985, Archives of CAR-PGa.

66. U.S. Consumer Product Safety Commission to Thomas Radecki, March 15, 1985, Archives of CAR-PGa.

67. Bivins, *The Religion of Fear,* 160.

68. Daniel Martin and Gary Alan Fine, "Satanic Cults, Satanic Play: Is 'Dungeons and Dragons' a Breeding Ground for the Devil?," in *The Satanism Scare,* ed. James T. Richardson, Joel Best, and David G. Bromley (Hawthorne, N.Y.: Aldine De Gruyter, 1991), 110–11; Carl A. Raschke, *Painted Black* (New York: Harper and Row, 1990), 181; "School Board Rules Out Children's Game," Associated Press, February 16, 1983.

69. James Brooke, "A Suicide Spurs Town to Debate Nature of a Game," *New York Times,* August 22, 1985, 1; Ruth Youngblood, "Firm Says Dungeons and Dragons is Safe," United Press International, July 23, 1985; "Putnam's High School Drops Dungeons and Dragon's Game," *New York Times,* October 9, 1985, 2.

70. Pulling, Dempsey, and Dempsey, *Dungeons and Dragons,* 5.

71. Robert A. Hamilton, "Game Is Target of Fight in Putnam," *New York Times,* May 26, 1985, 4.

72. Abington Township School District v. Schempp, 375 US. 203 (1963).

73. The *Impressions* curriculum was a set of fifty-nine books containing approximately 10,000 selections of literature with accompanying class exercises. Plaintiffs claimed that 32 of these selections involved witchcraft and that the activities required children to compose chants or discuss witchcraft. The case in Ohio was eventually dropped. Another case in California resulted in *Brown v. Woodland Joint Unified School District.* In this case, the Ninth Circuit Court confirmed the lower court's ruling that while the establishment clause prohibits schools from requiring students to participate in religious rituals, it does not apply to "school exercises that coincidentally resemble religious rituals." See Brown v. Woodland Joint Unified School District, 27 F.3d 1373 (9th Cir. 1994); Joan Delfattorre, *What Johnny Shouldn't Read: Textbook Censorship in America* (New Haven, Conn.: Yale University Press, 1992), 173.

74. Maia A. Gemmil and Daniel H. Nexon, "Children's Crusade: The Religious Politics of Harry Potter," in *Harry Potter and International Relations,* ed. Daniel H. Nexon and Iver B. Neumann (Lanham, Md.: Rowan & Littlefield, 2006), 79.

75. Paul Cardwell, "Setting the Record Straight on Law Enforcement Primer on Fantasy Role-Playing Games" (Bonham, Tex.: CAR-PGa, 1995), 1.

76. Patricia Pulling, "A Law Enforcement Primer on Fantasy Role Playing Games" (Richmond, Va.: B.A.D.D., n.d.), 10–11.

77. Patricia Pulling and B.A.D.D., "Interviewing Techniques for Adolescents" (Richmond, Va.: B.A.D.D., 1988), 6.

78. Quoted in Lisa Levitt Rickman, "Teens Involved in Satanism Commit Murder and Suicide," *Prescott Courier,* February 14, 1988, 11A.

79. "Dual Deaths Are Linked to Fantasy Game," *The Record,* November 4, 1984.

80. Howard Witt, "Fantasy Game Turns into Deadly Reality," *Chicago Tribune,* January 27, 1985, C3.

81. Jerry Hicks, "Lampasi Gets 25 Years Plus for Shootings," *Los Angeles Times,* October 18, 1985.

82. Jon Rabiroff, "Night of Carnage in Canaan: Looking at the Death of Family," *Times Union,* December 26, 1986, A1.

83. "Man Charged in Dungeons and Dragons Death," Associated Press, July 1, 1987.

84. "16-Year-Old Boy Sentenced for Murder of His Playmate," *New York Times,* December 6, 1986, 30; "16-Year-Old Is Convicted in Fantasy-Game Slaying of Boy, 11," *New York Times,* November 23, 1986, 47; "Youth Pleads Guilty in Fantasy Murder," *Spartanburg Herald-Journal,* May 21, 1988, A2.

85. Bob Larson, *Extreme Evil: Kids Killing Kids* (Nashville: Thomas Nelson, 1999), 59.

86. State of Missouri v. Darren Molitor, 729 S.W.2d 551; 1987 Mo. (March 31, 1987).

87. The People v. Daniel E. Kasten, No. 2862E (June 25, 1991); Henry G. Logeman, "Student Convicted in 'Dungeons and Dragons' Murder Case," United Press International, June 29, 1988. The mind flayer is a classic *D&D* monster. It was invented by Gary Gygax and appeared in the first issue of the *Strategic Review.* Gygax was inspired by the work of H.P. Lovecraft and the cover of the novel *The Burrowers Beneath* by Brian Lumley. The particular mind flayer cited by Kasten's attorney was named "Lord Derelith." This may be a reference to August Derleth, Lovecraft's first publisher.

88. Russell Chandler, *Understanding the New Age* (Grand Rapids, Mich.: Zondervan, 1993), 240; Joe McGinniss, *Cruel Doubt* (New York: Pocket Star Books, 1991), 427–30; Jerry Bledsoe, *Blood Games* (New York: Onyx Books, 1992), 446–48.

89. Ewing, *Kids Who Kill,* 85; State of Ohio v. William R. Anderson, Case No. 1288 (March 4, 1992); "Judge Dismisses Two Rape Claims," *The Columbian,* September 18, 1994, A11.

90. Thomas Claridge, "Brother and Sister not First Choice as Murder Victims, Doctor Tells Trial," *Globe and Mail,* February 28, 1985; Wes Keller, "Family Still Feels Pain of Children's Murder 25 Years Ago," *Orangeville Citizen,* October 29, 2009.

91. Alex Dobish, "Teen Ruled Sane, Gets Life Term for Slaying," *Milwaukee Journal,* June 9, 1985, 6; Associated Press, "Jury Poised for Crossbow Murder Trial Opening Statements Today," *Rochester Sentinel,* November 7, 1985, 12.

92. Ewing, *Kids Who Kill,* 85.

93. "Where the Dragons Are," *Globe and Mail,* March 25, 1985.

94. "Real Life Clerics: TSR Hobbies Needs You," *Dragon* 40 (August 1980): 49.

95. Carson Snow, "Emerald Article: Dragons in the Stacks; An Introduction to Role-Playing Games and Their Value to Libraries," *Collection Building* 27:2 (2008): 64; Helen L. Miternight, "Groups Blame Fantasy Game for Several Deaths," Associated Press, March 22, 1985.

96. Quoted in Pierre Savoie, "The Whole Loon Catalogue," *Shadis* 7 (May 1992): 7.

97. The most extreme example of this is White Wolf's viral marketing campaign to promote its game *Demon: The Fallen.* White Wolf created a phony website putatively run by a priest named Father Ramos. "Father Ramos" posted jeremiads about the dangers of White Wolf's new game. The site even featured a comic called "Demonic Deviltry." This was an over-the-top parody of *Dark*

Dungeons, in which the players use ecstasy and engage in deviant sex orgies. In the final panel, Father Ramos invites the reader to "join his crusade" against *Demon: The Fallen*.

98. Lizzie Stark, in her ethnography of LARPers, describes her surprise that so many gamers in their thirties and forties emphasized to her that they were not Satanists. Lizzie Stark, *Leaving Mundania: Inside the Transformative World of Live-Action Role Playing Games* (Chicago: Chicago Review Press, 2012), 92.

99. Wizards of the Coast, *30 Years of Adventure: A Celebration of Dungeons & Dragons* (Renton, Wash.: Wizards of the Coast, 2006), n.p.

100. "Inmate Sues to Play Dungeons and Dragons," United Press International, March 21, 1990.

101. Shigatani, "Forum Letter," 77.

102. "Student Petition to Restore 'Dungeons' to After School Program," Associated Press, February 9, 1983.

103. Nicholas Orndorff, "Games: Odds Are, They're Harmless," *Charleston Gazette*, December 27, 1998, 10E.

104. John Ankerberg and John Weldon, "Dungeons and Dragons and Fantasy Role-Playing Games," in *Encyclopedia of New Age Beliefs*, ed. John Ankerberg and John Weldon (Eugene, Ore.: Harvest House Publishers, 1996), 156.

105. "Why Gamers Should Support CAR-PGa," *Shadis* 7 (May 1992): 11.

106. Todd A. Stevenson, Freedom of Information Officer, to Paul Cardwell, Jr., December 7, 1988; Lloyd Bentsen to Paul Cardwell, January 10, 1989, Archives of CAR-PGa.

107. Savoie, "The Whole Loon Catalogue," 7.

108. Cardwell, "Setting the Record Straight," 8.

109. John Walliss, "The Road to Hell Is Paved with D20s: Evangelical Christianity and Role-Playing Gaming," in *The Handbook of Hyperreal Religions*, ed. Adam Possamai (Boston: Brill, 2012), 214.

110. Cardwell, "Setting the Record Straight," 12.

111. White, *Dungeons and Dragons*, 8.

112. Pierre Savoie to Rosemary McCracken, managing editor of *The Catholic Register*, August 15, 1987, Archives of CAR-PGa; Pierre Savoie, "Catholics! Have You Been Duped by *Anti*-Catholics?," Archives of CAR-PGa; Pierre Savoie, "Allow Games in Schools," *The Catholic Register*, November 14–November 20, 1987, 1.

113. Wendell Albright and Herbert Patton III, "Dungeons, Dragons and Great High Dudgeon," *Washington Post*, May 4, 1991, A21; Cindy Clayton, "Teens and the Occult Experts Say Parents Need to Learn What to Look for and How to Distinguish between the Dangerous and the Harmless," *Virginian-Pilot*, May 14, 2001, B3.

114. Carolyn Caywood, "Rescuing the Innocent: The Lure of Dungeons and Dragons," *School Library Journal*, March 1991, 138.

115. Anthony Moriarty, *The Psychology of Adolescent Satanism* (Westport, Conn.: Praeger, 1991), 5.

116. Strain, *Reload*, 56–57.

117. Cardwell, "The Attacks on Role-Playing Games." 162; State of Illinois Department of Professional Regulation v. Thomas E. Radecki, No. 91–6666-LEG (March 31, 1992); Brittany Boyer, "Local Doctor Accused of Exchanging Drugs for Sex Permanently Surrenders Medical License," WJACTV.com (September 27, 2012), http://www.wjactv.com/news/news/local-doctor-accused-exchanging-drugs-sex-permanen/nSNd9/ (accessed May 6, 2013).

118. Allen Varney, "The Current Clack," *Dragon* 242 (December 1997): 119–20.

119. Walliss, "The Road to Hell Is Paved with D20s," 213.

5. A WORLD OF DARKNESS: 1991–2001

Epigraphs: Rick Swan, "Role-Playing Reviews," *Dragon* 192 (April 1993): 83; William J. Bennett, John J. DiLulio, Jr., and John Walters, *Body Count: Moral Poverty and How to Win America's War against Crime and Drugs* (New York: Simon and Schuster, 1996), 26.

1. J.R.R. Tolkien, *The Monsters and the Critics and Other Essays* (Boston: Houghton Mifflin, 1984), 153–56.

2. Graeme Davis et al., *Vampire: The Masquerade,* 2nd ed. (Stone Mountain, Ga.: White Wolf, 1992), 29.

3. Allen Varney, "Role-Playing Reviews," *Dragon* 212 (December 1994): 91.

4. Ethan Gilsdorf, *Fantasy Freaks and Gaming Geeks: An Epic Quest for Reality among Role Players, Online Gamers, and Other Dwellers of Imaginary Realms* (Guilford, Conn.: The Lyons Press, 2009), 1.

5. Donald Miller and Arpi Miller, "Understanding Generation X: Values, Politics, and Religious Commitments," in *Gen X Religion,* ed. Richard Flory and Donald Miller (New York: Routledge, 2000), 6.

6. Michelle Belanger and Chris Miller, "Drama, Roleplay, and Ritual," *Shadowdance* podcast, June 25, 2007.

7. Bennett, DiLulio, and Walters, *Body Count,* 27.

8. Ibid., 14.

9. Ibid., 208.

10. Tom Morganthau, "The Lull before the Storm?," *Newsweek,* December 6, 1995, 40.

11. "Superpredators," *Sunday Mail,* January 21, 1996, 99. Other criminologists argued that an increase in homicide among youth was likely the result of easier access to firearms rather than an increase in the number of murderous teenagers. "Juvenile Divide," *Washington Post*, August 20, 1996, A2.

12. "Superpredators," 99.

13. Bennett, DiLulio, and Walters, *Body Count,* 16.

14. "Dole Vows 'Real War' on Youth Crime," United Press International, July 16, 1996.

15. Mark Rein-Hagen, "Games Are Serious Fun," TEDxTbilisi (March 14, 2013).

16. Shannon Appelcline, "History of Game #10: Lion Rampant, 1987–1990" (2007), http://www.rpg.net/columns/briefhistory/briefhistory10.phtml (accessed May 29, 2013).

17. Gary Alan Fine, *Shared Fantasy: Role-Playing Games as Social Worlds* (Chicago: University of Chicago Press, 1983), 36. An early player-designed adaptation of the *D&D* magic rules suggested that magic users have a reservoir of "goetic energy" used to cast spells. The term "goetia" (from the Greek word *goetia*, "sorcery") appears in medieval grimoires and suggests the players were conversant in magical traditions. See Jon Peterson, *Playing at the World* (San Diego: Unreason Press, 2012), 509.

18. Paul La Farge, "Destroy All Monsters," *The Believer*, September 2006, http://www.believermag.com/issues/200609/?read = article_lafarge (accessed December 17, 2012).

19. Appelcline, "History of Game #10."

20. Appelcline, "History of Game #10."

21. Sarah Lynne Bowman, *The Functions of Role-Playing Games* (Jefferson, N.C.: McFarland, 2010), 122.

22. Rick Swan, "Role-Playing Reviews," *Dragon* 205 (May 1994): 99.

23. The world created for *Vampire* was so compelling that producer Aaron Spelling consulted with Rein-Hagen to create a prime-time soap opera called *Kindred: The Embraced* that revolved around the vampire prince of San Francisco. *Kindred* aired on the Fox network in 1996. Only eight episodes were made before the show's star, Mark Frankel, died in a motorcycle accident. Despite the show's limited success, this was the first television series based on a role-playing game since CBS's *Dungeons and Dragons* cartoon.

24. Rick Swan, "Role-Playing Reviews," *Dragon* 192 (April 1993): 83.

25. Rick Swan, "Role-Playing Reviews," *Dragon* 202 (April 1994): 81–82.

26. Rick Swan, "Role-Playing Reviews," *Dragon* 213 (January 1995): 90–91.

27. Tolkien, *The Monsters and the Critics*, 153.

28. Bowman, *The Functions of Role-Playing Games*, 66.

29. Rein-Hagen, "Games Are Serious Fun."

30. David Ewalt, *Of Dice and Men: The Story of Dungeons & Dragons and the People Who Play It* (New York: Scribner, 2013), 160.

31. Not to be confused with the role-playing game *Cyberpunk*, first published by R. Talsorian Games in 1988.

32. Quoted in Philip Elmer-Dewitt and David S. Jackson, "Cyberpunk!," *Time*, February 8, 1993, 58.

33. Steve Jackson, "Press Conference Notes," April 24, 1990, Archives of CAR-PGa.

34. Kurt Lancaster, "Do Role-Playing Games Promote Crime, Satanism and Suicide among Players as Critics Claim?," *Journal of Popular Culture* 28:2 (1994): 70.

35. Steve Jackson to Pierre Savoie, May 23, 1990, Archives of CAR-PGa.

36. John Schwartz, "The Hacker Dragnet: The Feds Put a Tail on Computer Crooks—and Sideswipe a Few Innocent Bystanders," *Newsweek*, April 30, 1990, 50; "Feds vs. Cyberpunks: Part II," *Locus*, June 1990, 4, 64; "Feds vs. Cyberpunks: Part III," *Locus*, September 1990, 6, 70.

37. Steve Jackson to Pierre Savoie, May 23, 1990, Archives of CAR-PGa.

38. Jackson, "Press Conference Notes."

39. Lancaster, "Do Role-Playing Games Promote Crime, Satanism and Suicide?," 70.

40. "Feds vs. Cyberpunks: Part II," 64.

41. Jackson, "Press Conference Notes."

42. Mike Mather, "More 'Vampire' Victims Say They Were Bitten, Assaulted," *Virginian-Pilot*, January 19, 1996, A1; "In 'Vampire' Case, Dual Blame Judge," *Washington Post*, January 7, 1997, B2.

43. Donald Baker, "A Tale from the Dark Side," *Washington Post*, May 8, 1996, B01.

44. Mike Mather, "On Top of the Occult: The Detective Working Virginia Beach's 'Vampire' Case Is a Veteran at Investigating Alleged Forces of Darkness," *Virginian-Pilot*, February 5, 1996, B1.

45. *The 700 Club* (February 12, 1996; November 8, 1996); transcripts available at http://www.theescapist.com (accessed May 21, 2013).

46. Aphrodite Jones, *The Embrace: A True Vampire Story* (New York: Pocket Books, 1999), 332–83.

47. Michelle Belanger, *The Psychic Vampire Codex: A Manual of Magick and Energy Work* (Boston: Weiser Books, 2004), 25.

48. Lesley Clark, "For Some, Vampire Fantasy Can Be All Too Real," *Orlando Sentinel*, December 8, 1996. On December 16, 1996, Paul Cardwell of CAR-PGa called Lesley Clark, who reportedly admitted that no game materials had been found in the stolen Explorer. Cardwell feels this conversation helped to shift the *Orlando Sentinel's* coverage of the murders away from the anti-role-playing-game narrative.

49. Jones, *The Embrace*, 84.

50. Tony Thorne, *Children of the Night: Of Vampires and Vampirism* (London: Indigo, 2000), 176.

51. Ron Popeski, "Members of 'Vampire Clan' Arrested in Louisiana," Reuters, November 29, 1996.

52. Clifford Linedecker, *The Vampire Killers* (New York: St. Martin's, 1999), 272.

53. Ibid., 8.

54. Ibid., 271.

55. Dawn Perlmutter wrote a series of sensationalist articles for the online journal *Anthropoetics* that discussed the Ferrell murders and implied that the self-identified vampire community represents a serious threat to public safety because of their psychological need for ritual violence. Perlmutter's writings have also suggested that *Vampire: The Masquerade* lures young people into increasingly deviant and criminal subcultures. Perlmutter continues to publish alarmist articles but has since turned to writing about Islamic extremists and their alleged dependence on ritual violence. Don Rimer continued to hold seminars for churches and law enforcement groups on occult crime until his death in 2012. Informants from a conference held in 2002 indicate that he continued to talk about the dangers of fantasy games and to invoke the Ferrell murders. See Dawn Perlmutter, "The Sacrificial Aesthetic: Blood Rituals from Art to Murder," *Anthropoetics* 5:2 (2000), http://www.anthropoetics.ucla.edu/ap0502/blood.htm (accessed May 29, 2013); Perlmutter, "The Forensics of Sacrifice: A

Symbolic Analysis of Ritualistic Crime," *Anthropoetics* 9:2 (2004), http://www.anthropoetics.ucla.edu/ap0902/sacrifice.htm (accessed May 29, 2013); Kerr Cuhulain, "The Cycle Continues," *Witchvox,* January 16, 2005, http://www.witchvox.com/va/dt_va.html?a = cabc&c = whs&id = 8939 (accessed May 29, 2013).

56. Dan McComb, "Going Gothic: Spokane Vampire Community Sinks Imaginary Teeth While Searching for an Identity," *Spokane Review,* May 30, 1997, D1.

57. Interview for "Payback," *Wicked Attraction,* Investigation Discovery Network, 2009.

58. "The American Way of Murder," *The Times,* June 27, 1997, T18.

59. "Michigan School Alters Policy to Recognize Witch," Reuters News, March 22, 1999.

60. Dave Cullen, in his analysis of the Columbine Massacre, rejects the notion that "gothic culture" was responsible for Harris and Klebold's behavior. Cullen argues that Harris was a psychopath and that Klebold became his accomplice because he was suicidally depressed. A similar interpretation was applied to Anderson and Baranyi, with Anderson as the remorseless killer and Baranyi as the impressionable follower. Cullen suggests that mass violence lends itself to misinformation and mythologizing, including narratives that scapegoat deviant cultural forms. See Dave Cullen, *Columbine* (New York: Twelve, 2009).

61. Marc Fisher, "'Trenchcoat Mafia' Obsessed with Morose Culture of Death," *Spokesman Review,* April 21, 1999, A12.

62. Ted Anthony, "Summon Emotion, Prosecutor Speaks Out on Killings," *Argus Press,* April 24, 1999, 5.

63. Pat Robertson, *Bring It On: Tough Questions, Candid Answers* (Nashville: W Pub. Group, 2003), 238.

64. Carey Goldberg, "It's Gotten Even Harder to Be a Geek," *Tuscaloosa News,* May 1, 1999, 4A.

65. "WordCHECK Systems and Youth Magazine Team Up to Identify Violent-Prone Kids," PR Newswire, June 4, 1999.

66. In her ethnography of gothic culture, Julie Winden spoke with nightclub bouncers who reported that "goth night" always had the fewest incidents of violent altercations. According to her informants, this was because goths tended to be "introspective and nonviolent." See Julie Winden, "Spirituality Bites," in *Gen X Religion,* ed. Richard Flory and Donald Miller (New York: Routledge, 2000), 33.

67. Putsata Reang, *Deadly Secrets* (New York: Avon Books, 2001), 51.

68. Ibid., 339.

69. Ibid., 342.

70. Fine, *Shared Fantasy,* 44.

71. Daniel Mackay, *The Fantasy Role-Playing Game: A New Performing Art* (Jefferson, N.C.: McFarland, 2001), 150.

72. William Sims Bainbridge, *eGods: Faith versus Fantasy in Computer Gaming* (New York: Oxford University Press, 2013).

73. José Cassanova, *Public Religions in the Modern World* (Chicago: University of Chicago Press, 1994), 11; Rodney Stark, "Secularization, R.I.P.,"

Sociology of Religion 60:3 (1999): 249–73; William H. Swatos and Kevin J. Christiano, "Secularization: The Course of a Concept," in *The Secularization Debate,* ed. William H. Swatos and Daniel V. A. Olson (Lanham, Md.: Rowman and Littlefield, 2000), 2.

74. Wouter Hanegraaff, "How Magic Survived the Disenchantment of the World," *Religion* 33 (2003): 357–80.

75. See the footnotes of Christopher Lehrich, "Ritual Discourse in Role-Playing Games" (2005), http://www.indie-rpgs.com/_articles/ritual_discourse_in_RPGs.html (accessed May 29, 2013).

76. Mark Rein-Hagen, Sam Chupp, and Jennifer Hartshorn, *Wraith: The Oblivion* (Stone Mountain, Ga.: White Wolf, 1994), 265–66.

77. Sam Chupp, personal communication with author, August 12, 2008.

78. Venefica, "Mage the Ascension" (February 9, 2010), http://www.occult-forum.org/forum/viewtopic.php?f = 34&t = 29980&p = 447718 (accessed May 27, 2013).

79. Martin Ramstedt argues that the magical practices of modern pagans reflect a "metaphorical turn" in which ritual has increasingly converged with fantasy and play. See Martin Ramstedt, "Metaphor of Invocation? The Convergence of Ritual between Modern Paganism and Fantasy Fiction," *Journal of Ritual Studies* 21:1 (2007): 1–15.

80. For a detailed history of these groups, see Joseph Laycock, *Vampires Today: The Truth about Modern Vampirism.* (Westport, Conn: Praeger, 2009); "'We Are Spirits of Another Sort': Ontological Rebellion and Religious Dimensions of the Otherkin Community," *Nova Religio* 15:3 (2012): 65–90; Venetia Robertson, "The Beast Within: Anthrozoomorphic Identity and Alternative Spirituality in the Online Therianthropy Movement," *Nova Religio* 16:3 (2013): 7–30.

81. Belanger, *The Psychic Vampire Codex,* 14.

82. Ibid., 19–25.

83. Frater Shinobi, "Vampire/Lycanthrope: As Above, So Below," *Midnight Sun* 1:1 (1995): 6.

84. Frater Shinobi, "Of the Undead/Vampyre Order," *Midnight Sun* 1:5 (1996): 4.

85. Belanger, *The Psychic Vampire Codex,* 21.

86. Viola Johnson, *Dhampir, Child of the Blood: A Vampire's Babybook* (Fairfield, Conn.: Mystic Rose Books, 1996), 50.

87. This description was written as part of a survey of otherkin conducted by the Atlanta Vampire Alliance.

88. Lupa, personal communication with author, May 22, 2009; Lupa, *A Field Guide to Otherkin* (Stafford, Eng.: Megalithica Books, 2007), 16.

89. Gilsdorf, *Fantasy Freaks and Gaming Geeks,* 57; Mark Barrowcliffe, *The Elfish Gene: Dungeons and Dragons and Growing Up Strange* (New York: Soho Press, 2007), 77.

90. Laycock, "We Are Spirits of Another Sort," 71.

91. Ibid., 77.

92. Nick Mamatas, "Elven Like Me," *Village Voice,* February 21, 2001.

93. Mircea Eliade, *The Quest: History and Meaning in Religion* (Chicago: University of Chicago Press, 1969), iv.

94. Nachman Ben-Yehuda, *Deviance and Moral Boundaries: Witchcraft, the Occult, Science Fiction, Deviant Sciences and Scientists* (Chicago: University of Chicago Press, 1985), 99.

95. Ibid., 75; Danielle Kirby, "From Pulp Fiction to Revealed Text," in *Exploring Religion and the Sacred in a Media Age,* ed. Christopher Deacy and Elizabeth Arweck (Burlington, Vt.: Ashgate Press, 2009), 145; Christopher Partridge, "Alternative Spiritualities, New Religions, and the Re-Enchantment of the West," in *The Oxford Handbook of New Religious Movements,* ed. James R. Lews (New York: Oxford University Press, 2004), 55; and Robert Ellwood, "Notes on a Neopagan Religious Group in America," *History of Religions* 11:1 (1971): 131.

96. Partridge, "Alternative Spiritualities, New Religions, and the Re-Enchantment of the West," 56.

97. Jolyon Baraka Thomas, "*Shukyo Asobi* and Miyazaki Hayao's *Anime,*" *Nova Religio* 10:3 (2007): 73–95.

98. Danielle Kirby, "Alternative Worlds: Metaphysical Questing and Virtual Community amongst the Otherkin," *Sydney Studies in Religion,* 2006, 275–87; Kirby, "From Pulp Fiction to Revealed Text," 141–54; Kirby, *Fantasy and Belief: Alternative Religions, Popular Narratives and Digital Cultures* (Bristol, Conn.: Equinox, 2013).

99. Lupa, *A Field Guide to Otherkin,* 158.

100. Adam Possamai, *Sociology of Religion for Generations X and Y* (Oakville, Conn.: Equinox Publishing, 2009), 26.

101. Lynn Schofield Clark, *From Angels to Aliens: Teenagers, the Media, and the Supernatural* (Oxford: Oxford University Press, 2003), 228.

102. Lupa, *A Field Guide to Otherkin,* 27–29.

6. HOW ROLE-PLAYING GAMES CREATE MEANING

Epigraphs: Pablo Picasso, "Statement to Marius de Zayas" (1923), http://www.learn.columbia.edu/monographs/picmon/pdf/art_hum_reading_49.pdf (accessed June 13, 2013); Oscar Wilde, *The Decay of Lying and Other Essays* (New York: Penguin Books, 2010), 26.

1. J.R.R. Tolkien, *The Monsters and the Critics and Other Essays* (Boston: Houghton Mifflin, 1984), 148.

2. Peter Berger, *The Sacred Canopy: Elements of a Sociological Theory of Religion* (New York: Anchor Books, 1969), 5.

3. Clifford Geertz, *The Interpretation of Cultures* (New York: Basic Books, 1973), 90.

4. Alison Gopnik, *The Philosophical Baby* (New York: Farrar, Straus and Giroux, 2009), 28.

5. William James, *Principles of Psychology* (New York: Cosimo, 2007), 2:293.

6. Alfred Schutz, "On Multiple Realities," *Philosophy and Phenomenological Research* 5:4 (June 1945): 551.

7. Robert Bellah, *Religion in Human Evolution: From the Paleolithic to the Axial Age* (Cambridge, Mass.: Harvard University Press, 2011), 9.

8. Émile Durkheim, *The Elementary Forms of Religious Life* (New York: The Free Press, 1995), 170.

9. Gopnik, *The Philosophical Baby*, 14–15.

10. Victor Turner, "Liminal to Liminoid in Play, Flow, and Ritual: An Essay in Comparative Symbology," *Rice University Studies* 60:3 (1974): 59.

11. Ibid., 75.

12. Ibid., 61.

13. Daniel Mackay, *The Fantasy Role-Playing Game: A New Performing Art* (Jefferson, N.C.: McFarland, 2001), 76; Christopher Lehrich, "Ritual Discourse in Role-Playing Games" (2005), http://www.indie-rpgs.com/_articles/ritual_discourse_in_RPGs.html (accessed May 29, 2013); Sarah Lynne Bowman, *The Functions of Role-Playing Games* (Jefferson, N.C.: McFarland, 2010), 15.

14. Turner, "Liminal to Liminoid," 86.

15. Quoted in Mackay, *The Fantasy Role-Playing Game*, 85.

16. Turner, "Liminal to Liminoid."

17. Charles Taylor, *Sources of the Self: The Making of Modern Identity* (Cambridge, Mass.: Harvard University Press, 1989), 47.

18. Claude Levi-Strauss, *The Raw and the Cooked* (Chicago: University of Chicago Press, 1969), 16.

19. Joan Hake Robie, *The Truth about Dungeons and Dragons* (Lancaster, Pa.: Starburst Publishers, 1991), 13.

20. Jean-Paul Sartre, *The Psychology of Imagination* (Westport, Conn.: Greenwood Press, 1978), 90.

21. Mackay, *The Fantasy Role-Playing Game*, 26. Mackay makes the same point, using a different disciplinary tool kit. Where I have used the terminology of Turner and Levi-Strauss, Mackay incorporates Baudrillard's notion of the semiosphere to describe how role-playing games repurpose the signs of popular culture.

22. Wizards of the Coast, *30 Years of Adventure: A Celebration of Dungeons & Dragons* (Renton, Wash.: Wizards of the Coast, 2006), n.p.

23. Turner, "Liminal to Liminoid," 60.

24. Geertz, *The Interpretation of Cultures*, 94.

25. Geertz's essay was applied to *D&D* as early as 1986. See Terri Toles-Patkin, "Rational Coordination in the Dungeon," *Journal of Popular Culture* 20:1 (1986): 8. More recently, David Ewalt discusses this essay in *Of Dice and Men: The Story of Dungeons & Dragons and the People Who Play It* (New York: Scribner, 2013), 116–17.

26. John Eric Holmes, "Confessions of a Dungeon Master," *Psychology Today*, November 1980, 93.

27. Mark Barrowcliffe, *The Elfish Gene: Dungeons and Dragons and Growing Up Strange* (New York: Soho Press, 2007), 35.

28. Geertz, *The Interpretation of Cultures*, 443.

29. Again Mackay makes a similar point, using a different set of theorists. Following Roland Barthes, he suggests that role-playing games attempt to imitate not only the impression but also the structural foundations of reality. Mackay, *The Fantasy Role-Playing Game*, 67.

30. Wizards of the Coast, *30 Years of Adventure,* n.p.

31. Bowman, *The Functions of Role-Playing Games,* 177.

32. Mackay, *The Fantasy Role-Playing Game,* 68.

33. David Waldron, "Role-Playing Games and the Christian Right: Community Formation in Response to a Moral Panic," *Journal of Religion and Popular Culture* 9 (Spring 2005), http://utpjournals.metapress.com/content/v3503x532wxjoq28/.

34. Erik Erikson, *Identity, Youth, and Crisis* (New York: Norton, 1994), 156–57.

35. Gregory Bateson, *Steps to an Ecology of Mind* (New York: Ballantine Books, 1972), 191.

36. Gary Alan Fine, *Shared Fantasy: Role-Playing Games as Social Worlds* (Chicago: University of Chicago Press, 1983), 232.

37. Quoted in Ewalt, *Of Dice and Men,* 122.

38. Wayne D. Blackmon, "Dungeons and Dragons: The Use of a Fantasy Game in the Psychotherapeutic Treatment of a Young Adult," *American Journal of Psychotherapy* 48:4 (Fall 1994): 627.

39. Moira Johnston, "It's Only a Game—Or Is It?," *New West,* August 25, 1980, 39. Johnston's interview with Hargrave was directly quoted by several moral entrepreneurs. See John Weldon and James Bjornstad, *Playing with Fire* (Chicago: Moody Press, 1984), 53; Peter Leithart and George Grant, *A Christian Response to Dungeons and Dragons: The Catechism of the New Age* (Fort Worth, Tex.: Dominion Press, 1988), 6.

40. Barrowcliffe, *The Elfish Gene,* 227.

41. Johnston, "It's Only a Game," 39.

42. The computer game *Diablo* shares Arduin Gimoire's celebration of the gruesome and macabre. The game's manual contains a dedication to Hargrave, who died in 1988. See *Diablo* (Irving, Calif.: Blizzard Entertainment, 1996), 79.

43. Fine, *Shared Fantasy,* 44.

44. Ibid., 70.

45. Ibid., 248–49.

46. Holmes, "Confessions of a Dungeon Master," 88.

47. Fine, *Shared Fantasy,* 56.

48. Dorothy Singer and Jerome Singer, *The House of Make-Believe: Children's Play and the Developing Imagination* (Cambridge, Mass.: Harvard University Press, 1990), 257–58.

49. Fine, *Shared Fantasy,* 69.

50. Geertz, *The Interpretation of Cultures,* 444.

51. Kevin Schut, "Desktop Conquistadors: Negotiating American Manhood in the Digital Fantasy Role-Playing Game," in *Gaming as Culture: Essays on Reality, Identity, and Experience in Fantasy Games,* ed. J. Patrick Williams, Sean Q. Hendricks, and W. Keith Winkler (Jefferson, N.C.: McFarland, 2006), 116.

52. Barrowcliffe, *The Elfish Gene,* 267.

53. Bruno Bettelheim, *The Uses of Enchantment* (New York: Knopf, 1977), 120–22.

54. Dennis D. Waskul, "The Role-Playing Game and the Game of Role-Playing: The Ludic Self and Everday Self," in Williams, Hendricks, and Winkler, *Gaming as Culture,* 34.

55. Peter G. Stromberg, *Caught in Play: How Entertainment Works on You* (Stanford, Calif.: Stanford University Press, 2009), 60.

56. Richard Schechner, *Between Theater and Anthropology* (Philadelphia: University of Pennsylvania Press, 1985), 14.

57. Geertz, *The Interpretation of Cultures,* 119.

58. Paul La Farge, "Destroy All Monsters," *The Believer,* September 2006, http://www.believermag.com/issues/200609/?read = article_lafarge (accessed December 17, 2012). The first edition of the *Dungeon Master's Guide* did contain a "harlot table" featuring a dozen varieties of pimps and prostitutes with titles such as "brazen strumpet," "saucy tart," and "wanton wench." The table was obviously included as a joke but outraged moral entrepreneurs. See Gary Gygax, *Dungeon Master's Guide* (Lake Geneva, Wis.: TSR Games, 1979), 192.

59. Holmes, "Confessions of a Dungeon Master," 94: Robie, *The Truth about Dungeons and Dragons,* 43.

60. Fine, *Shared Fantasy,* 83.

61. Ian G. Barbour, *Myths, Models, and Paradigms: A Comparative Study in Science and Religion* (New York: Harper & Row, 1974), 33.

62. Anne H. Oman, "Dungeons and Dragons: It's Not Just a Game, It's an Adventure," *Washington Post,* February 20, 1981, 1.

63. Barrowcliffe, *The Elfish Gene,* 29.

64. Jon Cogburn, "Beyond Chaotic Good and Lawful Evil?," in *Dungeons and Dragons and Philosophy: Raiding the Temple of Wisdom,* ed. Jon Cogburn and Mark Silcox (Chicago: Open Court, 2012), 46.

65. Paul Cardwell, "Setting the Record Straight on Interviewing Techniques for Adolescents by Pat Pulling," (Bonham, Tex., n.d.), 6.

66. As early as the 1950s, psychological studies concluded that role-playing facilitates shifts in attitude. See Irving L. Janis and Bert T. King, "The Influence of Role Playing on Opinion Change," *Journal of Abnormal Psychology* 49:2 (1954): 211–18.

67. Bob MacKey, "Letter," *Dragon* 181 (May 1992): 80.

68. John Hughes, "Therapy Is Fantasy: Roleplaying, Healing and the Construction of Symbolic Order" (paper presented in Anthropology IV Honours, Medical Anthropology Seminar, Australian National University, 1988), http://www.rpgstudies.net/hughes/therapy_is_fantasy.html (accessed February 2, 2013).

69. Heather L. Mello, "Invoking the Avatar: Gaming Skills as Cultural and Out-of-Game Capital," in Williams, Hendricks, and Winkler, *Gaming as Culture,* 192.

70. Tanya Luhrmann, *Persuasions of the Witch's Craft* (Cambridge, Mass.: Harvard University Press, 1989), 106; Sarah M. Pike, *Earthly Bodies, Magical Selves: Contemporary Pagans and the Search for Community* (Berkeley: University of California Press, 2001); Michael Tresca, *The Evolution of Fantasy Role-Playing Games* (Jefferson, N.C.: McFarland, 2011), 15.

71. Isaac Bonewitz, "My Satanic Adventure or I Was a Teenage Satanist!" (2005), http://www.neopagan.net/SatanicAdventure.html (accessed June 13, 2013).

72. Isaac Bonewitz, *Authentic Thaumaturgy* (Austin, Tex.: Steve Jackson Games, 1998), 8.

73. James R. Cotter, "Dungeons and Dragons Lecture" (September 16, 1980), http://www.theescapist.com/archive-cotter.htm (accessed June 13, 2013); Bob Larson, *Satanism: The Seduction of America's Youth* (Nashville: Thomas Nelson Publishers, 1989), 51.

74. Gareth Medway, *Lure of the Sinister: The Unnatural History of Satanism* (New York: New York University Press, 2001), 289.

75. Barrowcliffe, *The Elfish Gene*, 170.

76. Pike, *Earthly Bodies, Magical Selves*, 171.

77. Luhrmann, *Persuasions of the Witch's Craft*, 336, 12.

78. Glenn Morris, *Path Notes of an American Ninja Master* (Berkeley, Calif.: North Atlantic Books, 1993), 59.

79. Glenn Morris, *Shadow Strategies of an American Ninja Master* (Berkeley, Calif.: Frog, Ltd., 1996), 311.

80. Luhrmann, *Persuasions of the Witch's Craft*, 13.

81. Ibid., 220.

82. Lupa, *A Field Guide to Otherkin* (Stafford, Eng.: Megalithica Books, 2007), 251.

83. Durkheim, *The Elementary Forms of Religious Life*, 63,

84. In 2008, I gave a talk on the real vampire community at the University of Michigan in Ann Arbor. An administrative assistant had brought her grade-school-age son to my talk because one of his friends claimed to be a vampire. After my talk, the boy explained to me that his friend said he was a vampire and that he was currently preparing for an apocalyptic war against the forces of evil. (Lupa warns that prophecies of a great war are extremely common among teenagers interested in magic.) The boy asked his friend why he was telling him this, pointing out that vampires do not reveal their identities to the public. His friend answered that he would need allies in the coming war. The boy replied, "So when a twenty-foot demon comes out of the ground, you'll be like 'It's a good thing I have two fourth-graders with me and that one of them has a yellow belt in Taekwondo?'" The boy concluded that his friend's fantasy was based on the novel *Cirque du Freak* by Darren Shan. In all likelihood, by the time these children reach high school, no one will remember any claims of being a vampire.

85. Quoted in John Walliss, "The Road to Hell Is Paved with D20s: Evangelical Christianity and Role-Playing Gaming," in *The Handbook of Hyperreal Religions*, ed. Adam Possamai (Boston: Brill, 2012), 217.

86. Donald E. Miller and Arpi Misha Miller, "Introduction" in *Gen X Religion*, ed. Richard W. Flory and Donald E. Miller (New York: Routledge, 2000), 5.

87. Olivia Grace, "What's Causing WoW Subscriptions to Drop?" (February 13, 2013), http://www.gamebreaker.tv/mmorpg/whats-causing-wow-subscriptions-to-drop/ (accessed June 13, 2013).

88. Barrowcliffe, *The Elfish Gene*, 3.

89. Ewalt, *Of Dice and Men,* 183.

90. William Sims Bainbridge, *eGods: Faith versus Fantasy in Computer Gaming* (New York: Oxford University Press, 2013).

91. Quoted in Bob Guerra, "Dungeons and Dragons: A Simulated Fantasy," *Compute!* 123 (November 1990): 64.

92. Quoted in Bowman, *The Functions of Role-Playing Games,* 23.

93. Cover, *The Creation of Narrative*, 48.

94. "Beloved Game Is Getting Poor Treatment in Computerized Versions," *South Burnett Times and Rural Weekly,* May 13, 2013, 38.

95. Pete Wolfendale and Tim Franklin, "Why Dungeons and Dragons Is Art," in Cogburn and Silcox, *Dungeons and Dragons and Philosophy,* 222.

96. Ethan Gilsdorf, *Fantasy Freaks and Gaming Geeks: An Epic Quest for Reality among Role Players, Online Gamers, and Other Dwellers of Imaginary Realms* (Guilford, Conn.: The Lyons Press, 2009), 204.

7. HOW THE IMAGINATION BECAME DANGEROUS

Epigraphs: Victor Turner, "Liminal to Liminoid in Play, Flow, and Ritual: An Essay in Comparative Symbology," *Rice University Studies* 60:3 (1974): 77; Joseph R. Chambers, "Barney: The Purple Messiah," a sermon booklet from Paw Creek Ministries in Charlotte, North Carolina, reprinted in *Harpers,* March 1994, 30–31.

1. "Preschool Wants to Ban 'Superhero Play,'" *The Naked City,* May 22, 2013, http://www.citypaper.net/blogs/nakedcity/Preschool-wants-to-ban-superhero-play.html (accessed June 3, 2013).

2. Dorothy Singer and Jerome Singer, *The House of Make-Believe: Children's Play and the Developing Imagination* (Cambridge, Mass.: Harvard University Press, 1990), 182. See also Marjorie J. Kostelnik et al., "Living with He-Man: Managing Superhero Fantasy Play," *Young Children* 4:4 (May 1986): 3–9.

3. "Preschool Wants to Ban 'Superhero Play.'"

4. Rebecca Klein, "Preschool Reportedly Bans Imaginary Superhero Play," *The Huffington Post,* May 24, 2013, http://www.huffingtonpost.com/2013/05/22/preschool-superhero-ban-reddit_n_3321630.html (accessed June 3, 2013); "Preschool Bans Superhero Play, Imagination, Fun," *Inquisitr.com,* http://www.inquisitr.com/671556/preschool-bans-superhero-play/#w47aH7ThHwW2MdAp.99 (accessed June 3, 2013).

5. Adam Edelman, "Boy, 7, Suspended for Throwing Imaginary Grenade," *New York Daily News,* February 5, 2013, http://www.nydailynews.com/news/national/boy-7-suspended-throwing-imaginary-grenade-article-1.1256200 (accessed June 14, 2013); Deborah Hastings, "Boy, Suspended for Chewing Pop-Tart into Shape of Gun, Gets Lifetime NRA Membership," *New York Daily News,* May 31, 2013, http://www.nydailynews.com/news/national/boy-suspended-gun-shaped-pop-tart-lifetime-nra-membership-article-1.1359918 (accessed June 14, 2013).

6. Bruno Bettelheim, *The Uses of Enchantment* (New York: Knopf, 1977), 117.

7. J.R.R. Tolkien, *The Monsters and the Critics and Other Essays* (Boston: Houghton Mifflin, 1984), 132–33.

8. Alison Gopnik, *The Philosophical Baby* (New York: Farrar, Straus and Giroux, 2009), 71.

9. Ibid., 31.

10. Gareth J. Medway, *Lure of the Sinister: The Unnatural History of Satanism* (New York: New York University Press, 2001), 291.

11. Nancy Ammerman, *Bible Believers: Fundamentalists in the Modern World* (New Brunswick, N.J.: Rutgers University Press, 1987), 6.

12. Alexander Nehamas, *Virtues of Authenticity: Essays on Plato and Socrates* (Princeton, N.J.: Princeton University Press, 1999), 282.

13. Brian Onken and Elliot Miller, "Fantasy Games People Play," The Christian Research Institute (1994), http://www.inplainsite.org/html/fantasy_games.html (accessed August 12, 2013).

14. Rick Jones, *Stairway to Hell: The Well-Planned Destruction of Teens* (Chino, Calif.: Chick Publications, 1988), 102 (bold in the original).

15. Bob Larson, *Satanism: The Seduction of America's Youth* (Nashville: Thomas Nelson Publishers, 1989), 54.

16. Rebecca Brown, *Prepare for War* (Chino, Calif.: Chick Publications, 1987), 134.

17. Larson, *Satanism,* 53.

18. Brown, *Prepare for War,* 134.

19. Larson, *Satanism,* 52.

20. William Schnoebelen, "Should a Christian Play Dungeons and Dragons?" (2001), http://www.chick.com/articles/frpg.asp (accessed July 1, 2013).

21. Brandon Cooke, "It's OK to Be Evil in Your Head," in *Dungeons and Dragons and Philosophy: Raiding the Temple of Wisdom,* ed. Jon Cogburn and Mark Silcox (Chicago: Open Court, 2012), 84–85.

22. Consider Larson's discussion of the computer game *Doom,* which suggests that the game designers' ability to imagine demons signifies the involvement of actual demons. He writes, "The color pictures on the box titillated my imagination with images of demons that, it seemed to me, only a mind possessed by them could conjure." Bob Larson, *Extreme Evil: Kids Killing Kids* (Nashville: Thomas Nelson Publishers, 1999), 41.

23. Peter Leithart and George Grant, *A Christian Response to Dungeons and Dragons: The Catechism of the New Age* (Fort Worth, Tex.: Dominion Press, 1988), 13.

24. John Ankerberg and John Weldon, "Dungeons and Dragons and Fantasy Role-Playing Games," in *Encyclopedia of New Age Beliefs,* ed. John Ankerberg and John Weldon (Eugene, Ore.: Harvest House Publishers, 1996), 156.

25. Leithart and Grant, *A Christian Response to Dungeons and Dragons,* 11.

26. Richard Abanes, *Harry Potter and the Bible: The Menace behind the Magick* (Camp Hill, Pa.: Horizon Books, 2001), 235–37.

27. In *The Silver Chair,* Lewis's protagonists, Jill and Eustace, enter Narnia by devising a ritual in which they face east with their hands in a particular gesture and chant Aslan's name. While preparing this ritual they have the following exchange:

> "How did you get there?" said Jill. She felt curiously shy.
>
> "The only way you can—by Magic," said Eustace almost in a whisper. . . .
>
> "You mean we might draw a circle on the ground—and write in queer letters in it—and stand inside it—and recite charms and spells?"
>
> "Well," said Eustace after he had thought hard for a bit. "I believe that was the sort of thing I was thinking of, though I never did it. But now that it comes to the point, I've an idea that all those circles and things are rather rot. I don't think he'd like them. It would look as if we thought we could make him do things. But really, we can only ask him."

Lewis is clear that the "magic" that allows the children to enter Narnia relies on divine intervention and not the manipulation of invisible forces as in Harry Potter. However, Jill and Eustace's ritual is just as imitable as the snippets of Latin that appear in J.K. Rowling's books. In fact, it seems almost a certainty that since *The Silver Chair* was published in 1953, young readers have performed this ritual just to see if it would work. Despite Lewis's theological caveat, this story seems no less likely to inspire an interest in magic than *Harry Potter.* C.S. Lewis, *The Silver Chair* (New York: HarperCollins Publishers, 1981), 7–8.

28. Jason Bivins, *Religion of Fear: The Politics of Horror in Conservative Evangelicalism* (New York: Oxford University Press, 2008), 18.

29. Mike Warnke, *Schemes of Satan* (Tulsa, Okla.: Victory House, 1991), 12–13.

30. Leithart and Grant, *A Christian Response to Dungeons and Dragons,* 4.

31. Rus Walton, *Biblical Solutions to Contemporary Problems: A Handbook* (Brentwood, Tenn.: Wolgemuth & Hyatt Publishers, 1988), 343. Judges 2:10 (KJV) reads: "And also all that generation were gathered unto their fathers: and there arose another generation after them, which knew not the Lord, nor yet the works which he had done for Israel."

32. Nicky Cruz, *Devil on the Run* (Melbourne, Fla.: Dove Christian Books, 1989), 24.

33. Gopnik notes that some fundamentalist Christians interpret their children's imaginary friends as demons. See Gopnik, *The Philosophical Baby,* 51.

34. Karen Armstrong, *The Battle for God* (New York: Alfred A. Knopf, 2000), xv–xvi.

35. Malise Ruthven, *Fundamentalism: The Search for Meaning* (New York: Oxford University Press, 2004), 85.

36. Paul Veyne, *Did the Greeks Believe in Their Myths? An Essay on the Constitutive Imagination* (Chicago: University of Chicago Press, 1988), 18.

37. Ibid., xi.

38. Dante Alighieri, *Purgatory,* trans. Dorothy Sayers (New York: Penguin Books, 1955), 196.

39. Ignatius, *The Spiritual Exercises of Saint Ignatius,* trans. George E. Ganss (Chicago: Loyola University Press, 1992), 48.

40. Ibid., 65.

41. Ibid., 35.

42. John Bunyan, *The Pilgrim's Progress,* ed. Roger Pooley (New York: Penguin Classics, 2008), 6.

43. Quoted in Veyne, *Did the Greeks Believe Their Myths?* 59–60.

44. Samuel Miller, *A Brief Retrospect of the Eighteenth Century* (New York: T. and J. Swords, 1803), 431.

45. E. Brooks Holifield, *Theology in America: Christian Thought from the Age of the Puritans to the Civil War* (New Haven, Conn.: Yale University Press, 2003), 159.

46. Ibid., 170.

47. Samuel Johnson, *The Works of Samuel Johnson* (London: Luke Hanford and Sons, 1810), 24.

48. Samuel Miller, "On Novel Reading," *The Panoplist and Missionary Magazine United,* October 1808, 205–6.

49. Quoted in M. Andrew Holochack, *Dutiful Correspondent: Philosophical Essays on Thomas Jefferson* (Lanham, Md.: Rowman and Littlefield, 2013), 11.

50. Quoted in Steven Starker, *Evil Influences: Crusades against the Mass Media* (New Brunswick, N.J.: Transaction Publishers, 1989), 62.

51. David W. Phillips, "The Influence of Suggestion on Suicide: Substantive and Theoretical Implications of the Werther Effect," *American Sociological Review* 39:3 (1974): 340; Larson, *Extreme Evil,* 33–34.

52. Sue Bohlin, "Dungeons and Dragons and FRPGS," Probe Ministries (2007), http://www.inplainsite.org/html/dungeons_and_dragons.html (accessed August 12, 2013).

53. Charles Dickens, *Hard Times* (New York: Harper & Brothers, 1854), 18.

54. Edward Burnett Tylor, "The Religion of Savages," *The Fortnightly Review,* ed. George Henry Lewes, August 15, 1866, 71–72.

55. Patricia Pulling, *The Devil's Web: Who Is Stalking Your Children for Satan?* (Lafayette, La.: Huntington House, 1989), 77.

56. Ruthven, *Fundamentalism,* 12.

57. James Barr, *Fundamentalism* (Philadelphia: Westminster Press, 1978), 40.

58. Karen McCarthy Brown, "Fundamentalism and the Control of Women," in *Fundamentalism and Gender,* ed. John Stratton Hawley (New York: Oxford University Press, 1994), 201–2.

59. Conrad Hyers, "Biblical Literalism: Constricting the Cosmic Dance," *Christian Century,* August 4–11, 1982, 823.

60. Karen Armstrong, *A History of God: The 4000-Year Quest of Judaism, Christianity, and Islam* (New York: Alfred A. Knopf, 1993), 363.

61. Tolkien, *The Monsters and the Critics,* 144.

62. Ibid. On Tolkien's relationship with Lewis, see Colin Duriez, "The Fairy-Story: J.R.R. Tolkien and C.S. Lewis," in *Tree of Tales: Tolkien, Literature, and Theology,* ed. Trevor A. Hart and Ivan Khovacs (Waco, Tex.: Baylor University Press, 2007), 13–24.

63. Warnke, *Schemes of Satan,* 91.

64. Quoted in Abanes, *Harry Potter and the Bible,* 1.

65. C.S. Lewis, *The Screwtape Letters* (New York: Harper Collins, 2001), 31–32.

66. Gary North, *Unholy Spirits: Occultism and New Age Humanism* (Fort Worth, Tex.: Dominion Press, 1988), 88.

67. Peter Berger, *The Sacred Canopy: Elements of a Sociological Theory of Religion* (New York: Anchor Books, 1969), 22.

68. Ibid., 23.

69. Sarah Lynne Bowman, *The Functions of Role-Playing Games* (Jefferson, N.C.: McFarland, 2010), 124.

70. Quoted in Gary Alan Fine, *Shared Fantasy: Role-Playing Games as Social Worlds* (Chicago: University of Chicago Press, 1983), 54.

71. Berger, *The Sacred Canopy*, 39.

72. Joan Hake Robie, *The Truth about Dungeons and Dragons* (Lancaster, Pa.: Starburst Publishers, 1991), 69–70.

73. Schnoebelen, "Should a Christian Play Dungeons and Dragons?"

74. Leithart and Grant, *A Christian Response to Dungeons and Dragons,* 10.

75. Jerry Adler and Shawn Doherty, "Kids: The Deadliest Game?," *Newsweek,* September 9, 1985, 93.

76. Jean-Paul Sartre, *Being and Nothingness: An Essay on Phenomenological Ontology* (New York: Philosophical Library, 1956), 47–67.

77. Leithart and Grant, *A Christian Response to Dungeons and Dragons,* 17.

78. Jean-Paul Sartre, *Existentialism and Humanism* (Brooklyn: Haskell House, 1977), 27.

79. Robert Hicks, *In Pursuit of Satan: The Police and the Occult* (Buffalo, N.Y.: Prometheus Books, 1991), 28.

80. Slavoj Žižek, *Welcome to the Desert of the Real! Five Essays on 11 September and Related Dates* (London: Verso, 2002), 2.

81. Antonio Gramsci, *Prison Notebooks* (New York: Columbia Press, 1992), 2:288.

82. Leithart and Grant, *A Christian Response to Dungeons and Dragons,* 8.

83. Ibid., 14–15.

84. Daniel Mackay, *The Fantasy Role-Playing Game: A New Performing Art* (Jefferson, N.C.: McFarland, 2001), 68.

85. Isaac Bonewitz, *Authentic Thaumaturgy* (Austin, Tex.: Steve Jackson Games, 1998), 8.

8. RIVAL FANTASIES

Epigraphs: Iris Murdoch, as quoted in *The Times,* April 15, 1983; Gary Gygax, interview for TheOneRing.net (May 30, 2000), http://archives.theonering.net/features/interviews/gary_gygax.html (accessed July 20, 2013).

1. Brian Onken and Elliot Miller, "Fantasy Games People Play," Christian Research Institute (1994), http://www.inplainsite.org/html/fantasy_games.html (accessed July 20, 2013).

2. Daniel Martin and Gary Alan Fine, "Satanic Cults, Satanic Play: Is 'Dungeons and Dragons' a Breeding Ground for the Devil?," in *The Satanism Scare,* ed. James T. Richardson, Joel Best, and David G. Bromley (Hawthorne, N.Y.: Aldine De Gruyter, 1991), 107–26.

3. For Robert Hicks's arguments on moral panic and civil liberties, see Robert Hicks, "None Dare Call It Reason: Kids, Cults, and Common Sense" (talk prepared for the Virginia Department for Children's Twelfth Annual Legislative Forum, Roanoke, Virginia, September 22, 1989).

4. Stanley Semrau and Judy Gale, *Murderous Minds on Trial: Terrifying Tales from a Forensic Psychiatrist's Casebook* (Toronto: The Dundurn Group, 2002), 292. The first edition of *Dungeon Master's Guide* contained rules for hiring evil creatures such as orcs and goblins to serve as mercenaries. The rules specified that such creatures are usually cheap to hire but cannot be controlled and will commit war crimes.

5. Robert Hicks, *In Pursuit of Satan: The Police and the Occult* (Buffalo, N.Y.: Prometheus Books, 1991), 288.

6. Paul Harvey, "Dungeons and Dragons Game Blamed in Suicides of Youth," *Press-Courier*, March 9, 1985, 4.

7. "Schoolboard Bans Fantasy Game," *Kingman Daily Miner,* February 16, 1983, A11.

8. Joan Hake Robie, *The Truth about Dungeons and Dragons* (Lancaster, Pa.: Starburst Publishers, 1991), 67–68. This litany also appears in Patricia Pulling, *The Devil's Web: Who Is Stalking Your Children for Satan?* (Lafayette, La.: Huntington House, 1989), 179; and John Weldon and James Bjornstad, *Playing with Fire (*Chicago: Moody Press, 1984), 57.

9. Gareth J. Medway, *Lure of the Sinister: The Unnatural History of Satanism* (New York: New York University Press, 2001), 286.

10. William Schnoebelen, "Straight Talk on Dungeons and Dragons," http://www.chick.com/articles/dnd.asp (accessed February 2, 2013).

11. Robie, *The Truth about Dungeons and Dragons,* 60.

12. Louise Shanahan, "Games Unsuspecting People Play: Dungeons and Dragons" (Boston: Daughters of St. Paul, n.d.), 17.

13. David Frankfurter, *Evil Incarnate: Rumors of Demonic Conspiracy and Ritual Abuse in History* (Princeton, N.J.: Princeton University Press, 2006), 126.

14. Jason Bivins, *Religion of Fear: The Politics of Horror in Conservative Evangelicalism* (New York: Oxford University Press, 2008), 159.

15. Frankfurter, *Evil Incarnate,* 32.

16. "Man Admits He Posed as FBI," *Chicago Tribune,* December 23, 2004.

17. Jerry Johnston, *Why Suicide? What Parents & Teachers Must Know to Save Our Kids* (New York: Oliver Nelson, 1987), 82.

18. In 2011, Johnston was forced to close down his church amid accusations of embezzlement and tax evasion. See Judy L. Thomas, "Jerry Johnston's New Day Church Shuts Down," *Kansas City Star,* October 10, 2012.

19. "Doctor's License Is Revoked for Diagnosis of Evil Spirits," *New York Times,* September 24, 1984; Hicks, "None Dare Call it Reason"; David Alexander, "Giving the Devil More Than His Due," *The Humanist,* March 1, 1990, 7–8; G. Richard Fisher, Paul R. Blizard, and M. Kurt Goedelman, "Drugs, Demons and Delusions: The 'Amazing' Saga of Rebecca Brown," *Cult Help and Information,* http://www.culthelp.info/index2.php?option = com_content&do_pdf = 1&id = 1091 (accessed July 10, 2013).

20. G. Richard Fisher and M. Kurt Goedelman, "The Course of Curse Theology: The Return of Rebecca Brown, M.D.," *Personal Freedom Outreach* (1996), http://www.pfo.org/curse-th.htm (accessed July 23, 2013).

21. Frankfurter, *Evil Incarnate,* 207.

22. David G. Bromley, Anson D. Shupe, and J.C. Ventimiglia, "Atrocity Tales, the Unification Church, and the Social Construction of Evil," *Journal of Communication* 29:3 (Summer 1979): 42–53.

23. Brant Wenegrat, *Theater of Disorder: Patients, Doctors, and the Construction of Illness* (New York: Oxford University Press, 2001), 57–80.

24. Alexander, "Still Giving the Devil More Than His Due," 27.

25. Richard Hofstadter, *The Paranoid Style in American Politics* (New York: Vintage Books, 2008), 25.

26. William Schnoebelen, *Lucifer Dethroned* (Ontario, Calif.: Chick Publications, 1993), 125 (bold in the original); Schnoebelen, "Should a Christian Play Dungeons and Dragons?," Chick Publications (2001), http://www.chick.com/articles/frpg.asp (accessed July 23, 2013).

27. William Michael Kelly, "Forum letter," *Dragon* 181 (May 1992): 79.

28. Quoted in Fisher, Blizard, and Goedelman, "Drugs, Demons and Delusions."

29. John Trott and Mike Hertenstein, "Selling Satan: The Tragic History of Mike Warnke," *Cornerstone* 21:98 (1992), http://web.archive.org/web/20110629063019/http://www.cornerstonemag.com/features/iss098/sellingsatan.htm (accessed July 23, 2013).

30. Mike Warnke, *Schemes of Satan* (Tulsa, Okla.: Victory House, 1991), 15.

31. Gary Metz, "The John Todd Story," *Cornerstone* 48, http://web.archive.org/web/20061006195908/http:/?www.cornerstonemag.com/pages/show_page.asp?437 (accessed July 13, 2013). Todd appeared equally interested in Christianity and witchcraft and vacillated between the two for much of his life. After being banished from the Melodyland Christian Center in Anaheim, California, in 1973, he moved to Dayton, Ohio, and opened a store called "The Witch's Cauldron." Todd's inventory may be the basis of the claim in *Dark Dungeons* that the works of Lewis and Tolkien are sold in occult bookstores. Todd was accused of using the Witch's Cauldron to seduce curious teenagers and served six months in prison for contributing to the delinquency of a minor. Ironically, Todd sought the help of Wiccan leaders, including Isaac Bonewitz, claiming that he was being persecuted as a religious minority. Gavin Frost of the National School and Church of Wicca investigated Todd and condemned him in a Wiccan newsletter as a dangerous individual. (The villainess of *Dark Dungeons* is named "Ms. Frost," possibly in reference to Gavin Frost.) Chick continued to support Todd and hired an attorney who got Todd an early release from prison for medical reasons.

32. William Schnoebelen, *Romancing Death: A True Story of Vampirism, Death, the Occult, and Deliverance* (Shippensburg, Pa.: Destiny Image Publishers, 2012), 38, 262.

33. Gary Alan Fine and Jeffrey Victor, "Satanic Tourism: Adolescent Dabblers and Identity Work," *Phi Delta Kappan* 76:1 (1994): 72.

34. Bob Larson, *Satanism: The Seduction of America's Youth* (Nashville: Thomas Nelson Publishers, 1989), 118–19. Larson regularly featured guests on *Talk-Back* to serve as foils in this fashion. Musicians from heavy metal bands such as Deicide, Morbid Angel, and Gwar were especially popular. One musician commented that Larson had a "great symbiotic relationship" with these transgressive artists. See Bivins, *Religion of Fear,* 111.

35. Patricia Pulling, "A Law Enforcement Primer on Fantasy Role Playing Games" (Richmond, Va.: B.A.D.D., n.d.), 4.

36. Rochelle Hines, "Protestors, Supporters Gather for Sellers Execution," Associated Press, February 4, 1999.

37. Richard Abanes, *Harry Potter and the Bible: The Menace behind the Magick* (Camp Hill, Pa.: Horizon Books, 2001), 181; Richard Monaco and Bill Burt, *The Dracula Syndrome* (New York: Avon Books, 1993), 58.

38. In his discussion of *bosozoku,* Ikuya Sato describes how play becomes real once irrevocable consequences ensue. One key factor that brings about such consequences is when the players feel challenged to "reach the limit" or see how far they can defy ordinary social norms in performing their role. Sato quotes a *bosozoku* he interviewed: "It's rather like raping a girl. It's the terribly thrilling feeling of doing something wrong, with the thought in mind, 'Hell, I'm doing something terribly wrong! Can I really do it?'" This desire to "reach the limit" is a plausible model of how Sellers's performance of a teenage Satanist led to the decision to murder a convenience store clerk. See Ikuya Sato, *Kamikaze Biker: Parody and Anomy in Affluent Japan* (Chicago: University of Chicago Press, 1991), 217–18.

39. Monaco and Burt, *The Dracula Syndrome,* 66.

40. Charles Ewing, *Kids Who Kill* (Lexington, Mass.: Lexington Books, 1990), 85.

41. Monaco and Burt, *The Dracula Syndrome,* 66.

42. Sean Sellers, *Web of Darkness* (Tulsa, Okla.: Victory House, 1990), 32.

43. Abanes, *Harry Potter and the Bible,* 183.

44. Bob Larson, *Extreme Evil: Kids Killing Kids* (Nashville: Thomas Nelson, 1999), 101–2.

45. Michael A. Stackpole, "The Pulling Report" (1990), http://www.rpgstudies.net/stackpole/pulling_report.html#65F (accessed July 23, 2013).

46. Sellers, *Web of Darkness,* 86.

47. Pulling, *The Devil's Web,* 136.

48. Ibid., 11.

49. Abanes, *Harry Potter and the Bible,* 186.

50. Pulling, *The Devil's Web,* 73.

51. Hicks, *In Pursuit of Satan,* 296.

52. A study concluded that even young children learn information about Satanism through popular culture, talk shows, and other media. See Gail S. Goodman et al., "Children's Religious Knowledge: Implications for Understanding Satanic Ritual Abuse Allegations," *Child Abuse & Neglect* 21:11 (1997): 1111–30.

53. Warnke, *Schemes of Satan,* 9.

54. Pat A. Pulling, Mary Dempsey, and Pat Dempsey, *Dungeons and Dragons: Witchcraft, Suicide, and Violence* (Richmond, Va.: B.A.D.D. Inc., n.d.), 9.

55. Gary Gygax, *Player's Handbook* (Lake Geneva, Wis.: TSR Games, 1978), 86. The cacodemon spell was removed from subsequent editions of *D&D*.

56. John Todd, "The Illuminati and Witchcraft" (1978), Tape 6a, http://www.kt70.com/~jamesjpn/articles/TAPE6A.pdf (accessed September 6, 2014).

57. Michael J. Tresca, *The Evolution of Fantasy Role-Playing Games* (Jefferson, N.C.: McFarland & Co, 2011), 61.

58. Bob Gretchen Passantino and Jon Trott, "Satan's Sideshow: The True Lauren Stratford Story," *Cornerstone* 18:90 (1990): 23–28.

59. Mike Mather, "Vampire-Hunting Detective Is Virginia Beach's Expert on the Weird," *Virginian-Pilot*, February 5, 1996.

60. Don Rimer, "Ritual Crime and the Occult (The New Youth Subculture)," 18, http://publicintelligence.info/OccultCrime.pdf (accessed July 18, 2013). Wiccan leader Kerr Cuhulain contacted Rimer and questioned him about the presence of traps at occult crime scenes. Rimer responded that police at occult crime scenes had encountered "poison, hallucinogenics, snares, nooses, tiger pits, guillotines, animal traps, etc." Cuhulain countered that if Rimer really encountered such traps it is odd that he does not include slide photos or any other physical evidence of this in his seminars on occult crime. See Kerr Cuhulain, "The Cycle Continues," Witchvox.com (January 16, 2005), http://www.witchvox.com/va/dt_article.html?a = cabc&id = 8939 (accessed July 18, 2013).

61. Michael Barkun, *A Culture of Conspiracy: Apocalyptic Visions in Contemporary America* (Berkeley: University of California Press, 2003), 29.

62. Hicks, *In Pursuit of Satan*, 28.

63. Schnoebelen, "Should a Christian Play Dungeons and Dragons?"

64. Metz, "The John Todd Story"; Jesse Walker, *The United States of Paranoia: A Conspiracy Theory* (New York: Harper Collins, 2013), 190–92.

65. Sellers, *Web of Darkness*, 40.

66. Carl A. Raschke, *Painted Black* (New York: Harper and Row, 1990), 183.

67. Wouter Hanegraaff, "Fiction in the Desert of the Real: Lovecraft's Cthulhu Mythos," *Aries* 7 (2007): 85–109.

68. Sellers, *Web of Darkness*, 45.

69. Dorothy Singer and Jerome Singer, *The House of Make-Believe: Children's Play and the Developing Imagination* (Cambridge, Mass.: Harvard University Press, 1990), 115.

70. For example, Kurt Lancaster mentions demons in accusing evangelicals of projection. He writes: "To believe that some role-playing games promote satanism is comparable to believing that one 'worships' Satan by reading Dante's *Inferno* or Milton's *Paradise Lost*. One must question the validity of arguments made by those who believe demons are real and dangerous in the real world, since there is no concrete evidence of their existence. At least the player knows he or she is exploring a make-believe game world." Kurt Lancaster, "Do Role-Playing Games Promote Crime, Satanism and Suicide among Players as Critics Claim?," *Journal of Popular Culture* 28:2 (1994): 77–78.

71. Susan Friend Harding, *The Book of Jerry Falwell: Fundamentalist Language and Politics* (Princeton, N.J.: Princeton University Press, 2000), 27.

72. Metz, "The John Todd Story."

73. Alan Dundes, *The Blood Libel Legend: A Casebook in Anti-Semitic Folklore* (Madison: University of Wisconsin Press, 1991), 353.

74. Dieter Petzold, "A Neverending Success Story? Michael Ende's Return Trip to Fantastica," in *Beyond Babar: The European Tradition in Children's Literature,* ed. Sandra L. Beckett and Maria Nikolajeva (Lanham, Md.: Scarecrow Press, 2006), 209–10.

75. Kath Filmer, *Skepticism and Hope in Twentieth-Century Fantasy Literature* (Bowling Green, Ky.: Bowling Green University Press, 1992), 79.

76. Michael Ende, *The Neverending Story,* trans. Ralph Mannheim (Garden City, N.Y.: Doubleday, 1983), 131–33.

CONCLUSION. WALKING BETWEEN WORLDS

Epigraphs: Roger Caillois, *Man, Play, and Games* (New York: Free Press of Glencoe, 1961), 43–44; Lord Dunsany, *The Hashish Man and Other Stories* (San Francisco: Manic D, 2006), 58.

1. Peter Berger, *The Sacred Canopy: Elements of a Sociological Theory of Religion* (New York: Anchor Books, 1969), 4.

2. Ibid., 42.

3. Ibid., 9.

4. Ibid., 90.

5. Ibid., 93.

6. Johan Huizinga, *Homo Ludens: A Study of the Play-Element in Culture* (Boston: Beacon Press, 1955), 11.

7. Berger, *The Sacred Canopy*, 37–38.

8. On the discursive functions of parody religions, see Joseph Laycock, "Laughing Matters: 'Parody Religions' and the Command to Compare," *Bulletin of the Study of Religion* 42:3 (September 2013): 19–26.

9. Michael Kinsella, *Legend-Tripping Online: Supernatural Folklore and the Search for Ong's Hat* (Jackson: University Press of Mississippi, 2011), 61.

10. David Szulborski, *This Is Not a Game* (Lulu.com, 2005), 31.

11. "Elf Defense for 'Lingerie Thief,'" BBC News, March 6, 2007, http://news.bbc.co.uk/2/hi/uk_news/northern_ireland/6425333.stm (accessed May 4, 2013).

12. Matt Baie and Verne E. Smith, "Evil to the End," *Newsweek*, March 8, 1999, 22.

13. United States of America v. David Brown Stone et al., Case No. 10–20123 (March 27, 2012).

14. Johan Huizinga, *In the Shadow of Tomorrow* (New York: W. W. Norton, 1936), 177.

15. Ibid., 172–73.

16. In 1975, Jane Tucker, a doctoral candidate at Columbia University, conducted an experiment to measure how well children between the ages of nine and twelve could recall a story. She found that children who engaged in imaginative play were better able to recall stories and demonstrated fewer incidences of omitting, distorting, or adding details than less imaginative children. See

Dorothy Singer and Jerome Singer, *The House of Make-Believe: Children's Play and the Developing Imagination* (Cambridge, Mass.: Harvard University Press, 1990), 142–45. More recently, Tanya Sharon and Jacqueline Woolley have measured the "fantasy orientation" of children ages three to five, using a combination of interviews and observation. The children were given pictures of a variety of real and imaginary entities (a clown, a dinosaur, a dragon, Michael Jordan, etc.) and asked to categorize them as either real, pretend, or "not sure." Children with a high level of fantasy orientation were more successful at discerning real ideas from imaginary ones. Sharon and Woolley suggest that spending more time engaged in imaginative play may help children to develop better concepts of what is plausible. See Tanya Sharon and Jacqueline Woolley. "Do Monsters Dream? Young Children's Understanding of the Fantasy/Reality Distinction," *British Journal of Developmental Psychology* 22 (2004): 293–310. However, there appear to be other factors besides imaginative play that determine how children discern fantasy from reality. A recent review of psychological literature on the developmental benefits of imaginative play found that much of the research in this area suffers from methodological flaws, and suggests that researchers in the Anglophone world may be predisposed to assume that imaginative play causes developmental benefits. The reviewers concluded that more research is needed with a higher degree of methodological rigor. See Angeline S. Lillard et al., "The Impact of Pretend Play on Children's Development: A Review of the Evidence," *Psychological Bulletin* 139:1 (2013): 1–34.

17. Robert Bellah, *Religion in Human Evolution: From the Paleolithic to the Axial Age* (Cambridge, Mass.: Harvard University Press, 2011), 91.

Bibliography

Abanes, Richard. *Harry Potter and the Bible: The Menace behind the Magick.* Camp Hill, Pa.: Horizon Books, 2001.

Abyeta, Suzanne, and James Forest. "Relationship of Role-Playing Games to Self-Reported Criminal Behaviour." *Psychological Reports* 69 (1991): 1187–92.

Alexander, David. "Giving the Devil More Than His Due." *The Humanist,* March 1, 1990, 5–34.

———. "Still Giving the Devil More Than His Due." *The Humanist,* September/October 1991, 22–42.

Alighieri, Dante. *Purgatory.* Translated by Dorothy Sayers. New York: Penguin Books, 1955.

Ammerman, Nancy. *Bible Believers: Fundamentalists in the Modern World.* New Brunswick, N.J.: Rutgers University Press, 1987.

Anderson, Poul. *Three Hearts and Three Lions.* Garden City, N.Y.: Doubleday, 1961.

Ankerberg, John, and John Weldon. "Dungeons and Dragons and Fantasy Role-Playing Games." In *Encyclopedia of New Age Beliefs,* edited by John Ankerberg and John Weldon, 156–61. Eugene, Ore.: Harvest House Publishers, 1996.

Anthony, T. Michael. *Suicide: Knowing When Your Teen Is at Risk.* Ventura, Calif.: Regal Books, 1991.

Armstrong, Karen. *The Battle for God.* New York: Alfred A. Knopf, 2000.

———. *A History of God: The 4000-Year Quest of Judaism, Christianity, and Islam.* New York: Alfred A. Knopf, 1993.

Bainbridge, William Sims. *eGods: Faith versus Fantasy in Computer Gaming.* New York: Oxford University Press, 2013.

Barbour, Ian G. *Myths, Models, and Paradigms: A Comparative Study in Science and Religion.* New York: Harper & Row, 1974.

Barkun, Michael. *A Culture of Conspiracy: Apocalyptic Visions in Contemporary America.* Berkeley: University of California Press, 2003.
Barr, James. *Fundamentalism.* Philadelphia: Westminster Press, 1978.
Barrowcliffe, Mark. *The Elfish Gene: Dungeons and Dragons and Growing Up Strange.* New York: Soho Press, 2007.
Bateson, Gregory. *Steps to an Ecology of Mind.* New York: Ballantine Books, 1972.
Belanger, Michelle. *The Psychic Vampire Codex: A Manual of Magick and Energy Work.* Boston: Weiser Books, 2004.
Bellah, Robert. *Religion in Human Evolution: From the Paleolithic to the Axial Age.* Cambridge, Mass.: Harvard University Press, 2011.
Bennett, William J., John J. DiLulio, Jr., and John P. Walters. *Body Count: Moral Poverty and How to Win America's War against Crime and Drugs.* New York: Simon and Schuster, 1996.
Ben-Yehuda, Nachman. *Deviance and Moral Boundaries: Witchcraft, the Occult, Science Fiction, Deviant Sciences and Scientists.* Chicago: University of Chicago Press, 1985.
Berger, Peter. *The Sacred Canopy: Elements of a Sociological Theory of Religion.* New York: Anchor Books, 1969.
Bettelheim, Bruno. *The Use of Enchantment.* New York: Knopf, 1977.
Bivins, Jason. *Religion of Fear: The Politics of Horror in Conservative Evangelicalism.* New York: Oxford University Press, 2008.
Blackmon, Wayne D. "Dungeons and Dragons: The Use of a Fantasy Game in the Psychotherapeutic Treatment of a Young Adult." *American Journal of Psychotherapy* 48:4 (Fall 1994): 624–32.
Bledsoe, Jerry. *Blood Games.* New York: Onyx Books, 1992.
Blum, Jason N. "Retrieving Phenomenology of Religion as a Method for Religious Studies." *Journal of the American Academy of Religion* 80:4 (December 2012): 1025–48.
Bonewitz, Isaac. *Authentic Thaumaturgy.* Austin, Tex.: Steve Jackson Games, 1998.
Bowman, Sarah Lynne. *The Functions of Role-Playing Games.* Jefferson, N.C.: McFarland, 2010.
Bromley, David G. "The Satanic Cult Scare." *Society* 28:4 (1991): 55–66.
———. "Satanism: The New Cult Scare." In *The Satanism Scare,* edited by James T. Richardson, Joel Best, and David G. Bromley, 49–74. Hawthorne, N.Y.: Aldine De Gruyter, 1991.
Bromley, David G., Anson D. Shupe, and J. C. Ventimiglia. "Atrocity Tales, the Unification Church, and the Social Construction of Evil." *Journal of Communication* 29:3 (Summer 1979): 42–53.
Brown, Rebecca. *Prepare for War.* Chino, Calif.: Chick Publications, 1987.
Burke, Kenneth. *Language as Symbolic Action: Essays on Life, Literature, and Method.* Berkeley: University of California Press, 1966.
Burroughs, Edgar Rice. *Jungle Tales of Tarzan.* New York: Grosset and Dunlap, 1919.
Caillois, Roger. *Man and the Sacred.* Glencoe, Ill.: Free Press of Glencoe, 1959.
———. *Man, Play, and Games.* New York: Free Press of Glencoe, 1961.

Cardwell, Paul. "The Attacks on Role-Playing Games." *Skeptical Inquirer* 18:2 (Winter 1994): 157–65.

Carroll, James L., and Paul M. Carolin. "Relationship between Game Playing and Personality." *Psychological Reports* 64 (1989): 705–6.

Cassanova, José. *Public Religions in the Modern World.* Chicago: University of Chicago Press, 1994.

Caywood, Carolyn. "Rescuing the Innocent: The Lure of Dungeons and Dragons." *School Library Journal,* March 1991, 138.

Chandler, Russell. *Understanding the New Age.* Grand Rapids, Mich.: Zondervan, 1993.

Chesterton, G.K. *The Ballad of the White Horse.* New York: John Lane, 1916.

Clark, Lynn Schofield. *From Angels to Aliens: Teenagers, the Media, and the Supernatural.* Oxford: Oxford University Press, 2003.

Cogburn, Jon, and Mark Silcox, eds. *Dungeons and Dragons and Philosophy: Raiding the Temple of Wisdom.* Chicago: Open Court, 2012.

Cohen, Stanley. *Folk Devils and Moral Panic.* New York: Routledge, 2002.

Corsini, Raymond J., and Raymond J. Corsini. *Role Playing in Psychotherapy.* New Brunswick, N.J.: Transaction Publishers, 2010.

Cover, Jennifer Grouling. *The Creation of Narrative in Tabletop Role-Playing Games.* Jefferson, N.C.: McFarland, 2010.

Cruz, Nicky. *Devil on the Run.* Melbourne, Fla.: Dove Christian Books, 1989.

Cullen, David. *Columbine.* New York: Twelve, 2009.

Dager, Albert James. "Dungeons and Dragons: A Look at Fantasy Role-Playing Games." *Media Spotlight,* 1980, 1–2.

Davis, Graeme, Tom Dowd, Mark Rein-Hagen, Lisa Stevens, and Stewart Wieck. *Vampire: The Masquerade.* 2nd ed. Stone Mountain, Ga.: White Wolf, 1992.

Dear, William. *The Dungeon Master.* Boston: Houghton Mifflin, 1984.

Delfattorre, Joan. *What Johnny Shouldn't Read: Textbook Censorship in America.* New Haven, Conn.: Yale University Press, 1992.

DeRenard, Lisa A., and Linda Mannik Kline. "Alienation and the Game Dungeons and Dragons." *Psychological Reports* 66 (1990): 1219–22.

Dunsany, Lord. *The Hashish Man and Other Stories.* San Francisco: Manic D, 2006.

Durkheim, Émile. *The Elementary Forms of Religious Life.* New York: The Free Press, 1995.

Eberle, Paul. *The Abuse of Innocence: The McMartin Preschool Trial.* New York: Prometheus Books, 1993.

Eisenstadt, S.N. *The Origins and Diversity of Axial Age Civilizations.* Albany: State University of New York Press, 1986.

Eliade, Mircea. *Myth and Reality.* New York: Harperbooks, 1963.

———. *The Quest: History and Meaning in Religion.* Chicago: University of Chicago Press, 1969.

Ellis, Bill. *Raising the Devil: Satanism, New Religions, and the Media.* Lexington: University Press of Kentucky, 2000.

Ellwood, Robert. *The Politics of Myth: A Study of C.G. Jung, Mircea Eliade, and Joseph Campbell.* Albany: State University of New York Press, 1999.

Elshof, Phyllis Ten. "D&D: A Fantasy Fad or Dabbling in the Demonic?" *Christianity Today,* September 4, 1981, 56.

Ende, Michael. *The Neverending Story.* Translated by Ralph Mannheim. Garden City, N.Y.: Doubleday, 1983.

Erikson, Erik. *Identity, Youth, and Crisis.* New York: Norton, 1994.

Ewalt, David M. *Of Dice and Men: The Story of Dungeons & Dragons and the People Who Play It.* New York: Scribner, 2013.

Ewing, Charles. *Kids Who Kill.* Lexington, Mass.: Lexington Books, 1990.

Filmer, Kath. *Skepticism and Hope in Twentieth-Century Fantasy Literature.* Bowling Green, Ky.: Bowling Green University Press, 1992.

Fine, Gary Alan. "Legendary Creatures and Small Group Culture: Medieval Lore in a Contemporary Role-Playing Game." *Keystone Folklore* 1:1 (1982): 11–27.

———. *Shared Fantasy: Role-Playing Games as Social Worlds.* Chicago: University of Chicago Press, 1983.

Fine, Gary Alan, and Jeffrey Victor. "Satanic Tourism: Adolescent Dabblers and Identity Work." *Phi Delta Kappan* 76:1 (1994): 70–72.

Fitzgerald, Timothy. *The Ideology of Religious Studies.* Oxford: Oxford University Press, 2000.

Flory, Richard W., and Donald E. Miller, eds. *Gen X Religion.* New York: Routledge, 2000.

Frankfurter, David. *Evil Incarnate: Rumors of Demonic Conspiracy and Ritual Abuse in History.* Princeton, N.J.: Princeton University Press, 2006.

Freud, Sigmund. *A General Introduction to Psychoanalysis.* New York: Washington Square Press, 1960.

Geertz, Clifford. *The Interpretation of Cultures.* New York: Basic Books, 1973.

Gemmil, Maia A., and Daniel H. Nexon. "Children's Crusade: The Religious Politics of Harry Potter." In *Harry Potter and International Relations,* edited by Daniel H. Nexon and Iver B. Neumann, 79–100. Lanham, Md.: Rowman & Littlefield, 2006.

Gilsdorf, Ethan. *Fantasy Freaks and Gaming Geeks: An Epic Quest for Reality among Role Players, Online Gamers, and Other Dwellers of Imaginary Realms.* Guilford, Conn.: The Lyons Press, 2009.

Gleaves, David H. "The Sociocognitive Model of Dissociative Identity Disorder: A Reexamination of the Evidence." *Psychological Bulletin* 120:1 (1996): 42–59.

Goffman, Erving. *Frame Analysis: An Essay on the Organization of Experience.* Cambridge, Mass.: Harvard University Press, 1974.

Goodman, Gail S., et al. "Children's Religious Knowledge: Implications for Understanding Satanic Ritual Abuse Allegations." *Child Abuse & Neglect* 21:11 (1997): 1111–30.

Gopnik, Alison. *The Philosophical Baby.* New York: Farrar, Straus and Giroux, 2009.

Gramsci, Antonio. *Prison Notebooks.* Vol 2. New York: Columbia Press, 1992.

Guerra, Bob. "Dungeons and Dragons: A Simulated Fantasy." *Compute!* 123 (November 1990): 64.

Gygax, Gary. *Dungeon Master's Guide.* Lake Geneva, Wis.: TSR Games, 1979.

———. *Player's Handbook*. Lake Geneva, Wis.: TSR Games, 1978.
Hall, Stuart, Chris Critchter, Tony Jefferson, John Clarke, and Brian Roberts. *Policing the Crisis: Mugging, the State, and Law and Order.* London: Macmillan, 1978.
Hanegraaff, Wouter. "Fiction in the Desert of the Real: Lovecraft's Cthulhu Mythos." *Aries* 7 (2007): 85–109.
———. "How Magic Survived the Disenchantment of the World." *Religion* 33 (2003): 357–80.
Harding, Susan Friend. *The Book of Jerry Falwell: Fundamentalist Language and Politics*. Princeton, N.J.: Princeton University Press, 2000.
Hicks, Robert. *In Pursuit of Satan: The Police and the Occult*. Buffalo, N.Y.: Prometheus Books, 1991.
———. "None Dare Call It Reason: Kids, Cults, and Common Sense." Talk prepared for the Virginia Department for Children's Twelfth Annual Legislative Forum, Roanoke, Virginia, September 22, 1989.
Hofstadter, Richard. *The Paranoid Style in American Politics*. New York: Vintage Books, 2008.
Holifield, E. Brooks. *Theology in America: Christian Thought from the Age of the Puritans to the Civil War.* New Haven, Conn.: Yale University Press, 2003.
Holmes, John Eric. "Confessions of a Dungeon Master." *Psychology Today*, November 1980, 84–94.
Holochack, M. Andrew. *Dutiful Correspondent: Philosophical Essays on Thomas Jefferson*. Lanham, Md.: Rowman and Littlefield, 2013.
Howard, Robert E. *The Savage Tales of Soloman Kane*. New York: Del Rey, 1998.
Hughes, John. "Therapy Is Fantasy: Roleplaying, Healing and the Construction of Symbolic Order." Paper presented in Anthropology IV Honours, Medical Anthropology Seminar, Australian National University, 1988.
Huizinga, Johan. *Homo Ludens: A Study of the Play-Element in Culture*. Boston: Beacon Press, 1955.
———. *In the Shadow of Tomorrow.* New York: W.W. Norton, 1936.
Hyers, Conrad. "Biblical Literalism: Constricting the Cosmic Dance." *Christian Century,* August 4–11, 1982, 823–27.
Ignatius. *The Spiritual Exercises of Saint Ignatius*. Translated by George E. Ganss. Chicago: Loyola University Press, 1992.
Isaacson, Walter. *Steve Jobs*. New York: Simon & Schuster, 2011.
Jaffe, Rona. *Mazes and Monsters*. New York: Delacorte Press, 1981.
James, William. *Principles of Psychology*. Vol. 2. New York: Cosimo, 2007.
Janis, Irving L., and Bert T. King. "The Influence of Role Playing on Opinion Change." *Journal of Abnormal Psychology* 49:2 (1954): 211–18.
Jenkins, Philip. "Weird Tales: The Story of a Delusion." In *The Last Pentacle of the Sun: Writings in Support of the West Memphis Three,* edited by M.W. Anderson and Brett Alexander, 35–41. Vancouver: Arsenal Pulp Press, 2004.
Johnson, Samuel. *The Works of Samuel Johnson*. London: Luke Hanford and Sons, 1810.

Johnson, Viola. *Dhampir, Child of the Blood: A Vampire's Babybook*. Fairfield, Conn.: Mystic Rose Books, 1996.

Johnston, Jerry. *The Edge of Evil*. Dallas: Word Publications, 1989.

———. *Why Suicide? What Parents & Teachers Must Know to Save Our Kids*. New York: Oliver Nelson, 1987.

Jones, Aphrodite. *The Embrace: A True Vampire Story*. New York: Pocket Books, 1999.

Jones, Rick. *Stairway to Hell: The Well-Planned Destruction of Teens*. Chino, Calif.: Chick Publications, 1988.

Kaminer, Wendy. *Sleeping with Extra-Terrestrials: The Rise of Irrationalism and Perils of Piety*. New York: Vintage Books, 1999.

Kinsella, Michael. *Legend-Tripping Online: Supernatural Folklore and the Search for Ong's Hat*. Jackson: University Press of Mississippi, 2011.

Kirby, Danielle. "Alternative Worlds: Metaphysical Questing and Virtual Community amongst the Otherkin." *Sydney Studies in Religion*, 2006, 275–87.

———. *Fantasy and Belief: Alternative Religions, Popular Narratives and Digital Cultures*. Bristol, Conn.: Equinox, 2013.

———. "From Pulp Fiction to Revealed Text." In *Exploring Religion and the Sacred in a Media Age*, edited by Christopher Deacy and Elizabeth Arweck, 141–54. Burlington, Vt.: Ashgate Press, 2009.

Kirschenbaum, Matthew. "How Reading Is Being Re-imagined." *Chronicle of Higher Education*, December 7, 2007, B20.

Kostelnik, Marjorie J., et al. "Living with He-Man: Managing Superhero Fantasy Play." *Young Children* 4:4 (May 1986): 3–9.

Kushner, David. *Masters of Doom*. New York: Random House, 2003.

La Fontaine, J. S. *Speak of the Devil*. Cambridge: Cambridge University Press, 1998.

Lancaster, Kurt. "Do Role-Playing Games Promote Crime, Satanism and Suicide among Players as Critics Claim?" *Journal of Popular Culture* 28:2 (1994): 67–79.

Larson, Bob. *Extreme Evil: Kids Killing Kids*. Nashville: Thomas Nelson Publishers, 1999.

———. *Satanism: The Seduction of America's Youth*. Nashville: Thomas Nelson Publishers, 1989.

Lawrence, T. E. *Seven Pillars of Wisdom: A Triumph; The Complete 1922 Text*. Charleston, S.C.: CreateSpace, 2011.

Laycock, Joseph. "Laughing Matters: 'Parody Religions' and the Command to Compare." *Bulletin of the Study of Religion* 42:3 (September 2013): 19–26.

———. *Vampires Today: The Truth about Modern Vampirism*. Westport, Conn.: Praeger, 2009.

———. "'We Are Spirits of Another Sort': Ontological Rebellion and Religious Dimensions of the Otherkin Community." *Nova Religio* 15:3 (2012): 65–90.

Leeds, Stuart M. "Personality, Belief in the Paranormal, and Involvement with Satanic Practices among Young Adult Males: Dabblers versus Gamers." *Cultic Studies Journal* 12:2 (1995): 148–65.

Lehrich, Christopher. "Ritual Discourse in Role-Playing Games." *The Forge*, October 2005. http://www.indie-rpgs.com/_articles/ritual_discourse_in_RPGs.html.

Leithart, Peter, and George Grant. *A Christian Response to Dungeons and Dragons: The Catechism of the New Age*. Fort Worth, Tex.: Dominion Press, 1988.

Levi-Strauss, Claude. *The Raw and the Cooked*. Chicago: University of Chicago Press, 1969.

———. *The Savage Mind*. Chicago: University of Chicago Press, 1966.

Lewis, C.S. *The Discarded Image*. New York: Cambridge University Press, 1994.

———. *The Screwtape Letters*. New York: Harper Collins, 2001.

———. *Surprised by Joy: The Shape of My Early Life*. New York: Harcourt, Brace, 1956.

Lifton, Robert Jay. "Protean Man." *Archives of General Psychiatry* 24:4 (1971): 298–304.

———. *Thought Reform and the Psychology of Totalism: A Study of "Brainwashing" in China*. Chapel Hill: University of North Carolina Press, 1989.

Lillard, Angeline S., Matthew D. Lerner, Emily J. Hopkins, Rebecca A. Dore, Eric D. Smith, and Carolyn M. Palmquist. "The Impact of Pretend Play on Children's Development: A Review of the Evidence." *Psychological Bulletin* 139:1 (2013): 1–34.

Linedecker, Clifford L. *The Vampire Killers*. New York: St. Martin's, 1999.

Luhrmann, Tanya. *Persuasions of the Witch's Craft*. Cambridge, Mass.: Harvard University Press, 1989.

Lupa. *A Field Guide to Otherkin*. Stafford, England: Megalithica Books, 2007.

MacCannell, Dean. *The Tourist: A New Theory of the Leisure Class*. Berkeley: University of California Press, 1999.

Mackay, Daniel. *The Fantasy Role-Playing Game: A New Performing Art*. Jefferson, N.C.: McFarland, 2001.

Martin, Daniel, and Gary Alan Fine. "Satanic Cults, Satanic Play: Is 'Dungeons and Dragons' a Breeding Ground for the Devil?" In *The Satanism Scare*, edited by James T. Richardson, Joel Best, and David G. Bromley, 107–26. Hawthorne, N.Y.: Aldine De Gruyter, 1991.

Mathews, Richard. *Fantasy: The Liberation of Imagination*. New York: Twayne Publishers, 1997.

McCarthy Brown, Karen. "Fundamentalism and the Control of Women." In *Fundamentalism and Gender*, edited by John Stratton Hawley, 175–202. New York: Oxford University Press, 1994.

McCutcheon, Russell. *Critics Not Caretakers: Redescribing the Public Study of Religion*. Albany: State University of New York Press, 2001.

McGinniss, Joe. *Cruel Doubt*. New York: Pocket Star Books, 1991.

Medway, Gareth J. *Lure of the Sinister: The Unnatural History of Satanism*. New York: New York University Press, 2001.

Miller, Samuel. "On Novel Reading." *The Panoplist and Missionary Magazine United*, October 1808, 204–9.

Monaco, Richard, and Bill Burt. *The Dracula Syndrome*. New York: Avon Books, 1993.

Montfort, Nick. *Twisty Little Passages: An Approach to Interactive Fiction.* Cambridge, Mass: MIT Press, 2003.

Moorcock, Michael. *Elric at the End of Time.* New York: Daw Books, 1984.

Moriarty, Anthony. *The Psychology of Adolescent Satanism.* Westport, Conn.: Praeger, 1991.

Morris, Glenn. *Path Notes of an American Ninja Master.* Berkeley, Calif.: North Atlantic Books, 1993.

———. *Shadow Strategies of an American Ninja Master.* Berkeley, Calif.: Frog, Ltd., 1996.

Nathan, Debbie, and Michael Snedecker. *Satan's Silence: Ritual Abuse and the Making of a Modern American Witch Hunt.* New York: Basic Books, 1994.

Nehamas, Alexander. *Virtues of Authenticity: Essays on Plato and Socrates.* Princeton, N.J.: Princeton University Press, 1999.

North, Gary. *Unholy Spirits: Occultism and New Age Humanism.* Fort Worth, Tex.: Dominion Press, 1988.

Partridge, Christopher. "Alternative Spiritualities, New Religions, and the Re-Enchantment of the West." In *The Oxford Handbook of New Religious Movements,* edited by James R. Lewis, 39–67. New York: Oxford University Press, 2004.

Paulos, John Allen. *Innumeracy: Mathematical Illiteracy and Its Consequences.* New York: Hill and Wang, 1988.

Penner, Hans. "Is Phenomenology a Method for the Study of Religion?" *Bucknell Review* 18:1 (1970): 29–54.

Perla, Peter P. *The Art of Wargaming: A Guide for Professionals and Hobbyists.* Annapolis: Naval Institute Press, 1990.

Perlmutter, Dawn. "The Forensics of Sacrifice: A Symbolic Analysis of Ritualistic Crime." *Anthropoetics* 9:2 (2004). http://www.anthropoetics.ucla.edu/ap0902/sacrifice.htm.

———. "The Sacrificial Aesthetic: Blood Rituals from Art to Murder." *Anthropoetics* 5:2 (2000). http://www.anthropoetics.ucla.edu/ap0502/blood.htm.

Peterson, Jon. *Playing at the World: A History of Simulating Wars, People and Fantastic Adventure, from Chess to Role-Playing Games.* San Diego: Unreason Press, 2012.

Petzold, Dieter. "A Neverending Success Story? Michael Ende's Return Trip to Fantastica." In *Beyond Babar: The European Tradition in Children's Literature,* edited by Sandra L. Beckett and Maria Nikolajeva, 209–40. Lanham, Md.: Scarecrow Press, 2006.

Phillips, David W. "The Influence of Suggestion on Suicide: Substantive and Theoretical Implications of the Werther Effect." *American Sociological Review* 39:3 (1974): 340–54.

Pike, Sarah M. *Earthly Bodies, Magical Selves: Contemporary Pagans and the Search for Community.* Berkeley: University of California Press, 2001.

Plowman, Edward E. "The Legend(s) of John Todd." *Christianity Today,* February 2, 1979, 38–51.

Possamai, Adam. *Sociology of Religion for Generations X and Y.* Oakville, Conn.: Equinox Publishing, 2009.

Pulling, Patricia. *The Devil's Web: Who Is Stalking Your Children for Satan?* Lafayette, La.: Huntington House, 1989.

Ramstedt, Martin. "Metaphor or Invocation? The Convergence of Ritual between Modern Paganism and Fantasy Fiction." *Journal of Ritual Studies* 21:1 (2007): 1–15.

Raschke, Carl A. *Painted Black*. New York: Harper and Row, 1990.

Reang, Putsata. *Deadly Secrets*. New York: Avon Books, 2001.

Reichert, Jenny, and James T. Richardson. "Decline of a Moral Panic: A Social Psychological and Socio-Legal Examination of the Current Status of Satanism." *Nova Religio* 16:2 (2012): 47–63.

Rein-Hagen, Mark, Sam Chupp, and Jennifer Hartshorn. *Wraith: The Oblivion*. Stone Mountain, Ga.: White Wolf, 1994.

Robertson, Pat. *Bring It On: Tough Questions, Candid Answers*. Nashville: W Pub. Group, 2003.

Robertson, Venetia. "The Beast Within: Anthrozoomorphic Identity and Alternative Spirituality in the Online Therianthropy Movement." *Nova Religio* 16:3 (2013): 7–30.

Robie, Joan Hake. *The Truth about Dungeons and Dragons*. Lancaster, Pa.: Starburst Publishers, 1991.

Rosenthal, Gary T., and Barlow Soper. "Role-Play Gamers and National Guardsmen Compared." *Psychological Reports* 92 (1998): 169–70.

Ruthven, Malise. *Fundamentalism: The Search for Meaning*. New York: Oxford University Press, 2004.

Santayana, George. *The Life of Reason: The Phases of Human Progress*. Auckland, New Zealand: The Floating Press, 2009.

Sartre, Jean-Paul. *Being and Nothingness: An Essay on Phenomenological Ontology*. New York: Philosophical Library, 1956.

———. *Existentialism and Humanism*. Brooklyn: Haskell House, 1977.

———. *The Psychology of Imagination*. Westport, Conn.: Greenwood Press, 1978.

Sato, Ikuya. *Kamikaze Biker: Parody and Anomy in Affluent Japan*. Chicago: University of Chicago Press, 1991.

Savoie, Pierre. "The Whole Loon Catalogue (A Thought Provoking Look at the Anti-RPG Movement)." *Shadis Magazine* 7 (1992): 5–12.

Schechner, Richard. *Between Theater and Anthropology*. Philadelphia: University of Pennsylvania Press, 1985.

Schick, Lawrence. *Heroic Worlds: A History and Guide to Role-Playing Games*. Buffalo, N.Y.: Prometheus Books, 1991.

Schnoebelen, William. *Lucifer Dethroned*. Ontario, Calif.: Chick Publications, 1993.

———. *Romancing Death: A True Story of Vampirism, Death, the Occult, and Deliverance*. Shippensburg, Pa.: Destiny Image Publishers, 2012.

Schutz, Alfred. "On Multiple Realities." *Philosophy and Phenomenological Research* 5:4 (June 1945): 533–76.

Schwartz, Benjamin. "The Age of Transcendence." *Daedalus* 104:2 (Spring 1975): 1–7.

Sellers, Sean. *Web of Darkness*. Tulsa, Okla.: Victory House, 1990.

Semrau, Stanley, and Judy Gale. *Murderous Minds on Trial: Terrifying Tales from a Forensic Psychiatrist's Casebook*. Toronto: The Dundurn Group, 2002.

Sewall, Gilbert T., ed. *The Eighties: A Reader.* New York: Perseus Books, 1998.

Sharon, Tanya, and Jacqueline Woolley. "Do Monsters Dream? Young Children's Understanding of the Fantasy/Reality Distinction." *British Journal of Developmental Psychology* 22 (2004): 293–310.

Shrader, Charles R. *History of Operations Research in the United States Army.* Vol. 1, *1942–1962*. Washington, D.C.: Office of the Deputy Under Secretary of the Army for Operations Research, U.S. Army, 2006.

Simon, Armando. "Emotional Stability Pertaining to the Game of Dungeons and Dragons." *Psychology in the Schools* 24 (October 1987): 329–32.

———. "Emotional Stability Pertaining to the Game *Vampire: The Masquerade.*" *Psychological Reports* 83 (1998): 732–34.

Singer, Dorothy, and Jerome Singer. *The House of Make-Believe: Children's Play and the Developing Imagination.* Cambridge, Mass.: Harvard University Press, 1990.

Snow, Carson. "Emerald Article: Dragons in the Stacks; An Introduction to Role-Playing Games and Their Value to Libraries." *Collection Building* 27:2 (2008): 63–70.

Sparks, Beatrice. *Jay's Journal.* New York: Pocket Books, 1979.

Stark, Lizzie. *Leaving Mundania: Inside the Transformative World of Live-Action Role Playing Games.* Chicago: Chicago Review Press, 2012.

Stark, Rodney. "Secularization, R.I.P." *Sociology of Religion* 60:3 (1999): 249–73.

Starker, Steven. *Evil Influences: Crusades against the Mass Media.* New Brunswick, N.J.: Transaction Publishers, 1989.

Strain, Christopher B. *Reload: Rethinking Violence in American Life.* Nashville: Vanderbilt University Press, 2010.

Stromberg, Peter G. *Caught in Play: How Entertainment Works on You.* Stanford, Calif.: Stanford University Press, 2009.

Sutton, Roger. "A D&D Phenomenon." *School Library Journal,* November 1984, 82.

Swatos, William H., and Kevin J. Christiano. "Secularization: The Course of a Concept." In *The Secularization Debate,* edited by William H. Swatos and Daniel V.A. Olson, 1–20. Lanham, Md.: Rowman and Littlefield, 2000.

Szulborski, David. *This Is Not a Game.* Lulu.com, 2005.

Taylor, Charles. *Sources of the Self: The Making of Modern Identity.* Cambridge, Mass.: Harvard University Press, 1989.

Thorne, Tony. *Children of the Night: Of Vampires and Vampirism.* London: Indigo, 2000.

Toles-Patkin, Terri. "Rational Coordination in the Dungeon." *Journal of Popular Culture* 20:1 (1986): 1–14.

Tolkien, J.R.R. *The Monsters and the Critics and Other Essays.* Boston: Houghton Mifflin , 1984.

———. *The Two Towers.* New York: Del Rey, 2012.

Tresca, Michael J. *The Evolution of Fantasy Role-Playing Games.* Jefferson, N.C.: McFarland, 2011.

Turner, Victor. "Liminal to Liminoid in Play, Flow, and Ritual: An Essay in Comparative Symbology." *Rice University Studies* 60:3 (1974): 53–92.

Tylor, Edward Burnett. "The Religion of Savages." *Fortnightly Review*, August 15, 1866, 71–86.

Veyne, Paul. *Did the Greeks Believe in Their Myths? An Essay on the Constitutive Imagination.* Chicago: University of Chicago Press, 1988.

Vygotsky, Lev. *Mind in Society.* Cambridge, Mass.: Harvard University Press, 1978.

Waldron, David. "Role-Playing Games and the Christian Right: Community Formation in Response to a Moral Panic." *Journal of Religion and Popular Culture* 9:1 (Spring 2005). http://utpjournals.metapress.com/content/v3503x532wxjoq28/.

Walker, Jesse. *The United States of Paranoia: A Conspiracy Theory.* New York: Harper Collins, 2013.

Walliss, John. "The Road to Hell Is Paved with D20s: Evangelical Christianity and Role-Playing Gaming." In *The Handbook of Hyperreal Religions*, edited by Adam Possamai, 207–23. Boston: Brill, 2012.

Walton, Rus. *Biblical Solutions to Contemporary Problems: A Handbook.* Brentwood, Tenn.: Wolgemuth & Hyatt Publishers, 1988.

Warnke, Mike. *The Satan Seller.* South Plainfield, N.J.: Bridge Publishing, 1972.

———. *Schemes of Satan.* Tulsa, Okla.: Victory House, 1991.

Weldon, John, and James Bjornstad. *Playing with Fire.* Chicago: Moody Press, 1984.

Wenegrat, Brant. *Theater of Disorder: Patients, Doctors, and the Construction of Illness.* New York: Oxford University Press, 2001.

Wilde, Oscar. *The Decay of Lying and Other Essays.* New York: Penguin Books, 2010.

Williams, J. Patrick, Sean Q. Hendricks, and W. Keith Winkler. *Gaming as Culture: Essays on Reality, Identity, and Experience in Fantasy Games.* Jefferson, N.C.: McFarland, 2006.

Wilson, Sheryl C., and Theodore X. Barber. "The Fantasy-Prone Personality: Implications for Understanding Imagery, Hypnosis, and Parapsychological Phenomena." In *Imagery: Current Theory, Research, and Applications*, edited by Anees A. Sheikh, 209–39. New York: Wiley, 1983.

Wizards of the Coast. *30 Years of Adventure: A Celebration of Dungeons & Dragons.* Renton, Wash.: Wizards of the Coast, 2006.

———. *Dungeon Master's Guide, Core Rulebook II, 3.5.* Renton, Wash.: Wizards of the Coast, 2003.

———. *Player's Handbook, Core Rulebook I, 3.5.* Renton, Wash.: Wizards of the Coast, 2003.

Žižek, Slavoj. *Welcome to the Desert of the Real! Five Essays on 11 September and Related Dates.* London: Verso, 2002.

Index